CPG Series of Comparative Constitutional Law,
Politics and Governance

Edited by the
German-Southeast Asian Center of Excellence
for Public Policy and Good Governance

Volume 7

Henning Glaser [ed.]

Doing Justice

Procedural Law and Procedural Law Reform in Comparative Perspective

Nomos

Onlineversion
Inlibra

The Deutsche Nationalbibliothek lists this publication in the Deutsche Nationalbibliografie; detailed bibliographic data are available on the Internet at http://dnb.d-nb.de

ISBN 978-3-8487-1388-2 (Print)
978-3-8452-5409-8 (ePDF)

1st Edition 2026

Table of Contents

Preface

Procedural law constitutes a central component of every legal system. It not only governs the course of judicial and extrajudicial proceedings but also plays a crucial role in the enforcement of substantive law, the safeguarding of state authority, and the upholding of constitutional principles.

The eleven contributions brought together in this volume explore key aspects of procedural law from a comparative legal perspective. While the primary focus lies on criminal procedure, the volume also addresses issues such as court organization, judicial independence, arbitration, and administrative procedure.

The contributions examine a range of legal systems—including those of the United States, Germany, Israel, Thailand, Vietnam, China, Malaysia, and the European Union. Alongside chapters that engage with foundational structural principles of procedural law in their doctrinal differentiation and practical application within various jurisdictions, the volume also offers in-depth analyses of the challenges to the development and reform of procedural law, particularly in Asia.

As such, the volume provides valuable insights into the procedural frameworks of individual legal systems and invites readers to engage in comparative reflection.

We extend our sincere thanks to all contributing authors whose expertise and commitment made this volume possible. Our gratitude also goes to the German Academic Exchange Service (DAAD) and the Federal Foreign Office of the Federal Republic of Germany for their generous financial support, without which this publication could not have been realized.

We also thank Duc Quang Ly for his technical support in the preparation of this volume.

Bangkok / Münster, April 2025

Henning Glaser

Balancing the Scales: Procedural Law in Comparative Perspective

Henning Glaser

Procedural law is a cornerstone of legal scholarship and practice, governing the mechanisms by which rights are asserted, disputes resolved, justice administered, the legal order upheld, and state authority affirmed. Its study, however, often seems to receive less attention than it deserves.

This volume seeks to pay tribute to the importance of procedural law by bringing together eleven contributions that examine key issues in procedural law across nine jurisdictions, primarily with a focus on criminal procedure, but also encompassing arbitration, mediation, court organization, general principles such as judicial independence, and administrative procedures within the European Union.

By analyzing legal procedures and procedural laws in regions as diverse as Europe, the Middle East, Asia, and the United States, these essays offer a broad comparative perspective that may prompt reflection on the feasibility of approaching procedural law through such a unified framework. This, in turn, raises the further question of whether the development of a general theory of procedural law is feasible and promising—a question that can be posed but not answered here.

In any case, it seems reasonable to take a broader approach to procedural law—one that encompasses diverse legal fields, procedural stages, and jurisdictions, as reflected in this volume. At the same time, there is good reason for placing particular emphasis on criminal procedural law, as it demands the highest standards of procedural integrity and fairness due to the severe intrusions on individual rights and the substantial costs associated with the administration of criminal justice.

In a liberal rule-of-law state, these heightened demands arise because criminal procedure involves the most profound infringements on citizens' rights. From a broader perspective, however, it reflects one of the fundamental responsibilities of any legitimate state—ensuring security, protection, and justice—at its most critical and sensitive frontier.

This thought leads from criminal procedural law back to procedural law as a whole. The demand on procedural integrity that applies in an intensified form to criminal procedure is equally relevant to procedural law in general. Its significance stems not only from the nature of the democratic constitutional state but also from the fundamental concept of the state itself—albeit with different emphases and varying degrees of intensity.

This is, again, particularly evident in criminal law. While procedural integrity in criminal justice embodies the essence of democratic constitutionalism, even autocratic and authoritarian states depend on some procedural integrity—albeit for different reasons, with often different objectives, and implemented in different ways. In such regimes, it is not the democratic community that owes its citizens procedural justice, but rather the state itself, whose legitimacy hinges on the provision and enforcement of some form of justice. Yet as much as justice constitutes a foundational condition for state legitimacy, it can only be perceived as such if a baseline of procedural adherence is maintained.

To once again return to the example of criminal procedure, both the absence of prosecution and arbitrary prosecution can severely undermine the stability of any regime. Accordingly, procedural law—including criminal procedure—long predates the modern democratic constitutional state. Even within a 'band of robbers,' to adapt Augustine's famous analogy,[1] regulated procedures are indispensable for maintaining order and preventing internal disintegration. In this sense, procedural requirements function as a universal principle of organization—arguably applicable even to robbers, and all the more so to the state.

Building on these introductory reflections on the significance of procedural law the discussion begins with a brief exploration of key dimensions of procedural law, before turning to the individual contributions.

---

1 In his famous analogy in *The City of God*, Augustine critiques the nature of political power divorced from justice recounting a dialogue between Alexander the Great and a captured pirate, wherein the pirate equates his own actions to those of the emperor, differing only in scale: "Justice being taken away, then, what are kingdoms but great robberies? For what are robberies themselves, but little kingdoms? The band itself is made up of men; it is ruled by the authority of a prince, it is knit together by the pact of the confederacy; the booty is divided by the law agreed on." The phrase "the booty is divided by the law agreed on" indicates that even robbers rely on normative procedural rules and must adhere to them. Augustine, Aurelius, Bishop of Hippo, *The City of God*, trans. E. M. Edghill, 2014, p. 140, at https://www.gutenberg.org/files/2412/2412-h/2412-h.htm#part01.

A. Selected Perspectives on Procedural Law

Given the breadth of themes and approaches in this volume, this introduction offers conceptual and comparative reference points to support orientation, inspire further inquiry, and foster deeper engagement with the chapters that follow. While not all aspects are addressed in each contribution, they may serve as starting points for further contextual reflection.

To this end, the initial question to be explored is what exactly should be understood as procedural law in this context and how broadly the concept should be defined. Building on this, the discussion will address the fundamental objectives of procedural law and examine the relationship between norms and procedures, as well as between substantive and procedural law.

Finally, an expanded perspective on procedural law is required—one that transcends positive law to capture its multidimensional nature, thereby bringing lived law into focus in its systemic character, structural and institutional prerequisites, conditions, and practical implementations.

I. Defining the scope of procedural law

The concept of procedural law can generally be defined more narrowly or broadly. In this case, a broad definition is adopted, which encompasses not only judicial proceedings but also other procedural legal regulations. At its core, procedural law thus initially consists of adversarial and non-adversarial judicial proceedings.

Adversarial proceedings primarily include civil and criminal trials, as well as contentious administrative or constitutional litigation, for example, as there are also other areas of law that could be mentioned here. Non-adversarial proceedings, on the other hand, involve matters of voluntary jurisdiction, such as probate or guardianship cases, non-contentious constitutional review proceedings, and certain administrative court procedures that do not involve conflicts between parties but rather focus on the formal recognition or authorization of a legal status.

While judicial proceedings constitute the core of procedural law, executive pre-trial procedures—particularly in criminal procedure for instance—can also be classified within this domain. Additionally, procedural law encompasses alternative dispute resolution mechanisms, such as mediation or arbitration. In all these cases, procedural rules serve to implement substantive law.

A second, distinguishable overarching area of procedural law can be described as the law of organization and competence. It regulates the structure, responsibilities, and processes within courts and administrative authorities. This includes, in particular, court organization law, which governs the structure and operation of judicial proceedings, including jurisdiction, procedural steps, and deadlines.

Finally, in the broadest sense of the term procedural law, even non-statutory methods of legal application, as well as professional practices and working styles of institutions responsible for legal application, can be included.

Since the exact scope of the concept of procedural law cannot be normatively derived and has no immediate normative implications, it can be determined based on heuristic criteria. Accordingly, a broad definition of procedural law is applied here to adequately reflect the selection of contributions presented and to support a comparative legal perspective on the individual contributions. After all, while the primary focus of the contributions is on issues of judicial procedure (*Philip M. Bender*, *Matthias Krüger*, *Rinat Kitai-Sangero*, *Pokpong Srisanit*, *Sorawit Limparangsri*, *Cheng Lei*, *Van Quang Nguyen*), some authors also address questions of court organization (*Sorawit Limparangsri*, *Van Quang Nguyen*, *Denise Wong and Makoto Hong*), alternative dispute resolution (*K. C. Vohrah* as well as *Denise Wong and Makoto Hong*), and administrative procedural law (*Anselm Küsters*).

II. Purpose and Principles of Procedural Law

Both the evaluation of the quality of procedural law and the comparison of different procedural law systems presupposes a fundamental understanding of the purpose and guiding principles of procedural law. If one follows the Kantian idea that law constitutes the condition of the possibility of right, then procedural law is the mechanism through which this condition is realized[2]—a thought that will be explored in more detail later. To this end, every procedural law system is guided by certain fundamental principles that are especially evident in judicial proceedings. Irrespective of the partic-

2 This formulation slightly modifies Kant's well-known dictum: "Right is therefore the sum of the conditions under which the choice of one can be united with the choice of another in accordance with a universal law of freedom." Immanuel Kant, "The Metaphysics of Morals," ed. Mary J. Gregor, 1996, p. 387.

ular area of law or legal tradition, three overarching procedural principles can be identified: first, justice; second, efficiency; and third, preserving legal peace.

These three principles must be considered when analyzing and understanding any procedural law system, each principle varying in its specific form and weighting, as well as in the way it is concretized through respective sub-principles and interacts with the other principles.

1. Justice

With respect to justice as the first of the three overarching guiding principles of procedural law, it can further be divided into a formal and a substantive dimension. The formal dimension—often referred to as "procedural fairness"—includes in particular the right to be heard (*audiatur et altera pars*), equal access to justice through the reduction of financial or social barriers, equal treatment of the parties, impartiality of the court, publicity of proceedings, and a fair and appropriate distribution of the burden of proof.

In its substantive dimension, the principle of justice primarily demands establishing the truth within the proceedings. In this context, the inquisitorial principle or, alternatively, the adversarial principle constitutes the most significant concretizing approaches (see also the contributions of *Bender* and *Srisanit*). Notably, the process of determining legal truth in judicial proceedings differs fundamentally from broader philosophical or scientific conceptions of truth. While the latter strive for objective truth, legal truth-finding seeks to establish a procedurally valid and legally recognized truth through structured mechanisms. This procedurally constructed legal truth serves the practical purpose of resolving disputes and maintaining legal order—even if, in certain cases, it diverges from a more comprehensive notion of truth. The extent to which such legal truth must align with principles of substantive justice varies across different legal traditions.

A notable distinction exists between most continental European legal systems and the Anglo-American legal tradition. In continental Europe, the principle of material truth prevails, aiming for the most thorough and objective clarification of facts. By contrast, the Anglo-American legal system places greater emphasis on formal truth, where truth is not determined independently of the procedural framework but instead emerges from the interplay of procedural rules—particularly the adversarial structure of litigation and evidentiary standards—which shape the boundaries of judicial decision-making more rigidly than in continental European legal systems.

Moreover, substantive justice also requires mechanisms for correcting erroneous decisions and—at least within the modern liberal constitutional state—the proportionality of procedural measures that interfere with the fundamental rights of the parties involved (see in this volume *Kitai-Sangero*, *Srisanit* and *Limparangsri*). Finally, the requirement of a speedy trial can, at least in part, be seen as a manifestation of the principle of justice in its substantive dimension, while at the same time leading into the second main principle, that of efficiency.

2. Efficiency

The second fundamental principle of efficiency aims to ensure that legal proceedings are concluded within a reasonable timeframe and with an acceptable level of effort. This leads to demands for expediting proceedings and controlling costs. Additionally, considerations of practicality and flexibility necessitate that procedures be designed to be user-friendly and streamlined where possible.

Particularly important in this regard are the principle of procedural acceleration and the imperative of cost-effective litigation. Speed is primarily achieved through rules governing deadlines and other mechanisms to streamline proceedings. These include judicial case management, procedural obligations for procedural advancement imposed on the parties, and, crucially, the organization of evidence collection. Further measures include facilitating settlements to achieve a final resolution at the first-instance level whenever possible, as well as promoting alternative dispute resolution methods such as mediation or arbitration.

The emphasis on cost-efficient proceedings varies across different legal systems. This divergence begins with the significance assigned to this sub-principle within the broader framework of procedural law and extends to its technical implementation.

The contrast between Anglo-American and continental European legal traditions is particularly pronounced. However, this difference is not only reflected in their respective approaches to efficiency in procedural law but also in their broader conceptualization of efficiency within legal systems. A notable example from U.S. law is Richard Posner's "Law and Economics" approach (Chicago School), which views efficiency as the primary objective of any legal system.[3] This approach focuses on minimizing transaction costs and achieving economically optimal outcomes.

By contrast, while continental European legal systems acknowledge the importance of economic efficiency, they typically subordinate it to more stringent justice considerations. Yet even within these traditions, efficiency should not be dismissed as a merely instrumental concern here. Rather, it must also be recognized as a structural prerequisite for a well-functioning procedure—and, in this sense, as a condition of the possibility of justice itself.

These divergent conceptions and weightings of efficiency are reflected in the way procedural laws are shaped and implemented within the respective systems. Whereas the continental legal tradition prioritizes the rationalization of proceedings while safeguarding justice, the Anglo-American approach places greater emphasis on market-driven mechanisms to shape and manage legal proceedings. This is evident, for example, in the significance of discovery procedures, which compel parties to disclose evidence to preempt disputes, in summary judgment, which allows cases to be resolved through preliminary judicial rulings, and in plea bargaining, which plays a central role in criminal proceedings.

However, an overriding focus on efficiency—particularly when interpreted solely as cost reduction rather than as a means to expedite proceedings in a manner that also upholds justice—can lead to deficiencies in substantive fairness. This is particularly the case when procedural truth-finding or protective mechanisms for litigants are treated as secondary concerns. For instance, strict limitations on fact-finding costs or an excessive preference for swift and low-cost dispute resolution may result in procedural frameworks that can tend to compromise formal and, more importantly, substantive principles of justice.

Regardless of the differing implementations in the two legal traditions, the principle of efficiency can both be in tension with and converge with the principle of justice. Such convergence is evident, for instance, where procedural gamesmanship is restricted in the interest of efficiency while simultaneously preventing a distortion of the truth-seeking function of the proceedings. In the present volume, the principle of efficiency is explored in depth particularly by *Wong and Hong*, *Lei*, and *Küsters*. It also underlies the reforms of Malaysian arbitration law described by *Vohrah*, and plays a more

3 Posner, *Economic Analysis of Law*, 1977. For Posner, the economic rationale is, in fact, the single unifying principle of law itself. Ibid., p. 189.

subordinate role in *Bender's* contribution, where it is briefly invoked in the context of negotiated agreements.

3. Legal peace

While justice and efficiency can be regarded as overarching objectives of procedural law more broadly, the establishment of legal peace is a goal specific to judicial procedure. After all, the judicial process ultimately fulfills the state's mandate to ensure internal security by reaffirming the authority of the legal order, resolving disputes between parties, and delivering a lasting, binding resolution to conflicts.

In establishing legal peace through conflict resolution and the enforcement of rights, the state fulfills one of its core responsibilities. While this principle is a universal feature of the modern state, both its conceptual foundations and practical application vary considerably. Some legal systems prioritize the strict enforcement of law, encapsulated in the Latin maxim *fiat justitia, ruat caelum* ("let justice be done, though the heavens fall"). Others place greater emphasis on achieving a pragmatic resolution to the specific dispute at hand.[4]

A key sub-principle is the requirement of procedural visibility, which, under the conditions of a liberal constitutional state, follows directly from the principles of democracy and human rights. Beyond that, however, it can also be derived from the function of legal proceedings in ensuring legal peace. In this regard, Lord Hewart's well-known maxim from *R v Sussex Justices, ex parte McCarthy* (1924) applies: "Justice must not only be done, but must also be seen to be done."[5] It is therefore important to recall that judicial proceedings can also be seen as ritualized processes of communication aimed at establishing normative validity—processes that, as a rule, presuppose public visibility.

In this sense, court proceedings, in particular, can be seen as staged enactments of justice, designed to uphold the legitimacy of the state, deterring unwanted (primary) behavior and providing a public forum to aggrieved parties. That said, one may debate whether procedural visibility—quite

4 Closely related to this is the question—primarily debated in the Anglo-American legal tradition—of whether the outcome of a trial should align more strictly with the parties' legal rights or with the substantive policies those rights are intended to promote. Bone, "Making Effective Rules: The Need for Procedure Theory," 2008, p. 330.

5 *Rex v. Sussex Justices, ex parte McCarthy* [1924] 1 KB 256.

apart from its derivation from human rights and democracy—must necessarily be regarded as an absolute requirement. One may finally also raise the question of whether some visibility of legal proceedings is directly linked to the development of the law—whether by enabling norm creation through precedent or by fostering doctrinal debate and differentiation.

Another fundamental sub-principle concerns the finality of decisions (*res iudicata*), which is reflected in the maxim *ne bis in idem*—prohibiting double jeopardy for the same offense—as well as in the requirement of legal force of judgments, the limited scope for appellate review, and the strictly confined possibilities for reopening proceedings.

Furthermore, the overarching principle of legal peace requires that legal proceedings and their outcomes be conducted in a manner that ensures broad societal acceptance. This implies that sanctions must be proportionate and socially sustainable, that institutional trust in the independence and neutrality of state interventions must be preserved, and, ultimately, that legal procedures must be both fair and efficient.

4. The broader system of procedural principles

As a final observation, it should be emphasized that, beyond the three fundamental aims of justice, efficiency, and legal peace, procedural law gives rise to a variety of additional structural principles. Some of these operate autonomously, others can be understood as functional extensions or concretizations of the aforementioned aims. The result is a complex constellation of normative coordinates that operate on multiple levels—sometimes reinforcing each other, sometimes generating internal tensions.

The precise configuration of this structural landscape varies across jurisdictions and areas of law, shaped by divergent doctrinal traditions and institutional priorities. While this introductory chapter does not seek to explore these further principles in detail, several contributions to the present volume do. *Krüger's* analysis, for instance, engages with the principle of immediacy as a structural expression of substantive justice understood in terms of the pursuit of truth.

III. Norm and Procedure

Instead of taking a deeper look at individual procedural law principles, the following section will examine the fundamental relationship between norms and procedures in its various dimensions. This perspective offers valuable insights not only into the function of procedural law itself, but also into the workings of the procedural legal system as a whole.

In this context, the focus lies, first, on identifying which specific areas of law—beyond procedural principles—are relevant for understanding a given procedural legal system. Second, it considers how norms and procedures can be related to one another in both practical and theoretical terms. This includes examining the regulatory scope of procedural law itself, its normative framing by international and constitutional law, those norms of (ordinary) substantive law that affect legal procedure, the functional and systems-theoretical interplay between substantive and procedural law and, finally, a foundational view of the anthropological dimension of law and procedure.

1. The positive legal framework of procedural realities

In positive law, the reality of legal procedure is governed both by procedural norms and by substantive law. In addition to procedural law itself, not only higher-ranking norms of international and constitutional law are relevant, but also those provisions of ordinary substantive law that influence the conduct of legal proceedings.

a) Procedural law

It is evident that procedural rules form the core of those norms within positive law that shape judicial procedures. Insofar, from a comparative perspective, particular interest lies not only in how procedures are structured, their guiding principles, and specific implementations, but above all in those numerous provisions that directly or indirectly influence the behavior and performance of participants in everyday procedural practice. This becomes especially clear when examining the judiciary, with civil proceedings offering the most illustrative examples.

Firstly, relevant areas of positive procedural law include norms concerning judicial management and procedural economy, such as those designed to concentrate procedural activities or prevent unnecessary delays. Specifically, these encompass rules empowering or requiring courts to set timeframes and deadlines for individual procedural stages, to determine whether the dispute is resolved in a single comprehensive oral hearing or across multiple sessions, and to stipulate parties' obligations regarding personal attendance and the consequences of their absence. Additionally, there are relevant provisions governing the extent to which courts may actively suggest settlements or even compel parties to engage in alternative dispute resolution methods.

Secondly, another significant cluster of rules addresses how courts handle parties' submissions and evidence. These regulations define the extent of judicial authority to request additional information from the parties and to provide parties with procedural guidance. Closely related are rules concerning possible procedural disadvantages, such as the court's discretion to reject late or incomplete submissions and its authority to independently order the gathering of evidence not explicitly proposed by the parties.

Thirdly, sanctions for procedural misconduct vary considerably between jurisdictions. Relevant issues here include the approach to contemptuous behavior, notably how regulations prioritize protecting the judge's person, function, or judicial authority itself, and whether freedom of expression or maintaining the court's authority is emphasized. Further aspects involve the court's power to exclude parties entirely or partially from further submissions or to apply alternative sanctions when procedural obligations are violated.

Fourthly, universally relevant across all procedural types are rules governing judicial decision-making and the evaluation of evidence. These provisions delineate the extent to which judges enjoy discretion or are constrained by formalized rules regarding the assessment of evidence and factual determinations, as well as the scope of judicial autonomy in conducting factual inquiries and independently evaluating the submitted evidence.

Fifthly, internal organizational rules and court management practices significantly shape procedural performance. These rules include case allocation within courts, criteria and procedures for judicial selection, promotion, professional training, and internal governance mechanisms (such as workload measurement systems), all indirectly influencing judicial behavior and effectiveness.

Closely related, sixthly, are provisions explicitly aimed at safeguarding judicial independence. Regulations and standards ensuring judicial independence—such as protections against external interference or clear disciplinary rules and procedures—vary considerably. Particularly important are clarifications on the limits of permissible administrative interventions by supervisory or executive bodies.

Beyond these judicial-centered provisions or aspects of the mentioned provisions, numerous other areas primarily concerning other procedural participants deserve attention, again differing often significantly across jurisdictions. These include for example rules governing third-party involvement (such as third-party intervention, amicus curiae participation, or collective litigation mechanisms), or provisions ensuring access to courts and procedural fairness, such as rules on legal aid, equality of arms, and general procedural equality between parties.

Furthermore, rules addressing digitalization and technological modernization of court procedures have become increasingly significant, including provisions for conducting virtual hearings or employing electronic case management and filing systems (e-filing). Equally relevant on a more general note are international and cross-border procedural norms, notably rules governing jurisdiction, recognition of foreign judgments, and procedures for international evidence gathering.

Finally, to give just one more example, transparency provisions aimed at ensuring public access and procedural openness play an important role in general as well. These regulations concern permissible media coverage, audio and video broadcasting of judicial hearings, and broader measures designed to foster public engagement in judicial decision-making processes.

b) Substantive law

In addition to the importance of procedural law itself, attention should also be given to the broader legal framework within which procedural rules operate—particularly constitutional provisions and specific substantive legal mechanisms—that shape the conduct of parties involved in legal proceedings. Beyond constitutional law, the judicial rights enshrined in the European Convention on Human Rights (ECHR) also have significant impact, most notably Article 6, which guarantees the right to a fair trial (see also the reference to international law in the contribution of *Srisanit* in this volume).[6]

6 Other relevant provisions include the principle of *nullum crimen, nulla poena sine lege* laid down in Article 7; the right to liberty and security under Article 5, regulating, for example, conditions and procedures related to detention and the right to prompt judicial review; and the prohibition of torture under Article 3. Further, Article 13 ECHR, providing the right to an effective remedy, directly influences procedural law

Regarding the concrete influence of constitutional law on the shaping of each procedural legal system, two factors are crucial: first, the specific procedural standards set forth by the constitution, and second, how consistently these standards are implemented in practice.

Both aspects ultimately depend on the underlying constitutional values that guide a given legal system as well as their actual importance for the reality of governance in the respective system. Among the various types of constitutional systems, the liberal democratic constitutional state typically provides the most comprehensive and coherent framework, built upon core principles such as democracy, human rights protection, and the rule of law which significantly impact the design and content of procedural rights.

These principles include for instance the right to effective judicial protection, the right to be heard and to access court-enforced remedies, the right to a fair trial, judicial independence, the principle of public trials, the prohibition against double jeopardy, and the requirement that any deprivation of liberty must be governed by law and proportionate.

Although some of these constitutional standards may also appear in constitutions of other non-Western or non-liberal-democratic systems, they are usually less consistently defined, less differentiated, and less rigorously enforced. At the outset, it is important to distinguish between constitutional law in general and the specific constitutional foundations that shape and constrain procedural law.

Every constitution contains not only normative provisions that vary in their legal enforceability but also a set of fundamental principles—what may be called the constitutional basic structure—which underpin a state's constitutional identity. It makes a considerable difference whether democracy, fundamental rights, and the rule of law form part of this basic structure and thereby reflect a hegemonic core consensus of a given society, or whether they merely exist as important elements within the constitutional order without enjoying such a foundational and paramount status.

This distinction marks a central fault line between liberal constitutional systems in the "West" and those found in much of Asia, a difference that

by requiring states to offer effective legal mechanisms through which violations of the Convention can be challenged, thereby shaping remedies and complaint procedures. Additionally, Article 8's protection of private and family life impacts procedural rules regarding evidence collection, such as surveillance measures, searches of suspects, testimonial privileges for family members, and detainees' communication rights. Further procedural implications can follow from Article 9's guarantee of freedom of thought, conscience, and religion, as well as from Article 14's prohibition of discrimination.

becomes particularly clear in the contributions by *Cheng Lei* on China and *Van Quang Nguyen* on Vietnam. In both countries, fundamental rights are recognized as relevant to procedural law and are increasingly used as reference points in the context of judicial or criminal justice reform. Yet within their respective constitutional frameworks, such rights are not only conceived differently than in liberal democracies; they also do not occupy the same structural rank. Rather, they remain subject to the overarching logic of the one-party state and subordinated to the structural primacy of democratic centralism—an organizing principle that, for example, precludes the Western conception of the separation of powers and the rule of law in the classical liberal sense.

Given that even within liberal democratic constitutional states, there exist notable differences in how constitutional principles are translated into procedural standards, the type of constitution—and its foundational structure—matters profoundly. Constitutional law is therefore a decisive factor in understanding how procedural law is implemented in practice, and in enabling meaningful comparison—particularly in the field of criminal procedure. It is no coincidence that criminal procedure has often been described as "applied" or "concretized" constitutional law—or, as the German scholar Claus Roxin famously put it, as the "seismograph of the state's constitution."[7]

Substantive legal provisions can significantly influence the practical implementation and quality of judicial proceedings by shaping the legal position of participants and particularly by guiding, disciplining, or incentivizing the behavior of actors involved in the process. Such provisions—primarily stemming from substantive civil and criminal law—serve diverse objectives, including ensuring truth-finding, maintaining procedural integrity, safeguarding the rights of participants, and disciplining parties within the proceedings.

Specifically, a wide range of substantive legal rules can be identified, which have found their way—often in distinctly different forms—into the procedural frameworks of various jurisdictions.

First, there are rules designed to ensure truth-finding and procedural integrity. These include, in particular, obligations to testify truthfully, criminal sanctions for perjury and false accusations, and provisions against the destruction or falsification of evidence. Additionally, in certain jurisdictions, substantive criminal offenses such as fraud explicitly address the

7 Roxin, *Strafverfahrensrecht*, 1998, para. 2, marg. n. 1.

manipulation of judicial proceedings through intentional deception or false statements.

Second, there are norms specifically aimed at disciplining state-appointed actors through sanctions. Particularly significant are provisions against abuse of office and judicial misconduct, which serve to prevent judges, prosecutors, or other officials from exercising their powers abusively or arbitrarily. Rules against obstruction of justice target judges, prosecutors, and attorneys specifically to prevent them from hindering proper criminal prosecution. Furthermore, civil liability provisions—especially state liability or official liability rules—can discipline authorities and judges by imposing personal financial accountability in cases of severe misconduct.

Third, some provisions aim to ensure the orderly conduct of proceedings as well as the authority and effectiveness of the judiciary. These include criminal offenses safeguarding the proper enforcement of judicial decisions, as well as rules against contempt of court or judicial defamation. The latter can contribute to preserving judicial authority, although depending on their specific formulation, they might simultaneously restrict the discursive freedom of the participants, thus significantly shaping courtroom culture.

Fourth, substantive rules may strategically influence the decisions of parties during proceedings. Among these are statutory limitation periods and exclusionary deadlines defined by substantive civil law, determining the timeframe within which claims can be pursued and thus influencing the behavior of parties and the dynamics of the litigation process. Equally important are substantive rules on cost recovery and damages, including sanctions for vexatious or obviously unfounded lawsuits (such as the Italian doctrine of *lite temeraria* or frivolous litigation), which can substantially affect the decision of whether to initiate litigation or seek settlement.

Fifth, there are provisions aimed at protecting fundamental rights of participants and specific groups involved in proceedings. These include rules protecting the confidentiality of communication, as well as data protection and privacy laws, which determine the admissibility of collecting and using sensitive information—for instance, through surveillance measures or communication monitoring. Moreover, special protective norms for vulnerable groups such as victims or minors directly shape procedural rights and the conduct of proceedings.

Finally, and sixth, general transparency provisions in substantive law (for example, freedom of information legislation), regulations regarding public participation, and anti-discrimination laws may substantially influence the openness and fairness of judicial proceedings.

c) On the relation of substantive and procedural law: Anglo-Saxon perspectives

A recurring theme in the theoretical engagement with procedural law is its relationship to substantive law.[8] Depending on how the question is framed and which analytical lens is applied, this relationship can give rise to a range of important insights. It is commonly conceptualized in one of several ways: as a dichotomy in which procedural and substantive law are treated as relatively autonomous spheres within the legal system;[9] as a one-directional influence, whereby either substantive law shapes procedure or procedure determines substantive outcomes; or as a model of mutual interaction, in which both domains exert equally significant influence on one another.

The first view—that of a broad autonomy between substance and procedure—was especially prominent in earlier stages of the Anglo-American legal tradition but has become increasingly difficult to maintain.[10] As Thomas Main has argued, this traditional distinction reflects a "false dichotomy at the core of our legal system."[11]

Rather, it can be said that procedure influences substantive outcomes as an "instrument of power that can, in a very practical sense, generate or undermine substantive rights."[12] At the same time, "procedure is embedded in substantive law,"[13] which shapes procedure by guiding the design of procedural law, procedural choices and their application. Contrary to the earlier conviction for example of the drafters of the 1938 Federal Rules that "substance played little, if any, role in shaping procedure,"—and that "procedural rules could largely be justified by process values alone, without reference to substance at all,"[14]—both dimensions of law are in fact rooted in the same underlying idea of justice.[15] This includes values such as justice

8 Robert G. Bone interestingly observes that "specifying more rigorously the precise nature of the relationship between procedure and substantive law" remains "a fundamental, but surprisingly difficult" task. See Bone, above fn. 4, p. 327.

9 Main, "The Procedural Foundation of Substantive Law," 2010, https://scholars.law.unlv.edu/facpub/741, pp. 801–841, especially pp. 804 f.

10 Ibid., p. 802.

11 Ibid., p. 803.

12 Ibid., p. 802.

13 Ibid., p. 803.

14 Bone, above fn. 4, p. 329.

15 Although substantive and procedural law share a common foundation in the general idea of law, their respective relationships to its core principles—such as justice,

and efficiency, and both are governed by the same constitutional principles, which claim system-conforming validity across both domains.

d) Substantive and procedural law: systems-theoretical perspectives

The recognition of a fundamental interdependence between substantive and procedural law does not yet answer the central question—it merely poses it. In other words, if we proceed on the assumption that such a constitutive relationship exists, the question then becomes how it is structured and functions. To address this, a systems-theoretical perspective proves particularly fruitful. Especially relevant is the systems theory developed by Niklas Luhmann, who was originally trained as a lawyer and repeatedly applied his theoretical framework explicitly to the legal system.

From the perspective of Niklas Luhmann's systems theory, law is understood as an autonomous, self-referential (autopoietic) social system that reproduces itself through legal communication. It operates in an operationally closed way—meaning that it decides according to its own internal binary code *legal/illegal*, without direct guidance from external systems like politics or morality. However, it remains cognitively open to such influences, which may irritate or prompt internal adjustments. The primary function of the legal system is to reduce societal complexity by stabilizing normative expectations and enabling reliable decision-making in conflict situations.[16]

Building on this elaborated understanding of the legal system, the relationship between substantive and procedural law can also be reinterpreted through the lens of systems theory. From this vantage point, procedural law no longer appears as a merely auxiliary instrument for implementing

legal certainty, and efficiency—differ significantly. Procedural law, as the structural precondition for the realization of substantive norms, occupies a distinct ontological position within the legal order. It is only through procedural form that substantive law attains full validity and effect in social reality. Consequently, the principle of efficiency—understood here as a condition for the functional viability of legal decision-making—assumes particular prominence in the procedural sphere, arguably to a greater normative and operational extent than in substantive law itself.

16 See for instance Luhmann, *Law as a Social System*, Oxford: Oxford University Press, 2004, originally published in German as *Das Recht der Gesellschaft*, 1993; Luhmann, *Social Systems*, 1995. Rottleuthner, "A Purified Sociology of Law: Niklas Luhmann on the Autonomy of the Legal System," 1989, pp. 779–796; Baxter, "Niklas Luhmann's Theory of Autopoietic Legal Systems," 2013, pp. 175–184, available at: https://scholarship.law.bu.edu/faculty_scholarship/140.

substantive norms. Rather, it emerges as a constitutive force within the legal system itself, actively shaping the way in which legal meaning is generated and legal reality constructed.

Procedure, in this sense, is more than an apparatus of enforcement. It lifts law onto a new level of realization, providing the structural conditions under which substantive norms become practically effective and socially visible. Law becomes operative through procedure. Crucially, this realization does not follow a linear logic of application, but rather unfolds through a recursive, self-referential process governed by the internal criteria of the legal system.

Central to this dynamic is the temporal structure of legal procedure. As Luhmann emphasizes, legal proceedings are not externally timed sequences imposed upon legal facts; rather, they are temporally autonomous operations that define their own beginning and end through formalized legal criteria.[17] While an external event—such as an accident, a breach of contract, or a crime—may serve as the initial irritant, it is procedural law that determines whether and how such an event becomes legally relevant in the first place. This capacity for temporal self-definition reinforces the autonomy of procedure and highlights its function as a selective filter for legal communication.

At the same time, legal procedure exhibits a paradoxical dual character. It serves both as a channel for applying substantive norms and as a generator of truth in accordance with the procedural logic of the legal system. This truth is not discovered in an external reality but produced within the structural constraints of the procedure itself. What counts as legally true depends not merely on facts or norms but on what procedural rules are allowed to be treated as relevant and admissible. In legal contexts, truth is not epistemological but systemic—a product of decision-making sequences bounded by form, time, and institutional ritual.

Yet this procedural construction of truth in all its contingency does not weaken the legitimacy of legal outcomes, quite the opposite: The very uncertainty of the outcome, inherent to the process, becomes a resource for legitimacy:[18] It opens up possibilities, invites participation, mobilizes argumentation, and fosters recognition of the result—even among those for whom the outcome may be unfavorable.[19] In this sense, procedure func-

17 Luhmann, *Das Recht der Gesellschaft*, 1993, p. 208.

18 Ibd., pp. 207 ff.

19 Ibd., p. 208.

tions not merely as a decision-making mechanism but as a legitimacy-generating form. As Luhmann suggests, participants become "prisoners of their own participation," bound to the process they have entered into and the distinctions it enacts.[20] This dual function of procedural law—as both the enabler of substantive decisions and the architecture of their legitimacy—leads to a further insight: law is not merely applied; it is brought into being.

This process is grounded in the procedure itself and, ultimately, in its boundary-drawing nature. At this point, George Spencer-Brown's foundational axiom becomes salient: "Draw a distinction, and a universe comes into being."[21] Each legal procedure draws such a distinction. It defines what is legally visible and relevant while simultaneously excluding what lies beyond the system's operative boundaries. In this act of distinction, law does not passively mirror social reality—it generates a reality of its own.

Accordingly, substantive law is not simply executed through procedure; it is constructed by and within it. Its operational validity depends on the selective, temporally bounded, and symbolically mediated architecture of procedural processes. Law is not found—it is produced. It arises not as an objective or ontological truth, but as decision-bound truth—a truth valid within the systemic logic of law itself. In this view, legal procedure is not a secondary mechanism of enforcement, but an epistemic architecture: a structured, communicative framework that renders the world of law visible, operable, and socially real.

As a conclusion, one might say—returning to the general legal-theoretical perspective indicated above—that procedure shapes how norms can be invoked, contested, and validated, while substance determines what is at stake when procedures are enacted. Their binding lies in their co-constitutive function: neither can fully function as law without the other. The legal system, in turn, depends on the continuous interplay between normativity and form, between meaning and structure—a dynamic that sustains both the internal coherence and the social relevance of legal operations.

20 Ibd., p. 209.

21 Spencer-Brown, *Laws of Form*, 1969, p. 1.

e) Legal-anthropological perspectives[22]

To further explore the relationship between substantive and procedural law, it is instructive to momentarily set aside the guiding assumption of their systemic unity within functionally differentiated legal systems. Instead, a legal-anthropological perspective shall be adopted transcending the focus on the internal relationship between substantive and procedural law. This shift brings into view a legal reality often overshadowed or displaced by the autopoietic logic of validity in modern legal systems—yet one that persists as a residual order in many societies, or gives rise to alternative forms of normative organization. The focus thus moves from the internal differentiation of juridical subsystems to the elementary building blocks of social order: order, law, procedure, ritual, and violence.

A focal point at which these elementary concepts condense in shifting constellations is the act of killing carried out as law enforcement. The point of departure for exploring this precarious zone is the initial observation that, in fully differentiated legal systems, substantive and procedural law form an integrated unity—one that presupposes and is conditioned by the existence of a functionally differentiated state with a monopoly on legitimate violence.

A first displacement of this unity becomes visible where state structures are ineffective or absent altogether. Here, some form of law may still regulate violence, even without recourse to institutional enforcement by a modern state.

This is particularly true for certain customary legal orders found in stateless or weakly institutionalized settings. Their function lies not in the prevention of violence but in its containment, its transformation into socially navigable forms. Such systems give rise to normative procedures—ritualized acts of revenge, mechanisms of compensation, mediation, or periods of protected immunity—that channel violence and make it legible.

22 While the individual contributions in this volume do not adopt an anthropological lens, the reflections offered in this section might serve to contextualize the normative foundations, structural possibilities, and potential dysfunctions of procedural law more broadly. They are aiming to illuminate the latent assumptions, symbolic operations, and performative dimensions that underlie any legal procedure, whether as a mere possibility or as a lived reality. Arguably, such a perspective is particularly helpful for the analysis and the comparative framing of procedural regimes, especially where such regimes diverge significantly in institutional form, normative foundations, or socio-political embeddedness.

Blood vengeance, in this context, operates not merely as retribution but as a form of symbolic equilibrium, restoring damaged honor and reaffirming social balance. It is, in this sense, a structured response embedded within a symbolically coded normative order.[23]

Crucially, such systems maintain a tight coupling between substantive norm and procedural form, even in the absence of a centralized enforcement apparatus. This suggests that some form of elementary unity of substance and procedure is not a modern invention, but, at least potentially, a structural feature of legal ordering per se. Yet this unity is not empirically necessary. One might further also account for forms of law devoid of procedure—where codified substantive norms exist but are enforced through unmediated acts of violence rather than structured legal process.

Nowhere is this more vividly dramatized than in the Western genre, which often stages the act of killing as a critical juridical moment. Insofar, the Western may be read as a myth of the co-evolution of law and statehood in American society, a narrative of legal order in formation. Many of these narrations portray a world in which substantive justice and legal procedure are not yet aligned, or even in tension. In movies like *Unforgiven* (Clint Eastwood) and *Django Unchained* (Quentin Tarantino) for instance, law appears in its nascent form, codified, but not yet fully institutionalized; present as substance, but absent as due process. Instead, immediate violence becomes the medium through which justice is enacted.

Django Unchained and *Unforgiven* articulate this structure in contrasting scenarios. In *Django*, the bounty hunter Dr. King Schultz operates under the guise of legal authority. Armed with wanted posters, he performs executions with ritualistic allusions to legality. The warrant's legal basis, however, is ultimately irrelevant; the killing is reduced to a minimal procedure.

23 As an example, the Kanun of northern Albania offers a paradigmatic example, with its criminal provisions governed by a logic of honor and blood feud. A powerful depiction of this logic can be found in Ismail Kadare's novel Broken April. Similar configurations appear for example in the *Pashtunwali* of Afghan Pashtu society, in the Somali *xeer*, or in the Arab *urf.* These orders, comprising both substance and procedure, not only regulate violence but, by virtue of their social embeddedness, stand as legitimate alternatives to state law where the latter is absent, rejected, or unrecognized. Law here emerges not as an instrument of sovereign imposition but as a medium of self-regulation under conditions of normative fragmentation. See for the Kanun, Cara and Margjeka, "Kanun of Leke Dukagjini Customary Law of Northern Albania," 2015, pp. 174–186, available at https://eujournal.org/index.php/esj/article/view/6383; Souleimanov and Aliyev, "Blood revenge and violent mobilization: evidence from the Chechen Wars," 2015, pp. 158–180.

Schultz identifies his target by means of a poster and carries out the execution himself—presenting the warrant with bureaucratic composure, as if enacting legality through repetition alone. The legal signifiers—warrant, poster, name—do not initiate a process, but merely mark the claimed difference between lawful killing and murder. In this nascent phase of legal differentiation, law is reduced to sanction without discourse-based procedure. There is no trial, no defense, no weighing of facts—only the unilateral decision of a figure who kills under the sign of authority, backed by violence and a literally paper-thin claim to legitimacy.

In *Unforgiven*, even this veneer of legality is absent. When a prostitute is disfigured by two cowboys, the sheriff refuses to impose criminal sanctions in due process, instead demanding compensation—paid not to the victim, but to the brothel owner. In response, the prostitute's colleagues place a bounty on the perpetrators' heads. With no access to law, they turn to violence as substitute justice. The man who ultimately carries out the killings has no badge, no warrant, just the injured party's mandate, acting as a private agent of revenge. Violence here is not the law's distortion, but its replacement, enacted in the void left by institutions that fail to recognize the victim and refuse the operation of due procedure.

The structural mechanisms governing the relationship between substantive and procedural law, as depicted in Westerns, are not confined to the past; rather, they reemerge in modern form. In state-directed killing campaigns—such as those in the "war on drugs" in the Philippines or Brazil, or in drone strikes against terror suspects within the framework of the Global War on Terror—violence is deliberately deployed to enforce substantive law without following the prescribed procedural path. This is achieved either by completely sidelining established procedures or by transferring decision-making into mere executive structures that escape judicial oversight and defy fundamental legal principles.

On the Philippines, for example, thousands of alleged drug users and traffickers have been killed by police or vigilante groups—often without trial and frequently without any tangible evidence. In the global war on terror, a parallel procedure has emerged within the executive branch to legitimize drone attacks. "Kill lists," secret legal memos, and executive review boards have supplanted the conventional processes of prosecution, defense, and adjudication. In these contexts, the symbolic tether to legality is replaced by administrative semiotics that only mimic a legal process—rather than embodying a genuine, normatively grounded procedural system.

These examples illustrate how substantive and procedural law can become decoupled, with procedural law supplanted by violence. This manifests in various ways. In drug wars like those in the Philippines and Brazil, either no legal procedure exists or only a faked façade of due process operates through fabricated evidence and staged self-defense claims, undermining fundamental principles of justice. In the War on Terror, a "procedure beyond law" emerged through protocols that failed to uphold legal ideals and constitutional principles. Ultimately, in all these cases, substantive and procedural law remain disconnected.

In all these examples, the separation of substantive law and procedure appears to be transitory and indicative of a deficient legal and state system, raising the question of whether substantive law without procedure can be conceived as a possible normal state of a functioning legal system. In an article on the relation between substantive and procedural law, Main underlines in this context that in the traditional courts of Equity in England—such as the Court of Chancery, the Court of Requests, and the Equity side of the Court of Exchequer—"there were no procedural rules and, instead, an all-encompassing substantive mandate."[24]

That raises the question of to what extent the courts of equity might indeed provide an example of such substantive law without procedural law. While the courts of equity operated without rigid procedural rules, instead exercising a broad substantive mandate as they did not rely on writs, single-issue pleadings, or strict procedural formalities, they were not entirely devoid of procedural elements. Entry requirements, such as petitions, and certain procedural practices still played a role. Thus, rather than representing a complete separation of substantive and procedural law, the courts of Equity exemplified a less formalistic procedural approach in contrast to the highly structured Common Law courts. Their distinguishing feature was thus not the absence of procedure but rather its flexibility and adaptability in the pursuit of fairness.

With this insight, we remain with the assumption of the exception or dysfunctionality of a separation between substantive and procedural law. Considering that in the examples mentioned—the enforcement of substantive law through the procedurally independent act of killing—the concept of the state of exception is at least implicitly present, a bridge can be made to a further iteration: the idea of order without law in a state of exception, thus the suspension not only of procedural law but of law as a whole.

24 Main, above fn. 9.

Instructive in this regard is Carl Schmitt's concept of the state of exception. According to Schmitt, in the state of exception, "the force of real life breaks through the crust of a mechanically frozen repetition," disrupting routine and established legal procedures.[25] In the exception, procedure without law—pure procedure accompanied by naked violence—replaces both substantive and procedural law.

The value of Schmitt's analysis for the point being made here lies in his explicit dissection of the concept of 'legal order' into its two components, effectively dissolving it into the terms 'law' and 'order,' thus establishing their principle separability.[26] This separability paves the way for Schmitt's state of exception. For him, it is a state in which law is suspended, but order—understood merely as order, no longer as a legal order—remains intact.[27]

Although a distinction can therefore theoretically be made between substantive law without procedural law and order without law, this transition will often prove fluid in practice. More importantly, one must consider whether, in both cases, the suspendable or suspended law in the state of exception, or substantive law enforced without procedural law, does not represent a fundamentally different entity from law that exists in the material unity of law and procedure.

Ultimately, for the first case of a separation between substantive law and procedural law, one can argue that the law enforced in this way is no longer identical to the law legitimized through an attached procedure. Only procedural binding ensures the integrity of a law that is rooted in the idea of law—not its enforcement through extralegal killings, which, even aside from the violation of procedural law, already contradict the very idea of law and the substantive law derived from it. It is precisely the procedure that ensures that substantive law does not degenerate into a mere legitimization of power interests but retains its normative validity.

If there can be such a thing as (substantive) law without procedure—even as an aberration—then the converse must also be asked: are there procedures that exert normative force without any connection to substantive law?

Such procedures do, in fact, appear across diverse contexts—in political institutions, economic systems, and social processes. Political bodies, for

25 Schmitt, *Politische Theorie. Vier Kapitel zur Lehre von der Souveränität*, 8th ed., 2004, p. 21.

26 Ibid., p. 19.

27 Ibid., p. 19.

instance, develop informal voting protocols, consultation mechanisms, or codes of conduct which, while neither codified nor legally recognized, exert binding effects in practice and demonstrate considerable regulatory capacity. In the economic sphere, rating agencies, certification bodies, and other actors establish procedures that generate normative expectations, effectively compelling market participants—despite the absence of any statutory foundation.

The very possibility that mere procedures can generate inherent normative force invites further reflection—one that may, in turn, deepen our understanding of the distinctive nature of legal proceedings and their constitutive linkage to substantive law, which stands as the conceptual opposite of "pure" procedure.

A particularly influential account of the normative force of such *pure* procedures—those untethered from substantive legal content—was developed by Michel Foucault. Drawing on concepts such as the *dispositif*, the power-knowledge nexus, and governmentality, Foucault demonstrates how administrative procedures, bureaucratic operations, and disciplinary practices exert power, regulate behavior, and constitute subjects—not by virtue of legal legitimacy or their connection to substantive law, but through their procedural form.[28]

28 In *Discipline and Punish* (1975), Foucault argues, for instance, that power operates not only through laws and punishments but also through procedural routines that define normality and deviance. Also, for him, governmental techniques derive their normative force not from juridical coercion but from mechanisms of regulation and control embedded in routine practices. This analysis is further developed in *The History of Sexuality* (Vol. 1, 1976), where Foucault introduces the concept of biopower and shows how modern regimes of knowledge and regulation generate normative effect on life and the body not through legal codification, but through procedures of management, classification, and control. Similar insights are expanded in his Collège de France lectures—particularly *Security, Territory, Population* (1977–78) and *The Birth of Biopolitics* (1978–79)—in which Foucault reconstructs a historical genealogy of governmental rationalities, ranging from early modern police regimes through classical liberalism to twentieth-century neoliberalism. Each of these regimes is characterized by distinct procedural logics—aimed at managing populations, optimizing circulations, and structuring freedom—often in ways that displace or bypass legal form altogether. Likewise, the power-knowledge that emerges from procedural structures exerts normative force in its own right—through mechanisms that operate alongside or beneath the law, rather than through it. Such procedural dispositifs, in which law is no longer the primary vector of normativity, produce classifications that acquire binding force within social practices—for instance, in medical or psychological labels such as "healthy" and "ill." This dynamic becomes especially visible in the institutions analyzed by Foucault—hospitals, psychiatric facilities, prisons, schools,

With a slightly different emphasis than Foucault—and drawing, not least, on insights from Niklas Luhmann again—one might thus indeed argue, in the present context, that procedures generate normative force by virtue of their own internal processual logic. With a slightly different emphasis than Foucault—and once again drawing, not least, on insights from Niklas Luhmann—one might argue, in the present context, that procedures generate normative force by virtue of their own internal processual logic. This effect is grounded in a kind of reality-producing evidence. Once established, a procedure generates a logic of facticity that confirms and thus reinforces itself. What has been procedurally fixed comes to appear as objective necessity—not because it is substantively compelling, but because its application produces social reality.

The recognition of this norm-generating function of procedures proves fruitful for analyzing legal constructs, including procedural law—whether for purposes of reform, comparison, or deeper conceptual understanding. At the same time, it highlights the central role of procedural law in securing the effectiveness of legal norms.

Two conclusions follow. First, by way of clarification, the independent normative force of procedures is not confined to "pure" procedures alone. It also arises within legally structured procedures that are integrated with substantive law. In this light—and particularly from a systems-theoretical perspective—the normative contribution of procedural law to the functioning of substantive law becomes apparent (see Luhmann's analysis of the relation between substantive and procedural law above).

Second, this perspective draws attention to the informal and often implicit elements that animate legal procedures in their concrete operation. It underscores the significance of unwritten procedural norms, practical routines, and role attributions that shape the unfolding of legal processes in practice. These elements, too, might manifest the normative force of procedure itself—an aspect that will be explored in greater depth in the analysis below.

At the same time—and to give the analysis another turn—the autonomous logic of procedure reveals its dystopian potential: when procedure becomes detached from substantive law, it risks transforming into a total form—a hollow, self-referential process no longer concerned with

the military—where procedures not merely administer order, but actively constitute identities, norms, and deviations through their structure.

justice, but only with its own perpetuation. In such a configuration, procedure becomes a mechanism of formalized power—unaccountable, opaque, and ostensibly neutral, yet in truth structurally violent. In this vein, procedure without law—or without reference to a legal idea rooted in justice—reduces its subjects to mere objects, caught within a closed procedural loop.[29]

The ever-present risk of procedural law degenerating into pure procedure becomes particularly evident when considering Luhmann's insight that legal procedures are defined by their capacity to establish beginnings and endings.[30] At precisely this point, it becomes evident that even legally codified procedural law is not immune to the pathological dynamic that may lead it to converge with its own degenerate version—the dystopian form of pure procedure. Such a convergence becomes visible, for instance, when the conclusion of legal proceedings is indefinitely delayed by procedural regulations, or—particularly in criminal proceedings—when punishment is procedurally advanced without the issuance of a final verdict.

These developments become possible when procedural steps are no longer assessed in light of their function within the framework of substantive law and the guiding principles of procedural justice—most notably the principle of justice itself—but are instead instrumentalized to discipline those subject to legal authority. This becomes particularly evident in cases where coercive measures under criminal procedure, such as house searches or pre-trial detention, are no longer regarded as constitutionally grounded instruments of investigation, but are in effect employed as anticipatory forms of punishment.

---

29 Perhaps the most striking literary allegory of this dystopia is Franz Kafka's *The Trial* (1914/15). One morning, Josef K. is arrested without ever learning the charge. What follows is an encounter with a bizarre, opaque, and interminable procedure—one that conforms to neither clear rules nor visible authority yet confines him to a bureaucratic labyrinth that generates real consequences. The center of gravity in this trial is not the verdict, but the procedure itself—in all its depersonalized and unintelligible power. Though the process unfolds without reference to prior wrongdoing or substantive norms, it instills in Josef K. an actual sense of guilt—anticipating the productive power of procedures later theorized by Foucault. Kafka illustrates the absence of substantive law even more starkly in the parable *Before the Law*, embedded within the novel. Here, "a man" seeks entry to the law but is continually denied by the "doorkeeper", who represents the procedural form. The "man" dies without ever gaining access. Again, the procedure does not enforce the law—it replaces it and simultaneously obstructs its realization.

30 Luhmann, above fn. 16, p. 208.

In conclusion, a final configuration in the relationship between law and procedure should be considered—one that is not marked by a separation of the two categories, but rather by their fusion. What is at stake here is a phenomenon that recalls the historical beginnings of law in customary practice, the fusion of procedure and substantive order in the form of ritual. In this context, legal validity is produced by the repetition of a ritual act, without the existence of a procedure or substantive law that is separate from it. There is no distinction between norm, procedure, and legitimacy; rather, the ritual practice itself becomes the source of law.[31] If one assumes that residues of this ritualistic form of ordering may still be embedded in modern procedural law, then this perspective opens up an easily overlooked insight into another aspect of power of procedure and its normative implications—an insight by which the modern rituals of justice might be reinterpreted.

From these variations on the relationship between substantive law and procedure—viewed within the broader anthropological context of order, law, ritual, and violence—an important insight emerges regarding the significance and contingency of their nexus in the legal systems of modern, functionally differentiated societies. In such systems, procedure cannot be normatively empty; its legitimacy and functionality depend on an intrinsic connection to substantive law, particularly under the normative horizon of justice.

31 The focus here is not on customary law as such, but rather on the legal ritual within customary law, which differs from the procedural dimension of customary law discussed earlier. Both rituals and procedures, however, generate normative force through processual structures that appear self-evident or without alternative—even though they are historically contingent and subject to change. The resulting normativity thus rests less on objective correctness or rational justification than on factual implementation and social acceptance. From a legal-historical perspective, early procedural forms and ritual practices are admittedly often difficult to distinguish with precision. All the more striking, then, is the contrast with modern law, which—despite the systemic interrelation of substance and procedure—permits their differentiation in principle. **By contrast,** in relation to tribal customary law, Bronisław Malinowski emphasized the need "to re-cast completely the traditional conception of law" in order to acknowledge the fact that "Law and order arise out of the very processes which they govern." Malinowski, *Crime and Custom in Savage Society*, 1926, available at https://wolnelektury.pl/media/book/pdf/crime-and-custom-in-savage-society.pdf, pp. 36.

2. Institutional preconditions: system infrastructure

From the abstract, systems-theoretical perspective on procedural law, we now turn to the empirical conditions necessary for a well-functioning procedural law system.

In the normative domain, foremost are the quality, consistency, and doctrinal elaboration of the applicable legal norms. Equally significant is the quality of judicial decision-making, as evidenced by the depth of reasoning, density of argumentation, and the traceability of judicial opinions. Added to this is the extent to which the law—both in practice and in theory—is reproduced as a coherent system, whether in individual subfields or in its entirety.[32]

At the institutional level, both the number and resources of courts and judicial authorities are important, as is the quality of the state bureaucracy. Moreover, the ratio of legally active professionals to the overall population, as well as the number and qualifications of the various legal professional groups, is decisive. These factors are closely linked to the performance of legal education institutions, particularly universities with law faculties possessing sufficient scientific and didactic substance.

A high-performing legal system is further characterized by the comprehensive reach of state legal enforcement—both in urban and rural areas. Closely connected to this is the density and availability of legal services and institutionalized access to justice, including supporting instruments such as legal aid.

Additional indicators shed light on the practical utilization and societal relevance of the law. These include, in particular, the number of pending cases, case volumes in different types of proceedings, the average duration of proceedings, clearance rates, and the actual enforcement of judicial decisions.[33] The evolution of demand for legal services—as manifested, for

32 See Luhmann, above fn. 16, p. 263 (freely translated from the German original text). "The differentiation of legal procedures constitutes merely a peripheral condition of possibility; the true carrier of the legal system's evolution lies in the specification of how legal discourse refers argumentatively to legal materials. This development marks the breakthrough to an autonomous legal culture—one capable of distinguishing itself from morality, from common sense, and even from the everyday semantics of language."

33 Negative indicators in this regard include the rates at which pending cases exit informally—either due to an 'informal withdrawal' or because of a lack of further action. See Hammergren, *Envisioning Justice: Improving Judicial Reform in Latin America*, 2007, pp. 73 ff.

example, in the proliferation of legal protection insurance or the uptake of external litigation financing—is also significant. An ultimate litmus test for the actual reach of the law is the impunity rate—that is, the presence or extent of legal action taken against those in positions of power.

The quality of a legal system is further reflected in the vibrancy of its academic and professional legal community. This is evident in the number, diversity, and quality of legal publications—such as monographs, handbooks, commentaries, law reviews, legal education literature, annotations of judicial decisions, or compendiums of case law—as well as in the activity and sophistication of legal professional associations and advocacy groups. The intensity and institutional anchoring of the theory-practice discourse also constitute a crucial criterion for the system's capacity for reflection and development.

Finally, the performance and legitimacy of a legal system are revealed in its societal impact: in the public's trust in the judiciary and the rule of law, in the acceptance of judicial decisions—even by losing parties—in actual access to justice, and in the lived equality before the law.[34] Moreover, the existence and societal relevance of alternative or competing normative ordering systems, such as informal social, cultural, or religious rules that serve functions of social regulation and conflict resolution in certain contexts, must also be taken into account.

Against the backdrop of the complexity expressed by these indicators and factors, the overall quality of a given legal system assumes particular importance for the analysis and comparison of law and its constituent parts.

Thus, for example, the simultaneous implementation of identical civil or criminal procedural codes in two different countries would, in a very short time, almost certainly lead to two markedly distinct procedural legal systems in practice—an outcome that underscores the fundamental importance of both the context and subtext of the law. In addition to the influence of the intrinsic quality of the legal system, several other factors also contribute to these marginal conditions of a given procedural system, which will be briefly discussed here.

34 See also Bone, above fn. 4, p. 337.

3. Institutional preconditions: actors and roles in procedural law

Within the framework of comparative procedural law and legal culture studies, a central determinant of the practical operation of any procedural legal system lies in the conduct and configuration of its institutional actors. Particularly significant in this regard are for instance their degree of professionalization, prevailing role conceptions and self-understandings, normative orientations, communicative practices, and the structure of professional supervision and accountability. While these dimensions are to some extent shaped by formal legal norms—especially, though not exclusively, by procedural law—they tend to crystallize into complex and relatively stable patterns of professional behavior and institutional expectation.

These patterns are best understood as the cumulative outcome of multiple intersecting influences, many of which originate outside the domain of codified law. Accordingly, to a significant extent, they form part of a broader set of extra-positive factors that are indispensable for understanding the functional reality of procedural systems. Such factors—often referred to in legal anthropology or legal sociology as components of a legal culture—reveal how law is interpreted, practiced, and internalized by its actors within a given institutional and societal context.

a) Degree of professionalization

A crucial factor influencing the concrete structure and performance of any given procedural system is the degree of professionalism among its key actors—primarily judges, prosecutors, and lawyers, but also notaries, court staff, and police officers. This level of professionalism is significantly determined by initial education and ongoing professional training, as well as by recruitment methods and the attractiveness of each professional field. In general, the overall professionalism of actors within a procedural system can be viewed as a reflection of the quality of the legal system as a whole.

The more numerous and renowned the universities, the higher the number of legal professionals, the more differentiated legal scholarship is, and the more dynamic the self-reflection within the legal system becomes, the greater the opportunities for achieving a high degree of professionalism, particularly within the core legal professions on which we primarily focus here, even though administrative personnel and police officers also represent important procedural actors.

Regarding the education of judges, prosecutors, and lawyers, differences among jurisdictions can be substantial. Variations result from factors such as entry requirements for law studies, the average quality level of incoming students, the duration and rigor of legal education, the failure rate, the focus on or amount of practical training included, and the question of whether the academic program qualifies students equally for all legal careers or imposes higher standards specifically for judges.

A particularly interesting model is the German legal education system. The course of study is relatively flexible in structure, typically lasts more than four years, emphasizes practical case-solving skills, and concludes with an examination administered not by the universities but by government authorities—thus termed a "state examination." This exam is characterized by a high failure rate, and successful completion qualifies graduates directly for doctoral studies. This is followed by a compulsory two-year period of practical legal training within public service, during which candidates receive a temporary salary as public employees and are trained through practical experiences as judges, prosecutors, and attorneys, often assuming real responsibilities from each professional perspective. This second stage concludes with the second state examination, comprising up to nine written exams (each lasting five hours) and an oral examination, serving as a prerequisite for entry into all legal professions equally.

By contrast, if judges undergo more thorough and rigorous training than other legal professionals, this creates a professional disparity that will be reflected in differences in competence and interpersonal dynamics among legal actors.

Equally varied are the opportunities and incentives for continuing professional education among judges, prosecutors, and attorneys. Particularly for attorneys, a key question is whether continuing education is legally mandated[35] and how accessible and practically useful the available programs are. Additionally, in some jurisdictions, such as Germany or Switzerland, attorneys can acquire formal specialization in specific legal fields, a process regulated by law. Obtaining such specialization requires attorneys

35 In Germany, for example, lawyers have a statutory obligation for continuing professional education alongside their regular professional practice according to § 43a of the Federal Lawyers' Act (Bundesrechtsanwaltsordnung, BRAO), which sets out the fundamental duties of attorneys. Specifically, subsection 8 of this provision imposes a duty of ongoing training, requiring lawyers to independently ensure that they possess and maintain the necessary knowledge and skills, meaning they must remain up to date on relevant legal developments.

to demonstrate extensive practical experience and advanced theoretical knowledge in order to carry the corresponding professional title.[36] In many other jurisdictions, attorney specialization is common but typically not regulated through formal specialist titles awarded by the state or professional associations; rather, it emerges informally based on practice, professional reputation, and certifications provided by private organizations.

b) Professional identity and self-image

The professional identity and self-image of key actors—particularly judges, prosecutors, and attorneys[37]—play a crucial role in shaping a procedural legal system. This self-perception is shaped by numerous factors and can be reflected through various indicators. Both formal legal provisions and informal role expectations, as well as unwritten norms, play a decisive role in this context.

Formal factors include institutional rules ensuring judicial independence, as well as explicitly articulated role models found in professional codes of conduct and disciplinary regulations. Additionally, professional cultures, historical traditions, educational standards, societal expectations, and the actual degree of independence, objectivity, and integrity significantly influence the self-perception of these professionals and their public image.

Formal and informal factors often align in promoting either judicial restraint or judicial activism.[38] International comparisons reveal considerable differences in judicial self-perception. In some jurisdictions, the dominant

36 This involves specific continuing education requirements that are additional to the general professional training obligation for lawyers. For example, in Germany, specialized lawyers ("Fachanwälte") must annually engage in scholarly publications or actively participate—as attendees or lecturers—in relevant professional training events (§ 15 Fachanwaltsordnung).

37 Other key actors, such as notaries, court personnel, and police officers, also play important roles in the functioning of procedural systems, but their specific professional identities cannot be explored within the scope of this discussion. Nevertheless, the significance of the non-judicial administrative (support staff of courts, who play a frequently underestimated yet crucial role in ensuring both effective access to legal remedies and the overall efficiency of proceedings) shall be briefly underscored. See Jongbloed, "Judicial Case Management and Efficiency in the Netherlands," 2008, p. 101.

38 See, regarding formal expectations, Farber and Sherry, *Judgment Calls: Principle and Politics in Constitutional Law*, 2008, pp. 56, 85.

judicial ideal is that of a neutral conflict resolver, whereas in others, judges are viewed as active promoters of social justice. Accordingly, some judicial cultures emphasize a reserved, formal style, while others demand a more active, pragmatic approach.

Similarly, attorneys' professional identities vary widely. These range from strictly partisan advocacy ('zealous advocacy'), as exemplified by U.S. lawyers, to the notion of attorneys as 'organs of justice' (Germany) or 'officers of the court' (British barristers).

Prosecutors' self-perception oscillates between two poles: being independent guardians of the law or instruments of state prosecution policies. This self-image often depends significantly on the degree of political oversight and whether prosecutors primarily see themselves as protectors of public security or defenders of individual rights. Specific scenarios in terms of prosecutorial independence arise in systems where prosecutors are either elected or politically appointed, as both is common in the United States. Moreover, the standing and authority of prosecutors can vary considerably. An extreme example of prosecutorial authority is seen in the Japanese and South Korean justice systems, where conviction rates approach extraordinarily high rates, in Japan nearly 100 %, establishing prosecutors as particularly authoritative and influential actors.[39]

Conversely, prosecutors in jurisdictions primarily functioning as mere indictment bodies without independent investigative powers (e.g., Thailand) often enjoy significantly less prominence compared to judges. Such functional limitations, however, can sometimes be overshadowed by historical influences rooted in the colonial era, as seen in Indonesia.

Historical experiences also significantly shape attorneys' professional identities. A prominent example is France, where Émile Zola's famous "J'accuse!" in the Dreyfus Affair continues to reflect an attorney's professional ideal, explicitly incorporating political and social engagement.[40]

---

39 The overall situation in Japan is popularly exemplified by the Japanese legal series "99.9: Keiji Senmon Bengoshi (99.9: Criminal Defense Specialist)," which features an attorney deliberately handling cases he believes belonging to the exceedingly rare 0.1 % acquittal category despite their official handling.

40 Émile Zola's "J'accuse!" was an open letter published in 1898 that accused the French military and government of wrongful conviction, anti-Semitism, and cover-ups in the Dreyfus Affair—a scandal that began as a spy case against Captain Alfred Dreyfus, falsely accused of espionage for Germany. Zola's letter not only exposed deep institutional corruption but also helped transform the affair into a broader crisis of justice and accountability in France. Even though Zola himself was not a lawyer,

This also highlights the political dimension inherent in the self-image of legal professionals. In Italy, this is exemplified by sometimes legendary judges who, despite substantial resistance and considerable personal danger, fought against organized crime in the 1990s, often paying with their lives due to their extraordinary courage, integrity, and independence—most notably Giovanni Falcone and Paolo Borsellino. Such judges embody a judicial ideal characterized not by reserved neutrality but by a determined and publicly visible defense of justice and the rule of law against powerful and violent adversaries. In this context, the institutional guarantees of judicial independence—such as Italy's Consiglio Superiore della Magistratura—play a critical and often politically contested role. Similar institutional influences also shape the legal profession, exemplified by organizations like the American Bar Association or, in Southeast Asia, the Malaysian Bar.

Another influential factor shaping professional self-perception and societal recognition can be the prevalence of family traditions within the legal profession. Such traditions can foster social closure and may contribute, at least tendentially, to an elitist perception of the profession. India serves as a pertinent example of this dynamic.

Nevertheless, it should always be emphasized that these observations are rarely exhaustive descriptions but rather illustrative of prevailing patterns and trends. A final, crucial element in this context is undoubtedly the predominant attitude of legal professionals themselves, encompassing aspects such as integrity and loyalty towards the legal system and its foundational principles—what one might call the "spirit of the laws." Ronald Dworkin aptly summarized this point by stating: "Law's empire is defined by attitude, not territory or power or process."[41]

Thus, while "attitude" constitutes a central quality of legal professionals, especially critical in politically polarized societies, it can also become the explicit focus of projects or broader campaigns. Examples include initiatives such as the Open Justice Project or consciously cultivated traditions of public interest litigation and cause lawyering.

---

the Dreyfus Affair played a significant role in shaping the ideal of legal advocacy in France, influencing perceptions of what lawyers could and should represent in the pursuit of justice.

41 Dworkin, *Law's Empire*, 1986, p. 413.

c) Communication and Interaction

The way legal actors communicate and interact represents one of the constitutive elements of every system of procedural law. Dominant communication patterns shape not only the specific appearance of the procedure but are directly related to its legitimacy, fairness, and efficiency.

A central dividing line is the formal structure of the procedural framework, particularly the prevailing tendency toward adversarial or inquisitorial systems. Communication dynamics are heavily influenced by the way the respective roles are shaped along these lines. In adversarial systems (e.g., common law), confrontational and rhetorically charged communication between the parties is more common, while judicial communication tends to be more reserved. In contrast, inquisitorial systems (e.g., many continental European civil law systems) see judges playing a more active role in the investigation of facts, with communication shaped by greater procedural guidance and generally more neutral interactions between parties. In such systems, parties typically engage in more measured exchanges, while communication with the bench is less deferential.

These distinct communication styles are partly already encoded in procedural law, as seen, for instance, in the regulation and significance of cross-examination. While cross-examination is one of the central procedural practices in the U.S., it does not exist in the German procedural code in the same form. The German, modified version—which restricts judicial discretion far less—has gained little practical significance despite its codification. This latter observation hints at the relevance of those dimensions of legal communication culture that are not governed by positive law.

Naturally, procedural codes also include numerous explicit rules governing communication structures. These partly reflect the procedural system's position on the adversarial-inquisitorial spectrum, but also follow other considerations, such as the implementation of higher principles like fairness or efficiency. While such rules are essential to a system's basic communication framework, they are never exhaustive. Examples include provisions on judicial case management, the sequence of party presentations, judicial duties to provide guidance, the requirement for oral hearings, and the duty to give reasons for judgments.

Equally—if not more—formative than codified procedural rules in shaping the communicative character of legal proceedings are the professional role conceptions and broader societal expectations surrounding legal actors. These normative frameworks emerge from an amalgam of social imaginaries, power structures, legal role relations, and cultural understandings—many of which operate beyond the reach of formal law. Often more dynamic than written procedural norms, they are often subject to critical discourse while also forming culturally consolidated elements of a legal system's communicative architecture.

Rooted in legal culture, professional socialization, and public perception, these informal patterns shape not only the tone and style of interaction between judges, attorneys, and litigants but also inform implicit hierarchies, expectations of deference or assertiveness, and shared notions of procedural decorum. They help constitute what may be described as the 'deep structure' of procedural communication—an unwritten but powerful layer of norms and practices that complements and sometimes supersedes the formal text of the law. This is evident, for instance, in tendencies to conduct proceedings in more authoritarian or cooperative, hierarchical or egalitarian, bureaucratic or theatrically[42] performative ways.

An independent dimension of a legal system's communicative structure—one that is largely uncodified in positive law—manifests in its symbolic expressions: whether in the physical design of the space where proceedings take place or in the ritual elements and their symbolic representations. In this context, it is worth directing attention, on the one hand, to the external architecture of the courthouse and the design of the courtroom itself—such as specific architectural styles, symbols of state authority, elevated judicial benches, or the overall seating arrangement.[43] On the other hand, ritualized status and behavioral norms are equally significant—for instance, the obligation to wear robes, the design of official attire depending on professional role, or the use of formal address when speaking to the court. All these elements vary across procedural systems and are emphasized to differing degrees, depending on how the ritual of justice is actually performed in practice.

Such arrangements may—put differently—reflect or evoke existing power relations. At the same time, however, they may contradict the actual power dynamics that emerge through communicative practice, and thus function more as cultural artifacts than as direct expressions of dominant social hierarchies.

42 For the contrast between bureaucratic and theatrical styles in the context of German procedural law, see Langbein, "The German Advantage in Civil Procedure," 1985, p. 831: "German civil proceedings have the tone not of the theatre, but of a routine business meeting—serious rather than tense."

43 See Mulcahy, *Legal Architecture: Justice, Due Process and the Place of Law*, 2011.

It is necessary to differentiate between various actor relationships. For example, whether state authority is primarily represented by the court or by the prosecution can shape communication patterns significantly. Other important relationships include those between the court and attorneys, between attorneys themselves, between the court and the public—including litigants and courtroom observers—and between attorneys and clients.

Particularly concerning citizens, the key issue is what kind and quality of interpersonal treatment they receive—not only in terms of respecting their procedural rights but also in acknowledging their dignity as individuals.[44]

Among professional actors, the question arises whether interactions are marked by collegiality and cooperation, by confrontation, or by dynamics shaped by significant power asymmetries or equal statuses.

Major differences exist in the relationship between judges and other procedural participants, especially attorneys—whether shaped by formal rules or informal practices. A litmus test for the boundaries of these relationships is often the doctrine of "contempt of court," which gives concrete shape to communicative boundaries in many respects. More generally, the factual configuration of judge-attorney interaction and the status and leeway attorneys enjoy impacts not only the effective representation of parties but also the transparency and accountability of judicial conduct and thus the overall quality of justice. An open and discourse-friendly relationship also supports the legal system's capacity for internal critique and development —its autopoietic self-reflection.

Exploring power structures embedded in dominant communication pattern can begin with simple questions: Who may speak when, for how long, and in what manner? Who is interrupted, and how often? Such inquiries offer insight into the communicative dynamics between professionals—e.g., whether attorneys in systems such as the U.S. or Germany can argue on equal footing with judges, or whether culturally embedded hierarchies restrict open discourse—as well as into the reproduction of social hierarchies within legal proceedings.[45]

Moreover, communication in legal proceedings is also relevant in light of the structuring—and potentially excluding—effects of ritualized procedures and technical jargon. These can pose significant access barriers for

44 See Tyler, *Why People Obey the Law*, Princeton; Oxford: Princeton University Press, 2006.

45 See Jacobi and Schweers, "Justice, Interrupted: The Effect of Gender, Ideology and Seniority at Supreme Court Oral Arguments," 2017, pp. 1379–1496.

laypersons and specific social groups. Such barriers become especially pronounced in multilingual legal systems or when participants do not speak the official language.

The counterpart to formalized and often ritualized courtroom communication is informal communication that occurs outside official records.[46] This includes pre-hearing discussions, hallway conversations, or phone calls between the professional actors in the proceedings, which can significantly influence the course of the process. The functions of these informal communication channels vary and may include effective information exchange, fostering cooperation, strategic planning, and alliance-building. While informal communication can contribute to the fairness and efficiency of the proceedings, it can also undermine them by leading to unjust outcomes or reinforcing structural inequalities—such as in the case of judicial agreements in criminal proceedings.

An intermediate space between formal and informal communication is occupied by institutionalized formats that explicitly incorporate informal elements. Examples include Italy's *camera di consiglio* deliberations or informal preliminary discussions in German criminal proceedings that may lead to formal agreements.[47]

A final aspect concerns the digitalization of procedural communication, which is gaining ground and holds the potential to fundamentally reshape courtroom interaction. This includes virtual hearings, e-filing systems, and digital platforms that influence not only accessibility but also immediacy and equality in proceedings. Digital transformation also introduces new challenges, such as data protection, cybersecurity, and systemic dependencies on technical infrastructure—potentially posing strategic risks. More broadly, the digitalization of procedural communication harbors the capacity to transform not only modes of interaction but the very nature of proceedings, including their symbolic and performative dimensions.

46 See Mulcahy, above fn. 43, p. 83, on "scripted" vs. "unscripted performances".

47 In contrast to plea bargaining, procedural agreements are possible under § 257c of the German Code of Criminal Procedure, but they are much more limited in scope. In this context, communication regarding procedural agreements must always take place during a public main hearing. However, preparatory, non-public discussions, referred to as "legal talks," are not prohibited.

4. Legal technique: practices, methods & styles

A key factor in the practical reality of the procedural legal system is legal technique, the "professional norms"[48] comprising prevailing practices, techniques, methods, and styles employed by the experts involved—judges, prosecutors, lawyers, court staff, and others, drawing from highly diverse sources, with varying degrees of binding force and specificity. However, in most legal systems, they are formulated with the greatest precision, differentiation, and authority for the judiciary.[49] While adjudication reflects an interplay between reason and discretion—balancing free judicial decision-making with formally guided constraint—it is precisely this 'guided constraint' that reveals marked differences across procedural law systems.

In this volume, for example, *Limparangsri* calls for stronger normative guidance in Thai law, while *Kitai-Sangero* highlights Israeli reforms aimed at reinforcing such constraint by positive law.

Accordingly, one must distinguish the level of doctrinal specificity at which positive law regulates such guidance or instead leaves it to informal norms or even judicial discretion, as well as the degree to which the applicable rules and techniques are differentiated, functional, and practically effective.

Generally, these techniques are inherently heterogeneous in nature. While their content and emphasis varies, they are, in most legal systems, partly derived from positive legal sources—laws, regulations, set rules of procedure, and court rulings—and are always influenced by individual preferences.[50] However, to a large extent, they are also shaped by professional norms and traditional practices, methods, and work styles that precede positive law and are characteristic of a particular procedural system. The latter may involve, for example, the rules of legal interpretation, the use of a specific, standardized legal language with its own implications, the practices and work techniques that shape the judicial workflow and the particular form of legal reasoning reflected in decisions. This shall be further examined through some selected examples.

---

48 Farber and Sherry, above fn. 38, p. 113.

49 That said, these professional norms, though framed much more broadly and vaguely, are typically already a core objective of legal education, which seeks to impart the particular skills of legal thinking and practice. See Gerber, *Lawyers, Courts, and Professionalism: The Agenda for Reform*, 1989, p. 29.

50 The individual working style relates to time management, preparation and follow-up of court hearings, and to some extent also the handling of forms and procedural orders.

It may be reiterated at this point that mere legal technique is typically accompanied by positive legal regulation, albeit only to a limited extent. The classical theory of legal methods of interpretation, for instance, is, in most legal systems, either not subject to positive regulation or only minimally so. However, this is hardly surprising. The subject of legal methodology is not always clearly distinguishable from general methods of reasoning, such as hermeneutics or syllogistic thinking and for this reason alone resists exhaustive legal regulation. This is less true, however, for the rules of interpretation, which form the core of legal methodology, as well as for judicial lawmaking.

Nevertheless, even in this regard, it should be noted that the specific concretizations and prioritizations of the rules of interpretation are often as contested as their actual application in practice, which is frequently called into question. Moreover, systemic and logical objections have been raised against the comprehensive regulation of legal application rules, as a mere set of norms cannot determine its own applicability.[51] At the same time, those rules concerning legal application, which are not regulated by law, can have a significant impact on the differences between individual procedural legal systems.

This is even more true for the second example, judicial work techniques that go beyond mere legal methodology. These techniques, largely not regulated by positive law, often nonetheless claim practical validity and can be governed by clearly defined and finely differentiated practices. An example of this is German civil procedural law, which follows a differentiated method for the routine application of law aimed at handling complex civil disputes in a structured manner, particularly distinguishing between the submissions of the plaintiff and defendant, as well as between factual and legal issues.

This approach, called the 'relation technique' (*Relationstechnik*) enables disputes to be sorted, processed, and evaluated clearly and efficiently. As a product of a tradition deeply rooted in legal history, the relation technique is taught to all German lawyers during the mandatory two-year court training that follows the completion of their university studies. This method has been contrasted with the "American obsession with judicial lawmaking" leading to a certain "indifference to judicial law applying" reflected by a practice of applying law to facts "haphazardly rather than routinely," relying

51 See Wank, *Grenzen Richterlicher Rechtsfortbildung*, 1978, p. 17.

"on the parties' lawyers to determine the subject for decision rather than on judges," which might be seen as ultimately to the vanishing of trial.[52]

Another issue with legal technique, whose varying handling in different legal systems can have significant impacts, is the judicial work with the case file. Here too, positive legal regulations, traditional practices, and individual handling intersect, with the most notable difference being found in the traditional practices related to handling the legal file.

While the order, form, and structure of case file management, particularly with regard to transparency, archiving, and access, are regulated by law in many countries, these regulations specify which documents must be included in a case file, under what circumstances files can be maintained digitally, who may access the files, how confidentiality and data protection are ensured, and how long files must be archived. However, non-codified dimensions and practices of case file management can differ significantly.

This begins with the basic understanding of the function of the case file as an element of the judicial process, which can vary greatly depending on the legal culture. While in the inquisitorial system the case file is actively used to guide the procedure and plays a central role, in the adversarial system it is primarily the responsibility of the parties, although judicial interventions, such as case management orders, may still occur.

In the inquisitorial legal tradition, however, case file management is usually not just a technical documentation requirement but is a central element of judicial work and a key tool of procedural control. The aim of this understanding is to reduce complexity through methodological control and formalized systematization, precisely manage the course of proceedings, and secure all relevant information. As part of this approach, a specific style of case management has developed, shaped by historical, administrative, and legal traditions.[53]

---

52 Maxeiner, "Imagining Judges that Apply Law: How They Might Do It," 2009, pp. 469–483.

53 Historically, the practice of keeping case files can be traced back to the medieval canon-law court system, with a particularly refined form emerging in the German Reich through the Imperial Chamber Court (*Reichskammergericht*, 1495–1806). This tradition was in parts subsequently codified by the Prussian General State Law (Allgemeines Landrecht, 1794). According to this tradition, enshrined in regulations or not, the case file must be complete, including, for instance, notes on non-written interactions such as telephone calls. It must clearly identify the author of each entry and comply with the principles of truthfulness and clarity. Additionally, regulations concerning the authority to maintain and manage case files must be observed to

Features of case-file management in the inquisitorial system of Germany for instance include chronological structuring—often accompanied by judicial annotations—, thematic categorization (e.g., evidence, expert opinions, procedural motions), and a hierarchical arrangement in which important documents, such as judicial orders, are separately identified. Additionally, a standardized language is employed to minimize room for interpretative ambiguity, and evidence is systematically preserved within the file.

Keeping in mind that working with the strictly formalized case file significantly steers the proceedings and constitutes a central element of case management, a key component of working with the case file in this regard is preparing judicial summaries or preliminary opinions ("Voten") ahead of court hearings. These concise summaries outline which factual questions need clarification, which legal instructions should be communicated to the parties, and how relevant case law informs the decision. In chamber decisions, the goal of these judicial summaries is to clearly identify pertinent issues and propose a substantiated resolution that takes into account applicable jurisprudence. Typically, case files are reviewed during workflow in reverse chronological order ("from the back").

To briefly mention a final example, another central aspect of the adjudication process concerns judicial reasoning, which plays a crucial role in shaping decisions. It serves as "both an institutional constraint and a psychological one," as well as a provider of transparency and accountability.[54] Significant differences across jurisdictions arise in this regard, depending on the requirements of both positive law and prevailing legal techniques.

B. Procedural Law in the Light of the Individual Contributions of this Volume

The first six contributions in this volume are dedicated to the field of criminal procedure law, drawing on examples from the United States and Germany in comparison (Philip M. Bender), Germany (Matthias Krüger), Israel (Rinat Kitai-Sangero), Thailand (Pokpong Srisanit, Sorawit Limparangsri), and China (Cheng Lei).

The first three contributions primarily examine some of the underlying purposes and guiding principles of criminal procedure in the respective

ensure file retrievability, protection against manipulation, and safeguards against unauthorized access.

54 Farber and Sherry, above fn. 38, p. 44.

jurisdictions. Bender's comparative analysis of the United States and Germany emphasizes the different weights placed on truth and fairness in each system. Krüger focuses on the principle of immediacy in German criminal proceedings, while Kitai-Sangero explores how the truth-seeking function is operationalized within Israeli criminal justice.

The two Thai contributions by Srisanit and Limparangsri adopt a broader institutional lens, addressing selected particularly salient challenges within Thailand's procedural framework and criminal justice practice.

A similarly expansive perspective shapes Cheng's analysis of Chinese criminal procedure, which offers a critical evaluation of major legal and structural reforms. Van Quang Nguyen's chapter complements this discussion by examining the challenges of judicial reform in Vietnam, particularly regarding judicial independence and court organization under socialist constitutional principles.

Subsequently, K. C. Vohrah turns to the topic of arbitration in Malaysia, while Denise Wong and Makoto Hong examine the structure and role of Singapore's International Commercial Court as a hybrid judicial forum for cross-border commercial disputes.

Finally, Anselm Küsters shifts the focus from adjudicative procedure to regulatory rule-making, analyzing the European Commission's stakeholder consultation on digital competition law as a case of participatory and data-driven procedure beyond the courtroom—yet one that raises core questions of procedural legitimacy, inclusion, and epistemic authority central to contemporary procedural law.

Based on this brief overview, focus can be shifted to a short discussion of the individual contributions.

In his article *"Same Ends, Different Means: Truth and Fairness in Criminal Procedure of the United States and Germany,"* Bender addresses a central question in the bilateral comparative study of American and German criminal procedure: the differing emphasis each system places on the principle of justice—both in its substantive dimension, thus the truth-seeking function of the trial ("truth"), and in its procedural dimension, thus the fairness of the proceedings ("fairness").

The starting point of his analysis is the structural divergence between the two procedural frameworks, the adversarial model that characterizes American criminal justice, and the inquisitorial model underlying the German system. At the core of his argument in comparing them lies a distinction originally articulated by Hans-Heinrich Jescheck—a leading scholar of German criminal procedure—and further developed by Bender himself, namely, the distinction between the ends of criminal proceedings and the means by which those ends are pursued.

In the course of his comparative analysis, Bender engages with the fundamental question of how unity and divergence in the implementation of the principle of justice—in its two core dimensions, truth and fairness—manifest within the respective legal systems. To do so, he draws on the aforementioned distinction between an ends-based perspective, which emphasizes the objectives of criminal proceedings, and a means-based perspective, which foregrounds the procedural methods employed to achieve those objectives.

In doing so, Bender deliberately centers his analysis on the justice-oriented purpose of criminal procedure, setting aside efficiency as the second overarching procedural objective and the varying emphasis that each system may place on justice and efficiency in its broader institutional design. By focusing exclusively on justice in its dual dimensions of truth and fairness, Bender is able to examine with conceptual precision how these principles are operationalized in both systems through the lens of ends and means. While the ends-based perspective tends to emphasize structural differences, the means-based perspective reveals notable procedural parallels and even points of convergence.

In his contribution *"Reflections on the Relationship between Immediacy and Credibility in German Criminal Procedure,"* Krüger likewise addresses the justice-oriented function of criminal procedure yet does so by focusing on the principle of immediacy, one of the fundamental principles of German criminal procedure. Enshrined in § 250 of the German Code of Criminal Procedure, this principle requires the court to perceive the facts essential to its judgment as directly and firsthand as possible. Accordingly, evidence should, in principle, be presented orally and in person during the main hearing, while written statements or transcripts of prior examinations may be substituted only in exceptional cases.

The aim of the principle is to enhance the truth-finding process by enabling the court to form an immediate impression of witness testimony, assess credibility, and evaluate the authenticity of evidence. As Krüger puts it, the principle "is intended to lead the court to substantive truth by ensuring the establishment of a solid and reliable factual basis for the decision."

Beginning with a debate that dates back to the 19th century over the actual significance of immediacy in criminal proceedings, Krüger focuses on the tension between the principle's normative primacy and its procedural exceptions.

He centers his analysis on the question of "how far one should stick to the criminal procedural law principle of immediacy because the court can optimally and properly determine the credibility of witnesses in this way."

In examining both legislatively codified and doctrinally contested exceptions, Krüger draws on extensive criminological and psychological research. He concludes that the principle of immediacy must be recognized as fundamentally significant to criminal proceedings, particularly with regard to the evaluation of witness credibility. While further discussion of possible exceptions beyond those already codified may be justified, such debate must remain grounded in and consistent with the foundational weight of the principle itself.

Krüger's analysis—firmly rooted in legal doctrine and enriched by empirical insight—also opens the door to broader reflection on the immediacy principle as a structural element of the communicative architecture of criminal trials. His argument provides a compelling starting point for considering to what extent immediacy is not merely a means of optimizing evidentiary evaluation, but part of a procedural logic in which truth is not simply accumulated but discursively constructed.

This perspective opens up both systems-theoretical and symbolic dimensions. What is at stake is not only what is said in court, but also how, when, and in whose presence—especially with regard to the defense's ability to shape the evidentiary process.

In this sense, the court is not merely observing the witness, but also observing its own observation, thereby contributing to the public legitimacy of the verdict. Viewed in this light, the form of truth production becomes as central to the legitimacy of the outcome as its content.

One may also reflect—comparatively—on the symbolic function of the immediacy principle within the broader performance of the rule of law, particularly in relation to the principle of publicity. In requiring the court to see, hear, and decide "for itself," the principle of immediacy affirms the judiciary as an autonomous, active subject of truth-finding—and thereby reinforces both the court's authority and the structural coupling of law and society.

Rinat Kitai-Sangero's contribution *"Developments in Israeli Criminal Law Procedure,"* examines key dimensions of justice in criminal proceedings during a formative period of Israeli criminal procedure. She focuses, first, on justice in sentencing, with particular attention to the 2012 sentencing reform, and second, on the Israeli Supreme Court's evolving jurisprudence since the early 2000s concerning the balance between truth-seeking and defendants' rights. While these two strands address distinct legal contexts, they can be connected by the underlying idea of a unified concept of justice as well, comprising concretizations as achieving a just sentence through reliable truth-finding and ensuring procedural fairness.

The sentencing reform, introduced through an amendment to the Penal Law, established proportionality as the guiding principle—understood as the balance between the severity of the offense and the offender's culpability—while granting retribution primary status among sentencing goals. Deterrence, rehabilitation, and the protection of public safety serve as secondary considerations. Judges, according to the law, must first determine a proportionate sentencing range based on offense-related factors, then select a specific sentence within that range in light of the defendant's individual circumstances. Limited deviations are permitted: harsher sentences may be imposed to protect public safety, and more lenient ones to support rehabilitation—though the latter is generally restricted to non-severe offenses or exceptional cases. From a comparative perspective, it is noteworthy how extensively sentencing is not left to unwritten conventions or broad judicial discretion but is instead explicitly codified and methodically structured by statute.

In parallel with these legislative developments, the Supreme Court has progressively strengthened procedural fairness by expanding the exclusion of unlawfully obtained evidence. Even without an explicit guarantee of the right to a fair trial in the 1992 Basic Law: Human Dignity and Liberty,[55] the Court has held this right to be implicit in the protection of personal freedom. The emerging exclusionary doctrine reflects a careful balancing act, acknowledging the importance of truth-seeking while affirming that certain investigative methods are incompatible with the normative core of human dignity. Although the framework leaves room for judicial discretion, it marks a clear shift toward embedding fair trial guarantees more firmly within constitutional interpretation—without, however, adopting the U.S. "fruits of the poisonous tree" doctrine in its entirety.

In his contribution *"Issues of Criminal Procedure Law Reform in Thailand,"* Pokpong Srisanit offers a structured and multidimensional analysis of key issues in Thai criminal procedure, combining descriptive exposition with concrete reform proposals. The article highlights structural inconsis-

55 Israel does not have a single written constitution, but a set of Basic Laws enacted gradually since 1950, which together serve as the constitutional foundation of the state.

tencies, normative tensions, and practical deficiencies that affect the fairness, coherence, and human rights compatibility of the Thai system.

A first area of concern relates to institutional contradictions between legal norms and judicial practice. Although the Thai Criminal Procedure Code formally assigns judges an active role in fact-finding—suggesting inquisitorial features—in practice, judges often adopt a more passive stance. This discrepancy, according to Srisanit, undermines the truth-seeking function of trials and should be addressed not through legislative reform, but through a change in judicial practice, which underscores the importance of unwritten professional culture. Another systemic issue lies in the lack of prosecutorial flexibility: prosecutors are limited to either pursuing or dismissing a case, leading minor offenses either to contribute to court congestion or to be prematurely dropped. As a solution, Srisanit proposes introducing conditional suspension of prosecution as a third option.

A second perspective concerns inequalities in the treatment of defendants, particularly regarding bail and charging practices. While the law does not require bail for provisional release, in practice it is routinely imposed and calculated using fixed scales, which disproportionately disadvantage low-income individuals. Likewise, the practice of overcharging—filing charges that exceed what the evidence justifies—distorts the principle of proportionality and can be used strategically to justify pre-trial detention or inflate bail amounts.

A third cluster of concerns centers on human dignity and compliance with international standards. Srisanit draws particular attention to the continued use of chains and irons, which contradicts the presumption of innocence and violates the UN Standard Minimum Rules for the Treatment of Prisoners. In this case, he calls not for stricter application of existing norms, but for their explicit prohibition in law.

Finally, Srisanit addresses the ambiguous role of victims in the Thai criminal justice system. Although victims are allowed to initiate prosecutions independently of the public prosecutor, Srisanit warns that such private prosecutions may distort the public character of criminal law, especially in cases involving out-of-court settlements or strategic litigation. Furthermore, the current state-run compensation scheme for victims remains inadequate. Srisanit proposes establishing a dedicated compensation fund financed by offenders' fines to improve both fairness and sustainability.

In perfect complement to Srisanit's analysis, Sorawit Limparangsri further elaborates on key challenges and reform perspectives within Thailand's criminal justice system. In his contribution, *"The Road Ahead: Challenging*

Issues in the Administration of Criminal Justice in Thailand," he begins from the central thesis that, despite institutional progress over time, the system continues to exhibit structural deficiencies in several critical areas. Through a critically oriented analysis with a strong legal-political focus, he explores a range of problem fields that expose both normative tensions and practical dysfunctions.

A primary area of focus is the criminal accountability of holders of political office. Within Thailand's constitutional framework, which subjects elected bodies to heightened institutional scrutiny, such office holders are governed by a distinct legal regime.[56] First introduced in the 1997 Constitution and retained, with modifications, under the 2007 and 2017 Charters, this special procedure mandates that cases involving political figures be brought directly before a special department of the Supreme Court to insulate proceedings from political interference and to expedite adjudication.

However, Limparangsri highlights the tension between the finality of these one-tier procedures and the right to appeal as recognized under the International Covenant on Civil and Political Rights (ICCPR). While the 1997 Constitution provided no avenue for appeal, the 2007 Constitution introduced a narrowly framed review limited to newly discovered evidence. The 2017 Constitution broadened this by allowing appeals on both factual and legal grounds, to be decided by a separate panel of justices.

An interesting point of connection between Limparangsri's and Srisanit's contributions arises in relation to prevailing styles of judicial decision-mak-

56 It is worth noting that, since the 1997 Constitution, Thai constitutionalism has been consistently characterized by a dichotomous regulation of constitutional authority, carefully distinguishing between powers derived from popular electoral legitimacy—such as the cabinet and the House of Representatives—and institutions considered partially or wholly detached from such legitimacy, notably the judiciary and the so-called independent constitutional bodies, including the Election Commission, the National Anti-Corruption Commission, and the Human Rights Commission. A central function of these non-political institutions is the containment of the perceived vagaries of electoral democracy within the framework of Democracy with the King as Head of State. See for the background Glaser, "Permutations of the Basic Structure: Thai Constitutionalism and the Democratic Regime with the King as Head," 2021, pp. 233–251. As a consequence of the prevailing institutional mistrust toward electoral politics, corruption in context of elected office is framed within the legal system as a particularly severe and systemic threat. This perception has led to a structural bias in anti-corruption enforcement, with elected office holders subject to especially strict legal and institutional scrutiny. A prominent manifestation of this asymmetry is the special treatment of political office holders in the criminal justice system through the Supreme Court's Criminal Division for Persons Holding Political Positions.

ing. While Srisanit explicitly addresses the predominance of adversarial tendencies in Thai criminal trial practice—even where these diverge from the formal legal framework—Limparangsri's analysis of proceedings against political office holders touches upon an area where legal and institutional actors have, in broader reform discussions, considered a more inquisitorial orientation.

The second issue in Limparangsri's article concerns deferred prosecution as a form of diversion from formal criminal proceedings. Intended to reduce case backlog, this mechanism allows prosecutors to suspend charges under certain conditions. While seemingly pragmatic from an efficiency standpoint, Limparangsri raises concerns about the lack of clear criteria, external oversight, and procedural transparency.

He criticizes the vague requirement that the suspension be "beneficial for the accused, the injured party, and society" as overly broad and prone to discretionary abuse. Moreover, since the scheme often does not require an admission of guilt or active responsibility-taking, he argues that it lacks meaningful restorative elements and risks facilitating unequal treatment, undue inducement, or coerced confessions.

Limparangsri then turns to the role of victims in criminal proceedings—long marginalized in Thailand's system, which used to center almost exclusively on the alleged offender. Legislative developments, particularly the 2010 Juvenile and Family Court Act and the 2007 Domestic Violence Protection Act, illustrate however, how restorative justice principles can empower victims and support social reintegration. These laws enable structured, consent-based forums where harm is acknowledged, and accountability expressed. Limparangsri advocates for a cautious extension of such mechanisms into adult criminal justice, emphasizing voluntary participation and procedural safeguards.

Finally, Limparangsri turns to sentencing as another domain he identifies as normatively fragile—thus addressing a field also examined in this volume by Kitai-Sangero for Israeli law. In Thailand, sentencing remains largely discretionary, with judges relying on unpublished internal guidelines based on accumulated practice rather than publicly accessible frameworks. While these guidelines are not binding, they often influence decisions in ways that remain opaque to the parties. Limparangsri notes that this lack of transparency and consistency undermines public trust and limits defendants' ability to anticipate legal outcomes. He therefore advocates for the development of a dedicated sentencing procedure—such as a separate sentencing hearing—that would allow for broader evidentiary input and more principled deliberation.

Additionally, he calls for empirically grounded, flexible, and publicly available sentencing frameworks to guide judicial discretion and reduce disparities. Finally, existing mechanisms such as sentence suspension or deferral for minor first-time offenders should, in his view, be applied more systematically to avoid unnecessary stigmatization and to support reintegration.

In conclusion, Limparangsri emphasizes that while Thailand's criminal justice system has evolved, meaningful progress demands ongoing reform. He calls for a forward-looking, legally sound, and socially responsive recalibration of criminal procedures—one that combines institutional robustness with fairness, transparency, and inclusivity. Justice, he argues, is not a fixed state but a dynamic process that must continually adapt to uphold its legitimacy in a changing society.

Cheng Lei's contribution "*The Second Revision of the Chinese Criminal Procedural Law and the Respect for and Protection of Human Rights,*" offers a detailed account on the Chinese Criminal Procedural Law, in particular after its 2012 revision, appreciating the reform as a pivotal step in the gradual transformation of the Chinese criminal justice system under the constitutional mandate to "respect and protect human rights." Framed against the backdrop of the 2004 constitutional amendment, which introduced this mandate into the Constitution's general principles, Cheng portrays the 2012 revision as a legal codification of years of experimental reforms and political initiatives serving both as a response to institutional shortcomings and as an affirmation of the state's ambition to modernize its procedural framework within the boundaries of one-party constitutionalism.[57]

57 To better understand the constitutional framework in which the reform dynamics discussed by Cheng unfold, it is helpful to view them in light of what might be labelled as "socialist one-party constitutionalism". This type of constitutionalism characterizes a constitutional order in which the Chinese Communist Party (CCP) holds a normatively and structurally superior position vis-à-vis all state institutions, including the legislature, courts, and procuracy. While the Chinese Constitution affirms principles such as legality, rights protection, and institutional differentiation, these operate within a political framework organized around the Leninist principle of democratic centralism—a structure of centralized authority and vertical discipline that governs both intra-party organization and the relationship between the Party and the state. Within this context, legal reforms—such as the 2012 revision of the Criminal Procedural Law—when introducing new procedural norms and rights protections must not disrupt the basic tenets of the constitutional system such as the

Three structural rationales underpin the reform effort. First, the law addressed systemic deficits in the criminal process—most notably, the absence of codified guarantees for key procedural rights, the vagueness of evidentiary standards, and the overreliance on internal ministerial interpretations. Second, it aimed to legalize a series of institutional practices—such as conditional non-prosecution, structured sentencing, juvenile-specific procedures, and the exclusion of illegally obtained evidence—that had previously operated on an ad hoc or experimental basis. Third, the reform advanced the political project of building a rule-based administrative and judicial system "with Chinese characteristics," thereby enhancing the legitimacy of legal institutions within the framework of state-led governance.

Thematically, the revision introduced substantial innovations across eight areas, including: the addition of an explicit human rights clause; improvements to evidentiary standards and the introduction of the exclusionary rule; revised rules on detention, bail, and residential surveillance; strengthened rights of defense and legal counsel; expanded procedural protections against investigative abuse; greater emphasis on witness participation; a new chapter on special procedures (e.g., for juveniles, mentally ill defendants, and confiscation in absentia); and updated enforcement provisions such as community correction.

In the Chinese context, procedural innovation generally serves a dual function by introducing elements of due process while simultaneously consolidating state control through the formalization of discretion. Cheng's analysis is particularly attuned to the tension between legal modernization and institutional constraints. While the revised law codifies numerous procedural safeguards—such as the presumption of innocence, access to counsel during the investigative phase, and prohibitions on coerced confessions—the implementation of these norms remains uneven. Cheng, moreover, emphasizes that many of the problems the 2012 revision sought to address—notably, the low rate of witness appearances and the persistence of informal police practices—have proven resistant to legal change.

---

primacy of centralized political leadership. This relationship has been succinctly articulated by President and Party General-Secretary Xi Jinping, who stated in 2019 that China must "never follow the path of Western 'constitutionalism,' 'separation of powers,' or 'judicial independence'." Xi, "Speech at the Central Conference on Party and State Institutional Reform," 2019., quoted in Tiezzi, "Xi: China Must Never Adopt Constitutionalism, Separation of Powers, or Judicial Independence," 2019, at https://thediplomat.com/2019/02/xi-china-must-never-adopt-constitutionalism-separation-of-powers-or-judicial-independence/.

In the years following its implementation, several of its central provisions, such as the exclusionary rule and the expanded role of defense counsel, have been clarified and extended through subsequent implementing regulations. Yet persistent challenges still remain. The underlying problems of opaque police discretion, weak evidentiary scrutiny, and minimal adversarial practice continue to constrain the realization of procedural fairness.

In this light, Cheng's chapter contributes not only as a substantive case study of legislative reform and criminal justice modernization in China, but also as a lens onto the broader phenomenon of authoritarian legality revealing how human rights discourse and procedural rationalization can coexist with—and be subsumed by—a system that maintains centralized political control.

Van Quang Nguyen's contribution examines the structural and normative challenges to judicial independence in Vietnam, highlighting the persistent tension between constitutional principles rooted in socialist legal thought and the broader ambitions of judicial reform. Rather than focusing on a specific area of procedural law, Nguyen develops his inquiry through a detailed examination of Vietnam's court organization as a whole. After outlining the institutional architecture of the Vietnamese court system, the article turns to the enduring obstacles to judicial independence—especially those that emerge from constitutional doctrines governing the structure and operation of the state apparatus.

Anchored in Vietnam's political-legal tradition—characterized by a form of socialist one-party constitutionalism similar to, though distinct from, that of China as analyzed by Chen—Nguyen shows how the existing administrative unit-based court system entrenches local political dependencies. These dependencies, which extend to judicial appointments, budgeting, and informal channels of oversight, systematically compromise judicial autonomy, particularly in politically sensitive administrative law cases. As a structural remedy, Nguyen explores the proposed transition toward a jurisdiction-based court system. In this model, newly established regional courts would operate independently of provincial authorities, thereby insulating the judiciary from local political interference while maintaining national political coherence.

What distinguishes Nguyen's analysis is its framing of judicial reform not merely as a question of institutional redesign, but as a constitutional problem. He identifies two principles that simultaneously guide and constrain the reform process, the leadership of the Communist Party of Vietnam (CPV) and the doctrine of concentrated state power. Rather than challenging these principles outright, Nguyen advocates their functional recalibration. He suggests, for instance, that Party leadership might be reoriented toward strategic policy formulation, with a clearer demarcation from operational or case-level judicial decision-making. In doing so, Nguyen situates judicial reform within Vietnam's constitutional tradition, offering a nuanced path forward that seeks to strengthen judicial independence without undermining the ideological and institutional foundations of the Vietnamese state.

Dato Karam Chand (K.C.) Vohrah's contribution *"Arbitration in Malaysia,"* offers a comprehensive and historically informed account of the evolution of arbitration law and practice in Malaysia, tracing its transformation from colonial-era reliance on English common law to a modern statutory framework aligned with international standards. The article situates the Arbitration Act 2005 within Malaysia's broader legal-political context, emphasizing the country's transition from fragmented British-influenced jurisdictions to a centralized federal legal order with a strong statutory orientation.

Structured in three parts, the article first provides a legal-historical overview of Malaysia's federated system and colonial legacy, then outlines the types and institutional modalities of arbitration—including both ad hoc and institutional proceedings—and finally delivers a detailed exposition of the Arbitration Act 2005.

The Act's model-law orientation, particularly its adoption of the UNCITRAL Model Law on International Commercial Arbitration, is presented as a decisive break from the outdated 1952 Act and its reliance on English precedent.

Vohrah highlights key features of the reformed regime, including enhanced party autonomy, judicial non-intervention, the principle of Kompetenz-Kompetenz, and the strengthened enforceability of arbitral awards. He also examines the role of arbitration institutions such as the Kuala Lumpur Regional Centre for Arbitration, now renamed Asian International Arbitration Centre (AIAC), noting its increasing international profile and regulatory innovations.

Rich in statutory and jurisprudential detail, the article provides both doctrinal orientation and practical insight into the operational dynamics of arbitration in Malaysia. At the same time, it situates these developments within a broader trajectory of legal modernization, thereby offering a valuable point of reference for comparative debates on arbitration reform and the domestication of international legal standards in Southeast Asia.

In their contribution *"Singapore's International Commercial Court,"* Denise Wong and Makoto Hong examine the structure, procedural design, and institutional positioning of the Singapore International Commercial Court (SICC), established in 2015 as a division of the Singapore Supreme Court with the aim of offering a forum for the resolution of complex cross-border commercial disputes. The SICC forms part of Singapore's broader strategy to consolidate its role as a hub for international dispute resolution in Asia, complementing its success in the field of arbitration.

Constitutionally integrated into the Supreme Court to ensure enforceability abroad, the SICC operates under a hybrid model that draws on both litigation and arbitration. Its bench includes both local and international judges, and it allows the participation of foreign counsel subject to simplified registration. Jurisdictionally, the SICC hears cases that are international and commercial in nature, with access conferred through submission agreements or court transfers. Its procedures diverge from standard domestic litigation by adopting flexible, internationally oriented practices, such as modified discovery rules inspired by the IBA Rules on the Taking of Evidence in International Arbitration and the possibility to apply foreign evidentiary standards upon party request.

The SICC's procedural innovations also include a differentiated approach to confidentiality: hearings are generally public, but offshore cases may be granted confidential treatment. Foreign law can be determined by submission rather than formal proof, allowing parties procedural flexibility. Decisions are published, subject to redactions where necessary, contributing to the development of a jurisprudential corpus.

Judgments of the SICC are enforceable as judgments of the Singapore High Court, and Singapore's accession to the 2005 Hague Convention on Choice of Court Agreements enhances the prospects for recognition in other jurisdictions. The authors contrast this with the arbitral model, whose confidentiality and ad hoc nature limit its contribution to the development of transnational commercial law.

The final section situates the SICC within the broader context of international arbitration and efforts to articulate a global lex mercatoria. Wong and Hong argue that the SICC's institutional features—public judgments, judicial continuity, and procedural transparency—position it to support the harmonization of commercial norms. In this way, the SICC offers a procedural alternative that retains judicial control while addressing the needs of international commerce, contributing to the evolution of dispute resolution formats beyond conventional adjudication.

Anselm Küsters' contribution *"EU Competition Law in the Digital Age: Substantive Challenges and Methodological Innovations Using the Example of the European Commission's Consultation Procedure,"* finally examines the European Commission's 2019 stakeholder consultation on competition law in the digital economy. The focus lies both on the substantive challenges posed by digitalization—particularly with regard to data, algorithms, and platforms—and on the procedural structure of consultation as an emerging regulatory format. Unlike the other contributions in this volume, which center on adjudicative procedure and judicial organization, Küsters turns to the rule-making phase of competition law and to informal, participatory processes preceding formal legal change.

The first part of the study outlines core structural features of digital markets. Data is presented as a competitive input, differentiated by source and type, with particular attention to legal and technical issues surrounding access, portability, and substitutability. Algorithms are analyzed in terms of their complexity, adaptive functions, and potential to facilitate collusion or price discrimination. Platforms are treated as multi-sided markets characterized by network effects and vertical integration, raising specific concerns related to abuse of dominance, merger control, and market definition. In each domain, existing legal categories—such as Article 102 TFEU or the essential facilities doctrine—are examined for their applicability to digital contexts.

The second part investigates the structure and content of the consultation process launched by DG COMP. Based on 108 written submissions, Küsters applies Structural Topic Modelling (STM), a computational method for identifying thematic clusters in large text corpora. The analysis reveals distinct patterns of argumentation across different stakeholder groups—undertakings, academics, NGOs, and authorities—and explores how these positions reflect institutional interests, funding structures, and geographic origin.

Finally, the contribution compares the consultation input with the subsequent Expert Report commissioned by the Commission. It traces how topics such as data access, platform governance, and merger thresholds were taken up or reframed. This comparative analysis is complemented by a procedural reflection on stakeholder participation as a form of informal pre-legislative engagement. Drawing on regulatory literature, the study identifies representativeness, effectiveness, and transparency as central features of such processes and considers their relevance for evolving understandings of procedural legitimacy.

Positioned at the intersection of competition law, regulatory theory, and digital methodology, the contribution concludes the volume by expanding the perspective beyond adjudication and formal legal procedure, illustrating how procedural questions arise not only in courts and hearings but also in the structuring of consultation, participation, and evidence generation within digital governance.

Bibliography

Augustine, Aurelius, Bishop of Hippo, *The City of God*, trans. E. M. Edghill, Urbana, IL: Project Gutenberg, 2014, https://www.gutenberg.org/files/2412/2412-h/2412-h.htm#part01.

Baxter, Hugh, "Niklas Luhmann's Theory of Autopoietic Legal Systems," *Annual Review of Law and Social Science* 9 (2013): 175–184.

Bone, Robert G., "Making Effective Rules: The Need for Procedure Theory," *Oklahoma Law Review* 2, 61 (2008): 319–340.

Cara, Arben, and Mimoza Margjeka, "Kanun of Leke Dukagjini Customary Law of Northern Albania," *European Scientific Journal* 11, 28 (2015): 174–186.

Dworkin, Ronald, *Law's Empire*, Cambridge, MA: The Belknap Press of Harvard University Press, 1986.

Ehrlich, Eugen, *Grundlegung der Soziologie des Rechts*, München, Leipzig: Duncker & Humblot, 1913.

Farber, Daniel A., and Suzanna Sherry, *Judgment Calls: Principle and Politics in Constitutional Law*, Oxford; New York: Oxford University Press, 2008.

Foucault Michel, *Discipline and Punish: The Birth of the Prison*, reprint edition, New York: 1995.

Foucault, Michel, *The History of Sexuality, Volume 1: An Introduction*, London: Allen Lane, 1976.

Foucault, Michel, *Security, Territory, Population: Lectures at the College De France, 1977–1978*, ed. Michel Senellart, trans. Graham Burchell, London: Palgrave Macmillan, 2007.

Foucault, Michel, *The Birth of Biopolitics: Lectures at the College De France, 1978–1979*, ed. Michel Senellart, trans. Graham Burchell, London: Palgrave Macmillan, 2008.

Gardner, James A., "The Sociological Jurisprudence of Roscoe Pound (Part II)," *Villanova Law Review* 2, 7 (1961): 165–192.

Glaser, Henning, "Permutations of the Basic Structure: Thai Constitutionalism and the Democratic Regime with the King as Head," in *Thai Legal History: From Traditional to Modern Law*, ed. Andrew Harding and Munin Pongsapan, Cambridge: Cambridge University Press, 2021, pp. 233–251.

Gerber, Rudolph J., *Lawyers, Courts, and Professionalism: The Agenda for Reform*, New York: Greenwood Press, 1989, p. 29.

Hammergren, Linn, *Envisioning Justice: Improving Judicial Reform in Latin America*, University Park, PA: Pennsylvania State University Press, 2007.

Jacobi, Tonja, and Dylan Schweers, "Justice, Interrupted: The Effect of Gender, Ideology and Seniority at Supreme Court Oral Arguments," *Virginia Law Review* 7, 103 (2017): 1379–1496.

Jongbloed, A. W., "Judicial Case Management and Efficiency in the Netherlands," in *Judicial Case Management and Efficiency in Civil Litigation*, ed. C. H. van Rhee, Antwerp: Intersentia, 2008, pp. 93–107.

Kant, Immanuel, "The Metaphysics of Morals," in *Immanuel Kant: Practical Philosophy*, ed, Mary J. Gregor, Cambridge, UK: Cambridge University Press, 1996.

Langbein, John H., "The German Advantage in Civil Procedure," *University of Chicago Law Review* 4, 52 (1985): 823–866.

Luhmann, Niklas, *Das Recht der Gesellschaft*, Frankfurt am Main: Suhrkamp, 1995.

Luhmann, Niklas, *Social Systems*, Stanford, CA: Stanford University Press, 1995.

Luhmann, Niklas, *Law as a Social System*, Oxford: Oxford University Press, 2004.

Main, Thomas O., "The Procedural Foundation of Substantive Law," *Scholarly Works* 741 (2010): 801–841.

Malinowski, Bronisław, *Crime and Custom in Savage Society*, New York, 1926, available at https://wolnelektury.pl/media/book/pdf/crime-and-custom-in-savage-society.pdf.

Maxeiner, James R., "Imagining Judges that Apply Law: How They Might Do It," *Penn State Law Review* 2, 114 (2009): 469–483.

McIntyre, Joe, *The Judicial Function: Fundamental Principles of Contemporary Judging*, Singapore: Springer, 2019.

Mulcahy, Linda, *Legal Architecture: Justice, Due Process and the Place of Law*, Abingdon: Routledge, 2011.

Posner, Richard A., *Economic Analysis of Law*, 2d ed., Boston, Massachusetts: Little Brown & Co, 1977.

Rex v. Sussex Justices, ex parte McCarthy [1924] 1 KB 256.

Rottleuthner, Hubert, "A Purified Sociology of Law: Niklas Luhmann on the Autonomy of the Legal System," *Law & Society Review* 5, 23 (1989): 779–796.

Roxin, Claus, *Strafverfahrensrecht*, 25th ed., München: C.H. Beck, 1998.

Schmitt, *Politische Theorie. Vier Kapitel zur Lehre von der Souveränität*, 8th ed., Berlin: Duncker & Humblot, 2004.

Souleimanov, Emil Aslan, and Huseyn Aliyev, "Blood revenge and violent mobilization: evidence from the Chechen Wars," *International Security* 40, 2 (2015): 158–180.

Spencer-Brown, George, *Laws of Form*, London: Allen & Unwin, 1969

Tyler, Tom R., *Why People Obey the Law*, Princeton; Oxford: Princeton University Press, 2006.

Walter, E. V., "Legal Ecology of Roscoe Pound," *University of Miami Law Review* 2, 4 (1950): 187–207.

Wank, Rolf, *Grenzen Richterlicher Rechtsfortbildung*, Berlin: Duncker & Humblot, 1978.

Xi, Jinping, "Speech at the Central Conference on Party and State Institutional Reform," *Qiushi* [求是], February 28, 2019, quoted in Shannon Tiezzi, "Xi: China Must Never Adopt Constitutionalism, Separation of Powers, or Judicial Independence," *The Diplomat*, February 28, 2019, https://thediplomat.com/2019/02/xi-china-must-never-adopt-constitutionalism-separation-of-powers-or-judicial-independence/.

Same Ends, Different Means: Truth and Fairness in Criminal Procedure of the United States and Germany

Philip M. Bender

A. Introduction

Both the adversarial, or coordinate, criminal procedure of the United States and the inquisitorial, or bureaucratic, system of Germany[1] must strike a balance between truth (substantive justice), on the one hand, and fairness (procedural justice), on the other.[2] Jescheck summarized this observation in the following way: "The goal of the German proceeding, like that of the American, is the determination of the objective truth on the basis of and within the framework of the procedural forms which the law prescribes."[3] Since both countries pursue truth and fairness, "[t]he difference between German and American procedural law does not lie [...] in the high ideals

1 See Kagan, *Adversarial Legalism: The American Way of Law*, 2001 (opposing adversarial legalism, as defined on p. 9, to bureaucratic legalism, as defined on p. 11); Damaška, "Structures of Authority and Comparative Criminal Procedure," 1975, pp. 480, 483–509 (continental bureaucratic model), 509–523 (U.S. adversarial model). See also Turner, "Limits on the search for truth in criminal procedure: a comparative view," 2016, p. 38; Walpin, "America's Adversarial and Jury System: More Likely to Do Justice," 2003, p. 175, 175; Weigend, "Is the Criminal Process about Truth?: A German Perspective," 2003, p. 157, 158 (using the distinction between adversarial and inquisitorial). See also Langbein, *Comparative Criminal Procedure: Germany*, 1977 (criticizing "inquisitorial" due to its negative connotation). See also Roxin and Schünemann, Strafverfahrensrecht: Ein Studienbuch, 2017, § 17 para. 6 (underlining that the difference only refers to the main hearing, not the initial accusation, and therefore describing the German model as accusation-based process with inquisitorial hearing).

2 On procedural and substantive legitimacy in general Christiano, "The Authority of Democracy," 2004, p. 266, 266 (in the context of democratic legitimacy). On the (parallel) distinction between output- and input-legitimacy Scharpf, *Governing in Europe: Effective and Democratic?*, 1999, pp. 6, 7 ff. (input-legitimacy), pp. 10 ff. (output-legitimacy).

3 Jescheck, "Principles of German Criminal Procedure in Comparison with American Law," 1970, p. 239, 240. On theoretical grounds on the conflict between factfinding accuracy and other values, see generally Damaška, "Truth in Adjudication," 1998, pp. 289, 305–307.

which have been set, but rather in the *methods* chosen to obtain them."[4] I will call this way of looking at comparative criminal procedure the *means-based narrative*. According to this narrative, criminal justice in both the United States and Germany pursues the same ends: truth *and* fairness. They only do so by different means.

In contrast to this means-based narrative, an important part of the academic contributions on criminal procedure tries to make sense of the differences between U.S. and German criminal procedure in terms of the ends pursued. I will refer to this other explanatory model as the *ends-based narrative*. According to the ends-based narrative, the German system aims at objective truth while U.S. criminal procedure is said to aim at formal, consensual, interpretive, or procedural truth only.[5]

In this strong version, the ends-based narrative is untenable from both an internal (doctrinal) and external (theoretical) perspective. From an *internal* perspective, the participants of both systems act at least as if there was something like objective truth, but they also recognize the need for limiting truth for the sake of fairness. The similar way in which U.S. and German courts articulate their legal decisions illustrates this point: yes, German courts do underline the important objective of finding the truth[6]—but not "at all cost."[7] And yes, U.S. courts do sacrifice truth for the sake of fairness—but they do so only reluctantly and likewise emphasize that the criminal process is about truth.[8] From an *external* perspective, the truth of criminal justice is determined through the legal process and therefore

4 Jescheck, above fn. 3, p. 241. See also Weigend, above fn. 1, p. 158.

5 See generally Weigend, "Should We Search for the Truth, and Who Should Do It," 2011, p. 389, 396 ("Traditionally, correspondence theory has been regarded as congruent with inquisitorial procedural systems, whereas the adversarial process prevalent in common law countries has been said to reflect consensus theory."); Pizzi, "Soccer, Football and Trial Systems," 1995, p. 369, 369 ("a trial system that seems to be more about winning and losing than it is about truth"); Grande, "Comparative Approaches to Criminal Procedure: Transplants, Translations, and Adversarial-Model Reforms in European Criminal Process," p. 67, 69 (objective versus interpretive truth); Roxin and Schünemann, above fn. 1, § 15 para. 6. This aligns with the focus of academia on substantive law, cf. Dubber, "Criminal Process in the Dual Penal State: A Comparative-Historical Analysis," 2019, p. 15 ("In German criminal law, substance has long been privileged over process.").

6 See, e.g., BGH NJW 2011, 2417, 2419.

7 Ibid.

8 See *United States v. Herring*, 555 U.S. 135, 141 (2009); *United States v. Leon*, 468 U.S. 897, 911 (1983).

procedural in both systems. Truth might only survive as some form of regulative idea.[9]

However, one could tell the ends-based narrative in a weak version. Indeed, one could underline that even though U.S. criminal procedure aims at truth as well, it is more prone to sacrifice truth for fairness than the German system.[10] The historic origins of both systems seem to support this interpretation. Besides, that version of the ends-based narrative seems to be a powerful tool to explain the procedural differences in terms of the presence or absence of jury trials, plea bargaining, exclusionary rules, and the impeachment of witnesses.

The weak version of the ends-based narrative might indeed capture some differences between the United States and Germany. But it also has its problems. Most legal institutions of the criminal process do not serve only truth *or* fairness. Rather, they can be conceptualized as different means to serve truth *and* fairness. Instead of focusing on the differences in the ends pursued, the study of comparative criminal procedure might benefit from emphasizing and further pursuing the means-based narrative.[11]

This essay aims at illustrating how historic developments in both countries and legal institutions can be explained in terms of both truth and fairness. It outlines a possible version of the ends-based narrative and at the

---

9 On the difference between the internal and external perspective concerning law, see eg Dworkin, "Hard Cases," 1975, p. 1057, 1090 ("internal logic of the law"). See also Litowitz, "Internal versus External Perspectives on Law: Toward Mediation," 1998, pp. 127, 127–128; Mandel, "Dworkin, Hart, and the Problem of Theoretical Perspectives," 1979, pp. 57, 59–60. In a particularly narrow sense Neumann, *Wahrheit im Recht: Zu Problematik und Legitimität einer fragwürdigen Denkform*, 2004, pp. 57–58. In the context of legitimacy (and with specific understanding) Herz, "Legitimacy: Can We Retrieve It?," 1978, pp. 317, 318–319; Christiano, above fn. 2, p. 269. Specifically on the concept of a "regulative idea" in the sense of Kant, see Neumann, in this fn., pp. 37–41; Canaris, "Richtigkeit und Eigenwertung in der richterlichen Rechtsfindung," 1993, p. 23, 41.

10 In that direction, cf. Thibaut and Walker, "A Theory of Procedure," 1978, pp. 541, 541–542 (associating adversarial procedures and justice as opposed to autocratic procedures and truth); Damaška, "Evidentiary Barriers to Conviction and Two Models of Criminal Procedure: A Comparative Study," 1973, pp. 506, 583–584, especially 583 ("Concern to establish the 'real truth' has serious competitors in 'collateral' considerations under the adversarial system [...].").

11 In that vein, see Jescheck, above fn. 3, p. 240. For this approach to comparative analysis, see generally Zweigert and Kötz, *An Introduction to Comparative Law*, 1998, p. 40. See also Pargendler, "The Role of the State in Contract Law: The Common-Civil Law Divide," 2018, p. 143, 178 (in the area of contract law).

same time relativizes this outline by pointing to the need for a means-based narrative, which completes the picture of comparative analysis.

In that spirit, I want to examine the legal origins of both systems (see B. below), the presence or absence of jury trials (see C. below), plea bargaining (see D. below), exclusionary rules, especially the fruit of the poisonous tree doctrine (see E. below), and rules concerning the impeachment of witnesses (see F. below). I will first interpret each of these points according to the ends-based narrative, associating the U.S. adversarial model with fairness and the German inquisitorial system with truth. Then, I will show that just as we can interpret U.S. rules in terms of truth, we can make sense of the German legal institutions in terms of fairness. I thereby provide concrete support for the thesis that the main difference resides in the means applied to reach the common ends, evoking the need for a means-based narrative. In a brief conclusion (see G. below), I will suggest that the means-based analysis should focus on the different design of legal norms in both systems—a point I develop in greater detail elsewhere.[12]

B. Historic Origins

Legal institutions develop over time, and many different factors certainly contribute to the emergence of the criminal procedure as we know it today in different countries. For the sake of simplicity, it is possible to illuminate some of these factors. Depending on where we shed light, either the ends-based narrative or a possible means-based narrative is more plausible.

I. The Ends-Based Narrative

At first glance, the ends-based narrative, which associates fairness with the adversarial and truth with the inquisitorial model, seems to find support in the historic origins of both systems. Indeed, the adversarial common law is sometimes presented as the legal successor of the medieval duel, a kind of trial by battle[13]—characterized by a fair fight with an open outcome. Of course, there is a big difference between fighting with swords and legal

12 See Bender, "Comparative Norm Design: The U.S. Rules Model and the German Standards Model in Criminal Justice and Beyond," 2024, p. 1.

13 See, e.g., Leeson, "Trial by Battle," 2011, p. 341, 341.

arguments. But even now, U.S. adversarial legalism is parties-driven and associated with litigant activism and passive judges.[14] In contrast, the continental criminal system is presented as the successor of the ecclesiastically inspired, medieval, judge-driven inquisition aimed at discovering the truth —even if by means of torture.[15] Of course, many things have changed here, too. Torture has been banned and a separation between the accusation (in the hands of the prosecutors) and the main judicial proceedings (in the hands of the judges) has been introduced.[16] But still, the idea of material truth is underlined over and over again in German criminal law, and at least the main judicial proceedings are still described as inquisitorial[17] and dominated by a powerful judge.[18] German Code of Criminal Procedure (*Strafprozessordnung [StPO]*),[19] section 244(2), prominently summarizes the point: "The court shall, in order to establish the truth, ex officio extend the taking of evidence to all facts and means of proof which are relevant to the decision." In short, history seems to explain the ends-based narrative: whereas adversarial legalism is the heir of the duel and organized around principles of fairness, German criminal procedure is the offspring of the medieval inquisition, aimed at revealing the truth.

II. The Need for a Means-Based Narrative

However, matters are more complicated. First, the historical lines are not as easy to draw. Trial by battle, for instance, was a classic Germanic way of settling disputes, which only came to England with the Norman Conquest.[20] Thus, it was a historical feature of continental Europe as well as

14 Kagan, above fn. 1, p. 9. See also Roxin and Schünemann, above fn. 1, § 69 para. 1 (still conceiving of U.S. criminal procedure as boxing).

15 On the inquisitorial heritage, see, e.g., Schroeder, *Strafprozessrecht*, 2018, pp. 265–266 (para. 392).

16 On these changes, see Jescheck above fn. 3, p. 239 (also pointing to the fact that jury trials existed for a brief time in Germany as well).

17 Critical of the common use of "inquisitorial" due to its negative connotation, see Langbein, above fn. 1, p. 1.

18 On this characteristic feature of (continental) criminal procedure, see Jescheck, above fn. 3, pp. 248–249.

19 Translation at http://www.gesetze-im-internet.de/englisch_stpo/ (accessed 14 July 2024).

20 Cf. Maitland, *The Constitutional History of England: A Course of Lectures Delivered*, 2001, p. 9; Thayer, "The Older Modes of Trial," 1891, p. 45 45

of England. Second, the association of duel and fairness on the one hand, and inquisition and truth on the other, is highly problematic. Through the external perspective of our modern eyes, both bloody duels and tortuous inquisitorial processes do not meet our perceptions of fairness. Nor are they particularly good tools for determining the truth.[21] However, if we take the historical, internal perspective of medieval societies seriously,[22] both procedures might have actually lived up to the ideals of both truth and fairness. The use of torture was heavily regulated by specific procedural rules, which implemented some sort of procedural justice.[23] The duel (trial by combat, trial by battle) can be interpreted not only in terms of fairness but also in terms of truth since it was a way to invoke the judgment of God to determine who is right. Indeed, it is important to see that trial by combat existed in parallel to different forms of trial by ordeal, in which the capacity of holding glowing irons due to divine miracles determined guilt or innocence.[24] Given all this, it is difficult to draw clear lines from fairness or truth to adversarial or inquisitorial criminal procedures. Rather, both systems seem to have developed following the same ideas pursued by different means.

---

21 On the ineffectiveness of torture to discover the truth, see, e.g., 1992 U.S. Army Field Manual FM 34–52 on Intelligence Interrogation, pp. 1–8 ("Use of torture and other illegal methods is a poor technique that yields unreliable results, may damage subsequent collection efforts, and can induce the source to say what he thinks the interrogator wants to hear."). On the possibility to explain the ban on coercive interrogation methods in terms of truth-seeking, see also Damaška, above fn. 3, p. 289, 306–307.

22 On this sociological approach of taking the internal perspective of a studied society, see Beetham, *The Legitimation of Power*, 2013, p. 11 ("A given power relationship is not legitimate because people believe in its legitimacy, but because it can be *justified in terms of* their beliefs."). See also Habermas, "Legitimationsprobleme im modernen Staat," 1976, pp. 39, 58–59 (taking the internal perspective even more seriously).

23 These were contained, among others, in imperial legislation, notably in the Constitutio Criminalis Carolina from 1532 (*Peinliche Gerichtsordnung Karls V.*), see Schroeder, above fn. 15, pp. 265–266 (para. 392). See also Langbein, "Torture and Plea Bargaining," 1978, p. 3, 7.

24 On (the decline of) judicial ordeals in detail Whitman, *The Origins of Reasonable Doubt: Theological Roots of the Criminal Trial*, 2008, pp. 51 ff. For a secular (economic) interpretation of trial by battle in land disputes, see Leeson, above fn. 13, p. 345 (para. 13).

C. Jury Trials

Let us now turn to the presence or absence of juries, which has been described as the core institutional difference between U.S. and German criminal procedure.[25] Can we make sense of this difference by analyzing it through the lenses of truth and fairness?

I. The Ends-Based Narrative

The ends-based narrative seems to suggest a plausible explanation of U.S. jury trials and their absence in Germany. The goal of adversarial legalism, one could say, is to tame the judicial power by means of procedure. In this case, the procedure dictates that not one, but two institutions are involved in determining punishment. The judge decides on the admissibility of evidence in pre-trial proceedings as well as the specific punishment to be imposed on the convicted person in sentencing proceedings. However, between these two procedural stages, a jury of laypersons determines the issue of guilt on the basis of admissible evidence.[26] This jury usually consists of twelve randomly selected citizens that do not receive special training and have no "privileged access" to the truth.[27] But the unanimity-requirement for jury verdicts[28] and the division of power between the jury and the judge procedurally control the power of those that act on behalf of the state.[29] The power is also strictly limited, for both jury and judge act rather passively so that the parties drive the procedure.[30] In addition to these checks and

25 Underlining this as one of the core aspects Jescheck, above fn. 3, pp. 243–245.

26 On the constitutional origins of the right to trial by jury in criminal cases, see U.S. Constitution, article 3, section 2, as well as the 6th Amendment. This right does not apply to petty offenses, where imprisonment is for six months or less, see *Baldwin v. New York*, 399 U.S. 66 (1970); *District of Columbia v. Clawans*, 300 U.S. 617 (1937).

27 In federal court, the number of twelve is constitutionally required, *Patton v. United States*, 281 U.S. 276 (1930). The jury requirement also applies to the states through the 14th Amendment. However, on the state-level, a number of six is still constitutional, see *Williams v. Florida*, 399 U.S. 78 (1970), but a number of five is not, see *Ballew v. Georgia*, 435 U.S. 223 (1978).

28 The unanimity-requirement applies to federal and state courts alike, see *Ramos v. Louisiana*, 20 April 2020, Docket No. 18–5924, 140 S. Ct. 1390.

29 On checks and balances as a feature of American criminal procedure, see Jescheck, above fn. 3, p. 250.

30 Cf. Kagan, above fn. 1, p. 9 ("litigant activism").

balances element, the jury introduces an element of direct democratic legitimation into the criminal procedure.[31]

In Germany, the picture is quite different. The judge determines without a jury whether the defendant is guilty or not.[32] The central norm on this point is German Code of Criminal Procedure, section 261, which reads as follows: "The court shall decide on the result of the taking of evidence at its discretion and conviction based on the entire content of the hearing." Besides the issue of guilt, the court also determines the intensity of the punishment (the sentence) that will be inflicted according to the guilt of the convicted person.[33] In other words, the determination of guilt and punishment is in the hands of the same institution: the judge. Few procedural safeguards prevent abuse of judicial discretion. However, the judge received extensive legal training[34] and is controlled by a well-structured hierarchy.[35] In this context, one could say, procedural safeguards are needed less.[36] The logic of legitimacy is substantive.[37] Whereas multiple checks and balances structure the U.S. criminal process according to values of procedural justice, the German system is based on substantive control. In sum, the contrast between an oppositional adversarial system that aims to convince a group of laypersons according to the rules of fairness in one case and a monolithic inquisitorial hearing driven by legal experts towards truth in another further seems to illustrate the common ends-based narrative.

---

31 In the field of torts, cf. James, "Functions of Judges and Jury in Negligence Cases," 1949, p. 667, 686.

32 On the free evaluation of evidence in the German system, see Roxin and Schünemann, above fn. 1, § 45 para. 43.

33 On that point, see German Criminal Code (*Strafgesetzbuch [StGB]*), section 46(1), translation at http://www.gesetze-im-internet.de/englisch_stgb/ (accessed 14 July 2024) ("The offender's guilt provides the basis on which the penalty is fixed."). On discretion in sentencing and the differences to the U.S. system, in which often sentencing enhancement statutes leave only very limited discretion to the judge, see Kaspar, "Sentencing Guidelines vs. Free Judicial Discretion – Is German Sentencing Law in Need of Reform?," 2020, pp. 345–347; Hörnle, "Sentencing in US-American Jurisdictions: A Commentary from a German Perspective," 2020, p. 183; Hörnle, "Moderate and Non-Arbitrary Sentencing Without Guidelines: The German Experience," 2013, p. 189.

34 On professionalism, see, e.g., Kagan, above fn. 1, pp. 68, 73; Damaška, above fn. 1, p. 492. See also Hörnle, above fn. 33, p.188.

35 On hierarchy as a feature of the continental system, see Damaška, above fn. 1, pp. 483 ff. See also Kagan, above fn. 1, pp. 11, 71.

36 Cf. Kagan, above fn. 1, p. 87.

37 See above, fn. 7.

II. The Need for a Means-Based Narrative

Yet again, the ends-based narrative cannot fully explain the procedural differences between the United States and Germany, even if it does capture some important disparities. The jury determines the *facts* of the case, and in that context, it evaluates evidence. The logic behind it is that a group of ordinary citizens does a better job in doing so than the judge.[38] Legal training might give the judge privileged access to *legal* answers. But this legal training does not necessarily imply better knowledge of facts. Therefore, the jury is not only an institution that splits power, multiplies decision-makers,[39] and implements democratic proximity,[40] but in its internal logic, it also serves truth.

Just as we could explain the legitimacy of the jury also in terms of substance, we can criticize it in terms of fairness. For instance, one could advance the argument that juries are more susceptible to the brilliant rhetoric of highly skilled lawyers, distorting the arm's length fight between equal parties if one side does not have the resources to match the other.[41]

Finally, it is important to see that the idea of multiplying decision-makers by involving several professional judges and the concept of creating proximity to the community by adding lay judges is common in the continental system as well. For instance, some criminal cases are decided by one professional judge and two lay assessors, each of them having one vote.[42] This can even lead to the judge being outvoted by two laypeople on a legal point since the majority decides the case.[43] Furthermore, lay participation and voting concern factual and legal issues alike, extending

38 In the field of torts, see James Jr., above fn. 31, pp. 685–686 (pointing to the common sense wisdom the jury is supposed to bring to the problems of finding facts and evaluating conduct).

39 Cf. Damaška, above fn. 1, pp. 512–513.

40 James Jr, above fn. 31, p. 686.

41 On inequality as a feature of the American criminal justice system, see Kagan, above fn. 1, pp. 67, 93–96. For an evaluation of juries compared to judges in general, see Robbennolt, "Evaluating Juries by Comparison to Judges: A Benchmark for Judging?," 2005, p. 469.

42 See German Courts Constitution Act (*Gerichtsverfassungsgesetz [GVG]*), section 29(1), first sentence, translation at http://www.gesetze-im-internet.de/englisch_gvg/ (accessed 14 July 2024) ("The bench shall consist of a Local Court judge as presiding judge and two lay judges.").

43 See German Courts Constitution Act, section 196(1) ("The court shall give its decision by an absolute majority vote unless otherwise provided by statute."). This, of course, will usually not happen due to the dominance of the professional judge, see

community participation even to areas in which in the United States the court decides without any participation of laypeople. In conclusion, both systems multiply decision-makers and include ordinary citizens because they are supposed to serve both truth and fairness. They just do so in different ways.

D. Plea Bargaining

After having briefly explored the division of decisional power between judge and jury, we can now turn to plea bargaining, one of the most (in)famous institutions of U.S. criminal procedure, and to its equivalent in Germany. We will see to what extent we can make sense of the differences in terms of truth and fairness.

I. The Ends-Based Narrative

At first glance, plea bargaining seems to illustrate the ends-based narrative, associating U.S. criminal procedure to fairness and the German system to truth. In the United States, the defendant can plead guilty and thereby avoid the jury trial, which determines the guilt in case the defendant pleads not guilty.[44] The plea is based on the consent of the defendant. This consent could be interpreted as a procedural approach to criminal justice at the expense of truth. As an institution based on procedural justice, the consent-based guilty plea can easily be combined with other institutions of procedural justice—for instance, with an agreement between the defendant and the prosecution in which the defendant trades a guilty plea for a reduction in punishment.[45] The guilty plea and plea bargaining describe, in that narrative, the procedural and fairness-oriented approach of U.S. criminal justice.

Damaška, above fn. 1, p. 493. See also Dubber, fn. 5, p. 14 (describing the participation of lay judges as largely ceremonial).

44 For the sake of plea bargaining, guilty pleas and nolo contendere pleas largely have the same effects, namely, to cut off the jury trial. For the sake of simplicity, we will concentrate on guilty pleas. On the different options, see U.S. Federal Rules of Criminal Procedure, Rule 11(a). See also Bender, above fn. 12, p. 27.

45 On the adversarial logic of plea bargaining, see Langer, "From Legal Transplants to Legal Translations: The Globalization of Plea Bargaining and the Americanization Thesis in Criminal Procedure," 2004, p. 1, 36.

In Germany, things are quite different. Initially, German criminal procedure did not mention any form of dealing or bargaining at all—to the point that Germany could be described as "land without plea bargaining."[46] The judge was supposed to decide on the basis of law and evidence alone. This corresponds to the idea that truth and punishment are beyond the disposition of the parties. In other words, in the German system, the search for truth is not only the default position but the mandatory and overarching goal of the whole criminal procedure. In that vein, even a confession does not relieve the judge of the duty to investigate what really happened.[47]

However, things are not as simple any more.[48] An article from 1982, published under a pseudonym, drew attention to informal dealing in the German criminal system at least since the seventies.[49] Of course, dealing in Germany takes slightly different forms: instead of the guilty plea, the defendant offers a confession[50] and instead of the parties alone, the deal involves the active court of the German system, which even takes a central place in the negotiations.[51] In that sense, we see the common phenomenon that migrating legal institutions are not simply transplanted into but always adapted to the context of the receiving legal system.[52] The same is true for legal institutions that develop in parallel in different legal systems: they also adapt to the specific context.[53]

---

46 Langbein, "Land Without Plea Bargaining: How the Germans Do It," 1979, p. 204.

47 Langer, above fn. 45, pp. 11, 37. See also Jescheck, above fn. 3, pp. 247–248.

48 The following presentation is also contained in Bender, above fn. 12, pp. 28–30.

49 Deal, "Der strafprozessuale Vergleich," 1982, p. 545. The real name of the author is Hans-Joachim Wieder.

50 Langer, above fn. 45, p. 40.

51 Ibid., pp. 40–41. See also Gilliéron, "Comparing Plea Bargaining and Abbreviated Trial Procedures," 2019, p. 713.

52 See Langer, above fn. 45, pp. 5, 32–35 (therefore speaking of legal translation). On a theory of legal transplants from a comparative law perspective cf. Watson, *Legal Transplants: An Approach to Comparative Law*, 1993. pp. 21 ff.; Watson, "The Evolution of Law: Continued," 1987, p. 537; Watson, "Aspects of Reception of Law," 1996, p. 335. Critically (due to the historicity and culture-dependence of law) cf. Legrand, "Comparative Legal Studies and Commitment to Theory," 1995, p. 262; Legrand, "The Impossibility of 'Legal Transplants'," 1997, p. 111. Critically at least as regards those legal institutions with a strong cultural imprint cf. Kahn-Freund, "On Uses and Misuses of Comparative Law," 1974, p. 1.

53 Indeed, according to Langer, above fn. 45, p. 39, in Germany, the deal rather developed due to the practical needs of the German system than due to the influence of American criminal procedure.

Even though the German confession-dealing adapted to the specificities of German criminal procedure and is, in many ways, quite different from U.S. plea bargaining, frictions and irritations remain.[54] First, there is an irreconcilable tension between the deal and the idea of seeking truth, since the very nature of the deal is to economize on investigative efforts (*truth problem*).[55] Moreover, there is a conflict between the idea of achieving a punishment proportionate to the guilt of the defendant because it is inherent in the deal that punishment deviates from guilt: in case the defendant actually committed the crime, she should receive no reduction in punishment; in case she didn't, she should receive no punishment at all (*proportionality problem*).[56] Finally, the deal is incompatible with the active, inquisitorial judge of the German system, whose dominant procedural position was designed to lead an inquisitorial proceeding, not to be a part of the deal at a level playing field (*dominant judge problem*).[57]

At first, the German Court of Justice (*Bundesgerichtshof*) tried to mitigate these problems.[58] Then, in 2009, the legislature officially recognized the negotiated agreement (*Verständigung*)[59] and codified requirements of legality in a bunch of provisions—most notably, but not only, in German Code of Criminal Procedure, section 257c. Section 257c(1) s. 2 states that the obligation to investigate the truth remains unaffected, presumably solving the truth problem. According to section 257c(4) s. 1, the court ceases to be bound to the punishment agreed upon if it believes the punishment no longer corresponds to the guilt of the defendant, presumably solving

54 On irritations caused by legal transplants, see Teubner, "Legal Irritants: Good Faith in British Law or How Unifying Law Ends up in New Divergences," 1998, p. 11.

55 On this conflict, see Roxin and Schünemann, above fn. 1, § 17 para. 20; Langer, above fn. 45, p. 39.

56 Roxin and Schünemann, above fn. 1, § 17 para. 21, § 69 para. 1.

57 On that point notably ibid., § 17 para. 24, 29, § 69 para. 1.

58 Notably the decision of the 4th Senate of the German Federal Court of Justice (*Bundesgerichtshof [BGH]*) from 1997, BGHSt 43, 195, 201 ff. See also BGHSt 50, 40, 63 (decision of the Joint Senate from 2005) pointing to the need for statutory regulation. From the decisions of the German Federal Constitutional Court (*Bundesverfassungsgericht [BVerfG]*), see BVerfG NStZ 1987, 419.

59 Initially, the agreement was commonly referred to as *Absprache*, see, e.g., Langer, above fn. 45, pp. 39–46, which is close to the meaning of deal. The statutory provision uses the more positive term of negotiated agreement (*Verständigung*), e.g., in German Code of Criminal Procedure, sections 35a s. 3, 257c, 273(1a) s. 1, 302(1) s. 2. These negotiated agreements are the product of previous discussions (*Erörterungen*), possible at every stage of the proceeding, see German Code of Criminal Procedure, sections 160b, 202a, 212, 243(4) s. 1.

the proportionality-issue. For that case, section 257c(4) s. 3 orders the inadmissibility of the confession, presumably limiting the power of the inquisitorial judge and solving the dominant judge problem.[60] Furthermore, according to German Code of Criminal Procedure, section 302(1) s. 2, a waiver of appellate remedies is without effect if a court decision preceded the judgment, thereby guaranteeing the control of the active and dominant judge by higher courts.[61]

Of course, for critics, this statutory regulation is nothing but lip service, unable to rescue the truth-seeking German criminal proceeding from its decline.[62] In 2013, the German Federal Constitutional Court (*Bundesverfassungsgericht*) declared the deal-regulation nonetheless constitutional if the statutory requirements are scrupulously respected[63]—which it had to emphasize since it diagnosed heavy shortcomings in the enforcement of the law and continued secret dealing. To sum up, in the eyes of the ends-based narrative, plea bargaining fits U.S. criminal justice because of its orientation towards fairness. In contrast, the German truth-seeking criminal procedure

60 In principle, the appellate court is not bound by the agreement. Therefore, it is neither bound by the prohibition to use the confession of the accused despite the withdrawal of the lower court from the deal. Nonetheless, it cannot inflict a harsher punishment on the accused based on the confession. If only the accused appealed, this follows from the prohibition of harsher punishment contained in German Code of Criminal Procedure, section 331 (so-called interdiction of *reformatio in peius*). If the prosecution appealed as well, German Code of Criminal Procedure, section 331, does not help. However, the fair trial principle of European Charter of Human Rights, article 6, is mainly interpreted in that the higher court has to be bound by the previously negotiated agreement, see, e.g., OLG Karlsruhe NStZ 2014, 294; OLG Düsseldorf StV 2011, 80. Differently OLG Nürnberg NStZ-RR 2012, 255. Details are far from being settled.

61 According to German Code of Criminal Procedure, section 35a s. 3, the convict is to be informed that she can always appeal the decision.

62 Notably Roxin and Schünemann, above fn. 1, § 17 para. 19–32, § 69 para. 1–3. Already before the legislative change with regard to jurisprudential rules Schünemann, *Wetterzeichen vom Untergang der deutschen Rechtskultur: Die Urteilsabsprachen im Strafprozess als Abgesang auf die Gesetzesbindung der Jusitz und den Beruf unserer Zeit zur Gesetzgebung*, 2005; Schünemann, *Absprachen im Strafverfahren?: Grundlagen, Gegenstände und Grenzen*, 1990; Schünemann, "Die Verständigung im Strafprozess – Wunderwaffe oder Bankrotterklärung der Verteidigung?," 1989, p. 1895.

63 BVerfGE 133, 168, especially 225–228 (paras 102–106) (on the compatibility with the constitutional requirement of proportionality of punishment according to the guilt, and the connected obligation to investigate the material truth). But see also 234 (para. 119) (pointing to the deficient implementation of the statutory provision [*Vollzugsmangel*]).

conflicts with dealing. These conflicts are either irreconcilable or heavy regulation is needed to preserve the orientation towards truth.

II. The Need for a Means-Based Narrative

At closer inspection, this ends-based narrative cannot fully explain the different approaches towards plea bargaining in criminal procedure. First, it is important to see that the deal is not only problematic in terms of truth but in terms of fairness as well. The defendant finds herself in a coercive situation that makes the negotiated guilty plea or confession inherently unfree—to the point that structural parallels between plea bargaining and medieval torture have been drawn.[64] In that vein, the deal conflicts with the right against self-incrimination (conceptualized in Germany as the *nemo tenetur* principle).[65] In U.S. criminal procedure, the coercive nature is particularly salient because enormous sanction gaps exist between a conviction after trial and a conviction after a guilty plea. The coercion is further increased by sentence enhancement statutes that mandate a specific punishment.[66] Even though these sanction gaps are not as great in Germany, the German system has to deal with an additional source of coercion stemming from the dominant position of the inquisitorial judge (dominant judge problem).[67] Given this, the deal is at odds with the adversarial and the inquisitorial system alike.[68] Neither truth nor fairness can explain negotiated agreements, but the logic of efficiency.[69]

Just as we are able to criticize the deal in terms of fairness, we can also explain it in terms of truth. To understand this point, we have to see that a judicial decision absent a deal can also go wrong. The defendant

---

64 See Langbein, above fn. 23, pp. 12–19 (arguing that both torture and plea bargaining developed as a subterfuge to excessively high procedural safeguards and that both are inherently coercive in nature).

65 The *nemo tenetur* principle is presupposed in German Code of Criminal Procedure, section 136a. On that, see (in the context of the deal) Roxin and Schünemann, above fn. 1, § 17 para. 11, § 44 para. 68b.

66 On that, see Kagan, above fn. 1, p. 85. See also Vogel, "Plea Bargaining under the Common Law," 2019, pp. 755–757.

67 See supra, fn. 57.

68 Grande, above fn. 8, p. 83.

69 Cf. ibid. Skeptical on whether plea bargaining actually serves efficiency, see Vogel, above fn. 66, pp. 758–759.

always faces the risk of an unjust conviction and punishment.[70] A particular challenge of the German system consists in the knowledge the judge has of the prosecutorial files (leading to perseverance) and the personal exchange between the prosecution and the bench (leading to a shoulder-to-shoulder stance), which might bias the judge in favor of conviction.[71] Therefore, even if truth is the goal in the internal logic of the trial, it need not be reached. In a system where dealing is strictly banned, the risk of incorrect decisions might even be particularly high. Indeed, resources available to the administration of justice are limited. Less dealing means more judicial decisions and fewer resources per case. This in turn might incentivize the judge to largely rely on the prosecutorial file,[72] which in the end leads to a higher error rate at the expense of the defendant. The deal takes these facts—particularly the possibility of error and the limitation of resources—into account. It is supposed to mitigate error risks and to reach a result that, overall, might come closer to the truth than the results of a system which completely bans dealing. Of course, it might fail in this endeavor as well. We have already pointed out the threats to truth and fairness. But it is possible to argue in favor of plea bargaining in terms of truth as well if we conceive of it as a tool to mitigate error risks.

Finally, dealing is connected to the truth-seeking function in another way since the very existence of a deal influences the determination of guilt. Even in the German system, cooperation by the defendant with the prosecution, e.g. by confessing, is and has always been a well-established guideline in determining the punishment.[73] The confession of the defendant is a

70 Cf. Turner, above fn. 1, p. 45. Compared to trials, plea bargaining seems to produce fewer errors in the form of acquittals of the guilty and more in the form of false convictions, see Vogel, above fn. 66, p. 752. Therefore, in terms of truth, they are particularly problematic for the defendant, not the punishing state.

71 On inertia or perseverance, see Schünemann and Bandilla, "Perseverance in Courtroom Decisions," 1989, pp. 182–183. See also Roxin and Schünemann, above fn. 1, § 1 para. 16, § 69 para. 1. On solidarity or the shoulder-to-shoulder stance between judges and prosecutors in Germany, see Roxin and Schünemann, above fn. 1, § 69 para. 2.

72 On the increasing importance of the prosecutorial investigation phase in German criminal procedure, see Roxin and Schünemann, above fn. 1, § 69 para. 1.

73 See, e.g., Langbein, above fn. 46, p. 221 (relativizing his statement of p. 219 that there is no reduction in punishment for a confession); Langer, above fn. 44, p. 42. The legal basis is German Criminal Code, section 46(2), point 7, which authorizes the court to take the offender's conduct in the period following the offense into consideration. The rewarded cooperation does not only concern the defendant's own proceedings. If she helps to uncover other crimes, the option to reduce punishment is even more official and substantial, recognized by German Criminal Code, section 46b.

mitigating factor. If this is the case, however, the defendant necessarily takes a tactical approach towards her confession, regardless of whether one institutionalizes this confession as part of a deal or not. In addition to the sentencing proceeding, this mitigating aspect of cooperation can also explain the greater leniency towards the accused in alternative proceedings to the trial hearing, such as the penal order proceeding (*Strafbefehlsverfahren*) or disposition of the case according to limited prosecutorial discretion, e.g. against payment of a fine.[74] In sum, plea bargaining, an institution that is best understood in terms of efficiency, conflicts with and residually fosters both truth and fairness. Therefore, a means-based analysis alone misses important aspects. Rather, the analysis of U.S. plea bargaining and its German equivalents suggests that a means-based analysis is needed to complete the comparative picture.

E. Exclusionary Rules

We can now have a look at the admission and exclusion of evidence and see how the ends-based narrative plays out here. More precisely, we will examine how violations of procedural rules by public officials affect the admissibility of evidence and examine the U.S. exclusionary rule in comparison to its German counterpart. One of the shining comparative law examples of this area is the fruit of the poisonous tree doctrine of U.S. criminal procedure. We will examine whether we can make sense of the presence and absence of this doctrine in terms of truth and fairness.

I. The Ends-Based Narrative

In the U.S. criminal system, evidence obtained in violation of the rights of the defendant is inadmissible. In addition, all evidence obtained based on information accessible only through the evidence illegally obtained is

74 On the Penal Order Proceeding, see Langbein, above fn. 46, pp. 213–218. On the limited role of the principle of expediency (*Opportunitätsprinzip*) for the disposition of petty crimes, see Langbein, above fn. 46, pp. 223–224 (on p. 224 referring to German Code of Criminal Procedure, section 153a, as "a mild form of plea bargaining").

also inadmissible.[75] It is considered a fruit of the poisonous tree. The U.S. system is ready to sacrifice truth if one party—the law-enforcing government—disregards the "fair play" rules of the game. It needs this fruit of the poisonous tree doctrine to sanction the public officials.[76] The prosecution is considered an interested party of the game that focuses not on truth but on winning. The only way to avoid disastrous outcomes is to scrupulously observe the procedural rules. If, for instance, the prosecution obtains a map indicating the location of the dead body in a search conducted in conscious violation of the warranty-requirement, not only is the map inadmissible but most likely also the dead body found only because the prosecution had previously violated the rules of the game. The dead body is (also) poisoned in a metaphorical sense.

In the German system, the court itself determines which evidence it considers admissible. In general, it is reluctant to exclude evidence since truth is best served when considering all relevant information. If a violation of the rights of the defendant occurred, the piece of evidence obtained in this context might still be admissible. The decision is taken according to a balancing test, in which the interest of society in punishment and the interest of the defendant in safeguarding the rights of the accused are evaluated. The severity of the offense of the defendant and the severity of the violation of the procedural rules of prosecution by public officials guide this balancing of interests.[77] Sometimes, a reduction in the punishment[78] or a stricter approach in appreciating the convincing nature of the evidence

75 See *Silverton Lumber Co v. United States*, 251 U.S. 385 (1920); *Nardone v. United States*, 308 U.S. 338 (1939); *Wong Sun v. United States*, 371 U.S. 471 (1963); *Taylor v. Alabama*, 457 U.S. 687 (1982). See also Bender, above fn. 12, p. 15.

76 On that origin, see Harris, "Verwertungsverbot für mittelbar erlangte Beweismittel: Die Fernwirkungsdoktrin in der Rechtsprechung im deutschen und amerikanischen Recht," 1991, pp. 313, 313–314; Hermann, "Neuere Entwicklungen in der amerikanischen Strafrechtspflege," 1985, p. 602, 608.

77 See, e.g., BGH NJW 1998, 959, 961; BGHSt 51, 285 (para. 20). On the factors, see also Harris, above fn. 74, p. 318. Of course, some (binding) statutory provisions on the exclusion of evidence, see German Code of Criminal Procedure, section 136a(3) or 100d(2) s. 1, as well as (non-binding) rules contained in judicial decisions attenuate the differences to the U.S. system to a certain degree. See also below fn. 104. See also Weigend, "Continental Cures for American Ailments: European Criminal Procedure as a Model for Law Reform," 1980, p. 381, 397 ("the German Code of Criminal Procedure contains but the vertiges of an exclusionary rule," referencing German Code of Criminal Procedure, section 136a).

78 See BGHSt 52, 48, 55 ff. (so-called *Vollstreckungslösung*).

is required as an alternative to the all-or-nothing solution of exclusion.[79] Even if the balancing favors exclusion, the counsel of the accused normally still has to object to the admission of the evidence.[80] Finally, this balancing only concerns the piece of evidence obtained directly through the violation. Even if this evidence is inadmissible, further evidence obtained on the basis of the inadmissible evidence might still be admissible.[81] In other words, this further evidence is not considered a fruit of the poisonous tree. There is, in principle, no "long-distance effect" (*Fernwirkung*) of the violation.[82] In the above-mentioned example, the map might be inadmissible (or not, depending on the balancing of interests), but in any case, this does not prevent the dead body from being evidence in court. The fruit of the poisonous tree doctrine is seen unfit for the German legal context: the prosecution is not the adversary of the defendant but an "objective" institution, looking for the truth (and not for victory).[83] Prosecutors also search for evidence that might help the defendant and they do not need the deterrence of the fruit of the poisonous tree doctrine. Their extensive training aims at minimizing mistakes and the hierarchical structure in which the state officials operate guarantees enough potential of sanctions.[84] Thus, exclusionary rules and

79 See, e.g., BGHSt 46, 93 (so-called *Beweiswürdigungslösung*). In contrast, the alternative of lowering the punishment by assuming that a part of the sentence has already been executed (so-called *Vollstreckungslösung*), see, e.g., BGHSt 52, 48, 55 ff., could not establish itself in the area of the admissibility of evidence, see contra that BGH NJW 2008, 1090, 1093.

80 On that, see, e.g., BGHSt 38, 214; 39, 349, 352 (so-called *Widerspruchslösung*). On the restriction of inadmissibility in case of procedural violations through the principle of proportionality, the necessity of counsel's objection, the option to reduce punishment, and the option to heighten the requirements in appreciating the evidence, see generally and critically Roxin and Schünemann, above fn. 1, § 24 para. 30.

81 From a comparative perspective, see Jescheck, above fn. 3, p. 246.

82 See, e.g., BGHSt 27, 355, 357; 34, 362, 364. See also Roxin and Schünemann, above fn. 1, § 24 paras 59–60. In the end, however, and as we will see, this depends on pondering different factors. One aspect here is—like in U.S. criminal procedure—the question of whether the evidence hypothetically could have been obtained legally, see on that BGHSt 32, 68; Harris, above fn. 76, pp. 320–321.

83 See, e.g., von Liszt, "Vortrag im Berliner Anwaltsverein am 23. März 1901," 1901, p. 179, 180 (ironically describing the prosecution as the "most objective office in the world" and contrasting this common description with the obligation of prosecutors to comply with the official instructions of their superiors according to German Court Constitution Act, section 146).

84 See, e.g., Roxin and Schünemann, above fn. 1, § 24 para. 60. On hierarchy and professionalization as features of continental systems, see Damaška, above fn. 1, pp.

especially the presence or absence of the fruit of the poisonous tree doctrine seem to align with the ends-based narrative.

II. The Need for a Means-Based Narrative

On closer inspection, however, strict exclusionary rules, and especially the fruit of the poisonous tree doctrine, are far less emblematic of the U.S. system than it seems at first glance. On the one hand, U.S. criminal procedure strictly limits their scope of application. On the other, the German system sometimes excludes evidence in a way that resembles the fruit of the poisonous tree doctrine.

Let us first turn to the limited scope of the U.S. exclusionary rule, especially of the fruit of the poisonous tree doctrine. Even though in practice largely presented as such, the exclusion of evidence is no automatism. Rather, conscious balancing is required: "the benefits of deterrence must outweigh the costs."[85] Just like in Germany, the U.S. Supreme Court is concerned with the exclusionary rule's "costly toll upon truth-seeking and law enforcement objectives."[86] Similar to Germany, the required balancing depends on the culpability of the police and the potential of the exclusion to deter wrongful conduct, as well as the costs of excluding the evidence.[87] Since U.S. criminal procedure needs to strike a balance between truth and fairness as well, the U.S. Supreme Court carved out many exceptions to the exclusionary rule.[88] For instance, the fruit of the poisonous tree doctrine does not apply for violations of Miranda warnings[89] in that physical evidence derived from confessions obtained in violation of the Miranda warnings is admissible. A violation of the knock and announce rule in case of a search will not lead to the exclusion of evidence, either.[90] Moreover, the exclusion of evidence requires a violation of the U.S. constitutional

---

483 ff. See also Kagan, above fn. 1, p. 11 (in general), pp. 68, 71 (in particular with regard to the criminal justice system).

85 *Herring v. United States*, 555 U.S. 135, 141 (2009). See also *United States v. Leon* 468, U.S. 897, 910 (1983).

86 *Herring v. United States*, 555 U.S. 135, 141 (2009). See also *Pennsylvania Board of Probation and Parole v. Scott*, 524 U.S. 357, 364–365.

87 *Herring v. United States*, 555 U.S. 135, 142 (2009). See also *United States v. Leon* 468, U.S. 897, 911 (1983).

88 On these exceptions, see also Bender, above fn. 12, pp. 15–16.

89 *United States v. Patane*, 542 U.S. 630 (2004).

90 *Hudson v. Michigan*, 547 U.S. 586 (2006).

rights of the criminal defendant and, therefore, does not apply to violations of state law[91] or internal agency rules.[92] The exclusionary rule is as well inapplicable in grand jury[93] or parole revocation proceedings[94] and it does not necessarily exclude the evidence for the purpose of witness impeachment.[95] Besides, the exclusionary rule only excludes tainted evidence: if the evidence was obtained through an independent act with no link to the initial misconduct, this evidence will be admissible.[96] Evidence will thus be admissible if the causal link was attenuated by an intervening act or circumstance,[97] especially an intervening act of free will of the accused.[98] The same is true for live witness testimony[99] and in-court identifications.[100] In addition, the evidence will be admissible if legal discovery had been inevitable (inevitable discovery),[101] or if police officers acting in good faith relied upon a defective but apparently authoritative judicial search warrant, judicial decision or statute (good faith exception).[102] Finally, to appeal a judgment based on prosecutorial misconduct, the defendant has to show how this affected the outcome to her detriment (harmless error test).[103] Given all these, one can ask whether it is still useful to formulate the fruit of

---

91 *Virginia v. Moore*, 553 U.S. 164 (2008).

92 *United States v. Caceres*, 440 U.S. 741 (1979).

93 *United States v. Calandra*, 414 U.S. 338 (1974). An exception applies for evidence obtained in violation of the federal wiretapping statute, *Gelbard v. United States*, 408 U.S. 41 (1972).

94 See *Pennsylvania Board of Probation and Parole v. Scott*, 524 U.S. 357 (1998) (in general with regard to the exclusionary rule).

95 *Harris v. New York*, 401 U.S. 222 (1971); *Oregon v. Hass*, 420 U.S. 714 (1975); *United States v. Havens*, 446 U.S. 620 (1980).

96 *Silverthorne Lumber Co v. United States*, 251 U.S. 385 (1920). See also Harris, above fn. 76, pp. 316–317.

97 *Brown v. Illinois*, 422 U.S. 590 (1975). Of course, if the link is completely missing because the evidence was obtained from an independent source, it is admissible as well, see *Murray v. United States*, 487 U.S. 533 (1988).

98 *Wong Sun v. United States*, 371 U.S. 471 (1963). On the attenuation, see also Harris, above fn. 74, pp. 315–316.

99 *United States v. Ceccolini*, 435 U.S. 268 (1978).

100 *United States v. Crews*, 445 U.S. 463 (1980).

101 *Nix v. Williams*, 467 U.S. 431 (1984). See also Harris, above fn. 76, p. 317.

102 *United States v. Leon*, 468 U.S. 897 (1983); *Massachusetts v. Sheppard*, 468 U.S. 981 (1984). See also *Herring v. United States*, 555 U.S. 135, 142 (2009).

103 See, e.g., *Chapman v. California*, 386 U.S. 18 (1967).

the poisonous tree doctrine as the principle rather than the exception.[104] At least, it is important to see that the doctrine is not a substitute but a kind of conceptualization of the German balancing test.

Let us now have a closer look at the presumable absence of the fruit of the poisonous tree doctrine in the German system. Even if, as a matter of principle, the evidence is not necessarily excluded when tainted by an initial violation, in some cases it is. The German Federal Court of Justice, for instance, has held that violations of procedural rules that protect privacy in the use of means of distance communication (such as the telephone) are actually sanctioned by a fruit of the poisonous tree doctrine: not only is the information obtained through illegal wiretapping inadmissible but also all further evidence obtained[105] on the basis of this information.[106] The same is true for information that belongs to the core of privacy, which cannot be used, even if obtained in the context of *legal* wiretapping.[107] Finally, it is important to see that even though "long-distance effects" (*Fernwirkung*) are not the rule, the illegality of a previous violation can persist (*Fortwirkung*) —for instance, if the accused is deceived about the admissibility of the evidence. In this case, her confession following the initial violation is also inadmissible.[108]

In conclusion, both systems follow the same principles and give weight to truth and fairness alike.[109] They balance the costs and benefits of excluding evidence. In that endeavor, they might formulate different starting points for their reasoning and employ different legal instruments. There-

104 Similarly, Hermann, above fn. 76, p. 609 (especially with regard to the good faith exception and interpreting the many exceptions as a general tendency of being harsher on crime).

105 Harris, above fn. 76.

106 See, e.g., BGHSt 29, 244, 247.

107 The statutory basis is German Criminal Code, section 100d(2) s. 1. On the constitutional background, which requires its interpretation in the sense of the fruit of the poisonous tree doctrine, see BVerfG NJW 2004, 999, 1007. Inadmissibility even applies in the case of *legal* behavior of authorities, which shows that sanctioning authorities is not the goal here. On that point, see also Harris, above fn. 76, p. 318.

108 On that, see BGHSt 31, 304, 308–309; 48, 240, 248.

109 See Harris, above fn. 76, p. 321 (relativizing the common idea that the fruit of the poisonous tree doctrine is unknown in German criminal procedure), pp. 321–322 (rightly pointing to the structural parallels regarding the attenuation of the taint, independent source, and inevitable discovery). See also Damaška, above fn. 5, p. 513 (underlining that the exclusion of evidence might be motivated by the pursuit of truth or reasons extraneous to truth—such as fairness, one might add).

fore, a means-based narrative needs to complete the ends-based narrative in comparative criminal procedure.

F. Impeachment of Witnesses

Let us now examine how U.S. and German criminal procedure determine the credibility of witnesses since the respective presence and absence of detailed rules of impeachment seems to be—yet again—a perfect illustration of the explanatory power of the ends-based narrative. Just like before, however, we will see that this narrative cannot fully capture the nuanced differences that exist between the United States and Germany.

I. The Ends-Based Narrative

In the U.S. criminal system, it is the jury that ultimately determines the credibility of a witness without any need to state reason.[110] But previous to this determination, a whole set of detailed rules of evidence formalizes the issue of credibility. According to these rules, a witness can be impeached in certain cases. These cases include prior inconsistent statements,[111] the character of truthfulness of the witness in a broad sense[112] determined through certain prior convictions[113] or bad reputation or opinion,[114] and specific case-related information such as bias, interest or motive.[115] If one party tries to impeach the witness, the other party can react and seek to rehabilitate her, e.g. by pointing to prior consistent statements[116] or by proving her good character for truthfulness.[117] A successful impeachment will not exclude

110 See Kagan, above fn. 1, p. 73. See also Damaška, above fn. 1, p. 492.

111 See Federal Rules of Evidence, Rule 613. In detail Steven Lubet, "Understanding Impeachment," 1992, p. 483, 492 ff. See also Ladd, "Some Observations on Credibility Impeachment of Witnesses," 1967, p. 239, 245.

112 Lubet, above fn. 111, pp. 530 ff.

113 See Federal Rules of Evidence, Rule 609.

114 See Federal Rules of Evidence, Rule 608(a) s. 1, first alternative.

115 Lubet, above fn. 111, pp. 335 ff. On these cases of impeachment, see Bender, above fn. 12, p. 20.

116 On that see Ladd, above fn. 111, pp. 255–256.

117 See Federal Rules of Evidence, Rule 608(a) s. 1, second alternative, and s. 2.

the witness, but it will lead to her being less credible.[118] Even though the impeachment rules do not automatically lead to the exclusion of evidence, they tend to discredit a witness at the expense of truth because jurors might be susceptible to anchor at the result of the impeachment proceeding and give it significant weight in determining the credibility of a witness.[119] These impeachment rules might be over- or underinclusive.[120] But at least, the rules of the game are clear. In that sense, they can be interpreted as fostering fairness.

In German criminal procedure, no detailed procedural rules of evidence and thus no rules of witness impeachment exist.[121] The court might take all the points of the impeachment procedure into consideration, but the German judge determines the credibility of the witness according to the general principle of German Code of Criminal Procedure, section 261: "at its discretion and conviction based on the entire content of the hearing."[122] The court's decision is discretionary, like the jury's, but without having a set of rules that structure the decision-making process in advance.[123] The rules of the game might not be clear for the defendant. It might seem opaque how the credibility of witnesses is determined by the court. But at

---

118 On this consequence of impeachment, see Lubet, above fn. 111, p. 485. On witnesses, see generally, Federal Rules of Evidence, Rules 601–615.

119 On anchoring, see Tversky and Kahneman, "Judgment under Uncertainty: Heuristics and Biases," 1974, pp. 1124, 1128 ff.; Korobkin and Ulen, "Law and Behavioral Science: Removing the Rationality Assumption from Law and Economics," 2000, pp. 1051, 1100 ff.; Thaler and Sunstein, *Nudge: Improving Decisions About Health, Wealth, and Happiness*, 2009, pp. 23–24; Bernecker, "Essays in Empirical Political Economics," 2014, pp. 96 ff. The importance of the rules of impeachment is also illustrated by the case *Jencks v. United States*, 353 U.S. 657 (1957), in which the U.S. Supreme Court ordered a new trial because documents containing an inconsistent statement have not been disclosed. On that, see Ladd, above fn. 11, p. 256.

120 On over- and underinclusiveness, see generally Tussman and tenBroek, "The Equal Protection of the Laws," 1949, pp. 341, 348 ff.; Schauer, *Playing by the Rules: A Philosophical Examination of Rule-Based Decision-Making in Law and in Life*, 1991, p. 31; Schauer, "Rules and the Rule of Law," 1991, p. 645, 685. See also Damaška, above fn. 5, p. 508.

121 On that observation, see also Jescheck, above fn. 3, pp. 244–245; Damaška, above fn. 1, p. 526.

122 On that, see Roxin and Schünemann, above fn. 1, § 45 para. 43. See also Pizzi, above fn. 5, pp. 374–375.

123 Indeed, the points governed by U.S. rules of impeachment will likely be known to the judge due to the written dossier or (quite informally) brought up by the parties in the context of their general right to ask questions, see German Rules of Criminal Procedure, section 240(2), or their closing speeches, see German Rules of Criminal Procedure, section 258.

least, no simplistic procedural rules will influence the judge in her objective inquiry towards truth.

II. The Need for a Means-Based Narrative

Yet again, this explanation does not fully capture the differences between both systems. Actually, impeachment can also be described as a means for guaranteeing truth. After all, the rules of impeachment are inspired by the idea that clear rules will help the jury to better appreciate the credibility and to prevent jurors from being misled. All they do is to procedurally capture this search for truth in a transparent way.[124] This might go at the expense of truth in some cases in which the impeachment rules are over- or underinclusive[125] and the jury decision-making anchors at the result of the impeachment process.[126] But it is not clear whether procedures that do not capture the suggested untrustworthiness in clear-cut impeachment rules would not mislead the jury in far more cases. Indeed, an evaluation of rules in terms of their potential to lead the legal process towards truth cannot be appreciated in terms of their over- and underinclusiveness alone. Rather, the negative effects of standards have to be part of the equation as well. As Schauer puts it,

> [i]n a world of non-ideal decisionmakers [...] one should calculate the virtues of ruleness based not only on an assessment of the costs of errors of under- or over-inclusion, but also on an assessment of the incidence and consequences of those errors that are more likely when decisionmakers are not constrained by rules.[127]

The rules of impeachment do not constrain a certain outcome, but at least they provide guidance. The German court must also consider all the aspects that, in the United States, constitute grounds for impeachment, but it is left to decide how exactly to deal with them. The rules of impeachment,

124 This point could be made for exclusionary rules as well since tainted evidence might have a lower probative value. On exclusionary rules motivated by the pursuit of truth, see above fn. 109 and especially Damaška, above fn. 5. However, in the context of (hard) exclusionary rules, the pursuit of fairness seems dominant, whereas (soft) impeachment rules seem more directly motivated by the pursuit of truth, which is why the argument is developed here.

125 See above fn. 120.

126 See above fn. 119.

127 Schauer, above fn. 120, p. 685.

maybe best understood as a regulated pregame to the discretionary factfinding, are missing. All that remains is discretion. No formal rules provide the backbone for concrete decision-making. If decision-makers are not ideal, this discretion might well go at the expense of truth.

Just as the rules of impeachment could be explained in terms of truth, certain elements of fairness appear to be lacking in U.S. criminal procedure. Indeed, in Germany, the immense degree of discretion is procedurally captured by an obligation to state reason for why one witness is more credible than the other.[128] In doing so, many judicial mistakes can be challenged on appeal.[129] In contrast, no obligation to give reason exists for the jury verdict.[130] In that sense, U.S. criminal justice lacks transparency as an essential aspect of procedural justice.[131] In conclusion, clear impeachment rules that guide decision-making, on the one hand, and free discretionary balancing combined with a strict obligation to state rationale, one the other, represent just two different ways of pursuing the same goals: truth and fairness. If we want to grasp the differences between U.S. and German criminal procedure, we have to focus on the means applied.

G. Conclusion

The ends-based narrative, which associates U.S. criminal procedure with fairness and the German system with truth, might explain some aspects of comparative criminal procedure. Therefore, we do not aim at replacing it. However, this essay aimed at showing that the ends-based narrative cannot fully capture the detailed differences between the ways both countries administer criminal justice. Indeed, legal developments and institutions in the realm of criminal justice generally serve both truth and fairness alike, depending on which further assumptions are made about the participants

128 On that, see German Code of Criminal Procedure, section 267. See also Kagan, above fn. 1, pp. 73, 87.

129 See, e.g., BGH, 2002 NStZ-RR 243 (underlining that the reasoning of the judgment has to indicate that the evaluation of evidence rests upon a sound basis and that the conclusion drawn by the court is not only an assumption or a mere supposition).

130 See Kagan, above fn. 1, pp. 73, 87. See also Damaška, above fn. 1, p. 492.

131 On "transparency and openness" as a source of empirical legitimacy (legitimacy as acceptability), see Tyler and Jackson, "Popular Legitimacy and the Exercise of Legal Authority: Motivating Compliance, Cooperation, and Engagement," 2013, p. 78, 82. On legitimacy and procedural justice, see generally Tyler *Why People Obey the Law*, 1990.

of the legal process. As we have seen, the historic origins of criminal procedure in the United States and Germany as well as the presence or absence of the jury trial, plea bargaining, exclusionary rules, and rules concerning the impeachment of witnesses could be explained in terms of truth and fairness alike. Therefore, a means-based narrative has to complete the comparative law analysis.

We have focused on demonstrating the need for this means-based narrative without fully developing what such a narrative might entail. Our concluding remarks are not the place to do that either. However, I would at least like to suggest here that many of the previously outlined differences can be understood by focusing on the different design of legal norms—an approach that I develop in greater detail elsewhere under the concept of *comparative norm design*[132]: whereas detailed rules structure the decision-making process in U.S. criminal procedure, the German system relies on standards that allow for broad judicial balancing. Through this focus on the design of legal norms within the means-based narrative, we can also make sense of some differences in other areas than those examined here. For instance, sentencing is largely governed by rules in the United States,[133] whereas in Germany, the court enjoys immense discretion.[134] The described difference in norm design can in turn be explained by the degree to which decision-makers are idealized in both countries. Indeed, if a legal system idealizes judges, it will foresee less control through detailed rules than a system which conceives of judges in a pragmatic way.[135] In that sense, the different means employed in the United States and Germany to pursue the

132 See Bender, above fn. 12. This article on comparative norm design provides a detailed explanation of the means-based narrative.

133 On that, see Kaspar, above fn. 33, pp. 345–347. See also Kagan, above fn. 1, p. 85; Pizzi, "Sentencing in the US: An Inquisitorial Soul in an Adversarial Body?," 2008, pp. 65–80. Even when these rules are not contained in binding sentencing enhancement statutes but in non-mandatory sentencing guidelines, they structure and thereby limit the discretion of the judge. On these two ways of limiting judicial discretion, see Aharonson, "Determinate Sentencing and American Exceptionalism: The Underpinnings and Effects of Cross-National Differences in the Regulation of Sentencing Discretion," 2013, pp. 161, 166–172.

134 See the vague guidelines of German Criminal Code, section 46, and the broad discretion granted by the codified criminal offenses. For instance, the German equivalent to assault and battery, regulated in German Criminal Code, section 223, allows the judge to punish either with a fine or with imprisonment of up to five years. For an overview, see Hörnle, above fn. 33. See critically Kaspar, above fn. 33, pp. 338–341. See also above fn. 33.

135 On that, see also Schauer's previously cited observation, see above fn. 120.

same goals reflect the broader idealistic or pragmatic theoretical underpinnings of their respective legal cultures.

Bibliography

Aharonson, Ely, "Determinate Sentencing and American Exceptionalism: The Underpinnings and Effects of Cross-National Differences in the Regulation of Sentencing Discretion," *Law and Contemporary Problems* 76, 1 (2013): 161–187.

Beetham, David, *The Legitimation of Power*, 2nd edn, Hampshire: Palgrave Macmillan, 2013.

Bender, Philip M., "Comparative Norm Design: The U.S. Rules Model and the German Standards Model in Criminal Justice and Beyond," *UCLA Journal of International Law & Foreign Affairs* 27, 2 (2024): 1–58.

Bernecker, Andreas, "Essays in Empirical Political Economics," Dissertation, Universität Mannheim, 2014.

Canaris, Claus-Wilhelm, "Richtigkeit und Eigenwertung in der richterlichen Rechtsfindung," in *Grazer Universitätsreden*, Nr. 50, 1993, pp. 23–41.

Christiano, Thomas, "The Authority of Democracy," *Journal of Political Philosophy* 12, 3 (2004): 266–290.

Damaška, Mirjan, "Evidentiary Barriers to Conviction and Two Models of Criminal Procedure: A Comparative Study," *Pennsylvania Law Review* 121, 3 (1973): 506–589.

Damaška, Mirjan, "Structures of Authority and Comparative Criminal Procedure," *Yale Law Journal* 84, 3 (1975): 480–544.

Damaška, Mirjan, "Truth in Adjudication," *Hastings Law Journal* 49, 2 (1998): 289–308.

Deal, Detlev, "Der strafprozessuale Vergleich," *Strafverteidiger [StV]* (1982): 545–552.

Dubber, Markus D., "Criminal Process in the Dual Penal State: A Comparative-Historical Analysis," in *The Oxford Handbook of Criminal Process*, ed. Darryl K Brown, Jenia I Turner, and Bettina Weisser, Oxford: Oxford University Press, 2019, pp. 3–24.

Dworkin, Ronald, "Hard Cases," *Harvard Law Review* 88, 6 (1975): 1057–1109.

Gilliéron, Gwladys, "Comparing Plea Bargaining and Abbreviated Trial Procedures," in *The Oxford Handbook of Criminal Process*, ed. Darryl K Brown, Jenia I Turner, and Bettina Weisser, Oxford: Oxford University Press, 2019, pp. 703–727.

Grande, Eliabetta, "Comparative Approaches to Criminal Procedure: Transplants, Translations, and Adversarial-Model Reforms in European Criminal Process," in *The Oxford Handbook of Criminal Process*, ed. Darryl K Brown, Jenia I Turner, and Bettina Weisser, Oxford: Oxford University Press, 2019, pp. 67–88.

Habermas, Jürgen, "Legitimationsprobleme im modernen Staat," *Politische Vierteljahresschrift Sonderhefte* 7 (1976): 39–40.

Harris, Kenneth, "Verwertungsverbot für mittelbar erlangte Beweismittel: Die Fernwirkungsdoktrin in der Rechtsprechung im deutschen und amerikanischen Recht," *Strafverteidiger [StV]* (1991): 313–322.

Hermann, Joachim, "Neuere Entwicklungen in der amerikanischen Strafrechtspflege," *JuristenZeitung [JZ]* 40 (1985): 602–609.

Herz, John H., "Legitimacy: Can We Retrieve It?," *Comparative Politics* 10, 3 (1978): 317–343.

Hörnle, Tatjana, "Moderate and Non-Arbitrary Sentencing Without Guidelines: The German Experience," *Law and Contemporary Problems* 76, 1 (2013): 189–210.

Hörnle, Tatjana, "Sentencing in US-American Jurisdictions: A Commentary from a German Perspective," in *Strafzumessung/Sentencing: Angloamerikanische und deutsche Einblicke/Anglo-American and German Insight,* ed. Kai Ambos, Göttingen: Göttingen University Press 2020, pp. 183–190.

James, Fleming Jr., "Functions of Judges and Jury in Negligence Cases," *Yale Law Journal* 58, 5 (1949): 667–690.

Jescheck, Hans-Heinrich, "Principles of German Criminal Procedure in Comparison with American Law," *Virginia Law Review* 56, 2 (1970): 239–253.

Kagan, Robert A, *Adversarial Legalism: The American Way of Law*, Cambridge, MA: Harvard University Press 2001.

Kahn-Freund, Otto, "On Uses and Misuses of Comparative Law," *The Modern Law Review* 37, 1 (1974): 1–27.

Kaspar, Johannes, "Sentencing Guidelines vs. Free Judicial Discretion – Is German Sentencing Law in Need of Reform?," in *Strafzumessung/Sentencing: Angloamerikanische und deutsche Einblicke/Anglo-American and German Insight,* ed. Kai Ambos, Göttingen: Göttingen University Press 2020, pp. 345–352.

Korobkin, Russell B., and Thomas S. Ulen, "Law and Behavioral Science: Removing the Rationality Assumption from Law and Economics," *California Law Review* 88, 4 (2000): 1051–1144.

Ladd, Mason, "Some Observations on Credibility Impeachment of Witnesses," *Cornell Law Review* 52, 2 (1967): 239–261.

Langbein, John H., *Comparative Criminal Procedure: Germany*, St. Paul, Minn.: West Publishing Co., 1977.

Langbein, John H., "Torture and Plea Bargaining," *University of Chicago Law Review* 46, 1 (1978): 3–22.

Langbein, John H., "Land Without Plea Bargaining: How the Germans Do It," *Michigan Law Review* 78, 2 (1979): 204–225.

Langer, Máximo, "From Legal Transplants to Legal Translations: The Globalization of Plea Bargaining and the Americanization Thesis in Criminal Procedure," *Harvard International Law Journal* 45, 1 (2004): 1–64.

Leeson, Peter T., "Trial by Battle," *Journal of Legal Analysis* 3, 1 (2011): 341–375.

Legrand, Pierre, "Comparative Legal Studies and Commitment to Theory," *The Modern Law Review* 58, 2 (1995): 262–273.

Legrand, Pierre, "The Impossibility of 'Legal Transplants'," *Maastricht Journal of European and Comparative Law* 4, 2 (1997):111–124.

Liszt, Franz von, "Vortrag im Berliner Anwaltsverein am 23. März 1901," *Deutsche Juristen-Zeitung [DJZ]* (1901): 179–182.

Litowitz, Douglas E., "Internal versus External Perspectives on Law: Toward Mediation," *Florida State University Law Review* 26, 1 (1998): 127–150.

Lubet, Steven, "Understanding Impeachment," *American Journal of Trial Advocacy* 15 (1992): 483–540.

Maitland, Frederic William, *The Constitutional History of England: A Course of Lectures Delivered*, Union, New Jersey: The Lawbook Exchange, 2001.

Mandel, Michael, "Dworkin, Hart, and the Problem of Theoretical Perspectives," *Law & Society Review* 14, 1 (1979): 57–82.

Neumann, Ulfrid, *Wahrheit im Recht: Zu Problematik und Legitimität einer fragwürdigen Denkform*, Baden-Baden: Nomos, 2004.

Pargendler, Mariana, "The Role of the State in Contract Law: The Common-Civil Law Divide," *Yale Journal of International Law* 43, 1 (2018): 143–189.

Pizzi, William T., "Soccer, Football and Trial Systems." *Columbia Journal of European Law* 1, 2 (1995): 369–377.

Robbennolt, Jennifer K., "Evaluating Juries by Comparison to Judges: A Benchmark for Judging?," *Florida State University Law Review* 32, 2 (2005): 469–510.

Pizzi, William T., "Sentencing in the US: An Inquisitorial Soul in an Adversarial Body?," *Crime, Procedure and Evidence in a Comparative and International Context: Essays in Honour of Professor Mirjan Damaška*, ed. John Jackson, Máximo Langer and Peter Tillers, Oxford: Hart Publishing, 2008, pp. 65–80.

Roxin, Claus, and Bernd Schünemann, *Strafverfahrensrecht: Ein Studienbuch*, 29th edn, München: C.H. Beck 2017.

Scharpf, Fritz W., *Governing in Europe: Effective and Democratic?*, Oxford: Oxford University Press 1999.

Schauer, Frederick, *Playing by the Rules: A Philosophical Examination of Rule-Based Decision-Making in Law and in Life*, Oxford: Clarendon Press 1991.

Schauer, Frederick, "Rules and the Rule of Law," *Harvard Journal of Law & Public Policy* 14, 3 (1991): 645–694.

Schroeder, Friedrich-Christain, *Strafprozessrecht*, 7th edn, München: C.H. Beck, 2018.

Schünemann, Bernd, "Die Verständigung im Strafprozess – Wunderwaffe oder Bankrotterklärung der Verteidigung?," *Neue Juristische Wochenschrift [NJW]* (1989): 1895–1903.

Schünemann, Bernd, *Absprachen im Strafverfahren?: Grundlagen, Gegenstände und Grenzen (Gutachten B für den 58. Deutschen Juristentag)*, München: C.H. Beck 1990.

Schünemann, Bernd, *Wetterzeichen vom Untergang der deutschen Rechtskultur: Die Urteilsabsprachen im Strafprozess als Abgesang auf die Gesetzesbindung der Jusitz und den Beruf unserer Zeit zur Gesetzgebung*, Berlin: BWV, 2005.

Schünemann, Bernd, and Wolfgang Bandilla, "Perseverance in Courtroom Decisions," in *Criminal Behavior and the Justice System: Psychological Perspectives*, ed. Hermann Wegener, Friedrich Lösel, and Jochen Haisch, New York: Springer, 1989, pp. 181–192.

Teubner, Gunther, "Legal Irritants: Good Faith in British Law or How Unifying Law Ends up in New Divergences," *The Modern Law Review* 61, 1 (1998): 11–32.

Thaler, Richard H., and Cass R. Sunstein, *Nudge: Improving Decisions About Health, Wealth, and Happiness*, 2nd edn, New York: Penguin Books 2009.

Thayer, James B., "The Older Modes of Trial," *Harvard Law Review* 5, 2 (1891): 45–70.

Thibaut, John, and Laurens Walker, "A Theory of Procedure," *California Law Review* 66, 3 (1978): 541–566.

Turner, Jenia I, "Limits on the search for truth in criminal procedure: a comparative view," in *Comparative Criminal Procedure*, ed. Jacqueline E. Ross and Stephen C. Thaman, Cheltenhem, UK: Edward Elgar 2016, pp. 35–74.

Tussman, Joseph, and Jacobus tenBroek, "The Equal Protection of the Laws," *California Law Review* 37, 3 (1949): 341–381.

Tversky, Amos, and Daniel Kahneman, "Judgment under Uncertainty: Heuristics and Biases," *Science* 185, 4157 (1974): 1124–1131.

Tyler, Tom R., *Why People Obey the Law*, New Haven and London: Yale University Press, 1990.

Tyler, Tom R., and Jonathan Jackson, "Popular Legitimacy and the Exercise of Legal Authority: Motivating Compliance, Cooperation, and Engagement," *Psychology, Public Policy and Law* 20, 1 (2013): 78–95.

Vogel, Mary, "Plea Bargaining under the Common Law," in *The Oxford Handbook of Criminal Process*, ed. Darryl K. Brown, Jenia I. Turner and Bettina Weisser, Oxford: Oxford University Press, 2019, pp. 728–760.

Walpin, Gerald, "America's Adversarial and Jury System: More Likely to Do Justice," *Harvard Journal of Law & Public Policy* 26, 1 (2003): 175–186.

Watson, Alan, "The Evolution of Law: Continued," *Law and History Review* 5, 2 (1987): 537–570.

Watson, Alan, *Legal Transplants: An Approach to Comparative Law*, 2nd edn, Athens, GA: The University of Georgia Press 1993.

Watson, Alan, "Aspects of Reception of Law," *The American Journal of Comparative Law* 44, 2 (1996): 335–351.

Weigend, Thomas, "Continental Cures for American Ailments: European Criminal Procedure as a Model for Law Reform," *Crime & Justice* 2 (1980): 381–428.

Weigend, Thomas, "Should We Search for the Truth, and Who Should Do It," North *Carolina Journal of International Law* 36, 2 (2011): 389–415.

Weigend, Thomas, "Is the Criminal Process about Truth?: A German Perspective," *Harvard Journal of Law & Public Policy* 26, 1 (2003): 157–174.

Whitman, James Q, *The Origins of Reasonable Doubt: Theological Roots of the Criminal Trial*, New Haven: Yale University Press 2008.

Zweigert, Konrad, and Hein Kötz, *An Introduction to Comparative Law*, transl. Tony Weir, 3rd edn, Oxford: Oxford University Press 1998.

Reflections on the Relationship between Immediacy and Credibility in German Criminal Procedure

Matthias Krüger

A. Introduction

The German criminal procedure is divided into several phases, two of which are of particular importance. In the beginning, there is the preliminary investigation conducted by the public prosecution which makes use of the police. The police interviews witnesses and drafts reports of these interviews. The guilty verdict or the acquittal is a matter of the actual court trial, however. De jure, the law is unanimous on the relationship between these two phases:

> The German Criminal Procedure Act puts the decisive importance for reaching a verdict on the actual trial, where the principle of orality and the principle of immediacy apply, and not on the findings made in the preliminary investigation, which is documented in writing.[1]

The principle is most clearly expressed in Section 250 German Code of Criminal Procedure (CCP). Pursuant to the provision, in the case that the proof of a fact relies on the perception of a person, the person has to give testimony in the actual trial (1st sentence) while this cannot be replaced by reading the minutes of the examination in the preliminary investigation (2nd sentence). Therefore, the minutes of the preliminary proceedings cannot be read offhandedly. There are some exceptions to this principle in Section 251 et seqq. CCP,[2] however, the actual trial has always been governed by the principle of immediacy.

This can be explained against the background of the importance of immediacy. In 1885 already, the maxim of immediacy was described as being a fundamental theorem ("*Fundamentalsatz*") of our criminal procedure law.[3] On the same line one spoke of the most important of all principles of

1 Translation of BGHSt 35, 164
2 See *Krüger, Unmittelbarkeit und materielles Recht,* 2014, pp. 66 ff.
3 RGSt 12, 104, 105.

procedural law.[4] Diametrically opposed to this is the sobering realization that the exact meaning of the principle of immediacy is considered not yet to be fully understood.[5] Already at an early stage it was said that it seemed to be wrapped in mist,[6] which has seemingly not yet cleared.

Therefore, it is not surprising that some authors disrespectfully comment on the principle of immediacy. According to them, the "splendor of the brand-new principle (of immediacy) is considerably reduced."[7] There are doubts being raised that the "theorems of orality and immediacy [...] can currently still sufficiently explain—and legitimate—our process model."[8] Others emphasize that the "principle of immediacy, which appears archaic today, [...] is a crucial element of the reformed inquisitorial procedure", too. But at the same time they are of the opinion that the "ideal of absolute immediacy" as a "nostalgic convenience solution [...] will possibly remain an academic dream" and detect an "unmistakable call for 'economic' solutions in criminal justice", that "unfortunately renders a return to the ideals of the 19th century unrealistic."[9] In this respect, it seems that one attempts—to take up a dictum of *Eser*[10]—to throw immediacy in the "dustbin" of criminal history.

On the other hand, there is no lack of voices which are of the opinion that immediacy as a major and characterizing pillar of the criminal trial has vital influence on the trial's design.[11] Even though "theorems are threatened to become not more than a false front", immediacy is counted among the "most important constituting principles."[12] Those positions could hardly be more opposite. While some want to dismiss the principle of immediacy in criminal procedure, others unabatedly support it.

---

4 See *Liszt, Reform des Strafverfahrens*, 1906, p. 29.

5 *See Schmoll, Videovernehmung kindlicher Opfer im Strafprozess*, 1999, p. 227.

6 *See Rupp, Beweis im Strafverfahren*, 1884, p. 125.

7 *Schmid*, "Der revisionsgerichtliche Augenscheinsbeweis," 1973, p. 913 (author's translation).

8 *Rieß*, "Entwicklungstendenzen in der deutschen Strafprozessgesetzgebung seit 1950," 2009, p. 469 (author's translation).

9 See *Weigend*, "Strukturelle Probleme im deutschen Strafprozess," 2013, pp. 45 ff.

10 *See Eser*, "Funktionswandel von Prozeßmaximen," 1992, pp. 395 ff.

11 *Stüber, Die Entwicklung des Prinzips der Unmittelbarkeit im deutschen Strafverfahren*, 2005, p. 21.

12 *Kühne*, "Einleitung," 2006, in *Löwe-Rosenberg, Kommentar zur StPO*, para. I, marginal no. 56 with marginal no. 54.

B. Possibilities for Enhancing the Establishment of the Truth by Better Assessment of the Credibility of Witnesses

The objective grounds for the existence of the principle of immediacy will be analyzed against this background. Therefore, the investigation and the determination of the truth as primary concerns of criminal procedure come in the focus of interest.[13] Its application is intended to lead the court to substantive truth by ensuring the establishment of a solid and reliable factual basis for the decision of the court. In this respect the claim for an immediate oral trial had and has the aim of providing the court with a better factual basis for its decision in the interest of the establishment of the truth.

Another aspect of immediacy is closely linked to this. Immediacy is intended to allow for a better assessment of the credibility of witnesses as, pursuant to Section 250 CCP, they have to testify in court (again) while this testimony must not be replaced by reading out the record of a previous statement. This provides the opportunity to address possible omissions or contradictions in the previous statement and to ask additional and follow-up questions. From this and from the confrontation with other witnesses informative conclusions can be drawn concerning the veraciousness and capacity for truth of the respective witness. And finally, one can get a personal impression of the witness. This goes hand in hand with the question if conclusions on the credibility of a witness can and/or must be drawn from the gesture, the facial expression, the sound of the voice and the alteration of the tone of the voice, the talkativeness on some issues on the one hand and the taciturnity on others on the other hand.[14] In any case, it cannot be denied that such circumstances can only be taken into account if one perceives them himself.

This raises the question if one should stick to the criminal procedural law principle of immediacy because the court can optimally and properly determine the credibility of witnesses in this way. This could be done away with, however, if the evaluation of credibility did not inevitably require the perception of an immediate oral testimony along with the (nonverbal) behavior of the witness.

13 On the following see *Krüger*, above fn. 2, pp. 40 ff., 49 ff., 60 ff.

14 See for the contents of the "personal impression" *Geppert, Grundsatz der Unmittelbarkeit im deutschen Strafverfahren*, 1979, p. 172.

I. Case Law on nonverbal witness behavior in particular criminal procedural law contexts

Although this does not clarify what exactly the advantage of the immediate personal examination is for the assessment of credibility, criminal courts tend to generally support it. This is shown by some issues in criminal procedure and how they are dealt with by the courts.

1. Credibility and blind judges

This is demonstrated particularly clearly in the discussion on the participation of blind judges.[15] Criminal courts regularly exclude blind judges from judging.[16] They argue that the principle of immediacy would be violated as visual impressions as posture and reactions of the participants of the proceeding were an integral part of the hearing. Such visual impressions are of crucial importance. It is not only the testimony as such

> that the judgment has to be based on concerning the forming of opinions, but the overall impression they create. For this, the immediate impression the judge gets during the hearing is crucial. For reaching the verdict, the Code of Criminal Procedure focuses on the main hearing which is bound to the principles of orality and immediacy and not to the written findings of the preliminary investigation.

Academic writing concurs. According to it

> the overall impression a witness or the defendant gives in court, the way he appears and behaves, his facial expression and gestures and the like are an important element of credibility.[17]

In this respect conduct and reactions of the participants of the proceeding can become important for the evaluation of evidence.[18] The evaluation of a testimony does not only depend on its contents and the acoustically

15 See *Geppert*, above fn. 14, pp. 147 ff., and *Stüber*, above fn. 11, pp. 79 ff.—each with further references.

16 On the following see BGHSt 35, 164 and BGH, NStZ-RR 2011, 349.

17 *Wimmer*, "Anmerkung zu BGH, Urteil vom 28.4.1953," 1953, p. 672 in his annotations to BGHSt 4, 191 (author's translation).

18 *Schmidt*, "§ 261 StPO in der neueren höchstrichterlichen Rechtsprechung," 1970, p. 340.

perceivable way in which it is formulated.[19] The credibility of witnesses is also substantially influenced by becoming personally acquainted and by their reactions to the judge's questions.[20] As this was of utmost importance, a fair evaluation was hardly possible without eyesight.

The Federal Constitutional Court also agrees:[21] According to it the removal of a blind lay judge from the list of lay judges because of his blindness and basing the decision on the criminal procedural law principle of immediacy is not unconstitutional. The principle "requires that every member of the trial court can get his own immediate—also visual—impression of the participants of the proceeding." in this respect, there is no doubt that a (certain) importance is attached to nonverbal behavior.

2. Credibility and Audio-Visual Transmission of Testimony

In a judgment of 1999 pointing in the same direction the German Federal Supreme Court (BGH) as the supreme German criminal court emphasizes that "the impression a defense witness makes—[...] nonverbal by his demeanor—during his examination can be of importance for the credibility of his testimony."[22] Relevant for the evaluation are, inter alia, "the appearance of the witness, his body language, a hesitant or fluent testimony or apparent emotions of the witness."[23] Concerning live stream witness examination the BGH argues along the same lines:

> It will have to be considered that a person who is examined remotely can more easily evade the tension created by the questions and answers than it would be the case in direct contact in the same room. The personal distance due to technical reasons makes it more difficult to reduce inhibitions prior to the testimony, to build trust, and to gain a sufficient impression of the witness's individual character and his *nonverbal behavior*.[24]

19 *Fezer*, "Anmerkung zu BGH, Urteil vom 27.11.1986," 1987, p. 335, 336.
20 *Schorn*, "Erblindeter Richter in der Gerichtsbarkeit," 1954, p. 299.
21 On the following see BVerfG, *NJW* 2004, 2150.
22 BGHSt 45, 354, 357 (author's translation).
23 BGHSt 45, 354, 360. (author's translation).
24 BGHSt 45, 188, 196 (author's translation, emphasis added).

With this, the courts—with general approval of academic writing[25]—consider the behavior of witnesses to be relevant when confronted with video technology.

3. Application of a polygraph

At first sight, BGH case law concerning the application of the polygraph in German criminal proceedings seems to go against this. The relevant (leading) decision of 1998 states that

> according to unanimous academic opinion it is not possible to find clear correlations between cognitive and emotional mental states and specific reaction patterns of the vegetative nervous system.[26]

However, it would be premature to draw the conclusion that, because of this, nonverbal behavior is of no relevance (any more).

This can be seen by the fact that the judgment of 1998 makes reference to an earlier decision of 1954, according to which a polygraph test must not be allowed into evidence—in contrast to open expressive movement.[27] Therefore, *internal*, from the outside non-perceivable states and body reactions are of no probative value, in contrast to *external* impressions, i.e. nonverbal behavior, as the parenthesis shows. The 1998 decision directly follows up on this when it states that, "uncontrollable expressive movements which the court perceives without technical aids (e.g. strong perspiration, blushing, speech impediments or other reactions of orientation, stress, or embarrassment) may be considered."[28] The wording unmistakably shows that nonverbal behavior plays a role or may play a role in assessing the credibility.

From this, it can be concluded that criminal case law awards (some) meaning to the behavior of witnesses in particular criminal procedural situations. However, this does not mean that it must be relevant for the assessment of credibility *in general.*

25 See for the relevance of nonverbal forms of expression for the evaluation of credibility based on behavior in connection with audio-visual transmission comprehensively *Rieck, Substitut oder Komplement? Die Videofernvernehmung von Zeugen*, 2003, pp. 157 ff., 181 ff.

26 BGHSt 44, 308, 316 (author's translation) and more recently BGH, *NStZ* 2011, 474.

27 See BGHSt 44, 308, 309 f., referring to BGHSt 5, 332, 335 f.

28 BGHSt 44, 308, 316.

II. Analysis of academic writing on the (non-)probative value of nonverbal behavior

Academic writing is divided when it comes to the question whether signs of credibility can *generally* (more or less reliably) be inferred from body language. *Bender/Nack* in particular looked in detail into this matter and, for this purpose, dealt with psychological literature on eyewitness testimony.

The following will deal less with the individual observations—*Bender/Nack* describe them as warning signs[29]—on the occasion of interrogations or examinations, but more with the relevance they can or should have. *Bender/Nack* initially state that characteristics of body language such as gesture, facial expression, posture and physical condition, eye contact and (inner) distance to the listener (favored by the speaker) can basically not expose the lie itself, but initially only portray emotional states such as fear, nervousness, embarrassment or exertion and concentration. Therefore, one should not talk about "symptoms for lies" but only about "warning signs of body language" because they can but not necessarily must be triggered by a lie but can also have other reasons.[30] Nonetheless those body reactions generally give rise to particular attention.[31]

Eventually *Bender and Nack* concede that the

> 'warning signs of body language' are not proven by empirical evidence. Nonetheless, they had found so many indications supporting the reliability of body language to at least classify them as 'informed hypothesis'.[32]

Later on, they only briefly deal with body language signs and conspicuities in situations of giving testimony.[33] At first, they state that the body language can hardly be interpreted reliably as it can have manifold causes. At the end, however, it is emphasized that this is different when body language signs go along with verbal conspicuities. Therefore, body language should not be ignored.

29 *Bender and Nack, Tatsachenfeststellung vor Gericht, Band I, Glaubwürdigkeits-und Beweislehre*, 1995, marginal no. 209.

30 Ibid., marginal no. 206.

31 Ibid., marginal no. 207.

32 Ibid., marginal no. 208. For the concurrence of verbal and nonverbal behavior during the testimony see the references in *Schneider, Nonverbale Zeugnisse gegen sich selbst*, 1991, p. 67.

33 On the following see *Bender, Nack, and Treuer, Tatsachenfeststellung vor Gericht*, 2007, marginal nos. 217 ff.

The literature in psychology of evidence follows the same approach. *Arntzen*, who intensely deals with psychology of witness evidence, denies full probative value of single sings of credibility and therefore negates the existence of direct "non-deficient" signs of untruthfulness and thus the existence of clear "signs of lie."[34] *Arntzen* attributes some probative value of psychology of evidence, although not free of sources of error, to the uncontrolled manner of giving testimony that can become a sign of credibility seen together with other criteria of credibility. For this, nonverbal elements of behavior do play a role. Concerning facial expression, the witness maintains casual eye contact and a casual facial expression if he is uninhibited. Impulsive and full-of-drive witnesses may show an uncontrolled behavior on a particularly wide field of expression while testifying what makes difficult any pretense. The lack of control of these witnesses does not only lead to lively facial expressions but to virtually pantomimic expressions—to the demonstration of the course of actions in the facial expression before managing to describe it verbally in particular. Finally, *Arntzen* refers to *Bender/Nack* according to whom the natural bodily and facial movements of a witness are particularly revealing if they remain unaltered when passing over from harmless topics to the relevant questions.[35] Psychology of evidence therefore does acknowledge a certain relevance of nonverbal expressions and be it only indirect relevance in connection with other side-effects of the statement.

Undeutsch handles the "usability of instinctive expressions in the evaluation of testimony" in a similar way in his article.[36] He starts with the characterization of the instinctive expressions while talking as being of great importance. Lying required more attentiveness, concentration, and tension than the true description of own experiences because of the risk of being discovered and found out. Therefore, the inner state of such a witness was characterized by intentional tenseness and emotional excitement. These characteristic features are reflected in the expressions of the witness—unintentionally. In this respect, discrepancies to an easygoing, free, and natural manner can be observed. In the process, expressions of intentional tenseness and emotional excitement on various fields of expression show at the

34 *Arntzen*, *Psychologie der Zeugenaussage*, 2007, pp. 22 and 109.

35 [See] ibid., pp. 71 ff.

36 *Undeutsch*, "Die Verwertbarkeit unwillkürlicher Ausdruckserscheinungen bei der Aussagenwürdigung. Eine Anfrage von psychologischer Seite," 1975, pp. 650 ff.

same time: in facial expressions, pantomime, speech mimics and in the vegetatively controlled and therefore unintentional bodily side-effects.

This is met with resistance by legal scholars. They are of the opinion that the behavior of witnesses is not of general importance but at most of inferior relevance, some deny any significance of the behavior at all. It is submitted[37] that empirical research in psychology of evidence led to the highly surprising result that behavior only gives highly unreliable indications of credibility. Instead, purely verbal symptoms were more reliable. Because a certain behavior can almost always have several causes and the hitherto postulated criteria of credibility could not yet be verified empirically, a research study was to be followed according to which the usability and reliability of such exterior phenomena have to be considered as being "extremely limited" and "greatest caution" is called for when evaluating exterior signs as indicating a lie.

Considering the relevance of nonverbal behavior to be "doubtful" for the evaluation of credibility as *today's* scientific knowledge in psychology would be that bodily language does *not* permit to draw reliable conclusions goes in the same direction.[38] Those authors concede that it is undisputed that emotions can be/are reflected in the facial expression as well as in gesture, posture, quality of voice and manner of speaking.[39] Eventually they do not conceal (even if mentioned in a hard-to-find place) that more studies are necessary to reject the nonverbal behavior as indicator for the evaluation of the quality of the testimony *altogether*.[40] Until then maybe the rule, which will be discussed below, applies that nonverbal behavior has to be at least noticed and taken into account on a case-to-case basis in order to take the—undisputed—rule of exhaustive assessment of evidence seriously.

---

37 On the following see *Lagodny*, "Videovernehmung in Strafverfahren: nur Risiken und Nebenwirkungen?," 2000, pp. 178 ff.

38 *Kilian-Herklotz*, "Einsatz von Videotechnik im deutschen Strafverfahren und richterliche Glaubwürdigkeitsbeurteilung," 2000, pp. 202 ff (emphasis in original). See in the same sense *Köhnken*, "Video im Gericht -Modelle und Erfahrungen aus Großbritannien," 1995, p. 379 as well as *Norouzi, Audiovisuelle Vernehmung von Auslandszeugen*, 2010, p. 251: "The nonverbal behavior, i.e., gesture, facial expression and posture, of a witness when testifying plays an inferior role and provides only barely usable inferences for evaluating the testimony" (translation).

39 *See Kilian-Herklotz*, above fn. 38, pp. 195, 202 ff.

40 See *ibid.*, p. 213 in N. 92 (emphasis added).

1. Assessment of credibility between the poles of psychology (of evidence) and jurisprudence

This leads right into the controversy about the (ir-)relevance of nonverbal behavior for the assessment of credibility. If one wants to participate in the discussion as a jurist, one inevitably finds himself in dilemmas. On the one hand "it is an uncomfortable and unpopular occupation for jurists [...] to invade the refuge of psychology and virtually break new ground."[41] Furthermore, psychology of evidence conveys a very indifferent and ambivalent picture of the relevance of nonverbal behavior.

Schneider in particular has dwelled on the evaluation of credibility from a legal-criminological and forensic-psychological perspective extensively and to that end he combined practitioners' studies and findings of psychology of evidence.[42] At the end of his reflections on this, he criticizes in particular the "lack of empirical research of nonverbal side-effects."[43] In addition, *Schneider* deals with empirical findings on side-effects of deception and states statistically relevant correlations between the credibility of statements and several (partly nonverbal) behaviors, only to summarize that these are mere average values and that these correlations occur not in every deceit or every deceitor.[44] But even if more valid empiric-statistical data were available, it should be borne in mind that judges in all branches of law do not decide according to rules (of weighing evidence) but according to the principle of free assessment of evidence and that they are bound only by normative aspects. Reviewing the previous discussion, one cannot help thinking that it is staying too close to the respective poles. Neither the abstinence of (criminal) jurists concerning the findings of psychology of evidence is convincing nor is this discipline's ignorance of the normative backgrounds of judges' decision-making. Subsequently, an attempt shall be made to bring the two closer together.

Legal scholars' statements are rather ambivalent towards psychological aspects of testimony and interrogation. However, they again concentrate too much on those and (overly) neglect the normative aspects. Some leave it at the terse statement that the trial judge must have the necessary expertise in

41 *Schneider*, above fn. 32, p. 3 (author's translation).

42 See ibid., pp. 60 ff., 70 ff., 102 ff.

43 Ibid., pp. 125 ff.

44 See ibid., pp. 195 ff., p. 201 at the bottom.

the field of psychology of evidence.[45] As stated elsewhere in more detail,[46] the judge has to try to get an idea of the ability to testify and of the credibility of a witness by virtue of his own ability to judge character, taking into account the particularities of each case and the findings of psychology of evidence. He has to decide on the basis of the appearance of the witness, his manner of testifying and other relevant factors such as personality structure, age, cognitive ability, and state of mind, as well as his affective involvement, whether his perceptions and his descriptions are reliable and whether he believes the statement to be true considering the other available evidence.

Others are much more cautious about the reliability of psychological criteria of credibility.[47] There would be doubts if a set of criteria of psychology of evidence could provide for reliable diagnostic instruments. Then these doubts are immediately dispelled (in part) by conceding that the criteria anyway include more or less reliable experience-based knowledge so that it is not their psychological value that appears to be problematic but rather their undifferentiated application to the individual case.

There are also authors who oppose the relevance of nonverbal behavior or consider it at least overrated in principle. Such a position is taken by *Schulze* for example,[48] who had not been able to remember

> to ever have read in a judgment that a testimony has to be considered to be noncredible *just because* the witness blenched or flushed. Such circumstances [...] may cause the court to ask critical questions. However, *in general*, they do not lead to calling into doubt the credibility of a statement afterwards.

With this statement he disavows his own position to some extent. In this respect, it should be noted that body symptoms may not be relevant *in gen-*

45 *Meyer-Goßner*, *Kommentar zur StPO*, 2013, § 261 marginal no. 4; *Kilian-Herklotz*, above fn. 38, pp. 195, 202 at the top.

46 On the following see *Sander*, in: Löwe-Rosenberg, Kommentar zur StPO, § 261 marginal no. 81b with referrals to case law and literature on individual relevant circumstances.

47 On the following see *Julius*, in: *Heidelberger Kommentar zur StPO*, 2012, § 261 marginal no. 27 at the end and further *Eisenberg*, *Beweisrecht der StPO*, 2013, marginal no. 1469: "Criminal law practice (should) be cautious when applying particular criteria of credibility as far as it is doubtful whether the respective set of criteria honor their claim to be able to evaluate credibility" (translation).

48 On the following see *Schulze*, "Zur Mitwirkung blinder Richter," 1988, p. 739 (emphasis added).

eral. This does not preclude, however, that they are relevant *in particular cases*. Apart from that *Schulze* admits—certainly unknowingly—that non-verbal behavior is of relevance insofar as it gives rise to critical questions by the court. Later, this aspect is thwarted by *Schulze* himself. He characterizes the recording of attributes over a longer period of time and weighing the information carefully—in contrast to jumping to conclusions based on the mere appearance—as an advantage "as far as there is no pressure to come to a quick evaluation."[49] But according to *Schulze* exactly this may become relevant when he states that blenching of flushing—in the ongoing examination of the witness—may at least cause the court to "ask critical questions."[50] A certain (self-)contradiction can therefore not be denied.

Furthermore, the court can only have reason for (critical) questioning if it can see the witness's body language. This cannot be replaced by perceiving merely acoustically. Only the correlation of verbal peculiarities and body language symptoms—in the spirit of *Bender/Nack/Treuer*[51]—allows for the court's critical questions. It is possible to ask critical questions about the content of the statement. But it is also possible to ask questions about the warning signals. The court can ask the witness whether e.g., there are anatomical or other non-mental causes for his sweating, flushing, blenching etc.—and will get an answer. Prerequisite is, however, that body language signals can be/are observed at all.

So far, one cannot agree with *Schulze*. Elsewhere he considers his assertion that blind judges can evaluate the credibility just as well as non-blind judges to be confirmed by a study of blind education. It characterizes the perception of others as a complex and manifold process that makes it "clear that the optically visible appearance of a person, that is not open to blind people in the same way as sighted people, is just one factor among many others."[52] Thereby he takes up his earlier thought that he could not remember "to ever have read in a judgment that a testimony has to be considered to be noncredible *just because* the witness blenched or flushed."[53] This does refer less to the (optical) perceptibility of nonverbal behavior than to its possible relevance for the evaluation of evidence—and denies it.

49 *Schulze*, "Blinde Richter – aktueller Stand von Diskussion und Rechtsprechung," 1995, p. 672 (author's translation).

50 *Schulze*, above fn. 48, p. 739.

51 *Bender, Nack, and Treuer*, above fn. 33, marginal no. 218.

52 *Schulze*, above fn. 49, p. 672.

53 On the following see Schulze, above fn. 48, p. 739 (emphasis added).

Schulze, however, misses out on the fact that the assessment of credibility in the course of evaluating the evidence is a (highly) complex process that will rarely depend on "just" one single aspect. Quite to the contrary: If one focuses too much on one aspect or one piece of evidence—the assessment of credibility being one part of it—when evaluating the evidence on the whole this may conflict with the obligation to exhaustively evaluate the evidence on the basis of a well-founded set of facts.[54] The same applies to the evaluation of witness testimony that is—just as every other part of the evaluation of evidence—subject to the rule of exhaustive evaluation of evidence.[55] This calls for an autonomous assessment of the ability to testify and the credibility by weighing all relevant circumstances.[56] This means that one single aspect must *per se* not be considered as solely decisive, because individual aspects must not be seen in isolation if one wants to remain true to the word "exhaustive".

2. Reflections on expert evidence on a witness statement's likely credibility

On the basis of this finding, more normative criteria may be identified on the question of the (ir-)relevance of nonverbal behavior that one cannot primarily and certainly not exclusively rely on studies and findings of psychology of evidence. Such studies entered criminal court practice in the form of expert evidence on a witness statement's credibility. In this regard, one important issue is the content requirements of such an expert opinion. Another issue, which has been dealt with by several supreme court decisions, are the requirements for obtaining expert opinions on psychology of evidence *ex officio* or denying a motion to take evidence.

BGHSt 45, 164 in particular dealt with scientific requirements (expert opinions on the credibility of witness statements). In the beginning of its reasoning, the BGH notes that the subject of such an expert opinion is not the general credibility of the examined witness in the sense of a permanent personal characteristic. The expert opinion is about the evaluation of whether the statements given on specific events are true, i.e., whether they correspond to the actual experience of the examined witness.

54 *See Julius*, above fn. 47, § 261 marginal no. 20 ff. with further references.

55 *See Brause*, "Glaubhaftigkeitsprüfung und -bewertung einer Aussage im Spiegel der höchstrichterlichen Rechtsprechung," 2013, p. 133 with further references.

56 *Julius*, above fn. 47, § 261 marginal no. 27 ff. with further references.

Subsequently the BGH deals with the scientific requirements of such expert opinions. The court mentions criteria (e.g. logical consistence, richness of detail, spatio-temporal interconnections, descriptions of unusual events and of mental processes, mentioning of exonerating details or of details intrinsic to the type of crime) which have to be compiled for the analysis of the quality of the statement and which may have circumstantial significance as quality criteria intrinsic to the statement whether the information given by the witness are based on actual experience. It is emphasized, however, that the identification of one (single) factor does not allow for a compelling conclusion about the credibility of the statement of the examined witness. Rather, an expert conclusion gains considerably higher significance and a corresponding circumstantial value for the credibility of the information to be evaluated only "if it is derived from the entirety of all indicators". This is the position of case law concerning the scientific requirements of expert opinions on the credibility of witness statements.

More often the BGH is confronted with the question whether there is an obligation of the trial courts to get such an expert opinion *ex officio* or at least pursuant to a motion to take evidence. In the beginning of 2013, the court addressed this issue again and consistently continued its line taken earlier.[57] According to it, the assessment of the credibility of witness testimony—as evaluation of evidence in general[58]—is in principle the trial court's original task. It can generally be assumed that professional judges have sufficient expertise in assessing the credibility of the witness and his statement to evaluate statements even in difficult and complex situations, and that they can pass on their expertise to the lay judges involved. The involvement of a psychological expert is therefore only necessary when there are particularities in the case which may raise doubts whether the trial judge's expertise is sufficient to assess the credibility of the witness and his statement under these particular circumstances. Such circumstances may be given if there are indications that the witness's ability to remember is impaired because of particular reasons that are psycho-diagnostically

57 BGH, Order of 8 Jan 2013 – 1 StR 602/12 and earlier BGH, *NStZ-RR* 2006, 241; BGH, *NStZ-RR* 2006, 242, 243; BGH, NStZ 2010, 51, 52. On this problem, see further *Fischer,* "Glaubwürdigkeitsbeurteilung und Beweiswürdigung – Von der Last der 'ureigenen Aufgabe'," 1994, pp. 1 ff.; idem, "Aussagewahrheit und Glaubhaftigkeitsbeurteilung. Anmerkungen zum Beweiswert von Glaub-haftigkeitsgutachten," 2008, pp. 191 ff; *Kett-Straub*, "Die Glaubwürdigkeitsbegutachtung minderjähriger Zeugen," 2005, pp. 354 ff.; *Brause,* above fn. 55, pp. 129 ff. – all with further references.

58 See only BGH, *NStZ* 2010, 51, 52; *NStZ-RR* 2013, 461.

determinable or if particular mental dispositions or burdens may call into question the reliability of the statement, and that the trial judge—in the given case—does not have the particular and scientifically sound expertise necessary to determine these factors and their possible influence on the contents of the testimony.

It follows from these principles that the assessment of credibility of witness testimony is in a relationship of rule and exception. Regularly, this is the original task of the trial courts, who may and must only resort to experts of psychology of evidence in case of particular circumstances in exceptional cases. If the trial court assumes that such a case is given, the expert opinion then obtained must also be evaluated on its quality criteria intrinsic to the testimony and on its indicators.

Irrespective of the relationship between the credibility of the witness and of the witness's statement[59] the following conclusions for the question under consideration here can be drawn from the observations above: If an exhaustive evaluation is necessary for expert opinions on the witness *testimony's* credibility, this must also be the case for the assessment of the *witness*'s credibility. As well as for psychology of evidence opinions, the identification of one (nonverbal) characteristic does not allow for a compelling conclusion about the credibility of a witness. For example, *Bender/Nack/Treuer* refer to this; according to them body language signs should not be ignored when they appear along with verbal particularities.[60] To completely ignore a significant part, namely the body language, conflicts with the rule of exhaustive assessment and evaluation of evidence. The personal impression is after all a significant part of evaluating the evidence which must not be ignored.[61] Apart from that, expert opinions on credibility should remain the exception. They are used mostly in cases involving sexual offences. Thus, it is questionable whether the findings gained from these exceptional expert opinions can be transferred to all witness testimony in criminal cases and therefore be universalized. If the personal interrogation is discarded as irrelevant *per se* referring to scientific studies in psychology of evidence concerning the (presumed or only possible) insignificance of nonverbal behavior for the assessment of the credibility of the witness, this would lead to an apodictic universalization in the assessment of the credibility

59 E.g. see *Schneider*, above fn. 32, pp. 13 ff.; *Kilian-Herklotz*, above fn. 38, p. 195, 201; *Kett-Straub*, above fn. 57, p. 364—all with further references.

60 *See Bender, Nack and Treuer, Tatsachenfeststellung vor Gericht*, marginal no. 218.

61 See *Brause*, above fn. 55, p. 129.

of witnesses against which one fights against vehemently concerning the assessment of the credibility of the witness's testimony. This has to be borne in mind when generalizing findings of psychology of evidence on nonverbal behavior from a legal perspective in the sense that it is irrelevant in general, and that the personal interrogation in the actual court trial therefore is irrelevant as well.

3. Multi-factor causation of nonverbal behavior

Finally, one more issue has to be resolved: The insignificance of nonverbal behavior is considered as being "appropriate" because flushing and so forth may well have another cause than the witness being aware of not telling the truth.[62] As a starting point one seems to be able to rely on respective scientific studies in psychology of evidence. According to a study—consulted by *Lagodny*—it is suggested that[63] "behavior is a highly unreliable criterion for the assessment of credibility". Such criteria were to be found exclusively in the contents of the statement. However, this opinion is not convincing.

Already *Lagodny*'s starting point is questionable. It is an odd view to rely on this study when stating that a "can process" poses no problems for the evaluation of the credibility of witnesses. What he describes by "can process" is a video-based trial where the statements of the accused and the witnesses which were recorded during the preliminary investigations are played back during the trial.[64] This seems strange as in the study on psychology of evidence a false version in TV, i.e. a false recorded statement, was identified as such less often than the false version disseminated by radio or newspaper.[65] If at all, one could ask for extending the possibilities to read out minutes of earlier interrogations because of the last-mentioned aspect.

In the end, a test can be made that argues in favor of adhering to immediate face-to-face witness testimony once and for all, or at least not ignore it because of asserted insignificance of nonverbal behavior. For this, *Kilian-Herklotz* will be consulted again who, on the one hand, considers the significance of nonverbal behavior for the assessment of credibility to be "questionable", but on the other hand—even if mentioned in a hard-

62 [See] *Schulze*, above fn. 48, p. 739.
63 On the following see *Lagodny*, above fn. 37, p. 178 and N. 26.
64 See ibid., p. 173.
65 See ibid., p. 178 in N. 26.

to-find place—emphasizes that more studies are necessary to *fully* reject the nonverbal behavior as indicator for the evaluation of the quality of the testimony.[66] Psychology of evidence therefore is dominated by a *non liquet* and the question arises how jurisprudence as a normative-judgmental science handles this. There are two possible scenarios: If one wanted to give up the immediate face-to-face witness interrogation *de lege ferenda* relying on critical studies on the reliability of nonverbal elements in evaluating credibility, it is in no way certain that this approach would be correct—from a psychology of evidence perspective—, it would, however, in any case, violate the rule of exhaustive evaluation of the evidence available. Therefore, the other scenario is more convincing, namely, to adhere to the principle of immediacy to get an impression of the nonverbal behavior and then—on a case-to-case basis—consider it in the judgement after an evaluative consideration of the evidence on the whole.

C. Résumé

These reflections show that nonverbal behavior of witnesses while testifying may be of relevance for assessing the credibility when evaluating the evidence, at least of indirect relevance in connection with other criteria, which, however, must not be seen in isolation but have to be correlated with each other. Therefore, as a starting point, it has to be adhered to the principle of immediacy. That does not mean that a (careful) development of the criminal procedural law principle of immediacy in the sense of further exceptions cannot be justified in another way.[67] However, such exceptions need to be justified in principle.

Bibliography

Arntzen, Friedrich, *Psychologie der Zeugenaussage: System der Glaubhaftigkeits-merkmale*, 4th ed., Munich: C. H. Beck, 2007.

Bender, Rolf, and Armin Nack, *Tatsachenfeststellung vor Gericht, Band I, Glaubwürdigkeits- und Beweislehre*, 2nd ed., Munich: C. H. Beck, 1995.

Bender, Rolf, Armin Nack, and Wolf-Dieter Treuer, *Tatsachenfeststellung vor Gericht*, 3rd ed., München: C. H. Beck, 2007.

66 *Kilian-Herklotz*, above fn. 38, p. 213 in N. 92 (emphasis added).

67 See. e.g. *Krüger*, above fn. 2, pp. 309 ff.

BGH, NStZ 2010, 51.

BGH, NStZ 2011, 474.

BGH, NStZ-RR 2006, 241.

BGH, NStZ-RR 2006, 242.

BGH, NStZ-RR 2011, 349.

BGH, Order of 8 Jan 2013 - 1 StR 602/12.

BGHSt 35, 164.

BGHSt 44, 308.

Brause, Peter, "Glaubhaftigkeitsprüfung und -bewertung einer Aussage im Spiegel der höchstrichterlichen Rechtsprechung," *Neue Zeitschrift für Strafrecht* 3 (2013): 129–135.

BVerfG, NJW 2004, 2150.

Eisenberg, Ulrich, *Beweisrecht der StPO: Spezialkommentar*, 8th ed., Munich: C. H. Beck, 2013.

Eser, Albin, "Funktionswandel von Prozeßmaximen," *Zeitschrift für die gesamte Strafrechtswissenschaft* 104, 2 (1992): 361–397.

Fezer, Gerhard, "Anmerkung zu BGH, Urteil vom 27.11.1986," *Neue Zeitschrift für das Strafrecht* 7 (1987): 335–336.

Fischer, Thomas, "Aussagewahrheit und Glaubhaftigkeitsbeurteilung. Anmerkungen zum Beweiswert von Glaubhaftigkeitsgutachten," in *Strafverteidigung, Revision und die gesamtem Strafrechtswissenschaften. Festschrift für Gunter Widmaier zum 70. Geburtstag*, ed. Heinz Schöch, Helmut Satzger, Gerhard Schäfer, Alexander Ignor, and Christoph Knauer, Köln: C. Heymanns, 2008, pp. 191–222.

Fischer, Thomas, "Glaubwürdigkeitsbeurteilung und Beweiswürdigung - Von der Last der 'ureigenen Aufgabe'," *Neue Zeitschrift für das Strafrecht* 1 (1994): 1–5.

Geppert, Klaus, *Der Grundsatz der Unmittelbarkeit im deutschen Strafverfahren*,, Berlin, Boston: De Gruyter, 1979, reprint 2012.

Julius, Karl-Peter, in: *Heidelberger Kommentar zur StPO*, ed. Björn Gercke, Karl-Peter Julius, Dieter Temming, and Mark A. Zöller, 5th ed., Heidelberg: C. F. Müller, 2012.

Kett-Straub, Gabriele, "Die Glaubwürdigkeitsbegutachtung minderjähriger Zeugen," *Zeitschrift für die gesamte Strafrechtswissenschaft* 117, 2 (2005): 354–378.

Kilian-Herklotz, Ines, "Einsatz von Videotechnik im deutschen Strafverfahren und richterliche Glaubwürdigkeitsbeurteilung," in *Strafprozess vor neuen Herausforderungen. Über den Sinn oder Unsinn von Unmittelbarkeit und Mündlichkeit im Strafverfahren*, ed. Otto Lagodny, Baden-Baden: Nomos, 2000, pp. 195–221.

Köhnken, Günter, "Video im Gericht. Modelle und Erfahrungen aus Großbritannien," *Strafverteidiger* 7 (1995): 376–380.

Krüger, Matthias, *Unmittelbarkeit und materielles Recht*, Berlin: Duncker & Humblot, 2014.

Kühne, Hans-Heiner, "Einleitung," in Löwe-Rosenberg, *Kommentar zur StPO*, 26. Aufl., Berlin: De Gruyter, 2006.

Lagodny, Otto, "Videovernehmung in Strafverfahren: nur Risiken und Nebenwirkungen?," in *Strafprozess vor neuen Herausforderungen. Über den Sinn oder Unsinn von Unmittelbarkeit und Mündlichkeit im Strafverfahren*, ed. Otto Lagodny, Baden-Baden: Nomos, 2000, pp. 167–182.

Liszt, Franz von, *Die Reform des Strafverfahrens*, Berlin: J. Guttentag, 1906.

Meyer-Goßner, Lutz, *Kommentar zur StPO*, 56th ed., Munich: C. H. Beck, 2013.

Norouzi, Ali B, *Die audiovisuelle Vernehmung von Auslandszeugen*, Tübingen: Mohr Siebeck, 2010.

Rieck, Patrick J., *Substitut oder Komplement?*, Berlin: Duncker & Humblot, 2003.

Rieß, Peter, "Entwicklungstendenzen in der deutschen Strafprozessgesetzgebung seit 1950," *Zeitschrift für Internationale Strafrechtsdogmatik* 10 (2009): 466–483.

Rupp, Erwin, *Der Beweis im Strafverfahren*, Freiburg i. B. und Tübingen: Mohr, 1884.

Sander, Günther M., in: Löwe-Rosenberg, *Kommentar zur StPO*, 26. Aufl., Berlin: De Gruyter, 2006.

Schmid, Werner, "Der revisionsgerichtliche Augenscheinsbeweis," *Zeitschrift für die gesamte Strafrechtswissenschaft* 85, 4 (1973): 893–915.

Schmidt, Eberhard, "§ 261 StPO in der neueren höchstrichterlichen Rechtsprechung," *Juristenzeitung* 11/12 (1970): 337–343.

Schmoll, Daniela, *Videovernehmung kindlicher Opfer im Strafprozess: Verfahrens- und verfassungsrechtliche Lösungen auf der Grundlage des Zeugenschutzgesetzes*, Frankfurt am Main, New York: P. Lang, 1999.

Schneider, Lothar, *Nonverbale Zeugnisse gegen sich selbst*, Tübingen: Attempto-Verl, 1991.

Schorn, "Erblindeter Richter in der Gerichtsbarkeit," *Juristische Rundschau* 8 (1954): 298–299.

Schulze, Hans-Eugen, "Blinde Richter – aktueller Stand von Diskussion und Rechtsprechung," *Monatsschrift für Deutsches Recht* (1995): 670–672.

Schulze, Hans-Eugen, "Zur Mitwirkung blinder Richter," *Monatsschrift für Deutsches Recht* (1988): 736–742.

Stüber, Michael, *Die Entwicklung des Prinzips der Unmittelbarkeit im deutschen Strafverfahren*, Frankfurt am Main et al.: Lang, 2005.

Undeutsch, Udo, "Die Verwertbarkeit unwillkürlicher Ausdruckserscheinungen bei der Aussagenwürdigung. Eine Anfrage von psychologischer Seite," *Zeitschrift für die gesamte Strafrechtswissenschaft* 87, 3 (1975): 650–662.

Weigend, Thomas, "Strukturelle Probleme im deutschen Strafprozess," *Strafverteidiger Forum* (2013): 45–53.

Wimmer, August, "Anmerkung zu BGH, Urteil vom 28.4.1952," *Juristenzeitung* 21 (1953): 671–672.

Developments in Israeli Criminal Law Procedure

Rinat Kitai-Sangero

A. Introduction

Two significant developments may be pointed to that occurred in Israeli criminal law procedure. The first of these was the sentencing reform of 2012, which delineated general principles in regard to imposing punishments. The second development is manifested in the growing readiness on the part of the Supreme Court to exclude unlawfully obtained evidence and to recognize the need for protecting the rights of accused persons as an independent value, even at the cost of harming the pursuit of truth. Despite the fact that the right to a fair trial does not explicitly appear in the Basic Law: Human Dignity and Liberty, which was enacted in 1992, the Supreme Court has held that this right stems from the Basic Law because it is a necessary condition for the protection of the fundamental right to personal freedom.[1]

B. Sentencing Reform and the Principle of Proportionality in Punishment

An amendment to the Penal Law generated a reform in the way punishment was meted out. The amendment has two objectives: the first aim was to lay down a hierarchy of the different considerations for sentencing; the second objective was to create greater unity in the sentences meted out by judges through the structuring of judicial discretion in sentencing.

Until the amendment to the Penal Law, legal rules did not determine a hierarchy of the different considerations for sentencing: retribution, general and special deterrence, incapacitation, and rehabilitation. Section 40b of the Penal Law provides now that the guiding principle in sentencing is proportionality between the seriousness of the offense committed and the degree of the offender's culpability, on the one hand, and the type and severity of the punishment, on the other. The Supreme Court made it clear

1 Crim. App. 8823/07, Anon. v. State of Israel, sec. 16 (February 11, 2010).

that the law grants senior standing to the principle of retribution and that this principle is what guides sentencing.[2] Along with retribution, the Penal Law gives voice to other considerations of punishment, such as protecting public safety, rehabilitating the defendant, and deterring the individual and the public.

The Penal Law states that the court is entitled to take deterrent considerations into account when passing sentence if it finds that there is a need to deter the defendant or the public from perpetrating offenses and that there is a real chance that a severe punishment will bring about this deterrence. Still, considerations of general and specific deterrence may be taken into account only in the framework of the principle of retribution. They cannot lead to a deviation from the principle of proportionality but only bring it about that the court will impose a punishment that is found on the topmost point of the proportionate sentencing range.[3]

The law allows deviation from the demand for proportionality in two cases. First, the severity of punishment may be increased in order to protect public safety. If the court finds that there is a real fear that the convicted person will commit further offenses, and that a harsher punishment and distancing the convicted from society are required to protect public safety, the judge is entitled to impose a longer sentence than one befitting the offense. The ability to deviate from proportionality in order to protect public safety is, however, limited. First of all, the sentence imposed cannot deviate significantly from the proportionate sentencing range. Second, the court can determine that the convicted person endangers public safety only if the latter has a significant criminal record or if the court is presented with professional opinion in regard to the convicted person's dangerousness.[4]

The second allowance for deviating from proportionality is for the sake of rehabilitation. The law does not restrict the extent of the permitted deviation on the side of leniency from the proportionate sentencing range for the purpose of rehabilitation. Nonetheless, the law grants limited standing to this consideration when a serious offense is involved, ruling that if the offense and the degree of guilt are of excessive severity, the court cannot normally deviate from the fitting punishment unless special and extraordinary circumstances exist and the court has been convinced that these

2 Crim. App. 8641/12, Saed v. State of Israel, sec. 21 (August 5, 2013).
3 Sections 40F and 40G of the Penal Law, 1977.
4 Ibid., sec. 40E.

circumstances outweigh the need for meting out a punishment within the proportionate sentencing range in accordance with the guiding principle.[5]

The second innovation of the sentencing reform has to do with structuring the judge's discretion when passing sentences. The process of the imposition of punishments needs to be done in two stages. First, the judge must determine the proportionate sentencing range for the offense that was committed. The range includes the minimum and maximum sentences, with each point along this continuum constitutes a reasonable punishment according to the demand for proportionality. The penal code contains no sentencing range apart from fixing the maximum penalty, and the task of determining the proportionate sentencing range is imposed on the individual judge, who needs to take into account the seriousness of the offense and the circumstances related to its perpetration. The law enumerates a list of circumstances related to the commission of the offense in the event that they are relevant to increasing or decreasing the defendant's culpability, such as premeditation; the relative role of the defendant in committing the offense; the degree of another person's influence on the defendant in perpetrating the offense; the damage caused by the commission of the offense; the circumstances that led the defendant to commit the offense; the degree of the defendant's ability to understand the wrongness of his or her misdeed, given, inter alia, his or her age; the ability of the defendant to refrain from doing the offense and the extent of the defendant's control over his or her acts, including provocation by the victim of the offense; the mental distress of the defendant owing to being abused by the victim; the proximity of the act to a defense to criminal responsibility, such as a case in which the defendant deviated only slightly from the requirements of self-defense; the cruelty, violence, and abuse aimed at the victim of the offense; the misuse of the defendant's power over the victim.[6]

In the second stage, upon determining the proportionate sentencing range, the judge has to decide the suitable punishment for the defendant. Thus, for instance, if the judge decided that, in circumstances that the value of the stolen property was slight and that the defendant had carried out the offense because of an addiction to drugs, the proportionate sentencing range for breaking and entering was one to three years imprisonment, a determination will then have to be made of the suitable punishment for this specific defendant. The judge can choose any point on this continuum of

5 Ibid., sec. 40D.
6 Ibid., sec. 40I.

one to three years imprisonment that, in his or her opinion, is fitting for the particular circumstances of the defendant.

At this second stage, the court examines additional circumstances that were not considered in the first stage. These circumstances relate to the defendant's individual circumstances unconnected to the offense itself, such as the harm that the punishment may cause the defendant and the defendant's family, the damage caused the defendant from having committed the offense and being convicted, whether the defendant has taken responsibility for the actions and returned or made efforts to return to the correct path, the defendant's attempts to compensate for the damage the offense caused, the defendant's cooperation with law enforcement authorities, the defendant's positive behavior and contribution to society, difficult life circumstances that may have had an influence on the commission of the offense, misbehavior on the part of law enforcement authorities, the passage of time since the offense was committed, the defendant's criminal or lack of criminal record.[7]

The judge, as stated, is entitled to deviate from the proportionate sentencing range when passing sentence in order to protect public safety or for the sake of rehabilitation. In the example presented just above, the judge can impose a sentence of less than one year if it is proved, for example, that the defendant had undergone a successful process of detoxification. By the same token, a harsher punishment can be imposed than three years imprisonment if the judge comes to the conclusion that the defendant is recidivist and that a harsher punishment may protect society.

The principal importance of the sentencing reform is the establishment of the proportionate principle as the guiding rule for meting out punishments and the determination of a hierarchy among the considerations for sentencing. As to achieving a higher uniformity in sentencing among different judges, although it is still too early to predict the outcome because a new law is involved, one may venture to say that the law will not succeed in attaining this goal and that judges will continue to pass sentence in accordance with their own free choice as was the case prior to the reform. Every judge, as mentioned, sets the proportionate sentencing range on his or her own. In doing so, the judge is entitled to take into account various circumstances relating to the commission of the offense. Even when the Supreme Court determines a suitable proportionate sentencing range for a certain offense, every judge can make a distinction between the case at

---

7 Ibid., sec. 40K.

hand and the case for which the Supreme Court issued its verdict and determine another proportionate sentencing range that is appropriate for the specific circumstances of the case at hand. Judges who know what they believe to be the proper punishment for a certain offense can simply adjust the proportionate sentencing range to that punishment. One may argue that lack of uniformity among judges is inevitable as long as free human beings determine verdicts, as reflected by the general technique in jurisprudence of distinguishing cases. The assumption underlying the amendment, however, was that punishment's disparity among judges violates the principle of equality. Nevertheless, in order to avoid dehumanization of the process of punishment, the legislator allowed taking into account a wide range of individual characteristics in determining the fitting punishment.

Given the awkwardness in determining the proper sentence, for the judge is required first to determine a general proportionate sentencing range that takes into account the circumstances which are relating to the perpetration of the offense and afterwards to adjust the punishment within the framework of this range, if the reform of the law does not succeed in achieving greater uniformity in sentencing, it is doubtful whether this awkwardness is justified and whether it is better to skip the phase of determining the sentencing range and to determine solely the fitting punishment for the specific defendant while taking into account all the relevant considerations.

C. The Exclusionary Rule as Protecting Accused Persons' Rights

In 2006, the Israeli Supreme Court held in the Issacharov case that a court has discretion to exclude evidence unlawfully obtained.[8] The Supreme Court based its opinion on the Basic Law: Human Dignity and Liberty, holding that this law created a new balance between the need to fight crime and the need to pay greater attention to accused persons' human rights. Therefore, courts have the discretion to reject the admissibility of incriminating evidence if it is of the opinion that this evidence was obtained unlawfully and that its acceptance by the court would substantially harm the defendant's right to a fair trial. The Supreme Court maintained that the exclusionary rule aims at obtaining a proper compromise between, on the one hand, the need of revealing the factual truth, the war against crime,

8 Issacharov v. Chief Military Prosecutor, 61(1) P.D. 461 (2006).

and the protection of public safety and of victims' rights, and, on the other hand, protection of accused persons' rights and of fairness and purity of the criminal procedure.[9]

In the Issacharov case, the court excluded the confession of a soldier regarding the use of soft drugs in the army that had been extracted without the investigator's informing him of his right to counsel.[10] Along with the innovation of the ruling, many doubts arose as to the issue of whether the exclusionary rule would indeed protect in practice accused persons' rights.[11] This fear stemmed principally from the list of criteria set down in the ruling regarding the appropriate exercise of judicial discretion. Thus, the Supreme Court held that physical evidence (such as a weapon, drugs, or stolen property) has an independent and separate existence from the illegality connected with obtaining it, and generally the illegality would be insufficient to affect its reliability or to cause its exclusion. The Supreme Court has also ruled that the essence and seriousness of the offense attributed to the defendant must be examined, in addition to the importance of the evidence for proving the defendant's guilt. When important evidence is involved that is decisive for convicting the defendant and when the offenses attributed to the defendant are very serious, then the inadmissibility of the evidence may overwhelmingly harm the opposing interests, which are concerned with fighting crime, protecting public safety and paying due attention to the victims. As opposed to the exclusionary rule in the United States, the doctrine of the "fruits of the poisonous tree" relating to evidence indirectly obtained by illegal conduct, has been rejected.

---

9 Ibid., sec. 76.

10 While sec. 12 of the Evidence Ordinance 1971 excludes involuntary out-of-court's confessions, the failure to apprise a suspect of the right to remain silent or the right to counsel is only one factor to be considered in the totality of the circumstances surrounding a confession and is not alone sufficient to automatically render the suspect's confession involuntary: Mooadi v. Israel, 38(1) P.D. 197 (1984).

11 See Sangero, "An Exclusionary Rule for Evidence Obtained Unlawfully as Established in the Issacharov Ruling – Good or Bad Tidings?," 2007, pp. 67 ff. Merin and Kitai-Sangero, "Miranda, Collins and Issacharov: The Gap between the Ideal and the Real in the Issacharov Ruling," 2007; Kitai-Sangero and Merin, "Israel: The Supreme Court's New, Cautious Exclusionary Rule," 2013, pp. 93–111; Etinger-Shapira and Shapira, "The Israeli Disqualification Rule Following Issacharov," 2007, pp. 429ff.; Blum, "Exclude Evidence, You Exclude Justice'? A Critical Evaluation of Israel's Exclusionary Rule after Issacharov," 2010, pp. 385–450.

Criticism has been leveled against these criteria arguing that the exclusionary rule that was established is too complex and too weak.[12] The discretion enabling the court not to exclude unlawfully obtained evidence is too broad. Additionally, some of the criteria that have been set down for the purpose of exercising discretion relating to the seriousness of the offense, the importance of the evidence, and the nature of the evidence are very problematic. Undoubtedly, these criteria weaken the protection, which the exclusionary rule provides to Israeli defendants, compared to their counterparts in the United States.[13]

Consequently, the fear was expressed that the doctrine would be applied only in cases involving less-serious offenses, whose enforcement the public has no great interest in, while in serious offenses, there would be no incentive for the police to act properly. Hence, the Supreme Court's declaration of the commitment to safeguarding the accused persons' rights would lack practical legal effect. The Supreme Court, however, surprised the critics by excluding evidence even in cases of serious crimes, such as rape and murder, in cases of physical evidence, like drugs or a knife, and in cases in which the excluded evidence was of vital importance for proving the defendant's guilt.

Thus, in the 2009 Alzam case, the Supreme Court dismissed the confession of a defendant, who was charged with murder.[14] Alzam confessed after the cover-agent, who was planted in Alzam's cell, stirred him up against his lawyer, convincing him that the lawyer had no interest in him and that the interrogators were the only ones he could trust. In this way, the police cover-agent violated Alzam's right to consult with counsel and his right against self-incrimination. It should be mentioned that the acquittal did not result in the freeing of a murderer, for Alzam was found dead in his cell for unknown reasons after his conviction by the district court and before the decision of the Supreme Court. Nevertheless, exclusion of a confession in a case of murder can constitute precedence for other cases in which the

---

12 See Sangero, above fn 11.

13 For a wide comparative discussion see Merin, "Lost Between the Fruits and the Tree: In Search of a Coherent theoretical Model for the Exclusion of Derivative Evidence," 2015, pp. 273–329.

14 Crim. App. 1301/06, Estate of the Late Yoni Alzam v. State of Israel (June 22, 2009). A detailed reference to the judgment may be found in Sangero, "The Use of Tricks and Cover-agents for the Sake of Gathering Evidence – Thoughts in the Wake of Crim. App. 1301/06, Estate of the Late Yoni Alzam v. State of Israel," 2011, pp. 399–417 (in Hebrew).

person charged with murder remains at large because the Court has not mentioned within the considerations to exclude the confession the fact that Alzam's death actually ensured public safety in future

In the 2011 Farhi case, physical evidence was set aside in a rape offense.[15] The defendant voluntarily gave a sample of his saliva, receiving police assurance that it would serve only a murder case. An examination made it clear that Farhi had no connection with the murder. However, Farhi's genetic profile, derived from the saliva sample, reminded the head of the DNA bank of the Israeli Police Criminal Identification Department of a DNA profile that had been collected and investigated in several rape cases. Comparison of the data in the computer found a match between Farhi's genetic profile and that found at several rape case sites.[16] After receiving this finding, police investigators obtained a cigarette butt that Farhi had smoked, and a match was found between Farhi's DNA profile and the DNA findings from the scenes of the sexual attacks. Farhi was put on trial in contradiction to the assurance given to him when he had agreed to give the saliva sample. The district court decided to admit the DNA evidence that had been unlawfully obtained and to base its conviction on this evidence, citing in support, among others, the considerations of the seriousness of the offense and the vital nature of the evidence for conviction.[17] Farhi was sentenced to 25 years in prison.

The Supreme Court held that in cases in which the offense was serious and the unlawfully obtained evidence was vital to the State's case against the defendant, the importance of safeguarding the accused persons' rights and the fairness of the procedure took precedence.[18] This correct judgment enabled the Court to add that not only had the original DNA evidence to be excluded—the saliva sample having been taken following a promise not to use it outside a murder case—but the secondary DNA evidence, taken from a cigarette butt, also had to be disqualified. The first piece of evidence was excluded because it was obtained unlawfully, harming the defendant's right to a fair trial and to privacy, as well as the image of the law enforcement system.[19] As to the second DNA evidence, the Court made it clear that although the American doctrine of "the fruit of the poisonous tree" had not

15 Crim. App. 4988/08, Eythan Farhi v. State of Israel (August 1, 2011).
16 Ibid., §1 to Justice Levy's verdict.
17 Ibid., §6.
18 Ibid., §19.
19 Ibid., §18–19.

been accepted in Israel, it was still possible to exclude secondary evidence. In the case at hand it should be disqualified, for a close causal relationship existed between it and the excluded original evidence.[20] Justice Levy stated that the fact that police investigators found a reason for obtaining the secondary evidence that made no contribution to clarifying the incriminating picture, testified in itself to the need that had arisen to whitewash the initial proof, the obtaining of which had been tainted. However, the Court decided not to exclude the rest of the secondary evidence to save the DNA from the cigarette butt. Therefore it had to decide the case according to the admissible secondary evidence: the defendant's refusal to give a sample of his saliva for laboratory testing; his refraining from participating in a line-up; the confrontation with the complainants and his choosing not to testify in court;[21] the testimonies of the complainants regarding the rapist's general appearance; the lower court's statement that incriminating admissions could be found in a number of the defendant's statements to his interrogators; and lastly the pinpointing of his cell phone close to three of the crime scenes. Based on all this admissible evidence, the defendant had been convicted. Sangero criticized the conviction, arguing that it had been based on quite weak evidence, which showed that the Supreme Court recoiled from paying the social cost connected with releasing a rapist and which, in his opinion, was compelled as a result of the DNA evidence's exclusion.[22]

The last verdict that I shall discuss in the context of the exclusionary rule is the 2012 Ben-Haim case.[23] There were several cases in which the police asked to conduct a search of people's bags without there being a reasonable suspicion that an offense had been committed. The police did not make it clear to these people that they had the right to refuse the search. In the course of a number of such searches, forbidden objects were found in the bags, such as drugs and a knife of a type whose possession was illegal.

Ben-Haim is an interesting and important verdict, for in handing it down the Supreme Court to a great extent abandoned considerations of the nature of the evidence and of the importance of the evidence for

---

20 Ibid., §20–21

21 Israeli law allows drawing adverse inferences from silence at court: sec. 162 of the Criminal Procedure Law, 1982.

22 Sangero, "The Exclusionary Rule Is Developing, but still without a Willingness to Pay the Social Cost and to Acquit a Person Guilty of a Serious Offense Who Is Still Living," 2012, pp. 25ff.

23 Crim. App. 10141/09, Ben-Haim v. State of Israel (March 6, 2012).

conviction as reasons not to exclude evidence. The main ruling in the Ben-Haim verdict was that in the absence of another source of authority, a person's consent to a search of his body, his possessions, or his home might constitute a source of independent authority for carrying out the search. However, the consent must be a true agreement, willingly given, and the person involved should be fully aware of the circumstances. Although the agreement to the search does not necessarily have to be given in writing in order to ensure the willingness of the consent, the mere agreement to a search is insufficient. Rather, the police should make it clear that the individual has a right to refuse the search request and that this refusal would not be held against him or her. A position protecting the rights of an individual to a greater extent was expressed by the dissenting Justice, Yoram Danziger, according to which without authority to conducting a search, the individual's consent does not create an independent authority for the police.

There was no dispute, in any event, over the fact that the evidence had been obtained by the police unlawfully, because the police officers did not make it clear that the individual had the right to refuse such a search. The Supreme Court held that the illegal search justified excluding the evidence. Although light offenses were involved in these cases—possession of a knife and possession of small amount of drugs—the importance of the decision lies in the Court's conceding the demand regarding the nature of the evidence and its importance as considerations against the exclusion of the evidence. Another conclusion that may be drawn from this decision concerns the hierarchy of evidence that is prone to exclusion. Tangible evidence, as opposed to confessions, is no longer immuned from exclusion despite its reliability.

D. Conclusion

This report has summarized two significant developments in Israeli criminal procedure. One was the sentencing reform of 2012, which gave priority to the principle of proportionality and attempted to structure judicial discretion in the imposition of punishments. It is difficult to evaluate at this time whether and how giving precedence to proportionality will impact the level of punishments and whether the amendment to the law will succeed in achieving greater unity of sentences.

Israel has seen a trend in Supreme Court judgments toward imparting greater significance to due process. I have shown this trend in relation to the exclusionary rule. The Supreme Court held that there was no place for a war on crime at any cost while sacrificing the basic values of democracy,[24] and that rules of criminal procedure have importance in themselves by ensuring fairness to accused persons, who stand against an enforcement system that is much more stronger than the individual.[25] This conception is translated to more readiness by the Supreme Court to exclude unlawfully obtained evidence and to rejection of considerations against exclusion raised in a previous holding that had to do with the seriousness of the offense, the nature of the evidence, and the vitality of the evidence for conviction.

Bibliography

Blum, Binyamin, "Exclude Evidence, You Exclude Justice'? A Critical Evaluation of Israel's Exclusionary Rule after Issacharov," *Southwestern Journal of International Law* 16 (2010): 385–450.

Crim. App 1790/06, Gusseinof v. State of Israel, sec. 3 (August 7, 2007).

Crim. App. 10141/09, Ben-Haim v. State of Israel (March 6, 2012).

Crim. App. 1301/06, Estate of the Late Yoni Alzam v. State of Israel (June 22, 2009).

Crim. App. 4988/08, Eythan Farhi v. State of Israel (August 1, 2011).

Crim. App. 8641/12, Saed v. State of Israel, sec. 21 (August 5, 2013).

Crim. App. 8823/07, Anon. v. State of Israel, sec. 16 (February 11, 2010).

Criminal Procedure Law, Israel, 1982.

Etinger-Shapira, Keren, and Ron Shapira, "The Israeli Disqualification Rule Following Issacharov," *Din Udvarim (Haifa L. Rev.)* 3 (2007): 429 ff.

Evidence Ordinance, Israel, 1971.

Kitai-Sangero, Rinat, and Yuval Merin, "Israel: The Supreme Court's New, Cautious Exclusionary Rule," in *Exclusionary Rules in Comparative Law*, ed. Stephen C. Thaman, Dordrecht: Springer, 2013, pp. 93–111.

Merin, Yuval, "Lost Between the Fruits and the Tree: In Search of a Coherent theoretical Model for the Exclusion of Derivative Evidence," *New Criminal Law Review* 18 (2015): 273–329.

Merin, Yuval, and Rinat Kitai-Sangero, "Miranda, Collins and Issacharov: The Gap between the Ideal and the Real in the Issacharov Ruling," *Mishpatim* 37, 2 (2007): 429 ff.

24 Alzam, above fn. 12.

25 Crim. App 1790/06, Gusseinof v. State of Israel, sec. 3 (August 7, 2007).

Mooadi v. Israel, 38(1) P.D. 197 (1984).

Penal Law, Israel, 1977.

Sangero, Boaz, "An Exclusionary Rule for Evidence Obtained Unlawfully as Established in the Issacharov Ruling – Good or Bad Tidings?," *Israel Defense Forces Law Review* 19 (2007): 67 ff.

Sangero, Boaz, "The Exclusionary Rule Is Developing, but still without a Willingness to Pay the Social Cost and to Acquit a Person Guilty of a Serious Offense Who Is Still Living," *Mishpatim Al Atar* 4 (2012): 25 ff.

Sangero, Boaz, "The Use of Tricks and Cover-agents for the Sake of Gathering Evidence – Thoughts in the Wake of Crim. App. 1301/06, Estate of the Late Yoni Alzam v. State of Israel," *Alei Mishpat* 9 (2011): 399–417. (Hebrew)

Issues of Criminal Procedure Law Reform in Thailand

Pokpong Srisanit

A. Introduction

This article is divided into two sections: overview of the Thai criminal procedure law (B.) and issues of its reform (C.).

B. Overview of the Thai Criminal Procedure Law

Thai criminal procedure comprises four main phases: investigation, prosecution, pre-trial court proceedings, and trial court proceedings.

I. The investigation

The police are responsible for conducting investigations. Specifically, some officers are designated by law as "investigators." Unlike the European system, there is a clear separation of powers between the police and the public prosecutor. This means that Thai investigators may carry out investigations independently, without consulting the prosecutor, and the prosecutor cannot intervene in the investigation. Once the investigation is complete, the police forward the case to the prosecutor, who decides whether to proceed with prosecution.

During the investigation, a suspect may be held in custody for up to 48 hours. If an extension of custody is required, the investigator or prosecutor must request a detention warrant by bringing the suspect before the court.

The judge must then decide whether to detain the suspect for a legally prescribed[1] period or release them, either with or without bail.[2]

Regarding investigative methods, the investigator may take any action necessary for fact-finding. They can summon individuals who may provide relevant information and conduct searches or arrests with a warrant issued by the court. In principle, court authorization is required for any actions that affect citizens' freedoms, except in specific circumstances prescribed by law.[3]

II. The Prosecutor

After receiving the police investigation, the prosecutor is obliged to decide whether to prosecute the suspect in court or take no further action. The prosecutor may also return the case to the investigator for additional investigation. Despite not having investigative authority, the public prosecutor plays a crucial role, as they ultimately decide whether or not to proceed with prosecution.

In line with the separation of powers and the system of checks and balances, Article 145 of the Thai Criminal Procedure Code states that when the prosecutor decides not to prosecute, the case must be forwarded to the Chief of the National Police. If the Chief of Police disagrees with the decision, the final ruling on the case will be made by the Attorney General.[4]

1 Article 87 of the Thai Criminal Procedure Code sets the detention periods for suspects as follows: for charges carrying a maximum sentence of up to 6 months' imprisonment, a suspect may be detained for a maximum of 7 days. For charges carrying 6 months to 10 years' imprisonment, detention may last up to 48 days, with each detention period limited to 12 days. For charges carrying 10 years' imprisonment or more, detention may last up to 84 days, with each detention period also limited to 12 days.

2 According to the Thai Criminal Procedure Code, bail is not a mandatory condition for the provisional release of a suspect or accused person. However, in practice, the court typically requires bail for such a release.

3 The Thai Criminal Procedure Code allows for arrests or searches without a warrant in certain circumstances, such as in cases of flagrante delicto or emergency situations, as outlined in Articles 65, 78, 92, and 135, paragraph 5 of the Code.

4 However, under the "private prosecution" system outlined in Article 34 of the Thai Criminal Procedure Code, a final decision not to prosecute does not bar the victim from initiating a criminal case in court.

III. The pre-trial court

Unlike the French system, which has a *Juge d'instruction*, the pre-trial chamber system in Thailand is available only to victims who wish to directly prosecute a case before the Criminal Court. In Thailand, when a crime is committed, the victim has two options for initiating criminal proceedings: either by filing a complaint with the police or by prosecuting the accused directly in the Criminal Court. In the first scenario, the Thai court does not open a pre-trial chamber for the prosecutor's action. However, in the second scenario, the case is always reviewed by the pre-trial chamber before being passed to the trial court.

There are two key principles regarding the pre-trial chamber in Thailand. First, the pre-trial chamber is strictly a matter between the judge and the victim, and the judge is prohibited from interrogating the accused if they are present. Second, during the pre-trial stage, the accused is never held in custody.

IV. The trial court

Trial proceedings in Thailand follow the accusatorial system, which is defined by three key characteristics: public, oral, and adversarial proceedings. First, the trial court allows public attendance at hearings, except in specific circumstances outlined by law. Second, during the hearing, communication between the judge and witnesses must be oral. Finally, since the prosecutor and the accused are the parties before an independent court, it signifies a character of contradictory proceeding.

The appellate courts in Thailand consist of the central Court of Appeal and nine regional courts, both of which have the authority to review both factual and legal matters. there is no debate or hearing before the Court of Appeal in Thailand.

The Supreme Court, on the other hand, has jurisdiction over all matters, and its judgments are final. Unlike other high courts that only address legal questions, the Thai Supreme Court rules on both legal and factual issues.

There is no debate or hearing before the Supreme Court of Thailand.

C. Issues of Reform

The following analysis analysis will address three issues related to the reform of the Thai criminal procedure: the system, the accused, and the victim.

I. The system

Two issues of reform are presented in the following: the active role of the judge in criminal proceedings and the suspension of prosecution.

1. Active role of the judge in criminal proceedings

The Thai Criminal Procedure Code is based on the civil law system, where the judge plays an active role in fact-finding while presiding over trials. Although I do not intend to conduct a deep analysis of the accusatorial and inquisitorial systems,[5] I would like to highlight Article 229 of the Thai Criminal Procedure Code, which clearly states that the judge is responsible for collecting witness testimony, and Article 228, which permits the judge to request additional witness testimony. In contrast, common law practice typically assigns a passive role to the judge in criminal proceedings, maintaining a neutral stance regarding witness testimony. Actually, Thai judges often prefer this common law approach.

This creates a contradictory situation between the intended purpose of the code and the actual conduct of judges. It is true that "two halves of the truth presented to the judge by both parties may struggle to reveal the whole truth." Furthermore, every criminal proceeding is conducted in the public interest rather than solely for the benefit of the parties involved. I advocate for an active role for judges in fact-finding during criminal proceedings, as this aligns with the code's prescriptions and significantly enhances our criminal justice system's ability to uncover the truth.

For this issue, the reform should be achieved solely by adjusting court practices, without the need for any amendments to the text.

5 See the clear distinction of accusatorial and inquisitorial system in LaFave, Israel and King, *Criminal Procedure*, 2000, p. 31.

2. The suspension of the prosecution

For a long time, Thai prosecutors adhered to the legality principle, which required them to prosecute every case with sufficient evidence. In 2010, we formally transitioned to the opportunity principle. Article 21 of the Public Prosecutor Act 2010 states that the Attorney General may refrain from prosecuting a case when such an action would not align with the public interest.

However, prosecutors have only two options for deciding a case: first, to refrain from prosecution in accordance with the opportunity principle; or second, to prosecute the case in court. Opting for the latter can lead to congestion in criminal courts, while choosing the former can negatively impact society. Consequently, we lack a third option for prosecutors: the suspension of prosecution, a practice common in many countries.

This proposed third option could benefit society by allowing us to retain the advantages of both existing approaches. In petty cases, where the maximum imprisonment does not exceed five years, prosecutors should have the authority to suspend prosecution and impose appropriate measures to monitor the suspect for a specific period.[6] If the suspect complies with these measures, the prosecutor would definitively refrain from pursuing the case. Conversely, if the suspect fails to comply, the prosecutor could proceed with prosecution.

To implement the suspension of prosecution, we need a new law. Since 1977, when the concept was introduced in Thailand, this law has yet to be established.

II. The accused

I would like to raise three issues regarding the rights of the accused: provisional release of the accused, excessive pressing of charges, and chain and irons as an instrument of restraint that is still applied.

6 According to the article 41–2 of the French Criminal Procedure Code, the public prosecutor, while applying the suspension of prosecution, could propose measures of control to the suspect: for example, paying fine or forfeiture, returning the driving licence, participating in a rehabilitation course, fulfilling a non payment social work, participating in a training course, not emitting the cheque, being absent from the place where the crime committed, not meeting the victim of crime, not leaving the country, fulfilling a training of civic education, or indemnifying the victim of crime.

1. Provisional release of the suspect or the accused

According to the Thai Criminal Procedure Code, a suspect or accused individual may be released during criminal proceedings through three methods: provisional release without bail, provisional release under an indemnity contract, and provisional release under an indemnity contract with bail.[7]

The Thai Code does not require bail for the provisional release of a suspect or accused individual. However, in practice, judicial authorities always demand bail to prevent the possibility of escape. Additionally, we have established bail guidelines that set bail amounts based on the severity of the charge.

For example, a suspect charged with involuntary manslaughter—such as a driver who caused a fatal accident—must deposit money or property equivalent to 90,000 Baht for provisional release during lengthy criminal proceedings. This amount increases to 120,000 Baht if the driver becomes the accused before the court. Conversely, if the driver cannot provide the required bail, they may be detained in custody, even if they do not pose a flight risk or exhibit dangerous behavior. This practice may be viewed as discriminatory, as it creates unequal opportunities for individuals seeking provisional release.

One reform suggestion is to adjust bail amounts based on the income of the accused or suspect. Alternatively, it may be appropriate to eliminate bail guidelines and implement other measures for control during provisional release, such as electronic monitoring.

2. Excessive pressing of charges

According to the Thai Criminal Procedure Code, the investigator is responsible for pressing charges against a suspect. However, police practices often lead to excessive charges, which may result from Article 192 of the Code stating that the court cannot impose a penalty greater than what the

7 Article 106 of the Thai Criminal Procedure Code outlines three possibilities for provisional release: 1. provisional release without conditions: The suspect or accused can be released without any requirements; 2. provisional release under an indemnity contract: The suspect or accused must sign a contract agreeing to pay indemnity to the court in the event of escape; 3. provisional release under an indemnity contract with bail: The suspect or accused must sign a contract and provide assets as bail.

prosecutor demands.[8]For example, most individuals involved in political demonstrations should be charged with rioting, which carries a maximum imprisonment of six months. Instead, investigators often charge these individuals with terrorism, which can result in capital punishment.

Excessive charges can negatively impact the suspect or accused in several ways. First, they may be more easily detained in custody.[9] Second, they may face longer periods of detention.[10] Third, the amount of bail, which varies based on the severity of the charge, may limit their opportunities for provisional release.

To address this issue, I recommend establishing better cooperation between investigators and public prosecutors. In petty cases, investigators may press charges independently; however, for cases with potential imprisonment of up to ten years, they should be required to consult with the public prosecutor before proceeding.

3. Chain and irons

It is necessary to use restraint instruments to maintain control over accused individuals or prisoners. However, these instruments must conform to international standards.

The international standard known as "The Standard Minimum Rules for the Treatment of Prisoners" (1955), specifically Article 33, prescribes that

> [i]nstruments of restraint, such as handcuffs, chains, irons and strait-jackets, shall never be applied as a punishment. Furthermore, chains or irons shall not be used as restraints. Other instruments of restraint shall not be used except in the following circumstances: (a) As a precaution against escape during a transfer, provided that they shall be removed

8 Article 192 of the Thai Criminal Procedure Code prohibits the court from imposing a harsher penalty than the charge demanded by the prosecutor. However, paragraphs 2 to 6 of the same article state that, under certain circumstances, the court may issue a judgment based on facts established during the proceedings, even if those facts were not raised by the prosecutor.

9 Article 109 of the Thai Criminal Procedure Code requires the court to consider the comments of the investigator or prosecutor before granting provisional release to a suspect charged with a crime carrying a potential imprisonment of 10 years or more.

10 Article 87 of the Thai Criminal Procedure Code states that a suspect charged with a crime punishable by imprisonment of no more than 10 years may be detained in custody for a maximum of 48 days. However, if the charge carries a potential imprisonment of 10 years or more, the suspect may be detained for up to 84 days.

when the prisoner appears before a judicial or administrative authority; (b) On medical grounds by direction of the medical officer; (c) By order of the director, if other methods of control fail, in order to prevent a prisoner from injuring himself or others or from damaging property; in such instances the director shall at once consult the medical officer and report to the higher administrative authority." Article 34 states that "the patterns and manner of use of instruments of restraint shall be decided by the central prison administration. Such instruments must not be applied for any longer time than is strictly necessary.

However, according to the Thai Prison Administration Act of 1936, a prisoner may be restrained with chains and irons, particularly in cases involving severe crimes. Additionally, the accused can be shackled upon arrival at court.

The proposed reform is to eliminate the use of chains and irons and to remove restraint instruments when the accused are seated in court. This change would align with standards for the treatment of prisoners and uphold the principle of presumption of innocence for the accused.

III. The victim

Three issues regarding the reform of the situation of crime victims are as follows: the impact of the victim's private gain on public interest, the effect of the victim's private gain on public administration, and the compensation for the victim.

1. Private gain of the victim affecting the public interest

The Thai Criminal Procedure Code allows victims of crime to prosecute their cases in court independently, without the involvement of the public prosecutor. It seems that such actions of the victim would be in the public interest. However, they may affect the public interest especially when the victim compromises with the accused.

I would like to present a real case. Charges for attempted murder were filed against D, and the case was under investigation by the police. D compromised with the victim and offered compensation, which seemed to address the victim's needs but did not consider the public interest. D then hired a lawyer for the victim to sue him as the accused in criminal court.

Although many witnesses saw the accused shoot, the victim's lawyer intentionally chose a sole witness who was present at the crime scene but did not see the shooting. As a result, the pre-trial court dismissed the case due to insufficient evidence to proceed to trial. Subsequently, the public prosecutor filed charges against D. The accused argued that he had already been prosecuted and acquitted, and therefore should not face prosecution again, in accordance with the principle of "ne bis in idem" as prescribed by Article 39(4) of the Thai Criminal Procedure Code. The Thai court dismissed the case.

However, two landmark cases led Thai courts to change their ruling, stating that the previous case brought by the victim was void. Therefore, the subsequent case filed by the public prosecutor was considered the first proceeding. As a result, the accused was not subjected to double jeopardy.[11]

While court intervention is important for maintaining public interest, there should be textual reforms to prevent the potential abuse of victims. The proposed reform is that a pre-trial court's decision regarding a victim's claim should not prevent the prosecutor from taking action aimed at preserving public interest.

2. Private gain of pseudo victims affecting the public administration

This issue pertains to the charge of misconduct in office as defined by Article 157 of the Thai Criminal Procedure Code. This article aims to punish public officials who engage in corruption while performing their duties. The primary victim of this crime is the state, which is directly affected by the officer's misconduct. This article does not penalize those who perform their duties incorrectly without criminal intent, as such cases fall under the jurisdiction of the administrative court. Consequently, individuals cannot be considered victims of this crime. However, a so-called "victim" under Article 157 may threaten the officer by bringing a case directly to criminal court, using it as leverage to pressure the officer into compliance with their demands. Such situations undermine the government's authority to effectively administer the country, leading to a climate where many officers may become passive in making important decisions.

11 Judgment of the Thai Supreme Court, number 9334/2538 rendered in 1995, and number 6446/2547 rendered in 2004.

3. Compensation of the victim by the state

According to tort law, victims have the right to claim compensation from those who commit crimes that cause damage.[12] However, the state is also required to provide initial compensation to crime victims based on the principle of state responsibility, which views crime occurring in society as a reflection of the state's failure to prevent it. In Thailand, the Victim Compensation Act of 2001 mandates that the state pay compensation to victims of three types of crimes: homicide, bodily injury, and sexual offenses.

Unfortunately, the state cannot provide full compensation to crime victims because all payments come from the state budget. For instance, the relative of a homicide victim may receive a maximum compensation of only 180,000 Baht (approximately 4,500 Euros), and only if there are no alternative avenues for seeking compensation. This situation limits the amount of compensation available and directly impacts the state budget.

The proposed reform is to establish a fund for victim compensation. This fund would be financed by fines paid by offenders. Additionally, as a legal entity, the fund could subrogate the victim's right to claim compensation from the perpetrator responsible for the harm. This approach could alleviate the financial burden on the state and expand compensation opportunities for more crime victims.

D. Conclusion

The credibility of the law and its enforcement directly impacts the credibility of the country. While challenges in reform are present in every nation, the key is to identify the issues and seek appropriate solutions. We have focused on critical issues within Thai criminal procedure law and are committed to reforming these laws and practices based on a balance between two fundamental models: crime control and due process.

Bibliography

Borricand Jacques, and Anne-Marie Simon, *Droit pénal, Procédure pénale*, 3rd ed., Paris: Sirey, 2002.

Guinchard, Serge, and Jacques Buisson, *Procédure pénale*, 2nd ed., Paris: Litec 2002.

12 See Article 420 of the Thai Civil and Commercial Code.

LaFave, Waynes R., Jerold H. Israel and Nancy J. King, *Criminal Procedure*, 3rd ed., St. Paul, Minn: West Group, 2000.

Pradel, Jean, *Droit pénal général*, 10th ed., Paris: Cujas, 2002.

The Road Ahead: Challenging Issues in the Administration of Criminal Justice in Thailand

Sorawit Limparangsri

A. Introduction

The criminal justice system has been one of the most vibrant areas in the administration of justice in Thailand during its development. Although several changes have been adopted to hopefully refine the system, there is still some room for improvement, and, in certain blind spots, it leaves a lot to be desired.

In the chain of the criminal process, it might be fair to say that changes and improvements can be imposed in almost every "link" or "connector", and each and every such "link" plays a very important role in the provision of justice to the people. A "defect" that occurs in a "link" may adversely affect the "link" that follows it. Therefore, to refine the process, we may have to take a look at the big picture and identify any possibly "defective link" in such process, no matter where the link is located.

The task of bringing the criminal justice system forward is already tough and painstaking in and of itself. When we add an extra factor, such as political-motivated conduct, the task becomes even more grueling and complicated. Bringing persons with political positions or holding political offices to justice has long been one of the challenging issues in the administration of criminal justice in Thailand. People called for such justice so loudly that a special system was specifically created for it. The system has been operating for quite a while and has been modified in the Constitution. It may be an appropriate time to examine the current system and see how it will work.

Diversion has been a fashionable phrase for many in the administration of criminal justice. But a question that should be asked is what we should divert it. We have to make sure that the final outcome of a diversion scheme is truly "just" and that all protections embedded in the conventional criminal justice system are transported into the scheme. One of the diversion schemes that have been proposed is the so-called "deferred prosecution". The scheme has some benefits that parties may obtain due to the seemingly faster justice that it offers. However, the primary goal of any civilized criminal justice system has never been the "speed" of the process, at any cost. We will therefore consider this diversion scheme, in the light of conventional, but indispensable, thinking in criminal justice.

One of the inherent characteristics of a criminal justice system is the focus on "bringing offenders to justice." The wheel of the system therefore goes around the "alleged" offender. It has often been criticized that the system neglects the injured party. The restorative justice movement has, at the very least, brought some attention back to those whom we have forgotten. It should be fruitful if we examine what the restorative justice movement can do for the Thai criminal justice system.

In the process of "bringing offenders to justice", we have to determine what the "justice" is that an offender deserves. The sentencing process is therefore a vital step that may affect the life and liberty of an offender, as well as the pursuit of the goals of criminal justice. It also needs careful attention and consideration. Otherwise, the tool will not be as effective as it is hoped for.

This paper will aim to point out some changes that have occurred, as well as a movement in the criminal justice system in Thailand that aspires to bring about more changes in the near future. Not all aspired changes are created equal, though. Some may be ready for adoption, while others need further refinement still. However, by its nature, this paper will not try to delineate all possible changes and improvements, and the basic theorems related to the issues that are discussed here. It will go from one issue to another. An answer for each issue is not what this paper will attempt to give. Rather, it aims to generate more questions that all concerned may give further thought to. It is hoped that more thought and more consideration will lead to more satisfactory progress in the administration of criminal justice.

B. Prosecution of Holders of Political Positions

When people feel that those who claim to work for public interest do not do so and betray their trust, they want justice to be done as soon as possible. Carrying out a political campaign always costs a significant sum of money. Such funds work just like an investment that is expected to be recouped after an election is won. Since no political term lasts forever, there must be some preparation for the next election that will surely come sooner or later.

No ordinary salary or income given for a political position is sufficient to run a campaign. Donation may come with some expectation for a favor. With this backdrop of the political scene, we may see some apparent motive for those who participate in the political arena to gather some funds in their war chest. Some may try their luck by using inappropriate means to gather the funds. For example, politicians may alter the policy regarding currency exchange, and exploit the benefit from the advance knowledge of the change to reap some financial gain. In that case, the administration of criminal justice may be called into action.

A primary concern for this type of case is that it needs to be carried out in a swift manner in order to send a strong message to those who might think of committing similar conduct that may cause great harm to the public interest. In the past, a criminal prosecution of this nature went through the traditional process of being investigated by the police, reviewed by the public prosecutors and then filed with the court. Even in the investigation stage, prosecution of those possessing political clout has never been easy. In terms of organizational structure, the police themselves might have come under extreme pressure from political forces, when there was any effort to investigate the conduct of a member of the political forces. When a case went to a court, the traditional trial could take quite some time before all witnesses and evidence could be properly adduced. Such kind of cases would also go through all three levels of the courts. By the end of the process, people had already forgotten what actually occurred in the first place.

Due to the potential for this type of criminal act to harm the public interest, it was felt that there was a need for a special procedure to tackle this awful behaviour. It started with the Constitution B.E. 2540 (1997) which set up such procedure, and the Constitution B.E. 2550 (2007) also adopted the approach with some modification. The procedure covers cases where holders of political positions are alleged to unduly enrich themselves, violate their official duties according to the Criminal Code, or violate duties or engage in corruption according to other laws.[1]

1 Constitution of the Kingdom of Thailand, B.E. 2550 (2007), Section 275, paragraph one and two:
In cases where the Prime Minister, ministers, member of the House of Representatives, senators or other holders of political positions, are alleged to unduly enrich themselves, violate their official duties according to the Criminal Code, or violate duties or corrupt according to other laws, the Supreme Court's Criminal Division for Persons Holding Political Positions shall have jurisdiction over such cases.

The Constitution established the National Anti-Corruption Commission to investigate allegations. The Commission is an independent body whose members are selected by a prominent panel.[2] If the Commission resolves that there are reasonable grounds to prosecute an accused, the case file and report will be submitted to the Attorney-General to file a case with the Court.

When a case is filed with the Supreme Court's Criminal Division for Persons Holding Political Positions, the plenary session of the Court will select nine justices to adjudicate the case. The Constitution requires that, in adjudicating the cases, the Court must use the case file of the Commission as the primary source of information, but the Court will always be empowered to inquire into any additional fact or evidence that the Court deems appropriate.[3] After all evidence and witnesses have been taken, the Court will decide the cases by majority votes of the justices in the quorum. Each justice shall prepare his or her own personal opinion.[4] The orders and

---

Paragraph one shall also apply to cases where such person or other persons act as the principal, the instigator or the supporter of the crime, including those who give, request for, or agree to give assets or other benefits to the persons in paragraph one, in order to induce those persons to act, omit to act or delay any action, which is contrary to their duties.

2 Constitution of the Kingdom of Thailand, B.E. 2550 (2007), Section 246, paragraph three:
Section 204 paragraph three and four, Section 206 and 207 shall apply to the selection and choosing of the commissioners in the National Anti-Corruption Commission *mutatis mutandis*. There shall be a Selection Committee comprising five members who are the President of the Court of Justice, the President of the Constitutional Court, the President of the Supreme Administrative Court, the Speaker of the House of Representative and the Leader of the Opposition.

3 Constitution of the Kingdom of Thailand, B.E. 2550 (2007), Section 277:
In adjudicating cases, the Supreme Court's Criminal Division for Persons Holding Political Positions shall use the case file of the National Anti-Corruption Commission or the independent inquirer, as the case may be, as the primary source of information in its consideration, and may inquire into any additional fact and evidence, as it deems appropriate.
The procedure of the Supreme Court's Criminal Division for Persons Holding Political Positions shall be in accordance with an act for the implementation of the constitution on criminal procedure with regard to persons holding political positions, and the provision of Section 213 shall apply to the discharge of the duties of the Court *mutatis mutandis*.
The provisions with regard to the immunity of members of the House of Representatives and the senators in accordance with Section 131 shall not apply to the adjudication of the Supreme Court's Criminal Division for Persons Holding Political Positions.

4 Constitution of the Kingdom of Thailand, B.E. 2550 (2007), Section 278:

decisions of the Court are final. Under the Constitution B.E. 2550 (2007), an accused may lodge an appeal with the plenary session of the Supreme Court within thirty days of the date on which a decision is passed, if there is any fresh evidence that may alter the material facts in the case.[5]

The procedure was drafted in such a way, because it aims to have a case become final as soon as possible. Therefore, it requires an extraordinary number of justices in a quorum. Usually, a quorum of justices in the Supreme Court consists of three justices. By increasing the number to nine,[6] it is hoped that there is sufficient scrutiny to justify the finality of the decision. Under the Constitution B.E. 2540 (1997), a case would become final without any mechanism for appeal.[7] Due to many criticism, the Constitution B.E. 2550 (2007) provided a bit more flexibility, by allowing an appeal to the plenary session of the Supreme Court.[8]

When the Constitution B.E. 2540 (1997) was in effect, a concern was raised that such procedure may not be compatible with the International Covenant on Civil and Political Rights which acknowledges the rights of those convicted of a crime to have his or her conviction and sentence

---

The decision shall be done by a majority of the quorum. Each justice in the quorum shall prepare his or her own opinion in writing, and make an oral statement with regard to the opinion to the meeting of the quorum, before votes are casted.
The order and decision of the Supreme Court's Criminal Division for Persons Holding Political Positions shall be disclosed to the public, and become final, except for the case of paragraph three.
In the case where those who are sentenced by a judgment of the Supreme Court's Criminal Division for Persons Holding Political Positions acquire new evidence that may alter the material fact, an appeal may be lodged with the plenary session of the Supreme Court within thirty days from the date of judgment of the Supreme Court's Criminal Division for Persons Holding Political Positions.
The criteria for lodging such appeal and the consideration of the plenary session of the Supreme Court shall be in accordance with the regulation prescribed by the plenary session of the Supreme Court.

5 Ibid.

6 Constitution of the Kingdom of Thailand, B.E. 2550 (2007), Section 219, paragraph four:
There shall be the Criminal Division for Persons Holding Political Positions in the Supreme Court. The quorum of justices shall consist of nine justices whose positions are not lower than a justice in the Supreme Court or a senior justice who held a position not lower than a justice in the Supreme Court. The quorum shall be selected, on a case by case basis, by the plenary session of the Supreme Court by means of secret ballot.

7 Constitution of the Kingdom of Thailand, B.E. 2540 (1997), Section 311, paragraph three.

8 Above fn. 4, para. three.

reviewed by a higher tribunal. The Constitution B.E. 2550 (2007) therefore added an appeal mechanism to be lodged with the plenary session of the Supreme Court. However, the criteria set forth for such an appeal was quite limited. A convict could lodge an appeal only on the grounds that there was fresh evidence that might alter material facts in the case. The model derived from those prescribed in the law on reopening of criminal cases which also provides for similar grounds.[9] It was extremely unlikely that any fresh evidence would appear within only one month from the date of judgment. What usually occurs was that a convict only raised a new argument based on the same evidence. Therefore, it did not pass the threshold for an appeal. When the bar was so high, its effect was that there was no practical channel for appeal.

Moreover, an essence of the review process is not that there is some fresh evidence or witness who can demonstrate that a person did not, in fact, commit the crime. Instead, it is a review of the same set of evidence and testimonies of witnesses, and then the reviewing panel decide whether a reasonable person could come to a different conclusion from that reached by the former panel, and whether there is any reasonable doubt that the accused might not be the one who committed the crime, when the information adduced is viewed from another perspective. It is, therefore, questionable that, by adding such appeal mechanism to the plenary session of the Supreme Court, the Constitution has already provided a suitable means in terms of a review process as envisaged by the International Covenant on Civil and Political Rights.

Although the drafters of the procedure attempt to justify finality by a single judgment by having a case decided by more justices, such procedure can hardly substitute an appeal by two different levels and panels of judges. It is definitely helpful in having more experienced justices considering the cases, because experience can enable the panel to look into the facts

---

9 Act on Reopening of Criminal Cases, B.E. 2526 (1983), Section 5:
A case that becomes final and imposes a punishment on a person may be reopened when it appears that
A witness whom the court relied upon in rendering the final judgment was later found by a final judgment that his or her testimony is a lie, or inconsistent with the facts;
Evidence other than the witness under (1) which the court relied upon in rendering the final judgment was later found by a final judgment to be a forged or false evidence, or inconsistent with the facts; or
A fresh and clear evidence pertaining to material facts which, if it had been adduced in the case that became final, would have shown that the person convicted by a final judgment did not commit the crime.

from the perspectives that less senior judges with less experience may not be aware of. However, the way the highest court in the land has worked for a century is different. In other cases, the Supreme Court will get the benefit of seeing the views of one or two lower courts: the issues become clearer and narrower in each stage of the proceedings and the arguments of the parties become more precise and forceful as the cases climb up the hierarchy of the courts. Acting in the first instance at the level of the Supreme Court will deprive the Court of such benefit.

Moreover, it is often the case that this kind of criminal allegation against a high-profile accused on a matter that affects the public in general will cause some negative mood, emotion, reaction and sentiment among the general public, taking into account the amount of media coverage. Separating the proceedings in the first instance from the review process will have a collateral benefit of providing a cooling off period for the public, so that they will see the matter with less emotion and sentiment.

Taking into consideration various views regarding the shortcoming of the appeal procedure and threshold for such appeal, the current Constitution B.E. 2560 tries to refine the procedure once more. Under the current Constitution, the party must still lodge an appeal with the plenary session of the Supreme Court. The appeal may be on the question of facts or law. There is no limitation regarding the appearance of fresh evidence as prescribed in the Constitution B.E. 2550 (2007).[10] The current Constitution also provides for the composition of the quorum of justices who will consider the appeal. Under the new provision, the justices who will form such quorum must be those who are, at least, at the level of presiding justices in the Supreme Court. The justices in the new quorum must not be the same justice who rendered the judgment against which the appeal is lodged.[11]

---

10 Constitution of the Kingdom of Thailand, B.E. 2560 (2017), Section 195 paragraph four:
An appeal agaist the judgment of Supreme Court's Criminal Division for Persons Holding Political Positions may be lodged with the plenary session of the Supreme Court within thirty days from the date of judgment of the Supreme Court's Criminal Division for Persons Holding Political Positions.

11 Constitution of the Kingdom of Thailand, B.E. 2560 (2017), Section 195 paragraph five:
The appeal lodged under paragraph four shall be considered by a quorum comprising justices in the Supreme Court who are, at least, presiding justices in the Supreme Court, or senior justices who were previously presiding justice in the Supreme Court. The justices in the quorum shall be those who did not previously adjudicate the case. The quorum shall consists of nine justices selected by the plenary session of

Such changes in the appeal procedure will definitely lessen the finality of the judgment, because parties may file an appeal both on question of facts and laws, and there the parties who are not satisfied with the outcome will almost always exploit the opportunity presented by the new procedure. In cases of this magnitude, parties will surely fight until the very end when all means are exhausted. So, there is no surprise if a party, or both parties, will lodge an appeal. Cases will then take longer time before they eventually become final, but at least the procedure provides better appeal procedure.

In practice, when the plenary session of the Supreme Court selects a quorum in cases against holders of political positions, the selected justices are usually among the most senior justices. Therefore, when a quorum to consider an appeal is formed, the justices in the appeal quorum may be those who are less senior than the justices in the original quorum. However, this issue is a practical one. It is not in itself a theoretical obstacle that might hamper the justification of the appeal procedure. Therefore, the appeal procedure in cases against holders of political position has come a long way from the procedure in the Constitution B.E. 2540 (1997). What we have to do now is to see how the procedure will be applied in practice, and what kinds of issues that will occur.

C. Deferred Prosecution

Diversion has become one of the catchphrases in the administration of justice in Thailand. The primary argument in favor of a diversion scheme is usually the speedy process that can alleviate the backlog that builds up in the conventional process for administering criminal justice. Any effort that tries to avoid the perennial problem of "justice delayed is justice denied" should be admired and given serious consideration. However, one of the critical differences between civil justice and criminal justice is that, in civil justice, the settlement of a dispute does not usually affect society and community, and the parties' main concern is to have their dispute resolved in one way or another. In criminal justice, there are several factors that we have to take into consideration, because criminal acts do affect society and community. We have established a criminal justice system at great cost

the Supreme Court, and shall be selected on a case by case basis. When the quorum renders a judgment, the judgment shall be deemed to be the decision of the plenary session of the Supreme Court.

in order to achieve several "goals", for example, incapacitation to commit another crime during a specified period of time, rehabilitation to become a decent member of society, retribution for past conduct, deterrence of future harmful conduct that might be committed by either the criminal being punished or any other member of society who might be frightened by the punishment of the criminal. Diversion or any other tool to be incorporated into the administration of criminal justice should therefore be able to achieve the same goals that conventional criminal justice process has long aimed at.

If a criminal does not receive a suitable consequence for the harm that he or she has caused to other members of society, this might result in the problem that economists call "moral hazard". The problem is, in essence, that a person might be more willing in the future to decide to behave in such a way that might cause the same harm again and again, because he or she realizes that even though harm might be caused, the person will not bear the consequences flowing from his or her conduct. Moreover, other members of society who are aware of the situation might as well decide to behave in a similar fashion in a similar situation.

Furthermore, any justice system, regardless of whether it is a civil or criminal one, cannot be conducted in an obscure manner and should be transparent enough to be able to stand up to any rigorous scrutiny and review from outsiders. The long history of the development of the criminal justice process has involved the protection of the rights of all concerned and the prevention of abuse by authority. One of the classic examples is the inadmissibility of a confession obtained by imposing undue influence on the accused. In court, an accused can always plea by his or her free will and denounce any undue influence that had been inflicted upon him or her in order to extract a confession. All information and facts will be disclosed and challenged for the public to see for themselves. Any obscure procedure will only encourage abuse of the process.

One of the diversion schemes that have been discussed and proposed is the so-called "deferred prosecution". Under the scheme, a public prosecutor may order that the prosecution against an offender be deferred for a certain period if the public prosecutor is of the opinion that a deferred prosecution will be beneficial to the accused, the injured party and society. The scheme is applicable to cases where the alleged offenses carry a maximum punishment not exceeding five years imprisonment, are punishable only by a fine, or involve negligent conduct. The order to defer the prosecution will be submitted for the approval of the Attorney-General. If the offender fulfills the conditions set forth in the order for deferred prosecution, the public prosecutor will grant an order for the termination of the prosecution. Then, no prosecution based on the same allegation can be initiated against the offender.

Despite some arguments that try to show the benefits to be derived from the diversion scheme, it is quite clear that the scheme is still in need of more careful consideration and refinement, and the balance of pros and cons should be weighed before any action to implement the scheme can go further. One of the issues that need comprehensive analysis is the transparency of the process and the review and safeguards to be given to the parties. The process as it currently stands has no mechanism to make the scheme transparent enough for the public and other interested persons to know what is actually going on behind the scenes, as well as how a decision to defer the prosecution has been reached and on what basis. The draft law does not even specify any criteria for such order, other than the ambiguous terms of "beneficial to the accused, the injured party and society" which can mean different things to different persons.

The review procedure is also in dire need of refinement. The only review procedure under the current draft law is merely an internal review process on the public prosecutor's side. There is no transparent process by which the public and other interested persons can ensure that discretionary power has been duly exercised.

Moreover, the goals that the scheme tries to bring about are also indistinct. The draft law governing the scheme has been merged with another draft law governing mediation in the interrogation process of the police. The merged draft law is called "measures in substitute of prosecution in court". It is argued that the scheme emulates the concept of "restorative justice" by providing opportunities for the accused to show his or her accountability. However, the draft law does not require that the accused has to confess to the crime before the scheme can be used. It is wondered, then, how an accused can show accountability when he or she does not even admit that he or she committed the very same act that caused harm to the injured party. It also creates an opportunity where an authority may unduly utilize their power to force an accused to admit a crime that he or she did not commit, or unfairly induce such confession by some promise of lenient treatment. A situation may also occur where an accused pays their way out of the case by over-indemnifying the injured party to obtain soft treatment. It is hardly seen how the goals of the criminal justice system mentioned above can be achieved under this scheme.

D. Restorative Justice

Proving the guilt or innocence of an alleged offender is at the pinnacle of most criminal justice systems and their processes. The evolution of the systems throughout their histories mainly focuses on the protection of the rights and liberty of an offender, so that the offender is not unduly treated and is punished only when it is proved beyond a reasonable doubt by evidence gathered in an appropriate manner.

The role of the injured party in a conventional process of criminal justice comprises mainly the provision of information regarding the alleged crime and the criminal involved, either in the investigation stage or in testimony before the court. The rights and protection that the process gives to an injured party, if any, pale in comparison with those bestowed upon an alleged offender. Very often do we find that an injured party is even "grilled" by the opposing lawyers who try to glean as much information as possible from the injured party who is called to the stand. The process cares only whether an inadmissible statement comes out of the mouth of the testifying injured party, and whether the fact finder may unduly be influenced by the statement.

What the process routinely forgets is that the injured party is actually injured or harmed by the criminal act. He or she suffers physically and mentally, incurs damage to property and endures emotional distress. He or she has his or her own needs that should be taken care of, and an injury that should be remedied and healed. Of course, a criminal justice system is not a procedure of therapy, but this does not mean that the criminal justice system should do away with, or turn a blind eye to, the needs and injury of the injured party.

Changes to a couple of laws have signified more attention for the rights and protection of the injured party and have provided means for offenders to express their accountability as well as mend broken relationships. In this paper, we will only point out some laws that have been trying to incorporate so-called "restorative justice" into the existing criminal justice system.

I. Procedural laws for juvenile and family cases

When the idea of "restorative justice" comes up, it is not difficult to see that juvenile and family cases will be an obvious candidate to put the idea into practice, because one of the goals of juvenile justice system have long been to provide an opportunity for juveniles to rehabilitate and reintegrate into society. The means and punishment in adult cases have been proved to be unsuitable for juvenile justice.

Under the newly-enacted Act on Juvenile and Family Court and Procedure for Juvenile and Family Cases B.E. 2553 (2010), the concept of "restorative justice" has been incorporated to create a tool by which, and a forum where, a juvenile can realize the consequences of his or her conduct, show accountability when he or she wants to do so as well as take part in designing a program for his or her own rehabilitation and reintegration into community.

In a case where the alleged offenses carry punishment not exceeding five years' imprisonment[12] and the juvenile has never been imprisoned by a final judgment, the Director of a juvenile observation center that supervises

12 The Act on the Juvenile and Family Court and Procedure for Juvenile and Family Cases B.E. 2553 (2010), Section 86:
In the case where a juvenile is alleged to commit a criminal offense with maximum punishment prescribed by the law not exceeding 5 years imprisonment, regardless of whether the offense contains a fine punishment or not, and the juvenile has never been sentenced to be imprisoned by a judgment that has already become final, except for an offense committed by negligence or a petty offense, if the juvenile shows his accountability prior to the commencement of prosecution in court, and, taken into account the age, background, behaviour, intelligence, education, physical and mental condition, status, and causes of the offense, and the Director of a juvenile observation center is of the opinion that the juvenile may be rehabilitated without the need to commence the prosecution in court, a plan for rehabilitation shall then be prepared for the juvenile. If necessary for the benefit of protection of the juvenile, the parents, the guardian, the person or organization with whom the juvenile lives may also be required to comply with the plan. The plan shall aim at transforming the juvenile's behaviour, redressing, restoring and compensating the injured party, as well as enhancing security in community and society. The Director shall give his or her opinion together with the plan and submit the same to the public prosecutor for consideration. Notwithstanding the above, the preparation of the plan shall be carried out with consents of the juvenile and the injured party.
When the public prosecutor receives the plan and the Director's opinion in according with paragraph one, the public prosecutor may, if there is any doubt, query the director or any relevant person for more information to be used in determination of the case. If the public prosecutor does not approve the plan, the public prosecutor shall order that the plan be modified, or the prosecution resumes. The director shall inform the interrogation officer and the relevant persons of the order. If the public prosecutor is of the opinion that the plan is in accordance with the utmost benefit of the juvenile, the public prosecutor shall approve the plan for the interest of justice. The plan may then be implemented immediately. Reports shall be submitted to the court.

juvenile cases may order that a rehabilitation plan for the juvenile be prepared. There are, however, some conditions that must exist before the order may be granted. The first condition is that the juvenile must, in the wording of the law, "show accountability". What is meant by the words is usually that the juvenile must confess to the alleged offense and realize the consequences of his or her conduct. Otherwise, any rehabilitation will not be achieved.

The second condition is that both the juvenile and the injured party consent to the process, because both the preparation and the implementation of a rehabilitation plan need cooperation from the juvenile and the injured party in order to be successful. Moreover, by requiring the consent of the injured party, the law gives a significant role in the process to the injured party. Such consent is compulsory both for the commencement of the process of plan preparation as well as for the finalization of the plan. The injured party therefore has been transformed from a mere witness in the process to one with a lot of say.

To prepare a rehabilitation plan that can be successfully implemented, various parties must play some role or provide some contribution. The law therefore requires that in some cases the plan may oblige the juvenile's parents, guardian or any person with whom the juvenile lives, to take part in the preparation of the plan and its implementation and allows[13]

In case where it appears to the court that the process for preparation of the plan was not in accordance with the law, the court may order as it deems appropriate.

The court shall render an order according to paragraph three within thirty days after receipt of the report. The President of the Supreme Court, with the approval of the plenary session of the Supreme Court, shall enact a regulation with regard to the proceedings to be carried out by court.

The plan for rehabilitation according to this section shall be prepared with consents from the injured party and the juvenile.

13 The Act on the Juvenile and Family Court and Procedure for Juvenile and Family Cases B.E. 2553 (2010), Section 87.

In preparation of the rehabilitation plan according to Section 86, the Director of a juvenile observation center shall invite those relating to the juvenile who is alleged to commit the crime, those relating to the injured party and a psychologist or a social worker to join the meeting. If appropriate, the director may also invite representatives from the community or the organization that has relevant responsibilities or is affected by the crime, or the public prosecutor. The plan shall be prepared and submitted to the public prosecutor for consideration within thirty days after the date on which the juvenile shows his or her accountability.

The rehabilitation plan shall not restrict the rights or liberty of the juvenile, except for restrictions prescribed for the benefit of the juvenile, or to protect public interest, and not violating human dignity of the juvenile.

the Director to invite any persons who may relate to the juvenile or the injured party, or representatives from the community, to participate in the preparation of the plan. The community can play a significant role in the rehabilitation process, because the juvenile has to go back and live in the same community. If the community does not welcome, or is not mindful of rehabilitation, it will be very difficult for the juvenile to be transformed into a decent member of the community.

Once the plan has been completely implemented, a non-prosecution order will be granted. In that case, the prosecution with regard to the alleged criminal offense will be terminated.[14] The juvenile will then have no stigma on his or her own personal record that might impede his or her future personal development and career. However, if there is still any residual civil claim, the injured party is still entitled to pursue the claim in civil proceedings.

In some cases, it might happen that the juvenile does not feel accountable for the criminal act that he or she is alleged to have committed while the case is still in the interrogation stage. The case will then go on and may be filed with the court. The law[15] still leaves some room for the

---

The rehabilitation plan according to paragraph one may require the instruction or warning to the juvenile and lay down conditions to be fulfilled by the juvenile. If necessary for the benefit of protection for the juvenile, the parents, the guardian, the person or organization with whom the juvenile lives may also be required to comply with the plan. The plan may also specify the restitution, the public service not exceeding thirty hours, or any other measures to be carried out for the benefit of rehabilitating the juvenile. The period of the plan shall not exceed one year.

The criteria, methods and conditions for the preparation of the rehabilitation plan shall be in accordance with regulations enacted by the Director-General.

14 The Act on the Juvenile and Family Court and Procedure for Juvenile and Family Cases B.E. 2553 (2010), Section 88:

Those who have duties to comply with the rehabilitation plan shall fulfill the duties in accordance with the rehabilitation plan. In case of violation or non-compliance, the Director of a juvenile observation center shall report the same to the public prosecutor and notify the interrogation officer to resume the prosecution.

When the rehabilitation plan is completely fulfilled, the Director of a juvenile observation center shall report to the public prosecutor. If the public prosecutor approves, the non-prosecution order shall be granted. Such order shall be final. The right to prosecute shall cease. However, the interested person shall still be entitled to enforce any civil claim. The Director shall report the non-prosecution order to the court.

15 The Act on the Juvenile and Family Court and Procedure for Juvenile and Family Cases B.E. 2553 (2010), Section 90:

When a criminal case alleging that a juvenile commits an offense with maximum punishment prescribed by the law not exceeding 20 years imprisonment, regardless

juvenile to express his or her accountability in the court proceedings, if he or she would like to do so at that later stage. The court may order that a rehabilitation plan be prepared if the juvenile expresses his or her accountability for the crime, the injured party consents and the prosecutor does not object. One of the distinctions with regards to the preparation of a plan prior to court proceedings and after the court proceedings start is that the court may order for such plan in cases where the offenses carry maximum punishment up to twenty years' imprisonment, while the process of rehabilitation plans may be carried out prior to court proceedings only in cases with maximum punishment not exceeding five years' imprisonment.

All in all, it can be fairly said that the process incorporated in the law tries to bring all stakeholders in the crime into the process and provides them with some meaningful roles. Therefore, no party will be left behind.

II. Law on the protection of those injured from domestic violence

Domestic violence inevitably involves those who have had a relationship prior to the incident and who are likely to have some form of relationship after the incident. Therefore, it is perceived that any procedure which puts the persons involved into a confrontational stance will do more harm than good. However, to heal or mend the shattered relationship is not a simple task. On the contrary, it is quite complicated due to the fact that it involves a long relationship between the parties.

---

of whether the offense contains a fine punishment or not is filed with the court, and the juvenile has never been sentenced to be imprisoned by a judgment that has already become final, except for an offense committed by negligence or a petty offense, the juvenile shows his accountability before a judgment is rendered, the injured party consents and the prosecutor does not object, it appears that the circumstances of the case do not seriously and unduly endanger society, and the court is of the opinion that the juvenile may be rehabilitated, the injured party may obtain suitable restitution, and the process for preparation of a rehabilitation plan, if carried out, will be more beneficial to the future of the juvenile and the injured party than the adjudication process, the court may order the Director of a juvenile observation center or any other person whom the court deems appropriate to carry out the preparation of the plan. The plan may contain conditions that the juvenile, the parents, the guardian, the person or organization with whom the juvenile lives be required to comply with the plan. A plan shall be submitted to the court for consideration with thirty days after the date of the court order. If the court approves the rehabilitation plan, the implementation shall then commence, and the case shall be temporarily disposed of. If the court does not approve, the court proceedings shall resume.

The Act on the Protection of Those Injured from Domestic Violence B.E. 2550 (2007) tries to provide a mechanism, in appropriate cases, for the parties to solve the problems together and lay down some guidance as to how they would like their relationship and their lives to proceed. Therefore, the law allows the court or the relevant official to try to use a conciliation process, regardless of how far the proceedings have been carried out[16]. A conciliation process of this nature needs some special training and practice, because not only have the parties endured a dreadful incident, but there is also an imbalance of power which may affect the process. Therefore, the law allows the court or the official to appoint the so-called "conciliator" to carry out the process.[17]

This kind of process does not aim at finding the "guilt" of an alleged offender. Instead, it opens a space in which the parties can share how they

---

16 Act on the Protection of Those Injured from Domestic Violence B.E. 2550 (2007), Section 15:
No matter how far a proceeding with regard to domestic violence case has been carried out, the court shall try to get the parties settle for the peace and harmony in family. In doing so, the following principles shall be taken into consideration:
The protection of rights of those abused in domestic violence;
The preservation and protection of the marital status as an institution where man and woman are willing to enter into matrimony; in case where such marital status cannot be preserved, the resulting divorce shall be fair and cause as little damage as possible, given the welfare and future prospect of their children;
The protection and help for the family, especially while the family has to care and provide education for children;
Any measures beneficial to the harmony and relationship among the couple and other family members.

17 Act on the Protection of Those Injured from Domestic Violence B.E. 2550 (2007), Section 16:
For the benefit of the settlement of domestic violence cases, the officials or the court, as the case may be, may appoint a conciliator composing of a person or group of persons which may include parents, guardian, relatives of the parties or any person whom the officials or the court deems appropriate, to provide consultation and assistance during the conciliation, or may assign a social worker or a social work organization or a person to help reconciling the parties.
When the conciliator or any person appointed under paragraph one has carried out the conciliation in accordance with orders of the officials or the court, the conciliator or the person shall report the outcome of the conciliation to the official or the court, as the case may be. In case where reconciliation is achieved, the conciliator or the person may have a settlement agreement prepared, or request the parties be called to enter into the settlement agreement before the officials or the court.
If the officials or the court deems that the agreement is not contrary to the law or public policy, the officials or the court shall proceed in accordance with the settlement agreement.

feel, what effect or suffering they have incurred, and how they want to deal with their lives and relationship in the future, including the future of their children, if any.

III. Potential for procedure in ordinary criminal cases

The movement of installing the concept of "restorative justice" into the administration of criminal justice in Thailand, so far, has occurred for some specific types of cases or offenders. However, its potential is beyond that. It can provide a tool and forum for the injured party to have some meaningful participation, other than the passive role of being a witness taking the stand.

The injured party may have several needs that the criminal justice system should pay attention to. They may suffer physical harm which is visible to those whom they come across. They may also suffer intangible wounds which are greater than the visible ones. To ask the injured party to recollect a painful memory in such a way that will subject him or her to ruthless cross-examination will not be helpful in curing the pain. Instead, it only exacerbates the situation. In many circumstances, the injured party may need only to share how they feel and what kind of suffering he or she has endured. Unfortunately, such information is mostly "irrelevant", in terms of the proof of guilt or innocence.

Thailand's criminal procedural law has recognized more of the harm incurred by the injured party and has opened up to the injured party. For example, following an amendment to the Criminal Procedure Code, the law allows the injured party to file a claim for damages in a criminal case, so that the court can decide the matter together in the same proceedings, without requiring the injured party to commence other proceedings.[18] However, the enhanced procedure still focuses on the monetary side of the matter.

---

18 Criminal Procedure Code, Section 44/1 paragraph one and two:
In case where the public prosecutor is a plaintiff, if the injured party is entitled to claim for damages due to the fact that he or she suffers harm to life, physical condition, mental condition or liberty, reputation or pecuniary damage because of the defendant's conduct, the injured party may file a request with the court in charge of the relevant criminal case to enforce the defendant to compensate for the damage.
In filing the request under paragraph one, the injured party shall file prior to the commencement of the trial. In case where there is no trial, the request shall be filed prior to the passing of judgment. Such request shall be deemed to be a complaint in

In this regard, if we can incorporate a similar procedure as found in the laws on juvenile and family cases and the laws on domestic violence, there will be a useful forum in which all parties including those relating to the matter, and not just the parties themselves, can participate and solve their problems together. If the offender or the defendant can see and realize for himself or herself what are the true consequences of his or her conduct, it may increase the likelihood that he or she may be more mindful in the future when facing a similar situation. It will also provide a chance for the offender or the defendant to express his or her accountability toward the injured party and those affected by the criminal act. Certainly, the importation of the mechanism from juvenile cases into adult cases needs careful consideration and may include a variety of safeguards and criteria which deserve serious thought.

E. Sentencing

At the closing stages of the prosecution procedure, there lies the time when a convicted offender will learn of his or her fate, and what punishment is to be inflicted. At least in Thailand, jurists who endure years of legal education mostly learn the theory and elements of crimes, so that they can decide whether the particular conduct is an offense prohibited by law and discern one crime from another. When it comes to the problem of what punishment should be imposed on a criminal, given the circumstances surrounding his background and the crime committed, jurists, at least in Thailand, will be more or less uncomfortable. The issue becomes even more complicated if we have to determine the punishment that can advance the traditional goals of criminal justice, e.g., rehabilitation, incapacitation, deterrence and retribution. Moreover, sentencing is within the realm of judicial discretion that a particular judge can exercise. Punishment imposed on two different convicts who commit the same offense in not so different circumstances may vary according to the discretion of the judges in each case. Judicial independence demands such liberty in making the decision. However, in the eyes of people who come to the court and observe such

---

accordance with the Civil Procedure Code, and the injured party shall be deemed to be the plaintiff with regard to the civil claims. The request shall contain appropriate details as to the damage and the amount of damages claimed. If the court is of the opinion that the request lacks some important feature, the court may order the injured party to modify the request to make it clearer.

difference, it might not be so easy to understand and appreciate the disparity of treatment. Hence, sentencing may be another area which we can polish.

In the various courts in Thailand that have to deal with criminal matters, usually there are some kinds of internal guidelines for sentencing. Such guidelines have been prepared from accumulated past practice and glean some common approaches to be used in future cases. They have never been compulsory or obliged judges, but judges usually will look and take them into consideration before giving a sentence. All such guidelines are confidential, but seasoned practitioners may be able to notice what the practices or approaches for a particular kind of offense are. Offenders always wonder what will happen to them if they are convicted. Such lack of knowledge often affects the way they choose to act in the process. To make sentencing more effective in advancing the goals of criminal justice, more attention and effort is required in this area. Currently, the factors that may be useful in determining the level of punishment will be adduced in conjunction with other kinds of evidence and witnesses. The court will then determine the punishment together with a determination on the issue of culpability. If we reconsider real practice, there might be some awkward stance in introducing evidence and witnesses for the purpose of sentencing in such a scenario. The intensive taking of evidence usually occurs when an offender pleads not guilty. Then, the prosecutor has to prove the culpability of the offender beyond a reasonable doubt. In turn, the offender has to introduce evidence and witnesses of his own to disprove the prosecutor's evidence. Therefore, the main focus of the process is on the issue of culpability. To require the offender to adduce evidence and witnesses to show that he or she deserves lenient punishment at the stage when he or she still insists on his or her innocence is a bit problematic in practice. It is quite likely that there will be little evidence and few witnesses that will be useful for sentencing. If there is a separate procedure exclusively for sentencing, like a sentencing hearing carried out in some countries, judges will benefit from larger sources of information directly pertaining to sentencing.

On the consistency of sentencing, while independent judicial discretion must be vehemently preserved, there should be more guidance and methodology for judges in rendering sentences, so that discretion by different panels of judges will not be too far apart. Any guidance and methodology in specifying a sentence for a particular crime committed with a particular set of factors should be prepared as best as social science can deliver and be responsive to the current state of affairs in society. Moreover, such guidance and methodology should be available for the public to voice any concern or appreciation, and the offenders can also take the likely outcome into his or her consideration when he or she decides on taking the next step in the proceedings.

Being a convict who is punished with a prison term can be a stigma that impedes rehabilitation of that person. The Criminal Code has provided that, in a case where the punishment to be imposed does not exceed five years imprisonment and the convict has never served a jail term, the court may defer sentencing or determine the sentence but suspend the infliction of punishment as the court deems appropriate. However, in practice, once a person is found guilty, courts will determine the sentence together with the guilty verdict. Even though the punishment may be suspended, the pending jail term will damage the personal record of the convict. Therefore, it may be more beneficial, in cases where the courts deem that the convict does not have to serve jail time just yet, to defer the determination of punishment.

F. Conclusion

On various fronts, the criminal justice system in Thailand has progressed over the years. However, we cannot be satisfied with the status quo, because as soon as we stop making progress we will regress. We have to pave the way to make sure that the criminal justice system in Thailand can serve the people and the public still better. To achieve that, there are several matters that can be dealt with. For example, the prosecution of persons holding political positions may be refined to ensure that the facts, evidence and testimonies of witnesses will be looked at from various perspectives by dividing the procedure into two tiers. Such a case may commence in the appellate courts and then be reviewed by the Supreme Court.

Some diversion from the conventional criminal justice system may expedite the process. However, any mechanism to be employed in a criminal justice system must contain the same protection and safeguards of the rights and liberty of the persons involved. It must also be transparent and be able to stand up to any kind of public scrutiny, and be equipped with an appropriate review mechanism, other than some internal stamp of approval.

The future course of criminal justice should also allow the injured party to have some say in the proceedings, and not neglect the harm caused and the persons who actually suffer the harm. Restorative justice can be an efficient tool in bringing the injured party to the forefront and provide a forum in which the injured party's pain and suffering can be acknowledged, and the offender can show his or her accountability.

The process of sentencing is another stage where we can do more, by devoting more time and effort to gathering and understanding the various factors that may affect the sentencing decision, probably in a process similar to a sentencing hearing. Moreover, more guidance and methodology to impose a sentence should be carefully prepared to the best of state of the art of social science and given to judges to take into consideration. Some useful tools such as deferring the sentence should be utilized more to allow a convict to have a better chance in reintegrating himself or herself into society.

We cannot know in advance how the road ahead in the administration of criminal justice in Thailand will be, but at least if we keep trying to improve and moving forward, no matter how bumpy it will be, we will still make progress.

Bibliography

Act on Reopening of Criminal Cases, B.E. 2526 (1983).

Act on the Juvenile and Family Court and Procedure for Juvenile and Family Cases B.E. 2553 (2010).

Act on the Protection of Those Injured from Domestic Violence B.E. 2550 (2007).

Constitution of the Kingdom of Thailand, B.E. 2550 (2007).

Constitution of the Kingdom of Thailand, B.E. 2560 (2017).

Criminal Procedure Code B.E. 2548 (2005).

The Second Revision of the Chinese Criminal Procedural Law and the Respect for and Protection of Human Rights

Lei Cheng

A. Introduction

"The State respects and protects human rights" (the "Human Rights Provision") was added to the Chinese Constitution as a result of the constitutional amendment of 2004. Since then, human rights protection has become a mission of the state. The Revision of 2012 of the Chinese Criminal Procedural Law (the "Revision" or "Revision of 2012") was another overhaul of the Chinese criminal procedures, which further improved human rights protection in the Chinese criminal justice system and directly implemented the Human Rights Provision in the Constitution.

This paper aims to discuss the changes made in the Revision of 2012 and their implications for human rights development, with a hope to help interested readers understand the context, process, and main objectives of the Revision, and assess the strengths and weaknesses of the Revision from a human rights perspective.

B. Context and Significance of the Revision

The Chinese Criminal Procedural Law was drafted in 1979 (the "Law of 1979"), and initially contained merely 164 articles. In 1996, the National People's Congress, China's legislature, made the first revision and increased the number of articles to 225. Sixteen years later, the Revision of 2012 was made, which further increased this number to 290, by revising 90 articles, adding 66 articles and merging one article of the Criminal Procedural Law of 1996 (the "Revision of 1996").

As the second "overhaul", after the revision of 1996, the Revision of 2012 proceeded from the basic reality in China, honored the constitutional principle of "the State respects and protects human rights", struck a proper balance between "punishing crimes" and "protecting human rights", and made the criminal procedural system more consistent with the rule of law, democracy, and science. This is a major achievement in China's efforts to deepen the reform of the judicial system and its mechanisms, and a remarkable accomplishment of the socialist legal system with Chinese characteristics.

I. Adaptation to rapid social and economic development

Since the reform and opening up policy was adopted in 1978, China has experienced rapid social and economic development, featuring improved quality of living and expansion of Gross Domestic Product (GDP) to be the second largest in the world. Against this backdrop, the evolving market economy shall be governed under the rule of law and be protected by the law. As a tool to implement the Criminal Law, the Criminal Procedural Law represents the basic law for regulating criminal justice, and thus plays a positive and crucial role in maintaining social stability and promoting social and economic development.

Thanks to such development, Chinese society has stepped into a period of in-depth reforms, intensive social tension and rising crime, particularly new types of crime. National security, social stability and public security face unprecedented challenges. All these situations require the Criminal Procedural Law to be adapted promptly, so as to effectively cope with the severity of the level and type of crime.

Alongside social and economic development, the people have become growingly aware of their rights and the rule of law and expect more from the system intended to safeguard justice and protect their rights. It is their hope that the Criminal Procedural Law, which is so essential to basic rights and freedoms as to be called the "mini-constitution", "constitution in action" and "seismometer of a country's constitution", can also advance with the times, and do more to honor and protect human rights.

Considering the current situation, judicial organs and other stakeholders have also called for the revision of the Criminal Procedural Law, expecting it to deliver more robust criminal procedures, and ensure crimes are prosecuted in an accurate and timely manner while the litigious and other rights of the people are duly protected.

In summary, people from all walks of life care deeply about, and demand for, a revision of the Criminal Procedural Law.

II. A necessary step to recognize and legalize the output of judicial reforms

At the end of 2008, the Central Committee of the Chinese Communist Party called for, in its Circular No.19, ever deeper reforms to the judicial system and its mechanisms. Fifteen out sixty reforms outlined in that Circular were about the improvement of criminal procedures. Coordinated and pushed by the Central Political and Legal Committee of the Chinese Communist Party, the various competent authorities have lost no time in rolling out high-profile, broad and deep judicial reforms across China. Some of these reforms have proven to be effective and yielded valuable experiences.

These results and experiences need to be perpetuated and legalized through legislation so that they can move Chinese criminal justice further forward. The Revision of 2012 embodied many new systems and breakthroughs gained from such judicial reforms, e.g. criminal settlement, conditional non-prosecution, standardized sentencing procedures, special procedures for minors, reformed procedures for arrests and procedures for the exclusion of illegal evidence.

III. Improvement for a more scientific and democratic system under the rule of law

While playing a huge role in the political, economic, cultural, and social dimensions, the Revision of 1996 had clearly shown its deficiencies and flaws in the course of the rapid economic and social development and fast changing social situations during the sixteen years of its implementation. Thus, there was an urgent need to remove this obstacle through legislation, and resolve the following two main problems with it:

1. Insufficient number of articles

The insufficient number of articles made the Revision of 1996 unable to cover all steps of criminal procedures. Case handlers often found the law to be either silent, or too general or vague to be operable. The 225 articles can hardly address every stage of each procedure. For example, there were only eight articles covering the collection, submission, cross-examination and admission of evidence despite the significance of evidentiary proof throughout the criminal procedures. In most advanced jurisdictions, there are at least 500 articles in their criminal procedural laws. For instance, there are over 500 articles in the Japanese, Korean, Russian and German criminal procedural laws. In Italy and France, this number is as high as 600 and 800, respectively. To make the rule of law work, one needs law first. This was largely not the case for the Chinese criminal procedure.

Furthermore, the lack of rules bred the excessive growth of judicial interpretations. To meet their practical needs, the Supreme People's Court, the Supreme People's Procuratorate and the Ministry of Public Security promulgated as many as 1,300-odd interpretations, rules, bylaws, and provisions. Many of these internal rules overstepped the authority of judicial interpretation and became legislation in disguised form. There also existed conflicts and inconsistencies among them, which undermined the coherence and solemnity of law.

2. Outdated Content of Legislation

Apart from its technicalities, a criminal procedural law shows a litigation system's level of democracy and civilization. The Law of 1979 reflected the mindset and knowledge level as of 1979. The Revision of 1996 constituted a significant improvement but did not alter the overall structure of the system. Therefore, the Revision of 1996 still fell short of the UN conventions, common rules in advanced jurisdictions and the minimum human rights standards. For example, the Revision of 1996 did not include such common rules as the presumption of innocence, self-incrimination, double jeopardy, detention as the exception instead of the default and access to timely and effective counseling.

C. Guiding Thoughts behind the Revision of 2012

I. Equal emphasis on, and proper balance between punishing crimes and protecting human rights

Criminal litigation serves dual purposes, i.e., punishing crimes and protecting human rights. Neither is negligible. As a law that implements the Criminal Law, the Criminal Procedural Law naturally emphasizes the purpose of punishing crimes, as necessarily required by the implementation of the Criminal Law and the maintenance of a safe and stable society. However, there existed misunderstanding about this purpose, causing an overemphasis on punishing crimes, and consequentially rampant non-compliant practices and widespread violation of citizens' rights, at the expense of human rights protection. As another important purpose of criminal litigation, protection of human rights shields the innocent from criminal liabilities. This is made possible by regulating state powers with procedural arrangements and keeping them on track towards the rule of law.

As mentioned above, the severe social reality does not permit the control over crimes to be relaxed. Otherwise, social harmony and economic well-being will become a luxury, and the protection of the citizens' personal, economic, and political rights will be futile. On one hand, therefore, it is necessary to ensure that criminal litigation does punish crimes, with facts discovered in an accurate and timely manner, and the criminals are penalized. On the other hand, human rights have taken root in social conscience, and have become a guiding philosophy of legislation, enforcement, and judicial activities. The constitutional amendment of 2004 clearly required "respect and protect human rights", enshrining this as a basic constitutional principle. Subordinate to the Constitution, the Criminal Procedural Law shall follow this constitutional requirement, by ensuring that while crimes are being punished, the innocent shall be shielded from criminal prosecution, human rights be respected and protected, and the citizens' litigious and other lawful rights be honored.

In summary, equal emphasis on, and total consideration of the relations between, protecting human rights and punishing crimes, became the paramount guiding thought behind the Revision of 2012, and guided its various work streams. On one hand, the Revision corrected and structured such content as compulsory measures, investigative procedures, trial procedures, enforcement procedures and special procedures, in order to more effectively discover, prosecute and try crimes. On the other hand, the Human Rights Provision was added to guide the operation of criminal litigations, prohibit compelled self-incrimination, and honor rights with structured procedures and mechanisms.

II. Resolution of urgent practical issues in the light of national conditions in China

While revising the Criminal Procedural Law, the legislature always acted prudently and upheld the principle of consideration of the national conditions in China. The evolution of criminal procedural systems in various countries has shown both commonalities and systemic differences. Germany and France are both civil law jurisdictions, but widely differ in criminal procedures. This is explained by the different national conditions and priorities. By the same token, China must base its solutions on its own national conditions. This is a populous country at the primary stage of socialism. During the ongoing economic and social transition, it faces many challenges that other countries may not have experienced, or even imagined. Copying a foreign system does not fit the reality in China and will not provide a fundamental solution. Such a solution is only possible when the lawmakers recognize the reality and look into the practical issues at present. Therefore, considering the national conditions became the starting point of the Revision of 2012.

Considering the national conditions requires the identification and solution of the urgent difficulties arising from practice. In the sixteen years after its adoption, the Revision of 1996 fell behind the changed society and ceased to function properly and effectively. The problems surfacing from practice called for revision of the legislation. Emerging challenges and difficulties facing law enforcers also needed legislative answers. For example, the National People's Congress made a law enforcement inspection in 2000, and discovered four major problems, namely torture, difficulty for lawyers to meet their clients, detention beyond legally prescribed time limits and the excessively low ratio of witnesses' appearances in court. Most of these problems were prioritized in the Revision of 2012.

Furthermore, special attention was paid during the Revision to the practical difficulties facing the procurators, such as corrupt officials fleeing the country and difficulty in enforcing procuratorial supervision. Judges found the time limit too short. The one and a half months legally prescribed for the first and second instances can hardly support the time required by the lawyers and procuratorates to read the case files, especially in the case of joint crimes involving dozens of, if not a hundred, defendants, which may generate hundreds of volumes of case files. The Revision of 2012 responded to the judicial call for longer time limits.

Gradual and Steady Improvement of the Criminal Procedures

As noted above, the Revision of 2012 was guided by the consideration of the national conditions in China. What are these conditions? The most prominent is that China is, and will long remain, at the primary stage of socialism. Thus, development is the paramount priority, and is not achievable without stability. All reforms, including those of criminal legislation, must fully consider what this stage can support, what society can afford, and how well society can be administered and controlled. It is wrong to disregard reality, and blindly leap towards perfection. Moreover, China suffers from political, economic, cultural, and social disparity. In some localities, there is chronic underinvestment of judicial resources and fiscal budget, and weak capacity of social governance and control. If the criminal procedures leapfrog to a level China is not yet ready for, such development will not help to resolve the problems in practice but will compromise social harmony and stability.

Of course, any revision of the Criminal Procedural Law must proceed within the judicial framework defined by the Constitution. During the Revision of 2012, some issues were tensely debated. For example, Article 113 was added to the draft Revision, providing that "the people's procuratorates may raise opinions and suggestions about murder and other major cases filed with and investigated by the public security organs." This addition originally aimed to introduce "procuracy guiding investigation" but was finally dropped amidst controversy. The reason is that the Criminal Procedural Law must comply with the judicial system established under the Constitution. Article 135 of the Constitution provides that "the people's courts, the people's procuratorates and public security organs shall divide responsibilities, support each other and check each other so as to ensure the law to be implemented accurately and effectively." Practically useful as it is, "procuracy guiding investigation" is exposed to unconstitutionality risk under the constitutionally established judicial system. The same problem lies with the procuratorial supervision of the failure of investigative organs to file cases and with the judicial review of investigative conduct.

In addition, any revision also needs to consider the status quo of the legislation. Among the special procedures introduced into the Revision of 2012, only those for minors are detailed, and the rest written in general terms and potentially poor in operability. This is because there was an existing model of, and a lot of judicial experience in, the principles, procedures, and practices for minor cases. It was easy to abstract these experiences into legal provisions. In contrast, there was no model or experience with respect to the brand-new systems created by the Revision, such as criminal settlement within a certain scope, flight of criminal suspects and defendants, confiscation of illegal gains in death cases and the compulsory medication of mental patients exempted from criminal liabilities. Thus, the Revision could only provide some rather principled provisions, broadly set up the procedural framework, and defer elaboration and improvement until experience would be accumulated through implementation.

In summary, a gradual and steady approach based on a total analysis of various factors is advisable for a revision of the Criminal Procedural Law. In practice, gradualism works, too. From the Law of 1979, through the Revision of 1996, to the Revision of 2012, steady progress has been made by constantly and realistically adapting the law to the social development and needs at the time, and by accumulating experience along the way. This approach has addressed the emerging needs, kept the law abreast with, but not far ahead of, the evolving reality, and ensured improvement of the criminal procedures.

D. Eight Highlights of the Revision of 2012

I. Addition of the human rights provision

Criminal Procedural Law is so crucial to the basic rights and freedoms of the citizens that it is called "the mini-constitution." Its sophistication reflects, to some extent, how well human rights are protected in a country. The Human Rights Provision entered the Constitution as early as in 2004.[1] Being so closely related to both the Constitution and the citizen's rights, the Criminal Procedural Law essentially needed to echo this addition, and enshrine its value proposition. To this end, Article 2 of the Revision of 2012 introduced the requirement to "respect and protect Human Rights." This did not only respond to mainstream values, but also marked a milestone of China's human rights cause. It is fair to say that this addition is the brightest highlight of the revision.

It is significant that this addition was made at the last round of review by the legislature. Such significance is interpreted to be: "helping to more clearly show the socialist nature of the country's judicial system, and to enable the judiciary to better follow and implement this constitutional principle in criminal procedures."[2] As a basic law with a direct bearing on personal freedom and other basic rights of citizens, and as "a constitution in action" or "mini-constitution", the Criminal Procedural Law took the lead in introducing the Human Rights Provision from the Constitution, in

1 Article 33(2) of the Constitution of the People's Republic of China provides that "the state respects and protects human rights."

2 Wang, "Explanation about the (Draft) Revision of the Criminal Procedural Law of the People's Republic of China at the Fifth Meeting of the Eleventh National People's Congress on March 8, 2012".

a way that is commensurate with its own status, conducive to its pursuit of human rights protection, and supportive of its future interpretation and improvement.

While acclaiming this legislative change, the author believes that three questions need to be answered by construing Article 2 before this Human Rights Provision can truly lead the Revision's interpretation and implementation.

First, the phrase "so as to" before "safeguard socialist legal system" was removed when the Human Rights Provision was drafted into Article 2. Given this removal, is "safeguard socialist legal system" the task or purpose of the Criminal Procedural Law? The removal caused Article 2 to be about nothing but the "task". Thus, "respect and protect human rights" should be seen as a task of this Law.

Second, is this a new task or an existing but rephrased one? In the Revision of 1996, Article 2 provided the requirement to "protect the personal, property, democratic and other rights of the citizens." If the citizens' rights were already protectable back in 1996, the Human Rights Provision would be a clearly unnecessary repetition. Therefore, the author would interpret the addition as a brand-new task, in parallel with "protect the personal, property, democratic and other rights of the citizens."

Third, the addition of the Human Rights Provision necessitates a logical interpretation of the tasks of the Criminal Procedural Law as set forth in Article 2. Such tasks fall into three categories: 1) ensure that facts are discovered in an accurate and timely manner, the law is applied correctly, the criminals are penalized and the innocent are not prosecuted; 2) respect and protect human rights, protect the personal, property, democratic and other rights of the citizens; and 3) educate the citizens to conscientiously observe the law, and actively fight against criminal conduct.

II. Improvement of the evidence system

The evidence system is a key component of the criminal procedures and safeguards the quality of criminal cases. The Revision of 2012 comprehensively overhauled the evidentiary system. For example, the concept of evidence changed from "facts" to "materials."[3] Documentary evidence

3 See Article 48, Criminal Procedural Law.

and physical evidence were separated as new types of evidence. "Forensic conclusion" was renamed as "forensic opinion". New types of evidence such as "identification transcript", "investigative experiment transcript" and "electronic evidence" were created.[4]

As a confirmation of the voluntary confession principle, the Revision required that "no one shall be compelled to incriminate himself."[5] This is a highlight of the revised evidentiary rules. The Revision also clarified the allocation of the burden of proof and modified the standard of proof. The "solid and adequate evidence" test was elaborated.

The brightest spot was the exclusory rules of illegal evidence.[6] The Revision set forth the scope and procedure of, and thus set up the legal framework for, illegal evidence exclusion. Another major area of improvement was made on securing witness appearances in court. The Revision made clear the protective measures for witnesses appearing in specific cases, and included allowances, salary, bonus and other benefits into the scope of protection.[7] Moreover, the Revision provided for the conversion and admission of physical, documentary, audiovisual and electronic/digital evidence collected in administrative enforcement.[8] After four-year implementation, the Supreme People's Court, the Supreme People's Procuratorate, the Ministry of Public Security etc. issued one implementing notice on the exclusionary rule on June 28, 2017, which shows the efforts of criminal justice system to make the rule alive strictly.[9]

III. Overhaul of compulsory measures

Compulsory measures are important tools that ensure the smooth operation of criminal procedures. As a result of social changes and development, many problems surfaced from the operation of the compulsory measures under the Revision of 1996 and required swift resolution.

The Revision of 2012 materially changed the procedures for detention, residential surveillance and bail. Considerable changes and improvements

4 See Article 48, ibid.
5 See Article 50, ibid.
6 See Article 54 – 58, ibid.
7 See Article 63, ibid.
8 See Article 52 (2), ibid.
9 See http://www.mps.gov.cn/n2254314/n2254409/n4904353/c5734089/content. html.

were made to detention, with the conditions for detention elaborated, and the detention approval procedure enhanced.[10] In particular, the Revision introduced requirements for a criminal suspect to be interrogated before his arrest is approved, the procedures for the necessity of his detention to be revisited after his arrest, and the duty to deliver an arrested person immediately to a detention center for detention. Adjustment was made to the controversial matter of notifying family members of detention on the basis that the investigation may be obstructed. As an exception permitting non-notice, "obstructing an investigation" was strictly restricted to two scenarios, i.e., crimes against national security and terrorist crimes. This is progress made compared to the Revision of 1996. These changes will help to better protect the rights of the arrested, reduce unnecessary detention, and prevent wrongful detention.

With respect to residential surveillance, the Revision adapted the criteria of application, the premise of implementation, the content to be reviewed, and permissible surveillance techniques. Notice to family members, defense by counsels, procuratorial supervision and other measures were stipulated to ensure the correct application of this compulsory measure. Moreover, it was made clear that the term of residential surveillance must be deducted from the term of imprisonment. All these modifications made residential surveillance a quasi-detention, whose severity level is between bail and arrest.

The Revision readjusted the matters to be reviewed for bail, set forth the duties of the bailees, and provided for the determination, custody, and refund of the bail.

IV. Protection of the Right to Defense

The right to defense is a basic right of criminal suspects and defendants. Protection of this right is a constitutionally recognized principle. In order to resolve the practical difficulty in obtaining effective defense and to align the

10 See Article 79 of Criminal Procedure Law, PR.C. In addition, on April 24, 2014, the Legislation body, NPC issued a legislative on condition for pre-trial detention, which provides suspects under one-year imprisonment penalty can be detained if he or she is against bail conditions seriously.

Criminal Procedural Law with the Law on Lawyers,[11] the Revision further improved the defense system, and strengthened the protection of lawyers' rights.

More specifically, the right to defense was made a basic principle, specifically recognized in the First Chapter. Legal aid was expanded to cover more kinds of beneficiaries.[12] A wider group of people were allowed to hire defense counsels.[13] The entry time of defense counsels was brought forward to the investigative stage. The lawyers' right to meet their clients and read case files set forth in the Law on Lawyers was brought into, and enhanced in, the Revision. With respect to the offense of lawyer's perjury, the liability provision was optimized, and special procedural safeguards put in place. The defense was granted remedies in case of obstruction of defensive duties.

V. Improvement of investigative measures

Investigative measures affect both the effectiveness of investigative organs and the protection of suspects' rights, and thus become a battlefield between powers and rights. In the Revision of 2012, appropriate readjustments were made to investigative measures by balancing various factors.

The brightest and most controversial was to bring technical investigation onto the path towards the rule of law by incorporating it into the purview of the Criminal Procedural Law, which clearly stipulates the applicable scope, targets, users, time limits and duty of confidentiality of such investigation, and permits secret investigation and controlled delivery under certain circumstances.[14]

In order to curb torture and other illegal means of obtaining evidence, the Revision explicitly required that suspects shall be delivered to detention

11 The Chinese legislature enhanced the protection of the right to defense in the revision of the Law on Lawyers in 2007. Nonetheless, the new rules in the Law on Lawyers conflicted with the then effective Criminal Procedural Law. These conflicts triggered many challenges in practice.

12 Under Article 34 of the Criminal Procedural Law, the public security organs, the procuratorates and courts shall provide free legal aid lawyers to the criminal suspects and defendants that may be sentenced to life imprisonment or death, the blind, the deaf, the dumb, minors and mental patients with limited or no capacity of action.

13 The Revision of 1996 only permitted criminal suspects and defendants to hire defense counsels. The Revision of 2012 also allowed their close relatives to do so on their behalf. See Article 33(3), Criminal Procedural Law.

14 See Article 148 – 152, ibid.

centers immediately after detention, detainees may be interrogated in detention centers only, and interrogations shall be audio/video taped. The interrogated shall be guaranteed food, drinks, necessary rest time and other basic needs. To protect the lawful rights and interests of the defendants, their attorneys and other relevant parties, the Revision also granted them the rights to report or prosecute non-compliant activities by the judiciary or its staff.

VI. Reshaping of trial procedures

Trials offer the platform for the parties to contend with each other, and the judges to hear the case. Their procedures bear on their fairness. Since the evolution of society necessitated changes to such procedures, the Revision of 2012 resulted in modification across the board.

The most remarkable was the reshaping of the summary procedures, comprising the changed criteria of applicability, widened scope of application by merging the existing summary procedures with those for guilty-plea cases, and the readjusted format and time limits. The parties' procedural options and procurators' duty to appear in courts received more emphasis. The changes made to summary procedures undoubtedly are conducive to better allocation of judicial resources and higher efficiency of litigation.

The most significant change to first-instance procedures is the enhancement of the court appearance procedure for witnesses and expert witnesses. Witness appearance is critical to factual discovery, evidence verification and correct judgments. In order to promote fair trials and resolve the frequent non-appearance of witnesses, the Revision of 2012 put forward clearer rules on the scope of witness appearance, inadmissibility of forensic evidence in the case of expert witness absence, establishment of a court appearance compulsion system, and necessary exceptions accommodating family relationships.

Civil actions are often filed as collateral actions to criminal prosecutions but were covered by merely two articles in the Revision of 1996, which can hardly cope with practical concerns. The Revision of 2012 allowed more diverse subjects to submit collateral civil actions, empowered the procuracy to take preservation measures *ex officio*, and confirmed that collateral civil actions may be settled.

With respect to the second instance, the Revision of 2012 expanded the scope of matters subject to appellate hearings and prohibited remanding a case more than once due to unclear fact finding. To provide full coverage of *reformatio in peius* and let the defendants safely exercise their right to appeal, it was generally disallowed for remanded case to increase the punishment of a defendant.

Two changes were made to the death penalty review procedures. One is to require that the Supreme People's Court must either approve or disapprove a death penalty case it reviews. The other is to allow the defense to participate in such review and, in particular, the procuracy to exercise procuratorial supervision over it.

VII. Development of special procedures with Chinese Characteristics

In the Revision of 2012, a specific chapter on special procedures made its debut in this code of criminal procedures. This was a logical product of the increasingly complex and sophisticated criminal practice. There is no doubt that this is the most forward-looking institutional development in this Revision, and an explicit manifestation of Chinese characteristics.

In this chapter, there are four sections, governing the procedures for minors, the settlement procedure for public prosecution cases, the flight of suspects and defendants, the confiscation of illegal gains in death cases and the compulsory medication of mental patients exempted from criminal liabilities. This chapter contains rules on their scope of application, procedure of application, legal remedies, and other matters.

With respect to minor cases, the suspects and defendants obtained stronger protective measures, including a social survey, the company of appropriate adults, conditional non-prosecution, and the sealing of criminal records. For the said compulsory medication procedures, assistance by lawyers and the supervision by the procuracy are particularly emphasized.

VIII. Refinement of enforcement procedures

Community correction was added to the Criminal Law through its Eighth Revision. As a law implementing the Criminal Law, the Criminal Procedural Law needed to be updated accordingly, by introducing community correction and defining the people eligible for it. Moreover, the Revision improved the rules for temporary service outside prison, expanded its scope of application, and clarified its application procedures. To ensure correct implementation of criminal punishments, the procuratorial supervision over their enforcement was reinforced.

E. Outlook beyond the Law of 2012

The Revision marked an important milestone in the development of the Chinese criminal procedures. But the journey of pursing better procedures and progress of criminal justice did not come to an end. Following the adoption of the Revision on March 14, 2012 after two readings, the legislature passed a package of revisions for seven related laws in October 2012[15], and resolved the conflicts and inconsistencies in the laws. Before the end of 2012, the legislature and supreme judicial organs issued four implementing regulations and judicial interpretations, which contained a total of 1,672 articles, and significantly elaborated the Criminal Procedural Law.

The Revision of 2012 has operated well as a whole since its entry into force on January 1, 2013. However, some problems still remain, such as the lingering difficulty of excluding illegal evidence and low appearance rate of witnesses. These two problems received a lot of attention when the Revision was contemplated but have not materially improved. Realizing how difficult it is to implement the law, the legislature has been using innovative approaches to advance its implementation, as represented by the preparation of a legislative interpretation since April 2014.

Implementation is the lifeblood of law. What holds back China from the rule of law is not the absence of law, but the failure to follow and strictly enforce it, and hold the culpable truly accountable. The implementation of the Criminal Procedural Law is a miniature of law enforcement in China. The solution to the flaws in implementation lies in the overall progress of the rule of law. While the enforcers and judiciary change their mindset, it takes reforms to both judicial systems and the system of rules to make the implementation of the law less difficult. Therefore, it is necessary to reform the judicial system and constantly identify and cure the vulnerabilities of the legal provisions while implementing the Criminal Procedural Law.

15 The seven laws are the Law on Prison, the Law on the People's Police, the Law on Public Security Administration and Punishment, the Law on Lawyers, the Law on State Compensation, the Law on the Protection of Minors and the Law on the Prevention of Minor Crimes.

Bibliography

Wang, Zhaoguo, "Explanation about the (Draft) Revision of the Criminal Procedural Law of the People's Republic of China at the Fifth Meeting of the Eleventh National People's Congress on March 8, 2012".

Establishing Regional Courts: A Quest for Judicial Independence in Vietnam

Van Quang Nguyen

A. Introduction

Over the last more than thirty years, in pursuing the establishment of a socialist law-based state (*nha nuoc phap quyen xa hoi chu nghia*),[1] Vietnam has done much to construct and develop its laws and legal institutions and one of its current tasks is judicial reform (*cai cach tu phap*).[2] Reforms of Vietnam's laws and legal institutions have in part been a response to the requirements of regional and international integration. In this context, the

1 The goal of the establishment of a law-based state was officially launched at the Seventh National Congress of Delegates of the Communist Party of Vietnam in 1991. This goal was then reaffirmed in *Van kien Dai hoi Dang toan quoc* [Documents of the National Congress of Delegates] in 1996, 2001 and 2006. It is also affirmed by the Constitution 2013 which came into force on 1 January 2014.

2 Judicial reform has been discussed in several important documents of the Communist Party of Vietnam, namely, *Nghi quyet so 08-NQ/TW cua Bo Chinh tri ve mot so nhiem vu trong tam cua cong tac tu phap trong thoi gian toi* [Resolution of the Political Bureau No 08-NQ/TW on Some Judicial Principal Tasks for the Forthcoming Period], *Nghi quyet so 49-NQ/TW ngay 02–6–2005 cua Bo Chinh tri ve "Chien luoc cai cach tu phap den nam 2020"* [Resolution of the Political Bureau No 49-NQ/TW on "Strategy on for Judicial Reform by the Year 2020"], and more recently *Nghị quyết số 27-NQ/TW ngày 09/11/2022 Hội nghị lần thứ sáu Ban Chấp hành Trung ương Đảng khóa XIII về tiếp tục xây dựng và hoàn thiện Nhà nước pháp quyền xã hội chủ nghĩa Việt Nam trong giai đoạn mới* [Resolution No. 27-NQ/TW dated November 9, 2022, of the Sixth Conference of the 13th Central Committee of the Communist Party of Vietnam on continuing to build and improve the socialist rule-of-law state of Vietnam in the new period]. For a summary of these Resolutions in the English language, see "Strategy for Judicial Reform to 2020," 2006; Cao, "Party Resolutions on Judicial Reform," 2006, and "Party Central Committee sets out major tasks and solutions for further improving the socialist law-ruled state in the coming time," 2023, *Vietnam Law & Legal* Forum at https://vietnamlawmagazine.vn/party-central-committee-sets-out-major-tasks-and-solutions-for-further-improving-the-socialist-law-ruled-state-in-the-coming-time-69791.html, last accessed on 8 Juanuary 2025. For a discussion of Vietnam's judicial reform reflected in Resolution of the Political Bureau No 08-NQ/TW on some judicial principal tasks for the forthcoming period, see Nicholson, "Vietnamese Jurisprudence: Informing Court Reform." 2005, pp. 160–170.

issue of judicial independence has emerged as a critical issue attracting many debates by legal experts and scholars. Judicial independence, as one of the most important characteristics of the rule of law, has been institutionalised since 1946, when the first constitution of the Democratic Republic of Vietnam (DRV) was enacted. The current Constitution 2013 of Vietnam clearly states that

> [j]udges and people's assessors independently hear cases and shall only obey the law; the interference into hearing of judges and people's assessors by state bodies, organisations and individuals is strictly prohibited.[3]

However, in reality, it is not an easy task to comply with this principle, and Vietnam has found it hard to guarantee the independence of its judiciary.[4] The lack of independence of Vietnam's courts, especially of local courts, in hearing law cases has been widely criticized. To deal with this problem, the law on organisation of Vietnam's courts has been significantly improved in responce to pursueing the goal of judicial indepence. Also, several solutions have been proposed, one of which is to establish a jurisdiction-based court system replacing the current administrative unit-based court system. Following the administrative unit-based model, courts are established corresponding with administrative levels, namely district, provincial and

3 See Article 103 of the Constitution 2013. It should be noted that the Constitution 2013 is the first constitution of Vietnam has affirmed that "the interference into hearing of judges and people's assessors by state bodies, organisations and individuals is strictly prohibited."

4 For a detailed discussion about judicial independence in Vietnam, see To, *Judicial Independence: A Legal Research on Its Theoretical Aspects, Practices from Germany, the United States, France, Vietnam, and Recommendations for Vietnam in Transitional Countries*, 2006, pp. 399–460; the issue in question has attracted many debates in present Vietnam, see for example, Tran, "Nguyen tac tham pham, hoi tham nhan dan xet xu doc lap va chi tuan theo phap luat – Thuc tien thuc hien và kien nghị [The Principle of Judges and Jurors Adjudicating Independently and Only Adhering to the Law – Practical Implementation and Recommendations]," 2018), at https://tapchitoaan.vn/nguyen-tac-tham-phan-hoi-tham-xet-xu-doc-lap-va-chi-tuan-theo-phap-luat-thuc-tien-thuc-hien-va-kien-nghi, last accessed on 8 January 2025; Truong and Nguyen, "Cac yeu to anh huong den su doc lap cua toa an o Viet Nam hien nay [Factors affecting the independence of the courts in Vietnam today]," 2018, pp. 12–18; Trinh, "Nguyen tac xet xu doc lap cua toa an: Thuc tien ap dung va nhung bat cap [The Principle of Independent Adjudication by the Court: Practical Application and Challenges]," 2023, at https://lsvn.vn/nguyen-tac-xet-xu-doc-lap-cua-toa-an-thuc-tien-ap-dung-va-nhung-bat-cap-1686783315-a131633.html, last accessed on 8 January 2025.

central levels; while the jurisdiction-based model requires that courts are established based on their jurisdiction to hear cases, namely courts to hear cases at first instance, court to hear cases of appeal and courts to hear cases of cassation. Regional courts as courts to hear cases at first instance will be part of that jurisdiction-based court system. While it is criticized that in Vietnam the administrative unit-based model easily creates the dependence of local courts on corresponding local governments and thus damaging the judicial independence, regional courts within the jurisdiction-based court system are expected to eliminate that dependence and thus making courts more independent in hearing cases. Whether the proposal of establishing regional courts would be promising for maintaining judicial independence in the Vietnamese context? What would be potential challenges for Vietnamese legal reformers while adopting those proposals? All these questions are the main concerns of this paper.

This paper begins with a brief introduction to the current Vietnamese court system in which some its typical features are specifically analyzed. That is followed by an analysis of the two core constitutional principles of Vietnam which are said to be critical to the issue of judicial independence in Vietnam. It then raises the issue of lack of judicial independence of Vietnamese courts and an analysis of the proposal for establishing regional courts as a solution to the issue in question will be provided. Finally, given that reforming the court system in a country in transition is not an easy task, this paper identifies several potential challenges facing the proposed reforms and contends that to overcome such challenges it is important to revisit the perception and the application of the constitutional principles underlying the organisation and operation of the state apparatus in general and of the court system in particular.

B. The Vietnamese Court System: Some Distinctive Features

I. Court Structure

The Vietnamese court system is organised and functions within the legal framework created by the Constitution 2013 and several other statutes. The Constitution 2013 sets forth the underlying principles which are concretised by a range of pieces of legislation governing the organisation and operation of the court system.[5] In terms of structure, the system of Vietnam people's courts is a bit complicated. It consits of the Supreme People's Court; the High People's Courts; the People's Courts of provinces and centrally governed cities; the People's Courts of districts, towns, townships, and cities under provinces or cities under centrally governed cities; the specialized first-instance People's Courts, including the Administrative Court, the Intellectual Property Court, and the Bankruptcy Court (hereinafter collectively referred to as specialized first-instance People's Courts); and the Central Military Court, Military Courts of Military Zones and their equivalents, and Regional Military Courts (hereinafter collectively referred to as Military Courts).[6]

The above-mentioned structure of Vietnam people's courts reflects the mixture of models of administrative unit-based courts and jurisdiction-based courts, but it is noted that the current Vietnam people's courts are mainly organised based on administrative territorial units.[7] Generally, they are structured by a three-level hierarchy, headed by the Supreme People's Court. The local people's courts are organised and operate within territories of provinces and districts. Currently Vietnam has sixty-three provinces and cities under direct central rule, within which sixty-three provincial people's courts operate. Similarly, hundreds of district people's courts are organised across the country, each of which operates within the territory of a district. This practice has led to the dependence of local people's courts

5 Chapter VIII of the *Constitution* 2013 named "People's Courts and People's Procuracies" consists of provisions which lay down the legal basis for the organisation and operation of the Vietnamese court system. The current law detailing the organisation of the court system is the *Law on the Organization of the People's Court* (Luat To chuc Toa an Nhan dan) 2024. Please note that the laws, regulations, and legal institutions of Vietnam described in this paper are accurate as of June 1, 2025.

6 See Article 4 of the Law on organisation of the People's Court 2024.

7 The Vietnamese territorial unit structure is provided by Article 110 of the Constitution of Vietnam 2013 according to which the whole country is divided into provinces (*tinh*) and cities under direct central rule (*thanh pho truc thuoc trung uong*). Each province normally includes a provincial city or town (*thanh pho or thi xa thuoc tinh*) and districts (*huyen*), while each city under direct central rule is divided into metropolitan districts (*quan*) and suburban districts (*huyen ngoai thanh*). Each district of a province or each suburban district of a city under direct central rule normally includes a district town (*thi tran*) and communes (*xa*) while each provincial city or town or each metropolitan district of a city under direct central rule and the town is divided into wards (*phuong*).

on corresponding local governments and it, arguably, threatens judicial independence.[8]

Within the Vietnamese court hierarchy, the Supreme People's Court is the highest body and enjoys the jurisdiction to supervise and direct the adjudicative work of its divisions, the military courts and special courts. The Supreme People's Court is headed by a president who is elected by the National Assembly for a five-year term, and vice presidents who are appointed by the State President on the recommendation of the President of the Supreme People's Court.

Prior to the enactment of the 2002 Law on the Organisation of the People's Courts, the Supreme People's Court had both original and appeal jurisdictions. At that time, the original jurisdiction was given to the Court for hearing certain cases under the special procedures called *so tham dong thoi chung tham* (roughly translated as the first instance and final-instance procedures). Under Vietnamese law, if a case was heard under the first-instance and final-instance procedures, the court decision would immediately take effect and there would be no chance for parties to appeal the court decision. This original jurisdiction of the Court is now no longer available.[9] The abolition of the jurisdiction to hear cases under the first-instance and final-instance procedure of the Court was a necessary task to ensure the right to appeal of parties. This also reflects one of the issues raised in the Judicial Reform Program that Vietnam is pursuing, according to which the Supreme People's Court is a court which enjoys the jurisdiction to supervise and instruct inferior courts on how to consistently apply the law, rather than having the jurisdiction to hear cases at first instance.[10]

Unlike the Supreme People's Court, provincial people's courts have both original and appeal jurisdictions.[11] In terms of structure, provincial people's courts are very similar to the Supreme People's Court. A provincial people's court consists of a criminal law division, a civil law division, a labour law division, an economic law division, an administrative law division and a family and juveline division. In cases of need, the Standing Committee of the National Assembly will decide to establish other divisions of provincial

8 See Lam, "Toà án và địa phương [Courts and local goverments]," 2023, at https://tapchitoaan.vn/toa-an-va-dia-phuong8057.html, last accessed on 8 January 2025.

9 See Article 46 of the *Law on the Organisation of the People's Courts* 2024.

10 See *Strategy for Judicial Reform to 2020*, above n 1.

11 See Article 55 of the *Law on the Organisation of the People's Courts* 2024.

people's courts on the recommendations of the President of the Supreme People's Court.[12]

District people's courts, which are the lowest courts within the Vietnamese people's court hierarchy, are organised based on the locality of the district units. Like provincial people's courts, district people's courts exercise a wide range of jurisdictions including administrative law jurisdiction, but their jurisdictions are explicitly defined by statute.

Figure: Diagram of the Vietnam People's Court System

II. Participation of people's assessors in hearing cases

Based on the notion that people's courts serve the people's interests, people's representatives who are chosen from amongst ordinary persons are required to participate in judicial processes to guarantee that the court judgements reflect the will and interests of the people. Trial by Vietnamese people's courts, based on this notion, is characterised by the presence of laypersons, namely *hoi tham nhan dan* (people's assessors; sometimes this term is translated as 'juror' or 'people's juror'). Shortly after the establishment of the DRV in 1945, the participation of people's assessors (*phu tham*

12 See Article 56 (b) of the *Law on the Organisation of the People's Courts* 2024.

nhan dan)[13] was first introduced in the court system. When the Constitution 1959 was passed, the institution of people's assessors, which totally followed the Soviet model, was adopted in Vietnam. Since then, there has been no change in the role of people's assessors in the hearing process of Vietnamese courts.[14]

Vietnamese law sets out several rules for selecting people's assessors and regarding their duties and powers in the judicial process. In relation to these points, people's assessors have much in common with judges. Thus, through Western lawyers' eyes, people's assessors, like judges, are classified as a type of legal officer.[15] The people's assessors are selected for a term of five years by local people's councils on the recommendations of the committee of the Vietnam Fatherland Front at the corresponding level.[16] They are released or dismissed by local councils on the recommendation of the president of the local people's court, with the approval of the committee of the Vietnam Fatherland Front at corresponding level. People's assessors are entitled to receive pay for their work. Each local people's court has a list of people's assessors who will be invited by the president of local people's courts to participate in trials.

---

13 Article 64 of the *Constitution* 1946 stated "[i]n hearing minor criminal cases the people's assessors are required to participate to give their recommendations, and in hearing serious criminal cases, they are required to participate to co-judge." In this Article, the term '*phu tham nhan dan*' was used. Regarding the meaning, the term '*phu tham nhan dan*' is slightly different from the term '*hoi tham nhan dan*'. The former term refers to those who function as judge's assistants while the latter refers to those who have power equal to that of judges.

14 The participation of people's assessors in court trials has become a constitutional principle. Article 103 (1) of the *Constitution* 2013 reads as follows: "Trials at first instance before People's Courts shall be attended by people's assessors except for cases with summary procedures."

15 See Penelope Nicholson, "Judicial Independence and the Rule of Law: The Vietnam Court Experience," (2001) 3 *Australian Journal of Asian Law* 37, 42–43.

16 See Articles 127 and 128 of the Law on the Organisation of People's Courts 2024. The Vietnam Fatherland Front (the VFF) as a socio-political organization plays an important role in the political life of Vietnam. This mass body represents all the masses in Vietnam and is involved in many important activities of the country. For instance, the VFF has responsibility to negotiate, select and introduce those candidates who run for elections as deputies to the National Assembly or local people's councils. Article 9 of the *Constitution* 2013 provides "[t]he Vietnam Fatherland Front and its member organizations constitute the political base of the people's government."

III. Vietnamese judges

For selecting and appointing judges, a range of criteria for candidates, covering moral, political and professional requirements is set out in Vietnamese law.[17] Legal provisions relating to criteria and procedures for selecting and appointing Vietnamese judges and the practice of implementing these provisions reflect the political influence involved in judicial appointments.[18] This means that selecting and appointing Vietnamese judges is not only a matter of professional concern but is also a political matter.

Vietnamese judges are appointed by the State President (for judges of the Supreme People's Court, the decision is made based on the Resolution of the National Assembly for approval recommended by the President of the Supreme People's Court and for judges of the other People's Courts, the decision is made based on recommendation of the President of the Supreme People's Court).[19] The term of office of a Judge of the Supreme People's Court is calculated from the time of appointment until retirement or transfer to another position while other judges of the People's Court appointed for the first time have a term of 5 years from the date of appointment and those who are reappointed have a term until retirement or transfer to another position.[20] The appointment of judges of Vietnam people's courts is made on the basis of recommendations of the Examination Council for the Selection of Judges of the People's Courts whose members represent some institutions, including the Ministry of Defence and the Ministry of Internal Affairs.[21] More importantly, the course of selecting and appointing judges always involves "the leadership of the Communist Party of Vietnam"

17 Article 94 of the *Law on the Organisation of the People's Courts* 2024 describes the criteria for judge candidates as follows: (1) As a Vietnamese citizen, loyal to the Fatherland and the Constitution, possessing good moral qualities, strong political integrity, a courageous spirit, and a firm determination to protect justice, integrity, and honesty; (2) Aged 28 years or older; (3) Holding a bachelor's degree in law or higher; (4) Having received judicial training; (5) Having experience working in legal affairs; and (6) In good health to ensure the completion of assigned duties.

18 For further discussion of this issue, see Nicholson and Nguyen, "The Vietnamese Judiciary: the Politics of Appointment and Promotion," 2005, pp. 1–34.

19 See Article 91 of the *Law on the Organisation of the People's Courts* 2024.

20 See Article 100 of the *Law on the Organisation of the People's Courts* 2024.

21 See Article 99 of the *Law on the Organisation of the People's Courts* 2024.

as one of the basic principles.[22] Despite being required to meet professional criteria, Vietnamese judge candidates, for example, are required to "strictly abide by the Communist Party of Vietnam's line" and to "firmly struggle against wrongdoings that can adversely affect the Communist Party of Vietnam's interests" and to have certificates of completion of political courses run by the CPV's political school system.[23] In practice, to satisfy these criteria, most judge candidates are members of the CPV who must gain the support of the competent Communist Party cell.[24] The strongly political influences in the process of selecting and appointing Vietnamese judges have led to discussions about the judicial independence of Vietnamese courts, especially that of local courts, and the quality of Vietnamese judges,[25] especially in the context that Vietnam is pursuing the goal of constructing a rule of law state.

C. Two Core Constitutional Principles Underpinning the Organisation and Operation of Vietnamese Courts

I. Leadership of Communist Party of Vietnam

Vietnam like China currently is a one-party state under the leadership of the communist party. It should be noted that in the past there were in Vietnam two other Parties existing in parallel with the CPV, i.e. the Social Party (*Dang Xa hoi*) and the Democracy Party (*Dang Dan chu*). These

22 See the Joint Circular No 01/2011/TTLT-TANDTC-BQP-BNV dated 20 October 2011 of the Supreme People's Court, the Ministry of Defense and the Ministry of Internal Affairs.

23 Ibid, Articles 1 and 10.

24 See Nicholson and Nguyen, above fn. 18, pp. 14–15.

25 Dealing with the problem of lacking judges, in a report to the National Assembly in 2006, the former Chief Justice Nguyen Van Hien acknowledged that Vietnamese courts have to employ some judges, especially judges of local courts at remote areas, who do not meet professional criteria (see Truong Uy, "'*Vo vet*' de co du tham phan!, ['To use the last resort' for appointing enough judges]," 2006, at http://tuoitre.vn/Chinh-tri-Xa-hoi/174877/%E2%80%9C-Vo-vet%E2%80%9D-de-co-du-tham-phan.html, last accessed on 9 January 2025). Given the fact that there are many lawyers who fully meet professional requirements of a judge, this practice indicates that political criteria for selecting and appointing Vietnamese judges are over emphasised while professional criteria are underestimated.

Parties, however, never obtained a ruling position in the socio-political life of Vietnam and were dissolved in 1988.[26]

The leadership role that the CPV has achieved is a result of Vietnam's historical development and objective reality. Since the 1930s when the Indochinese Communist Party—the predecessor of the CPV—was newly formed by President Ho Chi Minh, its leadership role has been confirmed. The great achievements of the Vietnamese people for more than seventy years, such as gaining independence from French colonialism, the great victory in the war against America, and the economic achievements in the *doi moi* (renovation) period, have consolidated the position of the CPV as the force leading the State and society. However, the leadership role of the CPV was not officially institutionalised until the Constitution 1980 was passed.[27] Since then it has been constitutionally reaffirmed, and the current Constitution reads in part as follows:

> The Communist Party of Vietnam, the vanguard of the Vietnamese working class, the faithful representative of the rights and interests of the working class, the toiling people, and the whole nation, acting upon the Marxist-Leninist doctrine and Ho Chi Minh's Thought, is the force leading the State and society.[28]

Examining the position of the CPV in the socio-political life of Vietnam, Mark Sidel is correct in his observation that '[a]ny discussion of Vietnam's formal political system, and therefore formal legal system, must begin with the role of the Vietnamese Communist Party'.[29] The leadership role of the CPV has been reflected in various functions that can be seen from both political and legal perspectives. From the legal perspective, there are two formal features which clearly indicate the ruling role of the CPV in leading the State and society.

First, the CPV leads the State and society through its policies on various aspects of political and socio-economic life. Party policy is directly binding on its members and functions as the political base for the law-making of the State. In other words, law must be enacted based on the Party policy,

---

26 See Tran, "Quy che phap ly hanh chinh cua cac to chuc xa hoi [Rules of Administrative Law Regulating Social Organisations]," 2004, pp. 247–248.

27 Although the Constitution 1946 and the Constitution 1959 did not formally mention the leadership of the CPV, the ruling role of the CPV during the period from 1945–1980 was maintained through various channels.

28 See Article 4 of the Constitution 2013.

29 See Sidel, "Vietnam: The Ambiguities of State-Directed Legal Reform," 1997, p. 364.

and it is regarded as a tool to institutionalise the Party line. Formally, this principle requires generally that "the programs for constructing Laws and Ordinances are made on the basis of the Party line."[30] However, in practice, complying with the leadership of the CPV principle, drafts of any statute are also required to pass the test of being consistent with the Party line before being officially approved. Thus, it is quite understandable that any suggestion for the reform of Vietnamese law and legal institutions has to be put in the context of the CPV's policy, and the case of reforming the administrative review system is not exceptional.

Secondly, the leadership role of the CPV can be seen in State personnel work. The law of Vietnam requires that "[t]he State personnel work is centralised under the control of the CPV."[31] This principle is concretised by several requirements reflecting the leadership role of the CPV regarding civil servants. For example, apart from complying with relevant legal provisions, the appointment, removal, and dismissal of State officials, especially high-ranking ones, is normally based on recommendations of corresponding Party organisations. The appointment of Vietnamese judges is another example reflecting political influence on State personnel in Vietnam.[32] Judge candidates, apart from meeting professional requirements, are normally members of the CPV, or at least are required to have a political knowledge certificate that is conferred on a person who takes a course in Marxism-Leninism, Ho Chi Minh Thought and Party-related policies.[33]

While acknowledging the leadership role of the CPV, there has been a call from the CPV and the public for reforming the forms and content of the CPV's leadership functions in relation to State management, especially for the separation of the Party from the day-to-day running of the State. The Party has gained the position to lead the State, but it cannot replace the State in managing society. In Vietnam, the phase 'the Party as leader, the State as administrator and the people as master' is commonly used to describe the mechanism for implementing the leadership role of the CPV

30 See Article 31 of *Law on Legal Normative Document Promulgation* (*Luat ban hanh van quy pham phap luat*) 2015.

31 See Article 5 of the *Law on Cadres and Civil Servants* (*Luat Can bo, Cong chuc*) 2008.

32 For a detailed discussion of the political influences in the appointment of Vietnamese judges see Nicholson and Nguyen, above fn. 18.

33 See the Joint Circular No 01/2011/TTLT-TANDTC-BQP-BNV dated 20 October 2011 of the Supreme People's Court, the Ministry of Defense and the Ministry of Internal Affairs.

in society.[34] This mechanism requires a distinction between the leadership of the Party and the administration of the State. The Party as a type of political bureaucracy that produces policy for the State, therefore, needs to be functionally separate from State institutions, though in reality it is not always easy to draw a clear boundary between the competence of the Party and that of the State.[35] Also, acting as the force leading the State and society, party organisations are required to operate within the Constitution and the law. Except for Article 4 of the current Constitution which generally recognises the leadership role of the CPV, a legal framework that specifically determines how the Party performs its role in managing the State and society is almost completely absent in Vietnam. Thus, there is a call from the public for laws to be made which specify mechanisms, content and principles that the Party must comply with in the course of its operation.[36] Enforcing such laws would ensure that the leadership of the Party cannot go beyond the boundary created by the law, and would coincide with Vietnam's goal of building a law-governed state.

II. Concentration of State Powers

Just as the doctrine of separation of powers is generally accepted in Western countries, the doctrine of concentration of state powers is widely accepted in socialist countries including China and Vietnam. This doctrine, which was developed based on the fundamentals of Marxism-Leninism, claims that in socialist states, all state powers must be united in their representative organs, which are organised at both the central level and the local level. The people make use of state powers through these representative bodies.[37] State bodies like people's councils in Vietnam (or soviets in the former Soviet Union) and the National Assembly (or the Supreme Soviet in the former Soviet Union) are selected by the people. The National Assembly (or the Supreme Soviet in the former Soviet Union) is the highest bodies of state

34 See Ngo, "The Constitution 1992 and the Rule of Law," 1994, p. 86.

35 See Gillespie, "Conception of Rule of Law in Vietnam," 2004, pp. 155–156.

36 See Diep, "Luat hoa su lanh dao cua Dang [Legally Particularising the Leadership of the Party]," 2006, at https://dantri.com.vn/xa-hoi/luat-hoa-su-lanh-dao-cua-dang-1145882750.htm, last accessed on 9 January 2025.

37 See Lenin, "The Tasks of the Revolution (Power to the Soviets)," 1964, pp. 61–62; "Can the Bolsheviks Retain State Power?," 1964, pp. 103–104; "Draft Program of the R.C.P. (B.)," 1965), pp. 106–109.

power, exercising the legislative power and supervising the operation of the entire state apparatus. Other state bodies (executive and judicial organs) must be established by the representative bodies and accountable to them.[38]

To justify the doctrine of concentration of powers, socialist theorists argue that under socialism the people, essentially, are united, which includes the classes of labourers under the leadership of the working class, with its vanguard party; thus, the existence of a body representing that united power is necessary. It is unnecessary to accept power separation, and if this doctrine were to be accepted, there would be no grounds for its existence.[39] This is particularly true in Vietnam, where the multiparty or pluralist concept is accepted neither in theory nor in practice, and where the leadership of the CPV is constitutionally recognised.

To be consistent with this doctrine, the National Assembly of Vietnam, for example, has the power to elect, release from duty, and remove from office the Prime Minister—the Head of the Government;[40] and the Government is accountable to the National Assembly and shall make its reports to the National Assembly.[41] Similarly, the Chief Justice of the Supreme People's Court is elected, removed and dismissed by the National Assembly and is responsible and reports to the National Assembly.[42] At the local level, the people' committees are elected by and accountable to the people's councils at the same levels.[43] Although local people's courts are no longer elected by local people's councils,[44] in many respects the dependence of local courts on local governments still remains.[45] In other words, a rather weak judiciary has been referred to as a feature of the government of Vietnam.

38 See Lenin, "Resolution on Setting up the Government of Working Class and Peasantry," 1966, pp. 28–29.

39 See Bui, "Van De Nhan Thuc Va Van Dung Nguyen Tac Tap Quyen Xa Hoi Chu Nghia Trong Dieu Kien Hien Nay [Issue of Perceiving and Applying the Socialist State Power Concentration Principle in the Current Conditions]," 2001, pp. 55.

40 See Article 70 of the *Constitution* 2013.

41 See Articles 70 and 94 of the *Constitution* 2013.

42 See Articles 70, 105 the *Constitution* 2013.

43 See Article 114 of the *Constitution* 2013.

44 It is noted that a strict application of the doctrine of concentration of state powers can be seen in the 1959 and 1980 Constitutions, according to which judges of the Supreme People's Court were elected by the National Assembly and those of local people's courts were elected by the people's councils at the same level.

45 For further discussion of this issue, see Part III of the paper below.

It is, however, noted that while building their state apparatuses, socialist countries applied this doctrine flexibly, consistent with their conditions.[46] In Vietnam this doctrine is currently applied based on the '*doi moi*' (literally, renovation) principle of the CPV. Shifting from 'a state of dictatorship of the proletariat' to 'a socialist law-based state' is an important step in reconceptualising the doctrine of the concentration of state powers in Vietnam.[47] The CPV argues that the doctrine of concentration of state powers is applied in Vietnam based on adopting relevant ideas of the doctrine of separation of state powers. In other words, in the new conditions of Vietnam this doctrine focuses on distributing state powers to state bodies which coordinate with each other in the exercise of legislative, executive, and judicial powers, rather than on uniting state powers in the National Assembly and other representative organs.[48] This idea is further developed by recognising the control of a state body over one another in the exercise of legislative, executive and judicial powers. Although there is still a lack of legal details particularising the application of 'relevant elements' of the doctrine of separation of powers in the Vietnamese conditions,[49] several propositions as 'conventions' have been acknowledged in legal practice of Vietnam. For example, it is generally accepted that the division of state powers amongst state bodies does not allow for the legislative body or the judicial body to perform the function of the executive body.[50]

46 See Bui, above fn. 39, p. 51.

47 The term 'state of dictatorship of the proletariat' was used in the 1980 Constitution in Vietnam. This state model was applied in all countries of the socialist bloc in this period. The state of dictatorship of the proletariat particularly stressed the supremacy of the representative state organs and regarded them as the political base of the entire state organ system; for example, according to the 1980 Constitution of Vietnam, judges of the Supreme People's Court were elected by the National Assembly, judges of the local courts were elected by the local councils at the same level. The term 'socialist rule of law state' has been known in Vietnam since the early 1990s. This state model inherited sensible elements of the doctrine of power separation. For more details about this state model in Vietnam see: Truong, "The Rule of Law in Vietnam: Theory and Practice," at https://biblioteca.cejamericas.org/bitstream/handle/2015/993/mcpa-rule-law-pacific.pdf?sequence=1&isAllowed=y, last accessed on 9 January 2025.

48 See Bui Xuan Duc, above fn. 39, pp. 53–54

49 See Le "Quyen giam sat toi cao cua Quoc hoi doi voi toan bo hoat dong cua Nha nuoc [The National Assembly's Right to Supremely Supervise All State Activities]," 2002, p. 17.

50 Bui, above fn. 39, p. 54.

Applying this principle more flexibly does not, however, mean that Vietnam is inclined to accept the doctrine of separation of state powers. The CPV affirms that concentration of state power is one of the fundamental principles in the organisation and operation of the state apparatus.[51] In fact, the Constitution 2013 states:

> State powers are unified and distributed to state bodies, which shall coordinate with and control one another in the exercise of legislative, executive and judicial powers.[52]

And:

> The people practice the state power under the forms of direct democracy and indirect democracy through the National Assembly and the People's Councils and other state bodies.[53]

D. Current Situation of Judicial Independence in Vietnam

As above noted, although 'judicial independence' has been recognised in the Constitution of Vietnam, the issue of how to maintain it in practice remains challenging and the lack of independence of Vietnam's courts, especially of local courts, in hearing law cases has been widely criticised.

Firstly, as above analysed, leadership of the CPV is one of the constitutional principles underpinning the organisation and operation of the machinery of state, including the court system. Complying with the principle of leadership of the CPV also requires a separation of the Party from the day-to-day running of the State. However, although there has been a call from the CPV and the public for Party organisations not to intervene in court cases to maintain judicial independence, cases where the local Party organisations interfere in daily court activities are still occurring. Much public attention was paid to the *Do Son* case.[54] In this case, some

51 Dang Cong san Viet Nam (CPV), "Cuong Linh Xay Dung Dat Nuoc Trong Thoi Ky Qua Do Len Chu Nghia Xa Hoi [Political Program for Constructing the Country in the Transitional Period Moving up to Socialism]," 1991, p. 20. See also Dang Cong san Viet Nam (CPV), "Van Kien Dai Hoi Dai Bieu Toan Quoc Lan Thu Viii [Document of the Party Congress Viii]," 1996, p. 129.

52 See Article 2 of the *Constitution* 2013.

53 Article 6 of the *Constitution* 2013.

54 See Quoc, "Bi thu Hai Phong xin xu nhe toi cho cac quan chuc nhung cham [The Secretary of the Party Committee of Hai Phong City Requests the

Party-State officials of Do Son Town, Hai Phong City, were convicted of abusing their power in the management of state land. The Criminal Code provides for penalties of up to three years re-education without detention or imprisonment for one to five years, or five to ten years in serious cases.[55] However, due to the interference of the Party Committee and the People's Committee of Hai Phong City, the People's Court of Hai Phong City decided to only warn the convicted Party-State officials. The public protested against the decision of the Court and it was set aside by the Supreme People's Court. This case indicates the difficulties local courts face in resolving cases involving local government.

Secondly, as above analysed, the entire state machinery of Vietnam is organised and operated based on the principle of concentration of powers. To comply with this principle, the Law on the Organisation of the People's Courts 2024 requires that local people's courts are accountable and that they report their activities to local people's councils at the corresponding level.[56] In terms of organisation, although local judges are no longer directly elected (*bau*) by local people's councils at corresponding levels,[57] the dependence of local courts upon local government is still clearly evident. In an interview conducted by a correspondent for a popular electronic newspaper in Vietnam, the Vietnam Net, the former Inspector General, Mr. Quach Le Thanh, admitted the difficulties regarding the organisation of local courts, which can influence their judicial independence in resolving administrative cases.[58] The most important reason for these difficulties, Mr. Thanh pointed out, is the dependence of local courts upon the local governments with respect to organisation, personnel and budget.[59]

Lightening of the Punishments Imposed on Party-State Officials Who Commit Crimes]," 2006, at http://vnexpress.net/tin-tuc/phap-luat/bi-thu-hai-phong-xin-xu-nhe-toi-cho-quan-chuc-nhung-cham-2069813.html, last accessed on 9 January 2025.

55 Article 281 of the Vietnamese Criminal Code.

56 See Articles 80 and 81 of *the Law on the Organisation of the People's Courts* 2024.

57 For a more detailed discussion of the changes in selection, appointment and removal of Vietnamese judges see Quinn, "Vietnam's Continuing Legal Reform: Gaining Control over the Courts," 2003, pp. 452–454.

58 See Le, "*Toa an tinh co the xu chu tich tinh?* [Can Provincial Courts Challenge Chairmen of Provincial People's Committees?]," 2004, at http://vietbao.vn/Xa-hoi/Toa-an-tinh-co-the-xu-duoc-Chu-tich-tinh/20052994/157/, last accessed on 9 January 2014.

59 For more details regarding this dependence, Article 2 of the Regulation on the Supreme People's Court's Cooperation with local people's councils in administering the organisation of local people's courts (enacted with the Resolution No 132/2002/

While the Supreme People's Court has been granted the authority to manage the local people's court system, the current law requires close coordination with the local government in local court administration regarding the following main functions:

assigning duties to local judges;
personnel management for local courts;
building new local court offices or upgrading facilities of local court offices.[60]

Such legal provisions make local courts dependent on the local government, which can easily lead to a breach of judicial independence. In fact, interference usually manifests itself in the uncooperativeness, unwillingness or opposition of government officials (especially of the high-ranking officials) when local courts are hearing cases in general and administrative cases in particular involving those officials. In the above mentioned interview of the former Inspector General, Mr. Quach Le Thanh published by the Vietnam Net in 2004, Le Tho Binh described the case of a Chairman of the people's provincial committee who not only ignored the court summons for his related administrative law case but also challenged the court with his intimidation words.[61] Similarly, in a research project conducted by the Supreme People's Court in 2006 the research team has pointed out that in practice government departments and officials dislike being defendants in administrative cases and are often uncooperative in providing the documents and evidence needed for the effective hearing of administrative cases.[62]

NQ-UBTVQH11 dated 04 April 2002 of the Standing Committee of the National Assembly).

60 See Article 2 of the Regulation on the Supreme People's Court's Cooperation with local people's councils in administering the organisation of local people's courts.

61 See Le, above fn. 58. See also "Nganh toa an kho kham noi viec xu ly tranh chap dat dai [It Is Very Tough for Courts to Resolve Land Disputes]," 2003, at http://vietbao.vn/An-ninh-Phap-luat/Nganh-toa-an-kho-kham-noi-viec-xu-ly-tranh-chap-dat-dai/10826857/218/, last accessed on 9 January 2014. In this newspaper article, the author quoted Mr. Nguyen Van Thuan, the Vice President of the Law Committee of the National Assembly who described the difficulties of local courts in hearing administrative cases involving local government officials.

62 See Toa an nhan dan toi cao (Supreme People's Court), "Nhung giai phap nang cao hieu qua cong tac giai quyet cac vu an hanh chinh tai Toa an nhan dan theo tinh than cai cach tu phap [Solutions for Promoting the Effectiveness of Resolving Administrative Cases at Court in Accordance with Judicial Reform]," De tai khoa hoc

E. Model of Regional courts: A Proposal for Judicial Independence in Vietnam

I. Some initial ideas

Being concerned about the lack of independence of courts, especially of local courts, many people in Vietnam start raising the issue of restructuring the court system. Several suggested models have been proposed. The main idea is that local courts should be independent of local governments in terms of organisation, personnel and budget allocation to prevent their interference in courts' decisions.[63]

The Strategy for Judicial Reform to 2020 of Vietnam (the Strategy) proposed by the CPV sets out the goal of court restructuring, according to which a jurisdiction-based court system would replace the current administrative unit-based court system.[64] In terms of structure, the jurisdiction-based court system, as proposed in the Strategy, would consist of the following courts:

Regional courts of first instance (*toa so tham khu vuc*) with jurisdiction to hear cases at first instance; regional courts are expected to be set up in geographical areas of one or more districts.

Appellate courts (*toa phuc tham*) with key jurisdiction to hear appeals from regional courts of first instance and jurisdiction to hear some cases at first instance; Appellate courts are expected to be set up in geographical areas of each province.

High courts (*toa thuong tham/toa cap cao*) with jurisdiction to hear appeals from appellate courts; High courts are expected to be set up in five regions of Vietnam (the North, the Centre, the Central Highlands, the South and the Mekong River Delta.[65]

The Supreme People's Court (*toa toi cao*) with the jurisdiction to sum up court practices, instruct inferior courts on how to apply the law, publish

cap Bo (the Ministerial level Project), 2006 (unpublished material on file with the author), p. 48.

63 Ibid.

64 See *Strategy for Judicial Reform to 2020*, above fn. 2.

65 See "Se thanh lap toa an khu vuc [Regional Courts Will Be Established]," 2005, at http://vietbao.vn/An-ninh-Phap-luat/Se-thanh-lap-toa-an-khu-vuc/40108555/218/, last accessed on 9 January 2014. This newspaper article is an interview conducted by *Phap luat Thanh pho Ho Chi Minh* (The law Ho Chi Minh City) newspaper with the former Deputy Chief Justice Dang Quang Phuong about the model of regional courts in Vietnam.

selected court decisions, and review and supervise the decisions of inferior courts (*giam doc tham, tai tham).*

In accordance with the Strategy, court divisions which specialise in hearing certain types of cases would be maintained in this new model. Together with the proposed structure of a jurisdiction-based court system, the Strategy also initiates the issue of reforming the regime of judicial appointment to secure judicial independence. Although the Strategy does not mention detailed proposals regarding this issue, a long-term appointment seems to be likely the case for Vietnamese judges in the future.[66]

Although the suggested model of jurisdiction-based courts has not been implemented in practice and there is a lack of many details as to how this system will work, the desire for the establishment of a jurisdiction-based court system indicates Vietnam's commitment to strengthening the judicial capacity of the court system in its move towards a law-based state. This suggested model, as the former Deputy Chief Justice Dang Quang Phuong commented, could overcome several inadequacies of the current court system, one of which is the administrative dependence of local courts on local governments.[67] Thus, it seems to be a promising model that could potentially solve the problem of the lack of independence facing local courts.

It should be noted that although the Constitution 2013 does not include any details regarding the model of jurisdiction-based courts, room for the possibility of establishing regional courts has been provided in the current Constitution. Instead of listing different courts including local people's courts as in the Article 127 of the Constitution 1992, Article 102(2) of the Constitution 2013 generally states that "the people's courts comprise the Supreme People's Court and other courts established by law". More importantly, the requirement that Presidents of local people's courts are accountable and responsible for reporting court activities to local people's councils at the corresponding level has been no longer available under the Constitution 2013.[68]

---

66 This viewpoint gains much support from Vietnamese legal scholars. Depute Chief Justice Dang Quang Phuong also has suggested that quasi-lifelong appointment should be applied for Vietnamese judges (see "Se thanh lap toa an khu vuc [Regional Courts Will Be Established]," above fn. 65).

67 See "*Se thanh lap toa an khu vuc* [Regional courts will be established]," above fn. 65.

68 Article 135 of the *Constitution* 1992 clearly stated that "Presidents of local people's courts are accountable and responsible for reporting court activities to local people's councils".

II. Some Challenges

Restructuring the court system, however, is a difficult task, especially for Vietnam, a country in transition. Several years ago, some people in Vietnam pointed out several potential difficulties that would arise from the process of setting up regional courts,[69] and their concerns remain current.

One of the difficulties lies in the question of compliance with the two constitutional principles relating to the organisation and operation of Vietnam's state apparatus: the principle of the leadership of the CPV and that of the concentration of powers. As many people argue, since regional courts would not be organised based on administrative units, it would be hard to maintain the leading role of executive committees of the CPV in court activities and the accountability of the courts to local state representative organs.[70]

It seems that it is not very difficult to suggest solutions for maintaining compliance with the above constitutional principles in the case of the model of jurisdiction-based courts. In fact, Nga suggested several ideas that could deal with the problem.[71] She, for example, proposed that to comply with the Party leadership principle, the Party-court relationship in regional courts should be maintained by the Party Committees of provinces.[72] However, what is more important is how to reconcile one of the significant purposes of the establishment of a jurisdiction-based court system, which is to secure the judicial independence of local courts, with compliance with the Party leadership and accountability to local state representative organs. Unless this ambivalence was dealt with, efforts to establish local courts which would be independent of local governments would appear to be meaningless.

---

69 See Le, "To Chuc Toa an Nhan Dan Khu Vuc – Nhung Van De Ly Luan Va Thuc Tien [Organising Regional People's Courts – Theoretical and Practical Issues]," 2003, pp. 51–57.

70 See for example, Duong, "May suy nghi ve doi moi to chuc va hoat dong cua toa an nhan dan [Some Thoughts on Reforms of the Organisation and Operation of People's Courts]," 2001, pp. 416–417 (Duong Thi Thanh Mai used to be Deputy Chief Justice of the Supreme People's Court of Vietnam); Dinh, "Xung quanh van de doi moi to chuc va hoat dong cua toa an nhan dan [On the Issue of Reforming the Organisation and Operation of People's Courts]," 2001, pp. 421–424 (Dinh Van Que used to be Depute Head of the Criminal Division of the Supreme People's Court).

71 See Le, above fn. 69, p. 55.

72 Ibid.

In my view, to deal with the above difficulty in the Vietnamese context the most important task is to revisit the perception and the application of the two constitutional principles underlying the organisation and operation of the state apparatus in general and of the court system in particular.[73] This means that, while the Party leadership is a constitutional principle, the Party can only guide courts through issuing court-related strategic policies, which will then be institutionalised as laws; Party organisations and Party members ought not to intervene in routine court activities. In the current Vietnamese context, a law which would set out details relating to the leadership of the CPV and responsibilities of Party-State officials for fully complying with these details at least may help to maintain a clear boundary between the Party leadership and the State activities. While it is acknowledged that it is not easy to deal with such sensitive political issues as the renewal of Party leadership and it would be hard to predict when such a law would be available,[74] open debates on the mode and content of Party leadership in the eleventh National Congress of Delegates of the CPV show promising signs for a future renewal process.

Another difficulty relates to the restructuring of related legal institutions and the amendment of several laws relating to the organisation and operation of the current people's court system. This would require much time, effort and money. Dealing with this difficulty would require an intensive search for relevant solutions, so it seems clear that the process of the restructuring of Vietnamese courts needs to be taken step by step. It however should be noted that implementing the Constitution 2013 which has come into force since 1 January 2014, a range of statutes relating to organisation and operation of state bodies including courts must be revised.[75] In such

73 There are many Western scholars' criticisms of the Party-court relationship and of the dependence of Vietnamese courts on local government, which leads to a lack of judicial independence. See for example, Nicholson, above fn. 2, pp. 167–168, Quinn, above fn. 57, pp. 449–455.

74 The case of China where the leadership of the Communist Party also is a constitutional principle may be worthwhile consulting. The Age Newspaper (Melbourne) had a report on the rejection by a China's top law and order official of the idea that rule of law prevails over Party rule. In this report, the correspondent Marry-Anne Toy referred to an essay by Mr Luo Gan, Security Chief, whose view was that 'an independent judiciary was not appropriate' and for judges, lawyers and prosecutors 'loyalty to the Communist Party was paramount'. See Toy, 'China Tells Courts to Toe Party Line, " 2007, p. 10.

75 According to Article 3(2) of the Resolution 64/2013/QH13 of the National Assembly dated 28 November 2013 on provision of some points to implement the Constitution

a context, much pressure has been put on Vietnamese law makers and it is expected a jurisdiction-based court system will be soon realised in Vietnam.

F. Conclusion

Vietnam is on the way to improving its court system for protecting the legitimate rights and interests of individuals and organisations and meeting the requirements of international integration. To deal with this task, Vietnam has committed itself to strengthening the quality of hearing cases by its courts and to a search for an effective model for maintaining judicial independence. The proposal for the model of regional courts offers an interesting story of how to transform the court system in a transitional country.

The Vietnamese court system has been established and developed in Vietnam's distinctive political and socio-economic conditions. It is obvious that any legal reform will involve dealing with relatively complex political and philosophical issues. As noted, several principles influenced by the socialist political and legal ideology, such as 'leadership of the CPV' and 'concentration of powers' have been maintained in the Constitution of Vietnam. Understanding the issue of judicial independence in Vietnam, and, more importantly, making any proposal for dealing with the issue in question must necessarily be put in the context of compliance with those constitutional principles.

Another factor affecting the reform of the Vietnamese court system is economic development. Since economic development is closely related to changes in perception and attitudes of people towards non-material values such as 'legality', 'fairness' or 'justice' and the willingness of people and government to pay the cost of legal institutions, proposals for reform need to be seriously considered regarding whether those reforms would be affordable in the economic conditions of Vietnam as a developing country.

Undoubtedly Vietnam has a long way to go in improving judicial independence of its courts. This will involve the adoption of experience suggested from concepts of laws and legal institutions of Western countries. Briefly

of the Social Republic of Vietnam, several laws relating to organisation and operation of state bodies including the revised Law on the Organisation of the People's Courts must be reviewed and passed by October 2015 as the latest.

speaking, the adoption of such Western notions would have to go through a complex process, including the observation, the assimilation and the application of foreign experience in the local conditions. During this complex process, Vietnamese law reformers would face a range of challenges. Also, it seems to be unavoidable that this reform process would involve a compromise between Vietnamese 'traditional' values shaped by socialist political and legal ideology, and Western liberal notions. This paper has pointed out specific potential challenges and dilemmas that would affect the process of reforming the Vietnamese court system, and the issues that need to be considered when looking at ways to encourage this reform process. As noted, while the model of regional courts is proposed as a way to encourage the judicial independence of local courts, especially in hearing administrative law cases, the question, however, remains as to how this model can be adopted and remain consistent with constitutional principles such as 'leadership of the CPV' and 'concentration of powers'. It is suggested that to deal with these dilemmas in the current Vietnamese context it is important to revisit the perception and the application of the constitutional principles underlying the organisation and operation of the state apparatus in general and of the court system in particular. In practice, debates in relation to the perception and the application of these constitutional principles and especially the passage of the 2013 Constitution in Vietnam have shown promising signals for the reform process. This trend has been supported by the context of globalisation and international integration in which fundamental values such as 'rule of law', 'separation of powers', 'democracy' and 'good governance' seem likely to be recognised even amongst countries that have different legal and socio-political traditions.

Bibliography

Bui, Xuan Duc, "Van De Nhan Thuc Va Van Dung Nguyen Tac Tap Quyen Xa Hoi Chu Nghia Trong Dieu Kien Hien Nay [Issue of Perceiving and Applying the Socialist State Power Concentration Principle in the Current Conditions]," in *Mot So Van De Ve Hoan Thien to Chuc Va Hoat Dong Cua Bo May Nha Nuoc Nuoc Cong Hoa Xa Hoi Chu Nghia Viet Nam* [Some Issues on Improving the Organisation and Operation of the State Apparatus of the Socialist Republic of Vietnam], ed. Le Minh Thong, Hanoi: Vietnam Academy of Social Sciences, 2001, pp. 47 ff.

Cao, Mai Phuong, "Party Resolutions on Judicial Reform," *Law & Legal Forum* 12, 139 (2006): 6–8.

Dang Cong san Viet Nam (CPV), *Cuong Linh Xay Dung Dat Nuoc Trong Thoi Ky Qua Do Len Chu Nghia Xa Hoi* [Political Program for Constructing the Country in the Transitional Period Moving up to Socialism], 1991.

Dang Cong san Viet Nam (CPV), *Van Kien Dai Hoi Dai Bieu Toan Quoc Lan Thu Viii* [Document of the Party Congress Viii], 1996.

Diep, Van Son, "*Luat hoa su lanh dao cua Dang* [Legally Particularising the Leadership of the Party]," 2006, at http://www.tuoitre.com.vn/Tianyon/Index.aspx?ArticleID=134274&ChannelID=3.

Dinh, Van Que, "Xung quanh van de doi moi to chuc va hoat dong cua toa an nhan dan [On the Issue of Reforming the Organisation and Operation of People's Courts]," in *Mot so van de ve hoan thien to chuc va hoat dong cua bo may nha nuoc nuoc Cong hoa Xa hoi chu nghia Viet Nam* [Some Issues on the Improvement of the Organisation and Operation of the State Apparatus of the Socialist Republic of Vietnam], ed. Le Minh Thong, Hanoi: Vietnam Academy of Social Sciences, 2001, pp. 418 ff.

Duong, Thi Thanh Mai, "May suy nghi ve doi moi to chuc va hoat dong cua toa an nhan dan [Some Thoughts on Reforms of the Organisation and Operation of People's Courts]," in *Mot so van de ve hoan thien to chuc va hoat dong cua bo may nha nuoc nuoc cong hoa xa hoi chu nghia Viet Nam* [Some Issues on the Improvement of the Organisation and Operation of the State Apparatus of the Socialist Republic of Vietnam], ed. Le Minh Thong, Hanoi: Vietnam Academy of Social Sciences, 2001, pp. 403 ff.

Gillespie, John, "Conceptions of Rule of Law in Vietnam," in *Asian Discourses of Rule of Law*, London: Routledge, 2004, pp. 146–182.

Lam, Uyen, "Toà án và địa phương,"[Courts and local goverments] (2023), *Tạp chí toà án nhân dân điện tử* [e-Journal of People's Courts] < https://tapchitoaan.vn/toa-an-va-dia-phuong8057.html>, last accessed on January 8, 2025.

Le, Minh Thong, "Quyen giam sat toi cao cua Quoc hoi doi voi toan bo hoat dong cua Nha nuoc [The National Assembly's Right to Supremely Supervise All State Activities]," *Nha nuoc va Phap luat (State and Law)* 12 (2002): 8.

Le, Thi Nga, "To Chuc Toa an Nhan Dan Khu Vuc – Nhung Van De Ly Luan Va Thuc Tien [Organising Regional People's Courts – Theoretical and Practical Issues]," *Nghien cuu lap phap (Legislative Studies)* 4 (2003): 51.

Le, Tho Binh, "*Toa an tinh co the xu chu tich tinh?* [Can Provincial Courts Challenge Chairmen of Provincial People's Committees?]'," 2004, at http://vietbao.vn/Xa-hoi/Toa-an-tinh-co-the-xu-duoc-Chu-tich-tinh/20052994/157/.

Lenin, Vladimir Ilyich, "Draft Program of the R.C.P. (B.)," in *V. I. Lenin: Collected Work*, Volume 29, 4th ed., Moscow: Progress, 1965.

Lenin, Vladimir Ilyich, "Resolution on Setting up the Government of Working Class and Peasantry," in *V. I. Lenin: Collected Works*, Volume 33, Moscow: 1966.

Lenin, Vladimir Ilyich, "The Tasks of the Revolution (Power to the Soviets)," in *V. I. Lenin: Collected Works*, Volume 26, 4th ed., Moscow: Progress, 1964.

Lenin, Vladimir Ilyich, "Resolution on Setting up the Government of Working Class and Peasantry," in *V. I. Lenin: Collected Works*, Volume 33, Moscow: 1966.

Ngo, Ba Thanh, "The Constitution 1992 and the Rule of Law," in *Vietnam and the Rule of Law*, ed. Carlyle A. Thayer and David G. Marr, Canberra: The Australian National University, 1993, pp. 81–115.

Nicholson, Penelope, "Judicial Independence and the Rule of Law: The Vietnam Court Experience," *Australian Journal of Asian Law* 3, 1 (2001): 37–58.

Nicholson, Pip, "Vietnamese Jurisprudence: Informing Court Reform," in *Asian Socialism and Legal Change: The Dynamics of Vietnamese and Chinese Reform*, ed. Pip Nicholson and John Gillespie, Adelaide: ANU E Press, 2005, pp. 159–190.

Nicholson, Pip, and Hung Quang Nguyen, "The Vietnamese Judiciary: The Politics of Appointment and Promotion," *Pacific Rim Law and Policy Journal* 14, 1 (2005): 1–34.

Quinn, Brian J. M., "Vietnam's Continuing Legal Reform: Gaining Control over the Courts," *Asian-Pacific Law & Policy Journal* 4,2 (2003): 431–468, at http://blog.hawaii.edu/aplpj/files/2011/11/APLPJ_04.2_quinn.pdf.

Quoc, Hung, "*Bi thu Hai Phong xin xu nhe toi cho cac quan chuc nhung cham* [The Secretary of the Party Committee of Hai Phong City Requests the Lightening of the Punishments Imposed on Party-State Officials Who Commit Crimes]," 2006, at http://vnexpress.net/tin-tuc/phap-luat/bi-thu-hai-phong-xin-xu-nhe-toi-cho-quan-chuc-nhung-cham-2069813.html.

Sidel, Mark, "Vietnam: The Ambiguities of State-Directed Legal Reform," in *Asian Legal Systems: Law, Society, and Pluralism in East Asia*, ed. Poh- Ling Tan, Sydney: Butterworths 1997, pp. 356–389.

To, Van-Hoa, *Judicial Independence: A Legal Research on Its Theoretical Aspects, Practices from Germany, the United States, France, Vietnam, and Recommendations for Vietnam in Transitional Countries*, Lund: Juristförlaget i Lund, 2006.

Toy, Mary-Anne, "China Tells Courts to Toe Party Line," *The Age (Melbourne)*, 5 February 2007, p. 10.

Tran, Thi Hien, "Quy che phap ly hanh chinh cua cac to chuc xa hoi [Rules of Administrative Law Regulating Social Organisations]," in *Giao trinh Luat hanh chinh Viet Nam* [Textbook on Themes of Vietnamese Administrative Law], ed. Tran Minh Huong, 2004, pp. 243 ff.

Tran, Thi Thu Hang, "Nguyen tac tham pham, hoi tham nhan dan xet xu doc lap va chi tuan theo phap luat – Thuc tien thuc hien và kien nghị [The Principle of Judges and Jurors Adjudicating Independently and Only Adhering to the Law – Practical Implementation and Recommendations]," 2018, Tap chi toa an nhan dan dien tu [e-Journal of People's Court], at https://tapchitoaan.vn/nguyen-tac-tham-phan-hoi-tham-xet-xu-doc-lap-va-chi-tuan-theo-phap-luat-thuc-tien-thuc-hien-va-kien-nghi.

Trinh, Van Dung, "Nguyen tac xet xu doc lap cua toa an: Thuc tien ap dung va nhung bat cap [The Principle of Independent Adjudication by the Court: Practical Application and Challenges]," 2023, Tap chi dien tu Luat su Viet Nam [e-Journal of Vietnamese Lawyers], at https://lsvn.vn/nguyen-tac-xet-xu-doc-lap-cua-toa-an-thuc-tien-ap-dung-va-nhung-bat-cap-1686783315-a131633.html.

Truong, Thi Thu Trang, and Nguyen Thi Ho Diep, "Cac yeu to anh huong den su doc lap cua toa an o Viet Nam hien nay." [Factors affecting the independence of the courts in Vietnam today], *Thong tin khoa học xa hơi* [Information on Social Sciences] No.2, 2018, 12–18;

Truong, Trong Nghia, "The Rule of Law in Vietnam: Theory and Practice," at http://www.mansfieldfdn.org/backup/programs/program_pdfs/10nghia.pdf.

Truong, Uy, "'Vo vet' de co du tham phan! ['To use the last resort' for appointing enough judges]," 2006, at http://tuoitre.vn/Chinh-tri-Xa-hoi/174877/%E2%80%9C-Vo-vet%E2%80%9D-de-co-du-tham-phan.html.

Vietbao, "Nganh toa an kho kham noi viec xu ly tranh chap dat dai [It Is Very Tough for Courts to Resolve Land Disputes]," 2003, at http://vietbao.vn/An-ninh-Phap-luat/Nganh-toa-an-kho-kham-noi-viec-xu-ly-tranh-chap-dat-dai/10826857/218/.

Vietbao, "Se thanh lap toa an khu vuc [Regional Courts Will Be Established]," 2005, at http://vietbao.vn/An-ninh-Phap-luat/Se-thanh-lap-toa-an-khu-vuc/40108555/218/.

Vietnam Law & Legal Forum, "Party Central Committee sets out major tasks and solutions for further improving the socialist law-ruled state in the coming time," (2023) *Vietnam Law & Legal Forum*, https://vietnamlawmagazine.vn/party-central-committee-sets-out-major-tasks-and-solutions-for-further-improving-the-socialist-law-ruled-state-in-the-coming-time-69791.html.

Vietnam Law & Legal Forum, "Strategy for Judicial Reform to 2020," *Vietnam Law & Legal Forum* 12, 139 (2006).

Arbitration in Malaysia

K. C. Vohrah

A. Introduction

This article comprises three parts. The introductory part will deal with a brief history of Malaysia, the coming together of several political entities in the Southeast Asian region as a nation state. These entities were under British political influence with ties to the English common law system, with reliance on English case law, the English legal system and basically the various statutory English Law on arbitration with adaptations that were accepted in these several entities.

The second part will deal, briefly, with the types of arbitrations which are resorted to in Malaysia, institutional or non-institutional whether under the old Arbitration Act 1952 or under the prevailing legislation on arbitration.

The third part will deal with the important Arbitration Act 2005 which replaced the Arbitration Act 1952. The Malaysian arbitration law since this legislation has moved away from the English Arbitration Acts of 1952, 1975 and 1979 and its heavy reliance on English case law. Its crucial provisions are modelled along the UNCITRAL Model Law on International Commercial Arbitration. The Malaysian legislation came into operation in 2006 for both domestic and international arbitration with the emphasis on party autonomy and restricted court intervention in the arbitration process and the arbitral award.

B. Malaysia

The Federation of Malaysia comprises eleven states and two Federal Territories in Peninsular Malaysia stretching from the Thai border in the north to the Straits of Johore (north of the Republic of Singapore) and two States and a Federal Territory some 650 kilometres across the South China Sea in the Island of Borneo.

I. Political entities in Peninsular Malaya and on Borneo Island before Second World War

Before the Second World War, when the Japanese Army occupied the Malay Peninsula and Singapore, there were three political entities in the peninsula.[1]

The four Federated Malay States formed in 1895 made up of the hereditary Malay Sultanate States of Negeri Sembilan, Pahang, Perak and Selangor where the British High Commissioner of the federation had the power to give advice to the State Governments and Rulers through the Resident appointed for each State;

The five unfederated hereditary Malay Sultanate States of Kelantan, Terengganu, Kedah, Perlis and Johore. Under Anglo-Siamese Treaty of 1909, the Siamese Government transferred rights including protection over Kelantan, Terengganu, Kedah and Perlis to Britain. In 1914 Johore became a crown protectorate of Britain. In all five states under British protection the executive authority was vested with the respective state government with a British Adviser for each state.

The Crown Colony of the Straits Settlement made up of Penang (ceded in 1786 by the Kedah Sultanate to the British), Malacca (acquired in 1824 from the Dutch by treaty), and the Island of Singapore (acquired in 1819 from the Johore Sultanate) and also Labuan in the north of Borneo Island, the Cocos Island and Christmas Island in the Indian Ocean.

As for the entities in Borneo Island they comprised North Borneo under the British North Borneo Company and Sarawak under the rule of the British Raja Brooke.

After the Japanese occupation and after a brief period of British military administration, the Malaya Union was constituted in 1946, made of the four Federated Malay Sultanate States and the five Unfederated Malay Sultanate States, the separate Crown Colonies of Penang and Malacca.

Singapore together with the Cocos Island and Christmas Island become a separate Crown Colony.

In Borneo Island, the British North Borneo Company surrendered their rights, and the new Colony of North Borneo became a Crown Colony. As for Sarawak, Raja Brooke gave up his rights and Sarawak also became a Crown Colony.

---

1 Aun, *The Malaysian Legal System*, 1972, pp. 3–34; Fong, *Constitutional Federalism in Malaysia*, 2016, pp. 1–22.

In 1948 the Malayan Union gave way to the Federation of Malaya with the Head of the new Federal Government being the British High Commission with legislative and administrative powers. On August 3, 1957, the independent Federation of Malaya headed by an elected King, the Yang di-Pertuan Agong, was established, and all the 9 Malay Sultanate States ceased to be British protectorates and Malacca and Penang ceased to be colonies with federally appointed governors as their head of state.

In 1963 the State of North Borneo (now known as Sabah), Sarawak and Singapore joined the Federation of Malaya, and the Federal Constitution was amended to accommodate the new States, and the Federation was renamed *Malaysia* and was established on September 16, 1963. Two years later, Singapore left the Federation. Malaysia now comprises eleven States and the two Federal Territories of Kuala Lumpur and Putrajaya in the peninsula and across the seas the two States of Sabah and Sarawak together with the Federal Territory of the island of Labuan.

II. The legal system

Since the 18th century, the English common law system became the main legal system that was administered over those political entities where the British had influence before Malaysia was established. English Law, either in statute form or common law, was received in these political entities, the English adversarial court system was established, and the law on civil procedure, evidence, criminal law and contract, based on legislations from the then British India and the all-important principle of *stare decisis,* according to which the decisions by a higher court are binding upon the lower courts, was applied. Needless to say, precedents, basically, English case law, were used extensively.

Malaysia has a written Federal Constitution with each of the States having its own State constitution ambited by provisions in the Federal Constitution which apply to the States. The competence of the Federal and State legislatures and the executive are spelt out in the Schedules to the Federal Constitution.[2]

Given the English influence in the States that make up Malaysia, it is not surprising that English is widely spoken in Malaysia. Although Bahasa

2 See Articles 74, 77 and Schedule 9 of the Federal Constitution; Vohrah, Koh and Ling, "Sheridan & Groves: The Constitution of Malaysia," pp. 317–376.

Malaysia (Malay) is the language of the courts, English is used extensively in the superior courts. In arbitration, the language used is almost wholly English unless the parties and the arbitrator opt for the use of Malay and that has happened occasionally.

The Malaysian Court System comprising the superior courts—the Federal Court, the Court of Appeal, and the High Court of Malaya and the High Court of Sabah and Sarawak—are federal courts and are established under the Federal Constitution.[3]

Each of the 13 states and the 3 federal territories has its own Syariah System and Syariah Courts.[4] Sabah and Sarawak have each its own native courts to administer native law and custom.[5]

III. The old laws on arbitration

The first arbitration legislation in the states in the peninsula was the Arbitration Ordinance XIII of 1890 of the Straits Settlements of Penang, Singapore and Malacca. Over the years, the British introduced this legislation into the Malay States. The Arbitration Ordinance 1890 replaced the legislation in the Straits Settlements which became the Arbitration Ordinance 1950 for all the states in the Federation of Malaya.

With the establishment of Malaysia in 1963, there were three pieces of legislation for Malaysia on arbitration. The Arbitration Ordinance 1950 of the Federation of Malaya (based on the English Arbitration Act 1899) was in force in Peninsular Malaysia, the Arbitration Ordinance[6] of Sabah was in force in Sabah and the Arbitration Ordinance of Sarawak[7] in Sarawak.

Under the Arbitration (Extension) Order made under section 74 of the Malaysia Act 1963, the Arbitration Ordinance 1950 of the Federation of Malaya and the Arbitration Ordinance of Sabah were repealed, and the Arbitration Ordinance of Sarawak was extended to apply throughout Malaysia and became known as the Arbitration Act 1952.

The Arbitration Act 1952 was modelled along the English Arbitration Act 1950 and was read subject to persuasive English cases which were adopted by the highest courts and were binding on lower courts because of the

3 See Federal Constitution, Articles 121, 122 & 122A.
4 See Federal Constitution, Schedule 9, List II, item 1 and List 1, item 27.
5 See Federal Constitution, Schedule 9, List II A, item 13.
6 Cap 7.
7 Cap 45.

principle of *stare decisis.* The Act and the decisions were impeding the development of the law in adopting trends and practices in international arbitration. Over the years until 2005, while other countries had revised or replaced their arbitration legislation to keep abreast with the UNCITRAL Model law on International Commercial Arbitration 1985, the Malaysian legislation with all its shortcomings continued to be used with its outdated provisions until 2005.

Regarding the Arbitration Act 1952, the well-known author Sundra Rajoo[8] noted:

> As applicable legislation now, there is a greater chance for the defaulting party to prolong matters as the arbitral tribunal does not have the same enforcement powers as a court of law.
> There is also a danger of arbitrations being converted into public litigation. There is no doubt that the archaism of the Arbitration Act 1952 contributes to some of the frustrations, delays court challenges and curial interferences which are part of Malaysian arbitration scene.
> Litigation may be more appropriate than arbitration where there are substantial legal questions; or the proceedings are multi-party proceedings; or the proceedings are likely to be difficult to control; or there are substantial allegations of fraud and dishonesty.

C. Types of Arbitration

There are many arbitration proceedings in Malaysia which are *ad hoc* proceedings, where the arbitration clauses allow the parties to choose their arbitrators, applicable law or procedure governing their arbitration. Others are administered institutionally if parties so choose.

One well-known institution to which recourse may be had in the Southeast Asian region and in Hong Kong is the Kuala Lumpur Regional Centre for Arbitration (KLRCA), now renamed Asian International Arbitration Centre (AIAC). Others are the Singapore International Arbitration Centre and the Hong Kong International Arbitration Centre.

Awards made are enforced in the High Court if the losing party does not honour its obligations after the award is made.

The KLRCA was established under the auspices of the Asian-African Legal Consultative Committee Organisation (AALCO), an inter-govern-

8 Sundra Rajoo, *Law, Practice & Procedure of Arbitration*, 2016, p. 39.

mental organisation, in co-operation with and with the assistance of the Government of Malaysia.

The Government of Malaysia and AALCO have renewed a host country agreement in Kuala Lumpur on March 26, 2013.

Among the main functions of the KLRCA[9] one is to administer international and domestic arbitrations under KLRCA Arbitration Rules (revised in 2013) which are the UNCITRAL Rules of Arbitration (as revised in 2010) with certain modifications.

There are other bodies offering the administration of arbitration proceedings. There is the Malaysian Institute of Architects Malaya known in the National Language as Pertubuhan Arkitek Malaya (PAM)[10] which was originally established in 1920. It is the governing body for architects. It appoints arbitrators when the contract used by the parties is a PAM standard terms contract. In addition to arbitration, it administers other forms of alternative dispute resolution.

Then, there is the Institution of Engineers Malaysia (IEM)[11] which is a professional society serving members in and outside Malaysia. It was formed in 1959. It was admitted as a member of the Commonwealth Engineers Council in 1962. The Institution is a qualifying body for professional engineers in Malaysia. It appoints arbitrators when the contract used by the parties is an IEM standard terms contract. It also administers other forms of alternative dispute resolution.

An arbitration agreement may provide for one arbitrator to be appointed and normally the claimant would suggest a number of persons (with their *curriculum vitae)* for the respondent to choose one of the named persons therefrom. Where there is more than one arbitrator to be appointed, each party will appoint one, and the two arbitrators will then appoint the third arbitrator who will be the presiding arbitrator. When there is no agreement or when the agreed procedure fails, the Arbitration Act 2005 provides for the intervention of the Director of the KLRCA[12] and where he is unable to act or fails to appoint an arbitrator, any party may apply to the High Court for the appointment of the arbitrator.[13]

9 www.klrca.org.my.
10 www.pam.org.my.
11 www.iem.org.my.
12 See s 13(4) – (6).
13 See s 13(7).

D. The Arbitration Act 2005

The new legislation, the Arbitration Act 2005 (the 2005 Act), was, according to its long title, enacted to "reform the law relating to domestic legislation, provide for international arbitration, the recognition and enforcement of awards and for related matters.[14]

It has been in operation for ten years since 15 March 2006. Practitioners of arbitration law over the years felt that there were shortcomings in the 2005 Act. In 2011, by the Arbitration (Amendment) Act 2011 which came into force on July 1, 2011, the 2005 Act was amended taking into account criticisms by the arbitration community and following the realisation of some shortcomings in the Act. Then, there was also a curial interpretation of some of the provisions which showed the shortcomings.

I. Agreement to refer to arbitration

It is a requirement under the 2005 Act that an arbitration agreement to submit to arbitration all or certain disputes which have arisen, or which may arise between the contracting parties in respect of a defined relationship, whether contractual or not, must be in writing.[15] This was recognised even under the old law. In *Malaysian Newsprint Industries Sdn Bhd v Bechtel International Inc. & Anor*,[16] the highest court in the country, the Federal Court, held that an agreement to refer disputes to arbitration under section 6 of the 1952 Act must be in writing and cannot be made by way of inference.

In Malaysia, parties may by agreement opt for institutional arbitration or non-institutional arbitration following the procedure agreed upon in the arbitration agreement.

The adoption of provisions of the UNCITRAL Model Law on International Commercial Arbitration 1985

The 2005 Act accords with the modern practice by modern States which have adopted the UNCITRAL Model Law on Commercial Arbitration (the Model Law) passed by UNCITRAL on June 21, 1985. The United Nations

14 In respect of arbitral proceedings under the 1952 Act which were commenced before the 2005 Act came into proceedings, the 1952 continues to apply; see s 51, 2005 Act.

15 See subsections (3) (4) and (5) of s 9.

16 [2012] 9 CLJ 993.

General Assembly recommended that all UN states give due consideration to introducing the Model Law in view of the desirability of the uniformity of the law of arbitral procedures and the specific needs of international commercial arbitration practice.[17]

The Model Law was amended by UNCITRAL on 7 July 2006, at the thirty-ninth session of the Commission. The General Assembly, in its resolution 61/33 of 4 December 2006, recommended "that all States give favourable consideration to the enactment of the revised articles of the UNCITRAL Model Law on International Commercial Arbitration, or the revised UNCITRAL Model Law on International Commercial Arbitration, when they enact or revise their laws ..."

The UN Secretariat in an explanatory note prepared in July 2007[18] comments in paragraph 5 "The Model Law was developed to address considerable disparities in national laws on arbitration. The need for improvement and harmonization was based on findings that national laws were often particularly inappropriate for international cases."

Paragraphs 6 and 7 in the Note go on to show the inadequacies of domestic laws –

> 6. Recurrent inadequacies to be found in outdated national laws include provisions that equate the arbitral process with court litigation and fragmentary provisions that fail to address all relevant substantive law issues. Even most of those laws that appear to be up-to-date and comprehensive were drafted with domestic arbitration primarily, if not exclusively, in mind. While this approach is understandable in view of the fact that even today the bulk of cases governed by arbitration law would be of a purely domestic nature, the unfortunate consequence is that traditional local concepts are imposed on international cases and the needs of modern practice are often not met.
> 7. The expectations of the parties as expressed in a chosen set of arbitration rules or a "one-off" arbitration agreement may be frustrated, especially by mandatory provisions of applicable law. Unexpected and undesired restrictions found in national laws may prevent the parties, for example, from submitting future disputes to arbitration, from selecting

17 Rajoo and Davidson, *The Arbitration Act 2005: UNCITRAL Model Law as Applied in Malaysia*, 2007, pp. 1–6; Rajoo, *The Malaysian Arbitration Act (Amended 2011), An Annotation* (2013), 2015.

18 See Explanatory Note by the UNCITRAL secretariat on the 1985 Model Law on International Commercial Arbitration as amended in 2006.

> the arbitrator freely, or from having the arbitral proceedings conducted according to agreed rules of procedure and with no more court involvement than appropriate. Frustration may also ensue from non-mandatory provisions that may impose undesired requirements on unwary parties who may not think about the need to provide otherwise when drafting the arbitration agreement. Even the absence of any legislative provision may cause difficulties simply by leaving unanswered some of the many procedural issues relevant in arbitration and not always settled in the arbitration agreement. The Model Law is intended to reduce the risk of such possible frustration, difficulties or surprise.

In regard to the UN Secretariat's Explanatory Note that "national laws were often particularly inappropriate for international cases," it has to be noted that in the case of Malaysia before the 2005 Act the High Court had power to invoke its inherent power under Order 92 rule 4 of the Rules of High Court to make any order as may be necessary "to prevent injustice and to intervene to prevent an abuse of the process of the Court" and to take over arbitration proceedings.[19] Section 8 of the 2005 Act has removed this power. Again, based on English common law principles, there was a limited inherent jurisdiction of the High Court to stay arbitration proceedings but s 10 on of proceedings negates such power.

The Malaysia 2005 Act, providing for international arbitration and the domestic arbitration in one act, is modelled in great part after the New Zealand Arbitration Act 1996.

One of the biggest criticisms of the arbitration process concerns judicial intervention (and some say judicial interference) in the arbitration process and also in the arbitral award and a lack of finality of an arbitral award as was seen in numerous court decisions, both English and Malaysian, before the coming into operation of the 2005 Act.

It will be noted that section 8 of the 2005 Act (as amended in 2011) under Part II (an adoption of article 5 of the Model Law), provides that unless otherwise provided, no court shall intervene in matters governed by this Act. In *JHW Reeds Sdn Bhd v Syarikat Borcos Shipping Sdn Bhd*[20], an application was made to aside an award and the application was made

19 See Bina Jati Sdn Bhd v Sum Project (Bros) Sdn Bhd [2002] 2 MLJ 71.

20 [2012] 6 AMR p 47.

beyond the prescribed time under section 37 of the 2005 Act. In this 2012 case Justice Mohammad Ariff Md Yusof rejected the application stating:[21]

> Having considered the submissions and the provisions in our Arbitration Act, I tend to be of the view that on a proper reading of s 37(4) the time limit imposed is mandatory. This view accords with the generally accepted view that under the Model Law. The time limit is strict and express power must be given under the law itself before the court can extend time. This view also accords with the principle of minimal intervention by the courts of law as strongly underlined in our s 8 of the Act. [See also the case KNM Process System Sdn Bhd v Mission Biofuels Sdn Bhd [2013] 1CLJ 993]

II. Parts of the 2005 Act

The Act has four parts. The long title of the Act and s 1 of Part I contain preliminary matters, s 2 contains the definitions of words and phrases used in the Act, s 3 deals with the application of the Act to domestic and international arbitration and awards in Malaysia, s 4 deals with the arbitrability of the subject matter where unless an arbitration is contrary to public policy any dispute which the parties have agreed to submit to arbitration under an arbitration agreement may be decided by an arbitrator.[22]

Part II is what makes the 2005 Act different from the old laws. It adopts section by section the articles of the Model Law with modifications to accord with Malaysian law and practice. Throughout Part II, there are numerous sections which clearly highlight party autonomy over default

21 [2012] 6 AMR p 52; see later observation in this article: with section 8 (and now in its clearer amended form) previous decisions allowing for court interventions on ground of "potent injustice" or the ground of the exercise of "the inherent jurisdiction" of the court no longer apply; see also Ashok, K.., The Arbitration 2011 (Amendment) Act 2011, http://www.skrine.com the arbitration-amendment-act-2011.

22 Rajoo and Davidson, above fn. 17, p. 25, where the authors states: "Since the Act is not limited to arbitration of commercial disputes, we see no reason why arbitration agreements to deal with disputes over distribution of a deceased's estate or other family matters, or to determine liability between parties to a claim in tort should be excluded from arbitration by section 4." It should be noted that section 4 may need to be read together with section 9 which defines an arbitration agreement and adds in the requirement for a defined legal relationship, whether contractual or not; see case "Tomolugen Holdings Ltd & Another v Silica Investors & Other Appeals," 2012.

provisions with phrases like "unless the parties agree" or "the parties are free to agree" in the sections.

In respect of deference to local law or practice when adopting the Model Law provisions, mention must be made and it will be elaborated later that, since the 2005 Act applies to both international and domestic arbitration, section 3 provides for the differentiation between them.

In Part II, there are other departures from the Model law provisions. Section 12(2) deals with the default provisions on the number of arbitrators to be appointed both in a domestic or an international arbitration where the parties cannot agree on the number. Another provision deals with the appointment of arbitrators and the role of the KLRCA where there is a failure to appoint and the role of the High Court where the KLRCA fails to act.[23]

Part III applies to domestic arbitrations and Part IV contains miscellaneous provisions, for example repealing previous Acts (it repealed the 1952 Act) and applies to both domestic and international arbitration.

III. Distinction between domestic arbitration and international arbitration

A distinction is made in the Act between domestic arbitration and international arbitration.

The terms "international arbitration" and "domestic arbitration" are defined in s 2(1) of the Act:

> international arbitration" means an arbitration where –
> (a) one of the parties to an arbitration agreement, at the time of the conclusion of that agreement, has its place of business in any State other than Malaysia;
> (b) one of the following is situated in any State other than Malaysia in which the parties have their places of business:
> (i) the seat of arbitration if determined in, or pursuant to, the arbitration agreement;
> (ii) any place where a substantial part of the obligations of any commercial or other relationship is to be performed or the place with which the subject matter of the dispute is most closely connected; or
> (c) the parties have expressly agreed that the subject matter of the arbitration agreement relates to more than one State

23 Section 13.

As was mentioned earlier, s 3 in Part I is an important provision. Section 3(2) provides which Parts of the Act apply to the arbitration after having determined whether an arbitration is to be classified as "international" or "domestic", i.e. the parties are free to "opt in" or "opt out", as the case may be from Part III of the Act. Section 3(2) states –

> 3.(1) ...
> (2) In respect of a domestic arbitration, where the seat of arbitration is in Malaysia -
> (a) Part I, II and IV of this Act shall apply; and
> (b) Part III of this Act shall apply unless the parties agree otherwise in writing.
> (3) In respect of an international arbitration, where the seat of arbitration is in Malaysia-
> (a) Part I, II and IV of this Act shall apply; and
> (b) Part III of this Act shall not apply unless the parties agree otherwise in writing.
> (4) For the purpose of paragraphs (2)(b) and (3)(b), the parties to a domestic arbitration may agree to exclude the application of Part III of this Act and the parties to an international arbitration may agree to apply Part III of this Act, in whole or in part. (emphasis added).

In other words, in respect of domestic arbitration, Part III of the Act applies unless the parties opt out in writing, and in respect of an international arbitration, Part III does not apply unless the parties agree in writing to apply it. The opting in or out on Part III can be in whole or in part.

IV. The Arbitral Tribunal

Under the definition section, s 2,[24] an arbitral tribunal means a sole arbitrator or a panel of arbitrators. The parties are free to determine the number of arbitrators under s 12(1). The default provisions, s 12(2) in the Act, provides that a sole arbitrator shall be appointed for a domestic arbitration whilst three arbitrators shall be appointed for an international arbitration.

There is ample liberty for the parties to the arbitral proceedings to determine the procedures that are to be adopted with regard to the appointment

24 See for the reasons why a three members arbitral panel is prescribed: Rajoo and Davidson, above fn. 17, p. 59.

of arbitrators under s 13. It also provides for a resolution procedure in the event that parties to the arbitral proceedings are unable to come to an agreement. As was stated earlier, recourse may be had to the Director of the KLRCA for the resolution of a disagreement on the arbitrator or arbitrators, and if he decides on the appointment his decision is not appealable. Should the Director be unable to make the appointment under the provisions of the Act, either party to the arbitral proceedings may then apply to the High Court for such an appointment. The High Court decision cannot be appealed against.[25]

V. Grounds on which arbitrators can be challenged

Under s 14 of the Act, it is mandatory for a person who is appointed to act as an arbitrator to disclose any circumstances that are likely to give rise to justifiable doubts as to his impartiality or independence as this is a ground for challenging arbitrators.[26]

The section also states that an arbitrator may be challenged if he does not possess the requisite qualifications agreed to by the parties.

A challenge should first be made before the arbitral tribunal and where the challenge is not successful an application can be made to the High Court for a decision of the High Court which is not appealable.[27] While the application before the High Court is pending, the arbitral tribunal including the challenged arbitrator may continue the proceedings,[28] and quite clearly this is to prevent dilatory tactics by a party who mounts the challenge.

There are provisions which deal with the situation when an appointed arbitrator fails to act or when it becomes impossible for the arbitrator to act,[29] and the appointment of a substitute arbitrator in the event the mandate of an arbitrator is terminated.[30]

---

25 See subsections (3) – (9) of s 13.

26 "Dr. Muhammad Ridzuan bin Mohd Salleh & Anor v Syarikat Air Terengganu Sdn Bhd," 2012, 737, on the need to disclose conflict of interest circumstances. This case is dismissed later in this article.

27 See s 15(1) and (3).

28 See s 15(4).

29 See s 16.

30 See s 17.

VI. Kompetenz-Kompetenz, Section 18

The German term "*Kompetenz-Kompetenz*" adopted for use in arbitration means that an arbitral tribunal is allowed to make a decision whether it has jurisdiction over an issue that needs to be settled and whether an arbitration agreement is valid. If an arbitral tribunal is not allowed to determine questions as to its jurisdiction, a recalcitrant party could cause delay to the proceedings by taking the issue of jurisdiction to court. The 2005 Act has adopted article 16 of the Model Law as s18 which grants the arbitral tribunal the authority to rule under its own jurisdiction, including matters relating to the validity of the arbitration agreement.

Section 18 also provides for the procedure and the limits on raising objections to the arbitral tribunal's jurisdiction and further provides for an appeal to the court which shall have the final say with regard to the arbitral tribunal's ruling on its jurisdiction. The High Court in *Standard Chartered Bank Malaysia v City Properties Sdn Bhd & Anor,*[31] *Chit Nyak Hasin Bin Nyak Ariff v Malaysia Technology Development Corporation Sdn Bhd v Ors*[32] and *CMS Energy Sdn Bhd v Poscon Corp*[33] have all observed that under the 2005 Act, an arbitral tribunal may determine its own jurisdiction. In the CMS Energy Sdn Bhd case the plaintiff had applied for an order on to restrain the defendant from proceeding with any arbitration proceedings against the plaintiff in respect of a sum of money. The plaintiff submitted that in this case the defendant could not rely on s 10 of the Arbitration Act 2005 because there was no arbitration agreement between the defendant and the plaintiff and that the arbitration, if any, was between the defendant and a joint venture company between the plaintiff, defendant and another party. The defendant submitted that the purchase orders purportedly raised by the joint venture company were in fact issued by the plaintiff to the defendant in Korea and each of those purchase orders contained an arbitration clause and relying on this arbitration clause had commenced arbitration proceedings against the plaintiff. The Court allowed the applica-

31 [2008] 1 MLJ 233; at pp 245 to 146 Vincent Ng J explained the ambit of s 10.

32 [2009] 9 CLJ 32; plaintiff opposed an application by the first defendant for stay of further court proceedings made under three arbitration agreements on ground that one of the agreements was null and void under s10(1) of the 2005 Act but the High Court allowed the stay stating that s 10 (application for stay) has to be read with s18 (competence of arbitration tribunal to rule on its competence).

33 [2008] 6 MLJ 561; see also TNB Fuel Services Sdn Bhd v China Civil Corp 2013 4 MLJ 587 (Court of Appeal).

tion for stay and held that the language used in s 18(1) of the Arbitration Act 2005 confers broad and wide powers on arbitration. It allows the arbitral tribunal to decide not only on the substantive issues raised before it but also on the point of preliminary objections as to its jurisdiction.

VII. Power of the Arbitral Tribunal to order interim measures

Under s 11, taking into account the equivalent article 9 in the Model Law, a party may, before or during arbitral proceedings, apply to a High Court for any interim measures on several matters including security for costs, the preservation, interim custody or sale of any property which is the subject matter of the dispute, and an interim injunction.[34] It is not clear whether the provisions of s 11 apply where the seat of arbitration is outside Malaysia as the Act has omitted article 1(2) of the Model Law. Article 1(2) in relation to article 9 (which is the equivalent of section 11 of the Act) states, "The provisions of the Model Law, except articles 8, 9, 35 & 36 apply only **if the place of arbitration is in the territory of the State**." (emphasis added).

Section 19 of the 2005 Act (corresponding to article 17 of the Model Law) allows an arbitral tribunal to grant interim measures on the application of a party for limited measures such as security for costs, discovery of documents and interrogatories, giving of evidence by affidavit, the preservation, interim custody or sale of any property which is the subject matter of the dispute.

VIII. Procedure for arbitration

What attracts most parties in a dispute to the process of arbitration over court proceedings is the flexibility of the process. Basically, parties can agree on most aspects of the conduct of the arbitration to sort their needs and the nature of the dispute. Chapter 5 in Part II of the Act meets the expectations of parties to a dispute in providing party autonomy[35] subject to the overriding principle that "the parties shall be treated with equality and

34 See the application of the section in Focal Asia Sdn Bhd & Anor v Raja Noraini bt Datuk Raja Nong Chik & Anor [2009] 1 LNS 913; Petrodar Operating Co. Ltd. V Nam Fatt Corp Bhd & Anor [2012] 5 MLJ 445.

35 See ss 20 to 28.

each party shall be given a fair and reasonable opportunity of presenting that party's case."[36]

Thus, the parties are free to agree on the rules of procedure applicable in the arbitration proceedings,[37] including the choice of institutional arbitration rules like the Arbitration Rules of the KLRCA, UNCITRAL Arbitration Rules (As revised in 2010) or the International Bar Association Rules on Taking Evidence in International Commercial Arbitration (2010). Parties are also free to choose the seat of arbitration,[38] the commencement of the arbitral proceedings,[39] the language to be used in the proceedings,[40] the time frame for filing pleadings,[41] the nature of the hearings whether they be conducted on the basis of documents or orally,[42] default of party,[43] and use of experts in the proceedings.[44]

IX. Court intervention

Article 5 of the Model Law on the extent of court intervention states:

> 5. In matters governed by this law, no court shall intervene except where so provided in this law.

Note 16 to this Model law provision is explained in the Seventh UNCITRAL Secretariat note of March 25, 1985, thus –

> … no court shall intervene, in matters governed by this Law. This is stated in the innovative article 5, which by itself does not take a stand on what is the appropriate role of the courts but guarantees the reader and user that he will find all instances of possible court intervention in this Law, except for matters not regulated by it (e.g., consolidation of arbitral proceedings, contractual relationship between arbitrators and parties or arbitral institutions, or fixing of costs and fees, including deposits). Especially foreign users and may be viewed as the primary addresses of any

36 See s 20.
37 Section 21.
38 Section 22.
39 Section 23.
40 Section 24.
41 Section 25.
42 Section 26.
43 Section 27.
44 Section 28.

special law on international commercial arbitration, will appreciate that they do not have to search outside this Law.

The 2005 Act had a weak adoption of article 5 of the Model Law when it came into operation as the then section 8 provided,

> Unless otherwise provided, no court shall intervene in any of the matters governed by this Act.

The Bar and arbitrators saw defects in the Act during its operation and called for amendments to the Act which included an amendment to this s 8. In 2011 s 8 was amended[45] and it reads:

> 8. No court shall intervene in matters governed by this Act, <u>except where so provided in this Act</u>. (emphasis added)

This provision hopefully takes care of conflicting Court decisions under the old 1952 Act which had, as previously mentioned, invoked the inherent and common law powers of the Court to intervene in arbitration decisions. Actually in 1998, the Court of Appeal had held that the Court had no power to intervene unless it was statutorily empowered to do so under the (1952) Act[46] but the Court of Appeal, in a different case, held that the courts had a supervisory jurisdiction over arbitrations and arbitrators and the court may invoke its "inherent powers" under Order 92, rule 4 of the Rules of High Court 1980 to make any order that may be necessary to prevent injustice.[47]

Among the first cases where the matter of inherent powers of the High Court to intervene under the 2005 Act came up is *Aras Jalinan Sdn Bhd v Trico Asphalt Public Company Ltd & Ors.*[48]

An application was made to the High Court of Malaysia in an arbitration involving a Malaysian Company and two foreign companies where the seat of the arbitration was in Singapore. The injunction relief was sought under section 11 of the 2005 Act. Federal Commissioner Badariah Sahamed of the High Court robustly interpreted the unamended section 8 of the 2005 Act on the restricted powers of the High Court to intervene in matters arising under the Act. She refused the injunctive relief because she held that section 11 (as it stood then) did not give jurisdiction to the High Court to grant injunctive relief in matters where the seat of arbitration is outside

45 See Act A1395; s 3

46 See Sarawak Shell Bhd v PPES Oil & Gas Sdn Bhd [1988] 2 MLJ 20.

47 See Bina Jati Sdn Bhd v Sum Projects (Bros) Sdn Bhd (2002) 1 CLJ 433.

48 [2008] 5 CLJ 654.

Malaysia. She observed that,[49] the High Court had not been expressly provided under the 2005 Act or any federal law with the jurisdiction to grant the relief sought by the plaintiff. Further, she adopted the Court of Appeal case of *Sarawak Shell Bhd v PPES Gel & Gas Sdn Bhd*[50] where the Court of Appeal deciding on an appeal from the High Court held (in 1998 in respect of the 1952 Arbitration Act) that the High Court had no statutory power to intermeddle in arbitrations whether by way of inherent jurisdiction or at common law.

In another case, Judicial Commissioner Lee Swee Seng in *Kelana Erat Sdn Bhd v Niche Properties Sdn Bhd and another,*[51] in an application dealing with s 37 (the setting aside of an award provision), in the context of the then unamended s 8, stated in regard to the extent of court intervention,

> When read together with the prior provision of s 8 which states that unless otherwise provided, no court shall intervene in any of the matters governed by this Act it would appear that there is a palpable paradigm shift and a discernible difference where arbitration under the 2005 Act is concerned compared to the Arbitration Act 1952 in that the court would tend to take a hands-off approach and would only intervene in matters specifically set out in s 37 where setting aside an award is concerned.

Since its amendment in 2011, section 8 has received robust application as well. In rejecting an application to set aside a partial award made under section 37 of the 2005 Act (the provision for setting aside awards), Mohammad Ariff Md Yusof, Judge of the High Court (as he then was), in *JHW Reeds Sdn Bhd v Syarikat Borcos Shipping Sdn Bhd*[52] dismissed the application stating that the time limit under s 37(4) is mandatory observing that under the Model Law, the time limit is strict and express power must be given under the law itself before the court can extend the time. The learned Judge stated that this accords with the principle of minimal intervention by the courts of law as strongly underlined in the amended s 8 of the 2005 Act.

49 Ibid, pp 667–676.

50 [1998] 2 MLJ 20; see above fn 47.

51 [2012] 5 MLJ 809 at p. 819.

52 [2002] 6 AMR 47.

X. Court intervention under the Act

There are several provisions in the Act which provide for court intervention in matters governed by the Act. Matters falling under provisions in Part II (i.e. Model Law provisions) are:

(1) obligation to stay court proceedings when there is a valid arbitration agreement;[53]
(2) power to grant interim measures of protection;[54]
(3) power to appoint an arbitrator in certain situations;[55]
(4) power to deal with challenges to an arbitrator;[56]
(5) power to hear appeals on the jurisdiction of the arbitral tribunal after the tribunal has made a decision;[57]
(6) power to assist in the taking of evidence on application of a party with the approval of the arbitral tribunal;[58] and
(7) power to set aside an arbitral award on specified grounds.[59]

There are also court intervention provisions not covered by matters covered under Part II but elsewhere and they are:

(1) power to determine a preliminary point of law on application by a party with consent of the arbitral tribunal or consent of every other party;[60]
(2) power to determine any question of law by reference arising from an award;[61]
(3) power to tax costs in certain circumstances;[62]
(4) power to order the arbitral tribunal to deliver the award in certain circumstances;[63]

53 Section 10.
54 Section 11.
55 Section 13(7).
56 Section 15(3).
57 Section 18(8).
58 Section 29.
59 Section 37.
60 Section 41.
61 Section 42.
62 Section 44(1).
63 Section 44(4).

(5) power to extend the time for commencing arbitration proceedings;[64] and
(6) power to extend the time for making an award.[65]
(7) power to grant or refuse recognition and enforcement of arbitral awards.[66]

XI. Arbitral Award

An arbitral award in the context of the 2005 Act is a decision of the arbitral tribunal on the substance of the dispute and it includes any final, interim or partial award and any award on costs or interest.[67]

All arbitral awards are final and binding.[68]

The award shall be in writing and signed by the arbitral tribunal and the arbitral award shall state the reasons upon which it is based unless the parties to the arbitral proceedings had agreed otherwise or if the arbitral award is on agreed terms.[69]

XII. Setting Aside of Arbitral Awards

As had been mentioned earlier, court intervention has been limited to specified grounds. There is no appeal procedure in regard to the arbitral award provided in the 2005 Act but s 37 (which is in Part II of the Act and which basically follows article 34 of the Model Law) provides for the setting aside of an arbitral award on proof of specified grounds.

Malaysian courts have since the coming into operation of the Act respected the clear intention of the Act not to interfere with arbitral awards except on proof of specified grounds. In the case of *Taman Bandar Baru Masai Sdn Bhd v Dindings Corporations Sdn Bhd*,[70] the High Court held, *inter alia*, that the 2005 Act makes it compulsory for courts to respect

64 Section 45.
65 Section 46.
66 Sections 38 & 39.
67 See the definition, s 2(1).
68 Section 36(1).
69 Section 33.
70 [2010] 5 CLJ 83; see also The Government of India v Lairn Energy India Pty Ltd v Others [2014] 9 MLJ 149; Open Type Joint Stock Co (EFKO) v Alfa Trading Ltd [2012] 1 MLJ 685.

the decision of the arbitrator. Only minimum intervention is allowed; real proof is required before the courts would meddle with an arbitral award.

Under s 37 the limited grounds according to which an award may be set aside are:

> 37. (1) An award may be set aside by the High Court only if –
> (a) the party making the application provides proof that –
> (i) a party to the arbitration agreement was under any incapacity;
> (ii) the arbitration agreement is not valid under the law to which the parties have subjected it, or, failing any indication thereon, under the laws of Malaysia;
> (iii) the party making the application was not given proper notice of the appointment of an arbitrator or to the arbitral proceedings or was otherwise unable to present that party's case;
> (iv) the award deals with a dispute not contemplated by or not falling within the terms of the submission to arbitrations;
> (v) subject to subsection (3) the award contains decisions on matters beyond the scope of the submission to arbitration; or
> (vi) the composition of the arbitral tribunal or the arbitral procedure was not in accordance with the agreement of the parties, unless such agreement was in conflict with a provision of this Act from which the parties cannot derogate, or, failing such agreement, was not in accordance with this Act; or
> (b) the High Court finds that –
> (i) the subject-matter of the dispute is not capable of settlement by arbitration under the laws of Malaysia; or
> (ii) the award is in conflict with the public policy of Malaysia.

With regard to the matter of "public policy" mentioned in s 37(1)(b)(ii) above, s 37(2) provides that, without limiting the generality scope of s 37(1)(b)(ii), an award is in conflict with the public policy of Malaysia where:

> (a) the making of the award was induced or affected by fraud or corruption; or
> (b) a breach of the rules of natural justice occurred-
> (i) during the arbitration proceedings; or
> (ii) in connection with the making of the award

In *Dato' Dr. Muhammad Ridzuan Bin Mohd Salleh & Anor v Syarikat Air Terengganu Sdn Bhd,*[71] mid-way through the arbitration proceedings the parties negotiated a settlement on the sole arbitrator's advice, withdrew their claims against each other and recorded a consent award, a consent order of costs payable by the plaintiff to the defendant. Unknown to the plaintiff, after the proceedings had started and before the arbitrator issued the consent award, he was appointed a non-executive director and member of the credit committee of the bank which financed the project under dispute. The High Court set aside the enforcement order under s 37(2)(a)(b) (i) and (ii) of the 2005 Act there being a breach of natural justice which was in conflict with the public policy of Malaysia on the ground that the arbitrator had a continuing duty of disclosure until the conclusion of the arbitral proceedings to disclose his appointment in the bank. His appointment to the Bank was not made known to the plaintiff after the date of the enforcement order made by the High Court. The fact that the bank was the financier of the project was sufficient nexus compelling disclosure. It was a nexus that raised the likelihood of circumstances giving rise to justifiable doubts as to the arbitrator's impartiality and independence. The High Court also held that "what was not given to the parties and in this case, more particularly the plaintiff was the right to decide whether or not to challenge the arbitrator's continuing arbitration on the ground that there is a likelihood he may not be impartial or independent.[72]

Where the decision on matters submitted to arbitration can be separated from those not so submitted, only that part of the award which contains decisions on matters not submitted to arbitration may be set aside.[73] This has relevance to the application to set aside an award on the ground that the award deals with a dispute not contemplated by or not falling within the terms of the submission to arbitration[74] and that the award deals with a dispute not falling within the terms of the submission to arbitration.[75]

71 [2012] 3 MLJ 737; see also the interpretation of public policy and natural justice in Open Type Joint Stock Co (EFKO) v Alfa Trading Ltd [2012] 1 MLJ 685.

72 Ibid, p 750.

73 See s 37(3).

74 See s 37(1)(a)(iv).

75 See s 37(1)(a)(v).

XIII. Recognition and enforcement of an arbitral Award

Malaysia is state party to the 1958 New York Convention on the Recognition and Enforcement of Foreign Arbitral Awards which presently has 156 state parties. Arbitral awards issued in Malaysia can be enforced in these countries and vice versa.

With the amendment of s 38 of the Act in 2011,[76] on an application in writing, an arbitral award made in respect of an arbitration where the seat of arbitration is in Malaysia, or an arbitral award from a foreign state shall, subject to s 39 (grounds for refusal of recognition and enforcement), be recognised as binding and be enforced by entity like a judgement according to the terms of the award or by action. The second alternative for enforcement appears to be recognition of the continued existence of the enforcement by action on the award, but if the applicant has met all the requirements of the section for recognition and enforcement and the court has rejected any of the grounds of refusal in section 39, there appears to be no conceivable purpose in the court directing enforcement by action.[77]

Recognition or enforcement may be refused under s 39 of the Act only at the request of the party against whom it is invoked and only on the grounds stated therein. If none of these grounds can be proven, the award must be recognised.[78]

The grounds for refusing recognition or enforcement are a mirror of the above-mentioned s 37 of the Act dealing with the setting aside of arbitral awards save for a provision similar to s 37(2) on the examples where an award is in conflict with the public policy of Malaysia.

The harshness of the decision to refuse recognition or enforcement under s 39 was reduced after the Act was amended in 2011.[79] According to the new s 39(3), where the decision on matters submitted to arbitration can be separated from those which have not been submitted, the court may recognise and enforce those parts of the award on matters that have been submitted for arbitration. This provision therefore refers to the grounds for the refusal of enforcement under s 39(1) (v) in that the award contains decisions on matters beyond the scope of the submission to arbitration.

---

76 See Arbitration Amendment Act 2011, s 7.

77 Rajoo and Davidson, above fn. 17, p. 183.

78 See Rossell NY v Oriental Commercial & Shipping Co (UK) [1991] 2 Lloyd's Rep 625.

79 See Arbitration (Amendment) Act 2011, s 8.

XIV. Reference on Question of Law Arising From Award Under s42 of the 2005 act.

Any party may refer to the High Court any question of law arising out of an award. This section as it stood at the commencement of the Act was being resorted to quite often because the provision had no mechanism to filter out frivolous appeals. In 2011 Parliament's amendment of the 2005 Act included the insertion of subsection (1A) in s 42 where the High Court "shall dismiss a reference... unless the question of law substantially affects the rights of the one or more of the parties". Section 42 (as amended) reads:

> (1) Any party may refer to the High Court any question of law arising out of an award.
> (1A) The High Court shall dismiss a reference made under subsection (1) unless the question of law substantially affects the rights of one or more of the parties.
> (2) A reference shall be filed within forty-two days of the publication and receipt of the award, and shall identify the question of law to be determined and the state of grounds on which the reference is sought.
> (3) The High Court may order the arbitral tribunal to state the reasons for its award where the award-
> (a) does not contain the arbitral tribunal's reasons: or
> (b) does not set out the arbitral tribunal's reasons in sufficient detail.
> (4) The High Court may, on the determination of a reference –
> (a) confirm the award;
> (b) vary the award;
> (c) remit the award in whole or in part, together with the High Court's determination on the question of law to the arbitral tribunal for reconsideration; or
> (d) set aside the award, in whole or in part.
> (5) Where the award is varied by the High Court, the variation shall be effect as part of the arbitral tribunal's award.
> (6) Where the award is remitted in whole or in part for consideration, the arbitral tribunal shall make a fresh award in respect of the matters remitted within ninety days of the date of the order for remission or such other period as the High Court may direct.
> (7) Where the high Court makes an order under subsection (3), it may make such further order as it thinks fit with respect to any additional costs of the arbitration resulting from that order.
> (8) On the reference under subsection (1) the High Court may –

(a) Order the applicant to provide security for costs; or

(b) Order that any money payable under the award shall be brought into the High Court or otherwise secured pending the determination of the reference.

The Court have been strict in interpreting s 42. In *Awangku Dewa Bin Pgn Momin & Ors v Superintendent of Lands and Survey, Limbang Division*[80] the arbitrator had disallowed the claim of Awangku Dewa for compensation over land which the Sarawak Government had acquired for public purposes. A reference was made to the High Court on eight questions of law. Mohd Hishammuddin, Court of Appeal Judge, dismissed the reference and held that the reference was an attempt to appeal against the award disguised as "reference on questions of law" under s 42 and went to state (as guidance for the benefit of High Court Judges in dealing with s 42 references) –[81]

> A High Court must ensure that the questions referred by the applicant were purely a question of law and not a question of mixed law and fact. The questions must be clearly and concisely framed, before embarking to entertain the application and to answer the question posed. A High Court must summarily dismiss the application under s 42 reference without even attempting to answer the question of law posed to the court if the question was in the first place, not properly and intelligently framed or where it was clear to the court that there was a disguised attempt by the applicant to appeal against the decision of the arbitral tribunal

There are other cases[82] where references to the High Court on questions of law under s 42 have also failed.[83] High Court Judge, Mary Lim, in *MMC Engineering Groups Bhd & Anor v Wayss & Freytag (M) Sdn Bhd*[84] has set out instructive guidelines for the use of Article 42,

> On the assumption that proper questions of law are before the court and that these questions of law substantively affect the rights of the plaintiffs, amongst the instructive guidelines that can be drawn, in no order of importance or priority and certainly, would be: (a) the court's ever aware-

80 [2013] 3MLJ 161.

81 Ibid, p 175.

82 SDA Architects (sued as a firm) v Metro Millennium Sdn Bhd [2014] 2 MLJ 625; Ahmani Sdn Bhd v Petronas Penapisan (Melaka) Sdn Bhd [2015] 11 MLJ 32.

83 But see where the High Court allowed the reference application; "Telekom Malaysia Bhd v Eastcoast Technique (M) Sdn Bhd and Another case." 2014.

84 [2015] 10 MLJ 689, p. 691.

ness of minimalistic intervention in arbitration matters; (b) that the general principle that the arbitral is both the master and final arbiter of the facts applies and there is no reason why any broad approach should be adopted just because one is now pondering a question of law arising out of an award; (c) that the court should not look beyond the award; but where necessary, the documents and correspondence referred to in the award may be examined for context and proper appreciation; (d) that the absence of an appeal or leave mechanism advocates for a strict approach; (e) that the power under s 42 is limited and should not be lightly exercised save in clear and exceptional cases; (f) the court should first determine whether questions of law have been properly identified; (g) these questions of law must arise out of the award and not from the arbitral proceedings; (h) these questions of law must not be academic but be questions of practical importance requiring the opinion of the court; (i) these questions of law cannot be the same questions that were referred to the arbitral tribunal for determination; (j) the determination of the questions of law must substantially affect the rights of the parties; (k) grounds for referring these questions of law must be given; (l) the interpretation of the applicable law by the arbitral tribunal is obviously wrong; (m) public law principles are not in play in what is otherwise a private contractual dispute; (n) the award must be viewed in its entirely in a fair and reasonable manner.

E. Concluding Remarks

By and large the present regime covering arbitration in Malaysia is a modern regime that accords with the Model Law and arbitration practice both for international and domestic arbitrations. Party autonomy in most practical matters guarantees that the parties can agree on matters which are not dealt with by the act in mandatory provisions with default provisions kicking in for the convenience of the parties. Arbitration proceedings are not being caught in the court system midway through the proceedings, avoiding delay in the arbitration process. There is more certainty in the arbitration system in Malaysia now under the new Act with the Courts respecting the pressure of party autonomy and non-intervention under the 2005 Act.

If parties want to resolve their dispute in the framework of an arbitration institution in Malaysia, there is the KLRCA which was mentioned earlier. The KLRCA[85] has a panel of over 700 experienced domestic and international arbitrators from diverse fields and expertise. Foreign lawyers are not barred from appearing in arbitration proceedings and there is no withholding tax imposed on the fees of foreign arbitration proceedings. It has to be noted that KLRCA's fee structure is about 20 % lower than other established international arbitration centres.

The KLRCA[86] has also developed new rules to cater to the growing demand of the global business community such as the KLRCA i-Arbitration Rules,[87] the KLRCA Fast Track Rules[88] as the Mediation/Conciliation Rules.[89]

The KLRCA also plays a pivotal role under the Construction Industry Payments and Adjudication Act 2012. This law was enacted to facilitate regular timely payment, provide a mechanism for speedy resolution through adjudication and remedies for the recovery of payment in the construction industry. Under s 32 of the legislation the KLRCA is appointed the adjudication authority. The Construction Industry Payment and Adjudication Regulations 2014 made under section 39 of the Act flesh out the areas of responsibility of the KLRCA.

Arbitration has become a modern, vibrant and viable adjudication process system in Malaysia.

Bibliography

"Arbitration in Malaysia: Taking it to the next level," *The Star Online,* 23 June 2013, at https://www.thestar.com.my/news/nation/2013/06/23/arbitration-in-malaysia-taking-it-to-the-next-level.

Aun, Wu Min, *The Malaysian Legal System,* 2nd ed., London: Longman, 1972.

85 "Arbitration in Malaysia: Taking it to the next level," 2013.

86 The KLRCA has been under the management of the experienced arbitrator Datuk Sundra Rajoo since 2010 and there have been very many innovative and modern measures introduced by him making it a vibrant arbitration centre.

87 These rules are suitable for arbitration arising from commercial transactions premised on Islamic principles.

88 These rules are designed for parties who wish to obtain an award in the fastest way (with strict timelines as to delivery of pleadings, the case management meeting, substantive hearings and the delivery of award).

89 There Rules are in fact a modified version of the UNCITRAL Conciliations Rules 1980 and cater to both domestic conciliation and international conciliation.

Fong, C. J., *Constitional Federalism in Malaysia*, 2nd ed., London: Sweet and Maxwell, 2016.

"KNM Process System Sdn Bhd v Mission Biofuels Sdn Bhd," *CLJ Law* 51 (2013): 993.

Davidson, W. S. W., "The Malaysian Arbitration Scene – The relationship between the Courts and the Arbitral Tribunal in the 21st Century," *The Malaysian Bar*, 2005.

"Dr. Muhammad Ridzuan bin Mohd Salleh & Anor v Syarikat Air Terengganu Sdn Bhd," 3 MLJ, *CLJ Law* 39 (2012).

Kumar, Ashok, "The Arbitration 2011 (Amendment) Act 2011," *Skrine*, 30 June 2011, at https://www.skrine.com/insights/newsletter/june-2011/the-arbitration-amendment-act-2011.

Menon, Sundaresh, "Tomolugen Holdings Ltd & Another v Silica Investors & Other Appeals," Case, SGCA 57, 2012, at http://www.uncitral.org/docs/clout/SGP/SGP_261015_FT.pdf.

Rajoo, Sundra, and W. S. W. Davidson, *The Arbitration Act 2005: UNCITRAL Model Law as Applied in Malaysia*," Thomson: Sweet & Maxwell Asia, Malaysia, 2007.

Rajoo, Sundra, *Law, Practice & Procedure of Arbitration*, Dayton: LexisNexis, 2016.

Rajoo, Sundra, and W. S. W. Davidson, *The Malaysian Arbitration Act (Amended 2011): An Annotation*, Dayton: LexisNexis, 2013.

"Telekom Malaysia Bhd v Eastcoast Technique Sdn Bhd," *CLJ Law,* Vol. 6, Chapter 8, Ampang: 2014.

Vohrah, K. C., T. N. Philip Koh, and Peter S. W. Ling, "The Constitution of Malaysia," *Singapore: Malayan Law Journal Sdn. Bhd*, 5. ed., Chapter 7, pp. 317–376.

Singapore's International Commercial Court

Denise Wong and Makoto Hong

A. Introduction

The first formal announcement of the Singapore International Commercial Court **("SICC")** came at the Singapore Opening of Legal Year Ceremony 2013. The Chief Justice of Singapore, the Honourable Chief Justice Sundaresh Menon, stated the grand vision to set up a court that was international in vision and scope. A senior minister of the Singapore government and a Judge of Appeal of the Supreme Court of Singapore were then appointed to co-chair a committee to develop a framework for the SICC. The impetus for the court was clearly set out in the Report of the SICC **(the "Report")** that was released in November 2013. The SICC would "enable Singapore to enhance its status as a leading forum for legal services and commercial dispute resolution".[1] The focus in Singapore had hitherto been on building the arbitration sector, with significant success.[2] The SICC sought to build on the already thriving litigation and arbitration sectors by creating a dispute resolution hub with a uniquely Asian flavor, in order to offer an alternative means of settlement for cases arising in this region.

The increase in demand for dispute resolution services cannot be understood separately from a rise in cross border investment and trade in the Asian region. As stated in the Report, the Asian economy is expected to triple in the period from 2010 to 2020.[3] The long-termfic region is also expected to have significant export growth over the next ten years.[4] This exponential growth phenomenon has created natural opportunities for disputes to arise in the course of long term trading and investment

1 Report of the Singapore International Commercial Court Committee (SICC Report), available at: http://www.mlaw.gov.sg/content/dam/minlaw/corp/News/Annex%20A%20-%20SICC%20Committee%20Report.pdf **("the Report")**.

2 See generally *Menon*, "International Arbitration: The Coming of a New Age for Asia (and Elsewhere)," available at: <http://www.arbitrationicca.org/media/0/13398435632250/ags_opening_speech_icca_congress_2012.pdf>.

3 The Report, p. 9.

4 Ibid.

relationships, which may require third party intervention in a swift and efficient manner. While the global harmonization of laws would be crucial in ensuring that such disputes are resolved with minimum cost, we are some ways away from achieving that ideal and a more immediately achievable aim was to establish a court that has the flexibility and expertise to address transnational issues in a cost-efficient manner. The SICC came into being on 1 January 2015 when the Supreme Court of Judicature (Amendment) Act 2014[5] came into operation. The legal framework to establish the SICC also includes legislative amendments to the Constitution, the Legal Profession Act, and the Rules of Court.

B. Key Features of the SICC

This next section highlights the key characteristics of the SICC that make it well placed to adjudicate upon cross-border disputes with an Asian focus.

I. Constitution and jurisdiction of the Court

The SICC is constituted as part of the Supreme Court of Singapore.[6] The SICC functions independently from the Singapore domestic court in terms of the cases that it hears, but is, in terms of set up and structure, a division or arm of the Supreme Court.

The necessity of this arrangement is grounded in the need for international enforceability of SICC judgments. All other courts in Singapore are considered to be subordinate as a result of Article 93 of the Constitution of the Republic of Singapore. Subordinate court judgments may face difficulties with enforcement in some jurisdictions. For example, the Foreign Judgments Act 1991 in Australia only applies to the enforcement of money judgments given by superior courts.[7] This is unless the Act is extended to specified inferior courts in a particular country by regulation passed by the Governor General.[8] As such, given that the success of the SICC will in part be predicated on the ease of enforcing its judgments in jurisdictions

5 Supreme Court of Judicature (Amendment) Act (Act No. 42 of 2014).
6 Supreme Court of Judicature Act Cap. 322, 2007 Rev Ed), section 18A.
7 Foreign Judgments Act 1991 (Act 112 of 1991) (Cth), section 5(1).
8 Foreign Judgments Act 1991 (Act 112 of 1991) (Cth), section 5(2).

in which the losing party has assets, such a structural arrangement is undoubtedly essential.

Judges hearing cases in the SICC comprise an international panel of jurists, as well as current judges of the Singapore Supreme Court.[9] Each member of the international panel of jurists is called an "international judge", who is appointed by the President acting in his discretion if he concurs with the advice of the Prime Minister.[10] International judges are appointed for a specified period and assigned cases on an *ad hoc* basis, without security of tenure.[11] Till date, 12 international judges, all of whom are eminent jurists from leading Commonwealth and civil law jurisdictions, have been appointed.[12] Apart from international judges, the relatively liberal rights of audience before the SICC for foreign lawyers also reflects the SICC's international character. Foreign lawyers need only submit an application form supported by an affidavit to be registered with the SICC.[13] Close to 50 foreign lawyers from 12 different nationalities, many of whom are renowned in international arbitration, had already registered with the SICC as early as October 2015.[14] Till date, 76 foreign lawyers have been granted full registrations.[15]

The SICC will be seised of jurisdiction to hear a case that satisfies all of the following conditions[16] –

(a) the action is international and commercial in nature;
(b) the action is one that the High Court may hear and try in its original civil jurisdiction; and

---

9 At the time of writing, 12 International Judges have been appointed. 19 Supreme Court judges have also been designated by the Chief Justice to hear cases in the SICC.

10 Art 95(4)(*c*) of the Constitution.

11 Art 95(5) of the Constitution.

12 See www.sicc.gov.sg/Judges.aspx?id=30 for a list of the judges of the SICC.

13 Legal Profession Act Section (Cap. 161), section 36P(5) read with rule 5 of the Legal Profession (Foreign Representation in Singapore International Commercial Court) Rules 2014 (G.N. No. S 851/2014).

14 Chong, "The Singapore International Commercial Court: A New Opening in a Forked Path," at para 37, available at http://www.supremecourt.gov.sg/Data/Editor/Documents/J%20Steven%20Chong%20Speeches/The%20SICC%20-%20A%20New%20Opening%20in%20a%20Forked%20Parth%20-%20London%20(21.10.15).pdf.

15 LeBherz and Walker, "The Singapore International Commercial Court – Two Years On" (29 May 2017), available at <http://www.kwm.com/en/au/knowledge/insights/singapore-international-commercial-court-two-years-on-20170529>.

16 Supreme Court of Judicature Act, above fn. 6, section 18D.

(c) the action satisfies such other conditions as the Rules of Court may prescribe.

The Rules of Court sets out 3 general scenarios in which the SICC has jurisdiction to hear a case. The first is where the parties have submitted to the SICC's jurisdiction under a written jurisdiction agreement and are not seeking any relief in the form of, or connected with, a prerogative order.[17] The second is where a case is transferred to the SICC under Rule 12 of the Rules of Court.[18] The third is where there is an originating summons under Order 52 of the Rules of Court for leave to commit a person for contempt in respect of any judgment or order made by the SICC.[19]

In the absence of a written jurisdiction agreement, the SICC may nevertheless be seised of jurisdiction if the High Court transfers proceedings to the SICC, either with the parties' consent or by the High Court on its own motion after hearing the parties, and where the following requirements are met:[20]

(a) the High Court considers that the claims are of an international and commercial nature, and is satisfied that the parties do not seek any relief in the form of, or connected with, a prerogative order; and
(b) the High Court considers that it is more appropriate for the case to be heard in the SICC.

II. Procedure and practice of the SICC

1. International best practices

Significantly, procedures in the SICC are not governed by domestic rules of procedure. Rather, a set of procedures that follow international best practices have been developed for the SICC. For example, the rules of document production (or discovery) in the SICC are similar to that in the International Bar Association Rules on the Taking of Evidence in International Arbitration.[21] The traditional discovery model in common law jurisdictions requires parties to disclose relevant documents in their

---

17 Rules of Court (Cap. 322, R 5), O 110 r 7(1).
18 Ibid., r 7(2)(*a*).
19 Ibid., r 7(2)(*b*).
20 Ibid., r 12(4).
21 See ibid., rr 14 to 22.

possession, custody or power. These comprise documents on which a party relies or will rely, as well as documents that could adversely affect his own case, adversely affect another party's case, or support another party's case.[22] In comparison, the default position for SICC cases is that each party must only provide to the court and all other parties documents available to it on which it relies.[23]

Like in international arbitration, a party may also serve a request to produce other documents on any person, and may apply to the SICC for an order for the production of the documents if the recipient of the request objects to the production.[24] The main differences between an order for production in SICC proceedings compared with that in domestic proceedings are firstly that the former is not limited to particular categories of documents.[25] A request to produce in SICC proceedings only has to fulfil certain formalities[26] in order for the recipient to be required to produce the documents.[27] If the recipient objects to the production, the court may nevertheless order the documents to be produced if the original request had complied with the formalities, and none of the specified objections apply.[28] Secondly, an order for production in SICC proceedings is not limited to circumstances where the order is "necessary either for disposing fairly of the cause or matter or for saving costs",[29] which applies to a domestic order for production.

Having regard to the international and commercial nature of the disputes, the SICC's procedures also provide for flexibility and customisation in various respects. For example, parties may apply for the court to adopt any other rules of evidence that they are familiar with, whether such rules are found in foreign law or otherwise.[30] At the same time, the SICC's model of dispute resolution remains "firmly underpinned by judicial control" and offers greater accountability and transparency compared with the arbitral

22 Ibid., O 24 r 2.
23 Ibid., O 110 r 14(1).
24 Ibid., rr 15 to 17.
25 See ibid., O 24 r 12(1), which sets out the categories of documents that a party may request for in a domestic order for production.
26 Ibid., O 110 r 15(3).
27 Ibid., r 15(4).
28 Ibid., r 17(2).
29 Ibid, O 24 r 13(1).
30 Ibid., O 110 r 23.

model.[31] For example, cases in the SICC are docketed so that interlocutory proceedings are heard by judges.[32] The policy of the SICC registry is, as far as possible, to assign interlocutory proceedings to the judge who will be hearing the trial or other dispositive hearings of the matter.[33]

2. Confidentiality

In terms of confidentiality procedures that govern court proceedings, the usual course is for SICC proceedings to take place in open court. This is a clear departure from the standard practice in international arbitration. The advantage of transparent proceedings lies in the ability of the court to quickly and effectively build a body of jurisprudence that may eventually build a transnational lex mercatoria,[34] and guide potential users of the court, both in terms of governing the relationship of the parties as well as predicting how the SICC is likely to decide in relation to a particular dispute.

Nonetheless, it is recognised that many parties would prefer that the details of the dispute be kept confidential. This is particularly the case where the parties are in a long-term and ongoing business relationship. The court does not give parties a free hand to choose whether proceedings will be confidential, but there are special rules that apply for "offshore" cases with no substantial connection with Singapore. In such cases, the court may order that the case be heard in camera, that no person must reveal or publish any information or documents relating to the case, or even for the court file to be sealed.[35] Another aspect of confidentiality is the publication of decisions. Consistent with the SICC's important responsibility of developing sound jurisprudence that is suitable for the purposes of commerce,[36] the general rule is for SICC decisions to be published. The general rule is

31 Man, "The Resolution of Disputes before the Singapore International Commercial Court," 2016, p. 447.

32 See Singapore International Commercial Court Practice Directions at para 105(1).

33 Ibid., at para 105(2).

34 *Dalhuisen*, "The Case for an International Commercial Court," 2014, available at SSRN: <http://ssrn.com/abstract=2433513 or http://dx.doi.org/10.2139/ssrn.2433513>.

35 Rules of Court, O 110 r 30.

36 Menon, "International Commercial Courts: Towards a Transnational System of Dispute Resolution," at para 27, available at http://www.supremecourt.gov.sg/docs/default-source/default-document-library/media-room/opening-lecture---difc-lecture-series-2015.pdf.

then subject to the necessary redaction and confidentiality safeguards for confidential cases.[37]

3. Treatment of foreign law

Another interesting aspect of the procedures of the SICC is the treatment of foreign law. The practice in many common law jurisdictions, including Singapore,[38] is that foreign law must be pleaded and proven. This is because foreign law is treated as a "fact" for the purpose of the law of evidence. In comparison, the procedures of the SICC empower the court to order that any question of foreign law be determined on the basis of submissions, which may be oral or written.[39] In the first case decided by the SICC, *BCBC Singapore Pte Ltd and anor v PT Bayan Resources TBK and anor*,[40] the parties successfully sought and obtained an order for certain questions of Indonesian law to be determined on the basis of submissions instead of proof.[41] At the same time, the SICC also received evidence on Indonesian law from various experts. Evidence on Indonesian law was taken from an Indonesian law academic and an Indonesian legal consultant, whereas submissions on Indonesian law were received from two members of the Indonesian Bar. This demonstrates the flexibility that SICC offers parties – foreign law can be determined using the traditional approach, the alternative approach under the SICC's procedures, or even a combination of both approaches.[42]

4. The SICC's judges and the right of appeal

The SICC's cases are heard by a single judge or by three judges at first instance.[43] Where three judges are appointed to determine the dispute, the

---

37 Rules of Court, O 110 r 31(1).

38 See *Greenline-Onyx Envirotech Phils, Inc v Otto Systems Singapore Pte Ltd* [2007] 3 SLR 40 at [24].

39 Rules of Court, O 110 r 25.

40 *BCBC Singapore Pte Ltd and anor v PT Bayan Resources TBK and anor* [2016] 4 SLR 1.

41 Teh, Yeo and Seow, "The Singapore International Commercial Court in Action – Illustrations from the First Case," 2016, p. 23.

42 Ibid., p. 23 and p. 28.

43 Supreme Court of Judicature Act (Cap. 322), section 18G.

Chief Justice shall appoint one of the judges to preside,[44] and the dispute is decided in accordance with the opinion of the majority of the judges hearing the case.[45] Cases are appealable to a Court of Appeal, whose coram may comprise international judges or Singapore Supreme Court judges.[46] Foreign counsel can also apply to represent parties before the SICC.[47] These features reflect the international character of the SICC. To provide maximum flexibility for parties, the SICC's practice directions allow parties to exclude, limit or vary the right and scope of appeal by prior agreement.[48] Model clauses are also available on the SICC's website to assist parties who wish to do so.[49]

III. International enforceability

A key factor in the SICC's success will be its accessibility and user-friendliness to litigants. A major aspect of this is that the judgment must be readily enforceable in jurisdictions in which the losing party has its assets. Under framework, judgments of the SICC are enforceable as judgments of the Singapore court. As such, unlike international arbitration awards that are enforceable via the New York Convention,[50] judgments of the SICC have the status of national court judgments and are dependent on the principles governing the recognition of foreign judgments in the relevant jurisdiction.

Recognising the limitations of national court judgments vis-à-vis arbitral awards, the Choice of Courts Agreements Act **("CCAA")** was enacted by Parliament on 14 April 2016[51] and came into operation on 1 October 2016.[52] The CCAA implements the 2005 Hague Convention on Choice of Court Agreements **("Convention")** to which Singapore is a signatory. Sin-

---

44 Ibid., section 18H(2).

45 Ibid., section 18H(3).

46 Ibid., section 29.

47 Ibid., section 18M.

48 SICC Practice Directions, para 139(3).

49 Model clauses to exclude the right of, or to limit the scope of, appeal to the Court of Appeal are available at http://www.sicc.gov.sg/documents/docs/SICC_Model_Claus es.pdf.

50 The Convention on the Recognition and Enforcement of Foreign Arbitral Awards, available at http://www.newyorkconvention.org/.

51 Choice of Court Agreements Act 2016 (Act No. 14 of 2016).

52 Choice of Court Agreements Act 2016 (Commencement) Notification 2016 (No. S 473/2016).

gapore ratified the Convention on 2 June 2016, shortly after the CCAA was enacted. These developments strengthen the SICC's position as a forum for international dispute resolution by ensuring that the courts of other contracting states suspend or dismiss parallel proceedings brought in their jurisdiction in favour of a Singapore court, where a Singapore court is the chosen court under an exclusive choice of court agreement.[53] It also enhances the international enforceability of SICC judgments by requiring other contracting states to recognise and enforce judgments of a Singapore court, including the SICC.[54]

While the Convention has only been ratified by the European Union, Mexico and Singapore till date, its potential impact should not be underestimated. It has been described as the "litigation counterpart"[55] to the New York Convention and as a "game changer"[56] in cross-border dispute resolution. When practitioners from the American Bar Association were surveyed before the US became a signatory to the Convention, more than 70 % indicated that they would be "more willing to designate litigation instead of arbitration" in their contracts, while 98 % indicated that the Convention would be useful for their practice.[57] With the interdependence of national economies in today's global economy, there is much room for optimism that more states will soon be drawn to sign or ratify the Convention.

IV. Forum non conveniens

In cases where parties have agreed via contract for the SICC to be the dispute resolution forum, any argument that the court is not the appropriate forum to hear the dispute would not be entertained. It should be noted that from 1 October 2016, an agreement to submit to the jurisdiction of the

53 Hague Conference on Private International Law, Convention of June 30, 2005, on Choice of Court Agreements, Art 6, available at: http://www.hcch.net/index_en.php?act=conventions.text&cid=98.

54 Ibid.

55 Brand and Herrup, *The 2005 Hague Convention on Choice of Court Agreements: Commentary and* Documents, 2008, p. 3.

56 Menon, above fn 36.

57 Chong, "The Singapore International Commercial Court: A New Opening in a Forked Path," at para 48, available at http://www.supremecourt.gov.sg/Data/Editor/Documents/J%20Steven%20Chong%20Speeches/The%20SICC%20-%20A%20New%20Opening%20in%20a%20Forked%20Parth%20-%20London%20(21.10.15).pdf.

High Court is to be construed as including an agreement to submit to the jurisdiction of the SICC.[58] A more interesting question is how the court will deal with cases where there is no exclusive jurisdiction agreement. The Rules of Court only require the parties to have submitted to the jurisdiction of the SICC under a written "jurisdiction agreement", which is defined to mean "an agreement to submit to the exclusive or non-exclusive jurisdiction of the Court".[59] In addition, the Supreme Court of Judicature Act contains a rebuttable presumption that an agreement to submit to the SICC's jurisdiction is an exclusive choice.[60] This approach is identical to that in the Convention, which provides that a choice of court agreement that designates the court or courts of one contracting state is deemed to be exclusive unless the parties have expressly provided otherwise.[61] The SICC's jurisdiction will therefore not be affected even if parties do not describe their jurisdiction agreement as either exclusive or non-exclusive.

V. The SICC Registry

It is undoubtedly the case that the efficiency of the court is of paramount importance. The registry of the SICC is the body tasked with the day to day administration of court matters. The Registry's key functions include:[62]

(a) assisting the SICC Judges and the Court of Appeal Judges hearing appeals in the SICC list in the provision of quality and timely adjudication services for the efficient management of the docket;
(b) assisting in administering the directions of the SICC Judges and the Court of Appeal Judges hearing appeals in the SICC list for the preparation of cases for hearing and appeal, including pre-trial and preliminary applications as well as pre-hearing conference;
(c) maintaining and managing the filing, production and certification of, and access to, court or hearing records and documents;
(d) convening court sittings and providing hearing support; and

58 Rules of Court (Cap. 322, R 5), O 110 r 1(2) (*ca*).
59 Ibid., 1(1).
60 Supreme Court of Judicature Act (Cap. 322), section 18F.
61 Hague Conference on Private International Law, Convention of June 30, 2005, on Choice of Court Agreements, Art 3(*b*), available at: http://www.hcch.net/index_en.php?act=conventions.text&cid=98.
62 The Report, p. 23.

(e) assisting in administering the directions of the SICC Judges and the Court of Appeal Judges hearing appeals in the SICC list in post-trial matters.

C. Role of the SICC in the Context of International Arbitration

This topic has been discussed elsewhere,[63] but the focus in this chapter is on the contribution that the SICC can make to the dispute resolution scene, both in Singapore, as well as in the Asian region more generally. The rise of arbitration in Asia is well-documented. An insightful speech delivered by Chief Justice Menon in 2012 highlighted as follows – "793 requests for arbitration were filed with the International Court of Arbitration of the International Chamber of Commerce (ICC) in 2010 involving 2,145 parties from 140 countries and independent territories. 95 of these cases were allocated to ICC Hong Kong; and another 10 % selected seats or venues in South and South East Asia. In 2010, the China International Economic and Trade Arbitration Commission (CIETAC) handled 1352 cases, nearly 5 times the number it handled in 1992; and between 2000 and 2010, the caseload of the Singapore International Arbitration Centre (SIAC) rose from 58 to 198 new cases."[64] In 2016, this number has almost doubled to 343 new cases.[65] Singapore can therefore be said to have successfully built itself as an arbitration hub in the region, boasting a strong infrastructure as well as an established set of rules and panel of arbitrators with good track records.[66]

The SICC, on one view, would detract from the success of arbitration as it may potentially cannibalize some of the cases that would otherwise have gone through the route of institutionalized arbitration. However, Chief Justice Menon has cited the experience of the London Commercial Court, which saw a burgeoning of its caseload alongside a vibrant arbitration

63 *Wong*, "The Rise of the International Commercial Court: What is it and will it work?," 2014, pp. 205–227.

64 *Menon*, above fn. 2.

65 Annual Report of the Singapore International Arbitration Centre 2016, available at <http://www.siac.org.sg/images/stories/articles/annual_report/SIAC_AR_2016_24pp_WEBversion_edited.pdf>.

66 See generally Annual Report of the Singapore International Arbitration Centre 2016, available at <http://www.siac.org.sg/images/stories/articles/annual_report/SIAC_AR_2016_24pp_WEBversion_edited.pdf>.

market, as support for the counterview that arbitration and commercial courts serve different needs and are complementary.[67] In the same vein, we argue here that in fact, the SICC can contribute to the dispute resolution scene generally and enhance international arbitration. We focus here on the advantage that the SICC has over arbitration in encouraging the harmonisation of commercial law, particularly in the Asian region.

Attempts to develop a law of commerce that transcends borders are not new, and academic consensus is in fact that such a mercantile law has been in existence for a very long time.[68] The dynamic and organic nature of such a law has meant that it has taken a variety of forms throughout the centuries, but its most recent manifestation exhibits unique characteristics. For one, it has been argued that global law in our high-speed economy deviates or at least minimally relies on classical legal forms.[69] More specifically, the need for high-speed dispute resolution in the globalised transactional world requires recourse to an easily accessible and highly efficient dispute resolution mechanism, but more specifically, an easily accessible and readily understandable set of legal norms.

In this vein, there is a growing trend of thought which posits that the time has come where it is possible for a freestanding body of commercial law to be created.[70] This was in fact raised by Lord Wilberforce as early as 1996, and twenty years on, may well become a reality.[71] While international commercial arbitration has to a large extent contributed to this rise,[72] other factors present challenges that we have yet to overcome, including historical factors, divergent interests and political factors, as well as inconsistent decision making by national courts.[73] The principal disadvantages of arbitration in this area are that its highly personalised approach, *ad hoc* nature and promise of confidentiality act as a counterweight to the development of transnational commercial law. In addition, arbitral awards have no

---

67 Menon, above fn. 36.

68 See *Mason*, "Cross-border Insolvency and Legal Transnationalisation," 2012, pp. 105–126.

69 Appelbaum, Felstiner and Gessner (eds), *Rules and Networks – The Legal Culture of Global Business Transactions*, 2001.

70 *Menon*, "Transnational Commercial Law: Realities, Challenges and a Call for Meaningful Convergence," Keynote Address for the 26th LAWASIA Conference, available at http://www.singaporelawwatch.sg/slw/files/SLW%20Headlines/131029_LAWASIA_Conference.pdf.

71 1996 English Arbitration Bill at the Second Reading before the House of Lords.

72 *Menon*, above fn. 70.

73 Ibid.

precedential value in the strict sense because even if they are published, a distinction nevertheless remains between the kind of precedent developed by arbitrators and that developed by institutional courts.[74] Fundamentally, arbitration by its very nature is not designed to provide an "authoritative and legitimate superstructure"[75] to facilitate global commerce. It therefore cannot single-handedly address issues like the harmonisation of substantive commercial laws, practices and ethics.[76]

In comparison, the SICC is uniquely placed to contribute to the growth of this transnational commercial law. As highlighted above, the judgments of the SICC will in the usual course be made public. This would allow a body of jurisprudence, whether it be greater convergence between domestic bodies of law or a harmonised body of international law, to develop in a far more sustained and systematic manner than hitherto permitted by the arbitral regime. Indeed, because the SICC is constituted for the purpose of resolving international commercial disputes and has a distinctly international bench, it has been said to have the capacity to facilitate the flow of information between judges and jurisdictions; "develop streamlined rules of procedure and harmonised rules for the taking of evidence", as well as clarify and promote the enhanced use of international conventions and standards such as the UN Convention on Contracts for the International Sale of Goods (**"CISG"**) and the UNCITRAL Model Law on Cross-Border Insolvency.[77]

The reception to the SICC's first written judgment, which was rendered on 12 March 2016, speaks volumes about its potential.[78] Among other things, the judgment has been hailed as a "masterclass" in the approach taken to deal with rules of interpretation, public policy and the implication of terms.[79]

In a speech delivered by Chief Justice Menon at the 35th Anniversary of the CISG, he spoke of the "4th chapter in the story of the lex mercatoria",

74 Bathurst, "Benefits of Courts Such as the Singapore International Commercial Court (SICC)," 2016, at paras 7 to 10, available at http://www.supremecourt.justice.nsw.gov.au/Documents/Publications/Speeches/2016%20Speeches/Bathurst%20CJ/Bathurst_20161121.pdf.

75 Menon, above fn. 36, *at para 14.*

76 Ibid.

77 Bathurst, above fn, 74, at para 14.

78 BCBC Singapore Pte Ltd and anor v PT Bayan Resources TBK and anor [2016] 4 SLR 1.

79 Teh, Yeo and Seow, above fn. 41.

which will be shaped by forces such as the deceleration of globalisation and the shifting of the global economy's centre of gravity away from OECD countries towards the East.[80] In this new global landscape, the development of lex mercatoria will come to be increasingly engaged by two themes – the creation of legitimacy and the necessity of imagination.[81] As the only international commercial court of its kind in Asia, the SICC is uniquely positioned to promote the legitimacy of international commercial practice in Asia and beyond through the systemic qualities such as openness, consistency and predictability, as well as the more substantive notions of fairness, justice and equality, that it embodies.

Bibliography

Annual Report of the Singapore International Arbitration Centre 2016, available at http://www.siac.org.sg/images/stories/articles/annual_report/SIAC_AR_2016_24pp_WEBversion_edited.pdf.

Appelbaum, Richard P., William L. F. Felstiner, and Volkmar Gessner (eds.), *Rules and Networks: The Legal Culture of Global Business Transactions*, Oxford: Hart Publishing, 2001.

Bathurst, Tom, "Benefits of Courts Such as the Singapore International Commercial Court (SICC)," 21 November 2016), at http://www.supremecourt.justice.nsw.gov.au/Documents/Publications/Speeches/2016%20Speeches/Bathurst%20CJ/Bathurst_20161121.pdf.

Brand, Ronald A., and Paul Herrup, *The 2005 Hague Convention on Choice of Court Agreements: Commentary and Documents*, Cambridge: Cambridge University Press, 2008.

Choice of Court Agreements Act 2016 (Act No. 14 of 2016).

Chong, Steven, "The Singapore International Commercial Court: A New Opening in a Forked Path," available at http://www.supremecourt.gov.sg/Data/Editor/Documents/J%20Steven%20Chong%20Speeches/The%20SICC%20-%20A%20New%20Opening%20in%20a%20Forked%20Parth%20-%20London%20(21.10.15).pdf.

Constitution of the Republic of Singapore 1999.

80 Menon, "Roadmaps for the Transnational Convergence of the Common Law: Lessons Learnt from the CISG" (23 April 2015) at para 27, available at http://www.supremecourt.gov.sg/docs/default-source/default-document-library/media-room/cisg-speech-(final---230415).pdf.

81 Menon, "Roadmaps for the Transnational Convergence of the Common Law: Lessons Learnt from the CISG" (23 April 2015) at para 29, available at <http://www.supremecourt.gov.sg/docs/default-source/default-document-library/media-room/cisg-speech-(final---230415).pdf>.

Convention on the Recognition and Enforcement of Foreign Arbitral Awards, at http://www.newyorkconvention.org/.

Dalhuisen, Jan Hendrik, "The Case for an International Commercial Court," 6 May 2014, available at https://papers.ssrn.com/sol3/papers.cfm?abstract_id=2433513.

English Arbitration Bill 1996 (at the Second Reading before the House of Lords).

Foreign Judgments Act 1991 (Act 112 of 1991).

Hague Conference on Private International Law, Convention of June 30, 2005, on Choice of Court Agreements, Art 6, available at: http://www.hcch.net/index_en.php?act=conventions.text&cid=98.

Hague Conference on Private International Law, Convention of June 30, 2005 on Choice of Court Agreements, Art 8, available at: http://www.hcch.net/index_en.php?act=conventions.text&cid=98.

Hague Conference on Private International Law, Convention of June 30, 2005 on Choice of Court Agreements, Art 3(*b*), available at: http://www.hcch.net/index_en.php?act=conventions.text&cid=98.

http://www.supremecourt.gov.sg/Data/Editor/Documents/J%20Steven%20Chong%20Speeches/The%20SICC%20-%20A%20New%20Opening%20in%20a%20Forked%20Parth%20-%20London%20(21.10.15).pdf.

Jones, Tom, "SICC Hands Down First Judgment," *Global Arbitration Review,* 24 May 2016, at https://www.sicc.gov.sg/docs/default-source/modules-document/news-and-article/-sicc-hands-down-first-judgment-global-arbitration-review_d80c1f6d-5166-4c94-8603-82bb95e9c94b-1.pdf.

LeBherz, Rebecca, and Zoe Walker, "The Singapore International Commercial Court – Two Years On," 29 May 2017, available at http://www.kwm.com/en/au/knowledge/insights/singapore-international-commercial-court-two-years-on-20170529.

Man, Yip, "The Resolution of Disputes before the Singapore International Commercial Court," *International and Comparative Law Quarterly* 65, 2 (2016): 439–473.

Mason, Rosalind, "Cross-border Insolvency and Legal Transnationalisation," *International Insolvency Review* 21, 2 (2012): 105–126.

Menon, Sundaresh, "International Commercial Courts: Towards a Transnational System of Dispute Resolution," available at http://www.supremecourt.gov.sg/docs/default-source/default-document-library/media-room/opening-lecture---difc-lecture-series-2015.pdf.

Menon, Sundaresh, "International Arbitration: The Coming of a New Age for Asia (and Elsewhere)", available at https://www.arbitration-icca.org/media/0/13398435632250/ags_opening_speech_icca_congress_2012.pdf.

Menon, Sundaresh, "Transnational Commercial Law: Realities, Challenges and a Call for Meaningful Convergence," Keynote Address for the 26th LAWASIA Conference, available at http://www.singaporelawwatch.sg/slw/files/SLW%20Headlines/131029_LAWASIA_Conference.pdf.

Report of the Singapore International Commercial Court Committee (SICC Report), available at http://www.mlaw.gov.sg/content/dam/minlaw/corp/News/Annex%20A%20-%20SICC%20Committee%20Report.pdf.

Singapore International Commercial Court Practice Directions, 2015, at https://www.supremecourt.gov.sg/rules/practice-directions/singapore-international-commercial-court-practice-directions.

Supreme Court of Judicature (Amendment) Act (Act No. 42 of 2014).

Supreme Court of Judicature Act Cap. 322, 2007 Rev Ed.

Teh Hwee Hwee, Justin Yeo and Colin Seow, "The Singapore International Commercial Court in Action – Illustrations from the First Case," *Singapore Academy of Law Journal* 28 (2016): 692–722.

Wong, Denise, "The Rise of the International Commercial Court: What is it and will it work?," *Civil Justice Quarterly* 33, 2 (2014): 205–227.

EU Competition Law in the Digital Age: Substantive Challenges and Methodological Innovations Using the Example of the European Commission's Consultation Procedure

Anselm Küsters

'[W]hoever possesses the rules of tomorrow possesses the markets of the day after tomorrow.'[1]

A. Introduction

In just a few years, the digitalisation of various areas of life and the economy has changed the strategic priorities of nation states and the European Union ("EU"), brought about significant investment in artificial intelligence ("AI"), and seemingly enabled large welfare increases for consumers.[2] Nevertheless, digitalisation raises numerous challenges, not least for the law and legal research.[3] On the one hand, competition law scholars and practitioners are usually concerned with digital technologies that potentially violate law or applications that necessitate the development of law, i.e., they are concerned with digital technology as an *object* of competition law. On the other hand, however, it is also possible to reflect on digital applications that could apply law or might help in applying it better, i.e., thinking about digital technology as *method*.[4] In short, digitalisation should not only be seen as a source of substantive challenges but also of methodological innovations.

---

1 Van den Abeele, "'Better Regulation': A Bureaucratic Simplification with a Political Agenda," 2015, p. 75. This article was written and submitted in early 2021 and reflects the literature up to that point; later literature and legislative developments could not be included due to the production process.

2 Havenstein, "Spring comes to AI winter," 2015, p. 28.

3 Overview: Faust, Schäfer, *Zivilrechtliche und rechtsökonomische Probleme des Internet und der künstlichen Intelligenz. 15. Travemünder Symposium zur ökonomischen Analyse des Rechts*, 2019.

4 I develop this argument more fully in: Küsters, "Artificial Intelligence, Law and Legal History," 2020, p. 27.

This paper captures both dimensions by dealing with the implications of the digital age on European competition law. In particular, it analyses two projects initiated by the European Commission in response to the digital revolution—a consultation of stakeholders and a subsequent export report—both quantitatively as well as qualitatively. At the end of 2018, DG COMP asked for written submissions on the impact of digitalisation, which resulted in a total of 108 submissions. Given a total volume of over 900 pages, this paper draws on computer-assisted quantitative methods to structure and analyse this large amount of semantic data.[5] On the basis of these stakeholder contributions, the Commission organised a conference on competition policy-making in early 2019 and commissioned *Schweitzer/ Crémer/de Montjoye* to produce a "Report on Competition Law in the Digital Age" ("Expert Report"), which was published in the course of the same year.[6] This expert report, written by three independent special advisors, is intended to guide the realignment of European competition norms in the digital age and has been praised in the literature as a very sensible initiative.[7] It is already influencing the work of public authorities.

In view of the planned involvement of stakeholders, however, the extent lobbying has influenced the reforms planned by the Commission ought to be questioned.[8] The influence of lobbyists is of particular relevance in

5 Overview: Grimmer, Stewart, "Text as Data: The Promise and Pitfalls of Automatic Content Analysis Methods for Political Texts," 2013, p. 267; Silge, Robinson, *Text Mining with R. A Tidy Approach*, 2020. For the application of these methods in legal research, see: Coupette, Fleckner, "Quantitative Rechtswissenschaft. Sammlung, Analyse und Kommunikation juristischer Daten," 2018, p. 379; Vogel, Hamann, Gauer, "Computer-Assisted Legal Linguistics: Corpus Analysis as a New Tool for Legal Studies," 2018, p. 1340. For examples, see: Kalbheim, "Der Einfluss der Richter des Europäischen Gerichtshofs auf dessen Rechtsprechung – eine empirisch-statistische Analyse der Rolle des Berichterstatters," 2016, p. 431; Siems, "Statistische Rechtsvergleichung," 2008, p. 354.

6 Schweitzer, Crémer, Montjoye, "Report on Competition Law in the Digital Age," 2019.

7 De Pablo, "Shortcuts and Courts in the Era of Digitization," 2019, p. 1, 2. See also: Podszun, "Conference Debriefing (6): Shaping the Future of Competition Policy," 2019.

8 Theoretical overviews: Speth, Zimmer, *Lobby Work. Interessenvertretung als Politikgestaltung*, 2015, esp. pp. 31–52; Hillman, *The Political Economy of Protection*, 1989; and Grossman, Helpman, *Interest Groups and Trade Policy*, 2002. For an empirical overview, see: Potters, Sloof, "Interest groups: a survey of empirical models that try to assess their influence," 1996, p. 403. Lobbying from a legal perspective: Brouwer, "Lobby-Compliance: Wege zu einer besseren und transparenteren Gesetzgebung," 2019, p. 2; Pischel, Kopp, *Compliance für Wirtschaftsverbände*, 2017.

the competition law treatment of digital markets,[9] not least because the complex assessment of Big Data and algorithms increases the risk of biased expert testimony[10] and is therefore addressed in the context of this paper. For example, observers increasingly point to the efforts of undertakings grouped under the acronym "GAFAM" (Google, Apple, Facebook, Amazon, Microsoft) to change competition law in their favour.[11] According to figures from the *EU Transparency Register*, the technology lobby spends a total of about 20 million Euros per year in Brussels.[12] In addition to political influence,[13] this lobbying also extends to academic discourse, as illustrated by the contradictory literature on the *Google Search* decision,[14] which even includes an article commissioned by Google.[15] Since 2009, Google has been funding university professors to produce publications supporting its competition law positions.[16] The complainants' arguments also took the form of an academic article.[17]

At the same time, lobbying efforts by non-governmental organisations (e.g., Oxfam; Konzernmacht beschränken; UnternehmerGrün; digi-

---

9 Zuboff, *The Age of Surveillance Capitalism*, 2019, p. 124. See also: Foroohar, *Don't Be Evil: The Case Against Big Tech*, 2019.

10 Patterson, "Conflicts of Interest in Scientific Expert Testimony," 1999, p. 1313.

11 D'Souza, "Tech Lobby: Internet Giants Spend Record Amounts, Electronic Firms Trim Budget", 2019.

12 See https://ec.europa.eu/transparencyregister/public/homePage.do (accesed 15 May 2020).

13 See https://www.techtransparencyproject.org/googles-revolving-door-explorer-us (accessed 15 May 2020).

14 Some found a concentrated market for search engines: Lianos, Motchenkova, "Market Dominance and Search Quality in the Search Engine Market," 2013, p. 419; Argenton, Prüfer, "Search Engine Competition with Network Externalities," 2011, p. 73. Others, however, questioned the economic assumptions of the Commission and asked whether the latter actually possessed the right to intervene: Manne, Wright, "Google and the Limits of Antitrust: The Case Against the Antitrust Case Against Google," 2011, p. 171; Crane, "Search Neutrality and Referral Dominance," 2012, p. 459; Verhaert, "The Challenges Involved with the Application of Article 102 TFEU to the New Economy: a Case Study of Google," 2014, p. 265; Luchetta, "Is the Google Platform a Two-sided Market?," 2013, p. 185; Camesasca et al, "Google: Why the EU and US Positions Are an Ocean Apart," 2013, p. 35.

15 Bork, Sidak, "What Does the Chicago School Teach about Internet Search and the Antitrust Treatment of Google?," 2012, p. 663.

16 Mullins, Nicas, "Paying Professors: Inside Google's Academic Influence Campaign," 2017. See also: Zuboff, above fn 9, pp. 125f.; Hamburger, Gold, "Google, Once Disdainful of Lobbying, Now a Master of Washington Influence," 2014.

17 Hoppner, "Google: Friend or Foe of Ad-Financed Content Providers?," 2013, pp. 14–30.

talcourage) demanding stricter competition law treatment of technology undertakings are also growing. *Podszun* comments:

> The non-governmental organisations have only discovered the topic of antitrust law in recent years, it seems to me. [...] Here comes pressure from the left, broadening the spectrum of opinion in competition policy.[18]

By classifying, summarising, and assessing the submissions made by stakeholders in the consultation process, this paper offers a survey of this 'spectrum of opinion'. By extending the analysis to the footnote apparatus and the financial support mentioned therein, this lobbying dimension can be objectively assessed.[19]

As a result, this paper contributes to the legal discussion in four main ways. First, the main substantive challenges for EU competition law arising from data, algorithms, and platforms are concisely summarised and explained (B). This is followed by a quantitative and qualitative review of the consultation on the reform of EU competition law in the digital age, which has not yet taken place in the literature (C).[20] On this basis, it can be asked whether the expert report has led to a productive involvement of stakeholders—or whether the existing "cacophony of polarization"[21] has been further strengthened due to lobbying (D). By employing digital methods to analyse both stakeholder contributions and the expert report, this contribution shows that besides challenging competition law from a substantive point of view, digital innovations can also enrich the methodological toolkit of competition law researchers and enforcers and thereby help to prepare EU

18 Podszun, "GWB10: Die Lage," 2020.

19 Conceptually: Hamann, "Die Fußnote, das unbekannte Wesen – Potential und Grenzen juristischer Zitationsanalyse," 2014, p. 501; Eckert, "Danksagungen gegen den Strich lesen," 2020; Schmidt, "Zueignung aus Zuneigung – Vorstudien zu einer juristischen Dedikationslehre," 1990, p. 1121.

20 There are only a few short comments, such as: Völcker, Benditz, "Die Entwicklung des europäischen Kartellrechts in den Jahren 2018 und 2019," 2020, p. 259, 268; Podszun, above fn. 7, 2019; Murray, "European Commission conference on 'Shaping competition policy in an era of digitisation': 5 key points and practical implications," 2019; Gassler, "Why the introduction of a new transaction-value jurisdictional threshold for the EUMR has been postponed, at least for now," 2019. Particularly the stakeholder contributions have not been assessed.

21 Colomo, "From a distance, literally and figuratively," 2020. See also: Shapiro, "Antitrust in a Time of Populism," 2018, p. 714.

competition law for the digital age.[22] This last point is fleshed out in more detail in the concluding section (E).

B. Competition Law Issues in the Age of Digitalisation

In recent years, technological progress has enabled the development of numerous 'Schumpeterian' markets, collectively referred to as digital markets or the New Economy.[23] The reform proposals for competition law in the digital age to be discussed here presuppose that one can name the economic peculiarities of this 'digital age' and analyse their effects on competition law. The aim of this rather extensive section is thus to present the essential economic concepts and jurisprudential problem areas that might later play a prominent role in either the stakeholder contributions or the export report.

The digital age is based on the synergy of mathematics, computing power, and the internet. Together, these enable the collection of large amounts of data, the patterns of which can be analysed algorithmically.[24] The basic categories can therefore be obtained through a business perspective:[25] On the one hand, there are the central 'inputs' of digital undertakings, namely large datasets (I) and algorithms trained on them (II). On the other hand, consumers obtain certain 'outputs' via digital platforms (III).

I. Input 1: Data

Data, the 'oil' of the digital economy, acts as a central resource of digital, and increasingly traditional, industries by enabling new business models, identifying competitive information, and monopolising access to certain in-

22 There is a growing legal literature that aims to incorporate digital methods: Coupette, *Juristische Netzwerkforschung. Modellierung, Quantifizierung und Visualisierung relationaler Daten im Recht*, 2019. For an overview: Coupette, Fleckner, above fn. 5, p. 379; Vogel, Hamann, Gauer, above fn. 5, p. 1340.

23 Robertson, "Delineating Digital Markets under EU Competition Law: Challenging or Futile?," 2017, p. 131, 132.

24 Mehra, "Antitrust and the Robo-Seller: Competition in the Time of Algorithms," 2016, p. 1323, 1331.

25 See: Zuboff, above fn. 9, pp. 63–97.

formation.[26] This has attracted the attention of not only the public but also of the Commission. In addition to a basic definition of data, an adequate assessment under competition law requires differentiation on the basis of the way in which it is collected.

In a broad sense, all information is ultimately 'data'. In view of the much-discussed question in the literature as to whether data are to be assessed as 'raw' or as 'made,'[27] the realization that data are always obtained in a theory-driven manner is often forgotten.[28] If one equates data uniformly with 'information,' one underestimates the importance of interpretation and construction, the necessary selectivity of data, as well as their temporal variety.[29] It has thus become established in the literature to distinguish four types of data for analytical purposes based on the way they are collected.[30] This is a purely conceptual, i.e. non-legal, differentiation and distinguishes: (1) data provided from the direct actions of individuals; (2) observational data obtained from third parties and digitally recorded; (3) derived data that can be produced by logical operations from other data; and (4) tapped data, which is the product of probability-based analytical processes and used in industry to make behavioural predictions. Since Big Data technologies rely mainly on categories (3) and (4),[31] while data protection requirements mainly concern data in categories (1) and (2), this differentiation is seen as a useful approach to better analyse the individual and societal impact of the data economy and to determine regulatory requirements.[32]

It is debated whether access to data constitutes a competitive advantage that can lead to market dominance of incumbents.[33] The value of data

26 Graef, *EU Competition Law, Data Protection and Online Platforms: Data as Essential Facility*, 2016; Telle, "Konditionenmissbrauch durch Ausplünderung von Plattform-Nutzerdaten," 2016, p. 814; Louven, "Datenmacht und Zugang zu Daten," 2018, p. 217; Louven, "Datenzugangsverhältnis, FRAND und Wettbewerbsrecht," 2018, p. 230.

27 Gitelman, "*'Raw Data' is an Oxymoron*," 2013.

28 Ritschel, Müller, "Big Data als Theorieersatz?," 2016, p. 4, 7.

29 Matzner, "Beyond data as representation: The performativity of Big Data in surveillance," 2016, p. 197.

30 OECD, Working Party on Privacy and Security in the Digital Economy, "Summary of the OECD Privacy Expert Roundtable. Protecting Privacy in a Data-driven Economy: Taking Stock of Current Thinking," 2014, p. 5; *ICO*, p. 35.

31 Fischbach, "Big Data – Big Confusion. Weshalb es noch immer keine künstliche Intelligenz gibt," 2020, pp. 136, 142 ff.

32 Broemel, Trute, "Alles nur Datenschutz?," 2016, p. 50, 52.

33 Furman et al, "Unlocking Digital Competition: Report of the Digital Competition Expert Panel," 2019, p. 33.

collection arises from high volume, high velocity, and high variety, which allow for optimal transformation of data into patterns that can be exploited for monetary gain.[34] Whether data represents a competitive advantage thus depends on its substitutability, complementarity and, not least, scale. This makes it more difficult for competition authorities to make counterfactual predictions, such as those that have to be made in merger control (see below). Data-based knowledge can also perpetuate market power: Established undertakings that extract extensive data on user behaviour and user preferences through customer relationships can not only estimate a person's future purchasing behaviour more accurately, but also predict preferences of previously unknown users more easily than competitors.[35] In the event that data collection results in a competition law violation, two regulatory solutions are discussed: data access via Art. 102 TFEU; or increased data mobility.

Most recommendations focus on data sharing to reduce barriers to entry.[36] Reference is made to the essential facility doctrine,[37] an offence of abuse of a dominant position developed in case law (Art. 102(1) TFEU).[38] For such an abusive refusal to deal with facilities essential for entry into upstream or downstream markets, the test developed in *Magill*, *Bronner*, *IMS Health*, and *Microsoft* sets out cumulative requirements.[39] Abusive conduct occurs when access is essential, results in foreclosure of all competition in the downstream market, and cannot be objectively justified. Moreover, if an intellectual property right is involved, the denial of access must restrict

34 Stucke, Grunes, *Big Data and Competition Policy*, 2016, p. 26; Hu, Wen et al., "Toward Scalable Systems for Big Data Analytics: A Technology Tutorial," 2014, p. 652.

35 Monopolkommission, "Wettbewerbspolitik: Herausforderung digitale Märkte," 2015, paras. 67 ff.; Bundeskartellamt, "Arbeitspapier Marktmacht von Plattformen und Netzwerken," No. B6-113/15, 2016, pp. 91ff.; Autorité de la concurrence, Bundeskartellamt, "Competition Law and Data," 2016, pp. 11–25.; Podszun, Leber, "Internetkartellrecht," 2015, p. 316.

36 Bundesministerium für Wirtschaft und Energie, "Ein neuer Wettbewerbsrahmen für die Digitalwirtschaft: Bericht der Kommission Wettbewerbsrecht," 2019, p. 150, 156.

37 ECJ, Cases 6 and 773, ECLI:EU:C:1974:18 – *Commercial Solvents*; Jones, Sufrin, *EU Competition Law*, 2014, p. 496.

38 Emmerich, *Kartellrecht: Ein Studienbuch*, 2008, § 10, para. 35.

39 ECJ, Cases C-241/91 P and C-242/91 P, ECLI:EU:C:1995:98 – *Magill*, Rn. 56; ECJ, Case C-7/97, ECLI:EU:C:1998:569 – *Bronner*; ECJ, Case C-418/01, ECLI:EU:C:2004:257 – *IMS Health*; ECJ, Case T-201/04, ECLI:EU:T:2007:289 – *Microsoft*. For a discussion of the test with respect to data access: Bruc, "Data as an essential facility in European law: how to define the "target" market and divert the data pipeline?," 2019, p. 177, 182–186.

technical progress. For the competitive assessment of data access in terms of the essential facility doctrine, it is decisive whether a certain dataset constitutes an 'essential facility' and whether the respective access is 'indispensable.'[40] In principle, any asset and thus physical infrastructure facilities, movable tangible assets as well as intangible assets, can be considered as an essential facility. Data is rarely an indispensable input, as most data is generally available and non-rivalrous in nature.

Moreover, depending on how the data is collected, there are different impacts on entrepreneurial incentives to innovate[41] that can be raised under objective justification and then require balancing.[42] Requiring only data made available (category 1) or derived from routine user interactions (category 2) could limit unintended negative consequences on business incentives to innovate, while taking into account collisions with privacy and data protection requirements.[43]Access to derived or tapped data (categories 3 and 4) would be more useful for potential competitors, but could have negative consequences for technological development as trade secrets are likely to be revealed. Furthermore, Art. 102 TFEU does not take precedence over the fundamental right to privacy (Art. 8 EU Charter of Fundamental Rights). Finally, granting data access would be technically complicated and require the determination of FRAND rates for remuneration.[44]

Lack of data portability is a barrier to customers switching providers and is targeted by dominant digital undertakings to foreclose the market.[45] These barriers to entry between the platform and other competitors can be reduced through portability and interoperability. While portability allows one to seek another provider, interoperability allows providers to effectively integrate the new customer. Such a bottom-up approach to facilitating user switching is more proportionate than the previously described top-down approach of mandated data access.[46] Moreover, it could promote innova-

40 Graef, above fn. 26.

41 Graf, Mostyn, "European Union – Access to Online Platforms and Competition Law," 2019.

42 Bethell, Baird, Waksman, "Ensuring innovation through participative antitrust," 2020, p. 41.

43 WEF, "Competition Policy in a Globalized, Digitalized Economy," 2019, p. 11.

44 Dolmans, Pesch, "Should we disrupt antitrust law?," 2019, p. 1, 7.

45 Van Gorp, Batura et al, "Challenges for Competition Policy in a Digitalised Economy," 2015, p. 10.

46 Dolmans, Pesch, above fn. 44, p. 7.

tion competition if undertakings are incentivised to exchange data on a voluntary basis or at the instruction of the user.[47]

Portability is initially regulated by Art. 20 GDPR, which provides for a right to data portability. As *Graef* points out, observed and derived data (categories 2 to 4) are outside the scope of this provision.[48] Data interoperability is defined as the ability to transfer and make usable data and other information across systems, applications, or components. The decision in *Microsoft* highlights that a lack of interoperability can be classified as abusive behaviour.[49] Vendors do not gain access to information about users collected on a competing platform through interoperability,[50] so even if interoperability were present, access to certain databases would only be possible through the Bronner jurisprudence set out above.[51]

II. Input 2: Algorithms

Advanced algorithms have, in recent years and in certain application areas such as Go or poker, been able to learn complicated non-linear relationships while acting as complexly as humans. Before the disruptive potential of this technology can be assessed from a competition law perspective, algorithms need to be defined and differentiated. Algorithms are step-by-step procedures for solving problems.[52] A formal, broadest possible definition of 'algorithm' understands the latter as a unique, precise list of simple operations applied mechanically and systematically to a set of inputs to produce an output.[53]

The functioning of algorithms is largely determined by their design and the available data. In static algorithms, the generated sequence is followed unchanged, whereas dynamic algorithms can vary both the instruction sequence and the target.[54] Dynamic algorithms learn the optimal strategies with the data provided to them, evolve these strategies, and can thus

47 Bethell, Baird, Waksman, above fn. 42, p. 41.
48 Graef, above fn. 26, p. 146.
49 ECJ, Case T-201/04, ECLI:EU:T:2007:289 – *Microsoft*, paras. 649–659.
50 Graef, above fn. 26, p. 153.
51 Bruc, above fn. 39, p. 199.
52 Mehra, above fn. 24, pp. 1324 f.
53 Autorité de la concurrence, Bundeskartellamt, "Algorithms and Competition," 2019, pp. 3 f.
54 Bernhardt, Dewenter, "Collusion by code or algorithmic collusion," 2020, p. 1, 4.

quickly adapt to a changing context. Again, a distinction is made between supervised and unsupervised learning.[55] In supervised learning, a given solution is sought as an optimisation problem, whereas in unsupervised learning no objective function is given. In contrast to these variants of machine learning, the much-cited 'deep learning' does not refer to the type of learning, but to the type of computer programme used, the so-called artificial neural networks.[56]

These design decisions regarding the overall design and specific modifications imply that different types of algorithms can be distinguished. In particular, algorithms are designed for different application contexts, so they produce knowledge of varying quality[57] and exhibit significant differences in performance depending on market structure and market dynamics.[58] The following application types are predominantly discussed in the literature: Algorithms that help collect various data; algorithms for dynamic pricing; algorithms for personalising products and services (especially advertising); and algorithms for ranking purposes (e.g. search engines).[59]

Another significant differentiation results from the degree of algorithmic complexity. While so-called white-box algorithms are almost completely visible and understandable to humans with appropriate knowledge and equipment, most algorithms used in industry, especially if they are based on 'deep learning' methods, are so-called black-box algorithms whose results are no longer comprehensible to human observers.[60] For example, recent simulations show that algorithms based on neural networks can learn to communicate with each other independently and that the language produced in the process can only be partially interpreted by humans.[61] Overall, algorithmic performance comes at the price of limitations in its comprehensibility. From a regulatory point of view, the question is therefore raised

---

55 Autorité de la concurrence, Bundeskartellamt, above fn. 53, p. 85.

56 Goodfellow, Bengio, Courville, *Deep Learning*, 2016, p. 1.

57 Broemel, Trute, above fn. 32, pp. 53–60.

58 Van de Geer et al, "Dynamic Pricing and Learning with Competition: Insights from the Dynamic Pricing Challenge at the 2017 INFORMS RM & Pricing Conference," 2019, p. 185.

59 Overview based on: Autorité de la concurrence, Bundeskartellamt, above fn. 53, pp. 4–14.

60 Delibašić, "White-Box or Black-Box Decision Tree Algorithms: Which to Use in Education?," 2012, p. 287.

61 Sukhbaatar, Szlam, Fergus, "Learning Multiagent Communication with Backpropagation," 2016. See also: Abadi, Andersen, "Learning to Protect Communications with Adversarial Neural Cryptography," 2016.

as to whether algorithms should be designed in such a way that competition authorities can comprehend their logic in individual cases.[62]

In view of the different use cases and complexity of algorithms, a case-by-case assessment is appropriate.[63] For the question of assessment under competition law, the efficiency and welfare effects of algorithms must be contrasted with any possibilities of an infringement of competition.

On the one hand, the increasing use of algorithms can lead to considerable efficiency gains for undertakings and welfare gains for consumers. Algorithmic analysis of mass data promises to help undertakings make more, faster, better, and cheaper decisions.[64] The use of algorithms is not new or limited to digital businesses, but algorithmic pricing is easier in online environments, as the latter allow real-time data collection and automatic as well as frequent price adjustments.[65] By using pricing algorithms, undertakings can more easily monitor their own prices as well as competitors' prices and make quick adjustments to changing market conditions if necessary.[66] Algorithms can also contribute to greater transparency by analysing large amounts of data in a short time,[67] which in turn benefits consumers. According to *Gal and Elkin-Koren*, the use of price comparison and prediction platforms reduces transaction costs as well as the time spent searching and comparing alternative products.[68]

On the other hand, the high degree of market transparency brought about by algorithms can benefit possible collusion and thus lead to welfare losses.[69] For the assessment under competition law, two scenarios have to be distinguished.[70] When sellers use algorithms as a tool to form and maintain a cartel, they serve as a tool to facilitate collusion (collusion by code). Due to greater accuracy in detecting price changes, faster reaction to market pricing and automation, algorithms make it easier for firms to

62 Bernhardt, Dewenter, above fn. 54, pp. 24 f.

63 Broemel, Trute, above fn. 32, pp. 53–60.

64 Mehra, above fn. 24, p. 1363.

65 CMA, "Pricing Algorithms: Economic Working Paper on the Use of Algorithms to Facilitate Collusion and Personalised Pricing," 2018, pp. 1, 17–19.

66 Bernhardt, Dewenter, abobve fn 54, p. 5.

67 Autorité de la concurrence, Bundeskartellamt, above fn. 53, pp. 18 f.

68 Gal, Elkin-Koren, "Algorithmic Consumers," 2016, pp. 309, 326–28.

69 Bernhardt, Dewenter, above fn. 54, pp. 12 f.

70 Schwalbe, "Algorithms, Machine Learning, and Collusion," 2018, p. 568. See also: Ezrachi, Stucke, "Artificial Intelligence & Collusion: When Computers Inhibit Competition," 2017, p. 1775.

overprice[71] as well as stabilise collusive outcomes.[72] Such a scenario can still be assessed as an 'agreement' or 'concerted practice' under Art. 101 TFEU. Since it is plausible that in some cases algorithms reduce marginal costs to a greater extent than they increase marginal costs for consumers, a balancing within the meaning of Art. 101(3) TFEU is required in the individual case. If a third party is involved in the coordination by means of algorithms, it must be asked, according to the case law in *VM Remonts* and *Eturas*,[73] whether the competitors knew of the third party's anti-competitive actions or at least could have reasonably foreseen them.[74]

Moreover, pricing algorithms could coordinate price fixing without any human intervention (collusion of code), raising novel questions of liability or intent. While better monitoring and adaptation by advanced algorithms in the sense of 'conscious parallel behaviour' does not constitute a violation of Art. 101 TFEU,[75] such a violation would be found if these algorithms coordinate themselves and thus lead to concerted practices of two competitors.[76] *Ezrachi and Stucke* in particular assume that algorithmic collusion is indeed possible and very simple.[77] In contrast, both the computer science literature on cooperation between algorithms and the economic literature on collusion in oligopolies suggest that tacit collusive behaviour can only be achieved under difficult conditions.[78] Moreover, some basic assumptions of this theory of harm, such as homogeneous goods and equal algorithms, do not hold in most digital markets.[79] Finally, there is a lack of empirical evidence.[80]

71 Mehra, above fn 24, p. 1323, 1340–51, 1357.

72 Ezrachi, Stucke, "Virtual Competition," 2016, p. 585.

73 ECJ, Case C-542/14, ECLI:EU:C:2016:578 – *VM Remonts*, paras. 27ff.; ECJ, Case C-74/14, ECLI:EU:C:2016:42 – *Eturas*, para. 44.

74 For a discussion: Ezrachi, Stucke, above fn. 70, p. 1775, 1801; Autorité de la concurrence, Bundeskartellamt, above fn. 53, pp. 68–74.

75 Weck, "Current Issues of Competition Policy in E Commerce, 2nd CoRe Conference Proceedings: Current Issues of Competition Policy in E-Commerce," 2019, p. IX, XII; Wiedemann, *Kartellrecht*, 2020, § 8 Rechtsgrundlagen para. 12.

76 Bernhardt, Dewenter, above fn. 54, p. 1, 8.

77 Ezrachi, Stucke, above fn. 72, p. 585; Ezrachi, Stucke, above fn. 70, p. 1775; Ezrachi, Stucke, "Two Artificial Neural Networks Meet in an Online Hub and Change the Future (of Competition, Market Dynamics and Society)," 2017. Similar: Woodcock, "The Bargaining Robot," 2017; Pasquale, *The Black Box Society: The Secret Algorithms that Control Money and Information*, 2016.

78 Schwalbe, above fn. 70, p. 596.

79 Petit, "Antitrust and Artificial Intelligence: A Research Agenda," 2017, p. 361.

80 Ballard, Naik, "Algorithms, Artificial Intelligence, and Joint Conduct," 2017, p. 29.

In addition to opportunities for collusion, the automation of pricing by algorithms could lead to different consumers being charged different amounts for the same good or service, which has led to a debate on algorithmic price discrimination.[81] By algorithmically evaluating consumer preferences, buying habits, search histories, etc., undertakings can charge personalised prices by exploiting differences in willingness to pay.[82] Well-known examples are the pricing algorithms of modern airlines and Google's dominant auction algorithm for personalised ad placement. Such price discrimination between customers has in principle ambiguous effects on competition and consumer welfare.[83] In addition to disclosure obligations,[84] abusive discrimination under Art. 102 TFEU may follow from individualised pricing.[85]

For legal regulation, this may give rise to a need for protection against algorithm-based attributions,[86] for example by excluding influencing factors that are normatively classified as abusive, which in turn requires the algorithms to be certified accordingly.[87] *Harrington* proposes to prohibit the use of algorithms with certain features that allow undertakings to set prices above the competitive equilibrium price.[88] Such concerns are also reflected in the call for 'algorithmic neutrality' to prevent economically or socially harmful distortions.[89] However, due to the heterogeneity of algorithms outlined above, a review of them by competition authorities would be a task that would be virtually impossible to fulfil, especially since most algorithms used are constantly modifying themselves through machine learning.[90] Whether the use of algorithms ultimately increases

81 Borgesius, Poort, "Online price discrimination and EU data privacy law," 2017, pp. 347–366.

82 Schwalbe, above fn. 70, p. 571.

83 Autorité de la concurrence, Bundeskartellamt, above fn. 53, pp. 61 ff.

84 For those, see: Zander-Hayat, Reisch, Steffen, "Personalisierte Preise – Eine verbraucherpolitische Einordnung," 2016, p. 403, 407; Paal, "Missbrauchstatbestand und Algorithmic Pricing," 2019, p. 43, 44.

85 Paal, above fn. 84, p. 47.

86 Broemel, Trute, above fn. 32, p. 55.

87 Schweitzer, Fetzer, Peitz, "Digitale Plattformen: Bausteine für einen künftigen Ordnungsrahmen," 2016, pp. 12 f.

88 Harrington Jr, "Developing Competition Law for Collusion by Autonomous Price-setting Agents," 2017.

89 Mehra, above fn. 24, pp. 1326, 1332. See also: Borocas and Selbst, "Big Data's disparate Impact," 2016, p. 671.

90 Schwalbe, above fn. 70, p. 599.

competitive pressure or reduces consumer welfare is not obvious in the end. A case-by-case assessment is necessary.

III. Output: Platforms

Based on the algorithmic analysis of large datasets, platforms—key players in digital markets—generate increases in consumer welfare by reducing transaction costs, creating new products, enabling innovative transaction types, or bringing about better 'matching' between market participants. Understanding the competitive dynamics in the relevant market requires differentiation by business model. Certain characteristics of platforms such as multi-sidedness, free pricing, and network effects require the adaptation of traditional competition law instruments.

Digital markets are typically enabled and dominated by platforms that involve the interaction of different but independent groups of users.[91] Such multi-sided markets thus bring together two (or more) distinct product markets, whose interconnectedness makes it impossible to consider one market without also considering the other. While this phenomenon is by no means limited to digital markets, platforms are particularly common in the new economy.[92] Such platforms are intermediaries that reduce transaction costs for market participants.[93] In contrast to traditional firms, platforms usually focus first on creating a critical mass of participants to generate network effects before exploiting the latter for monetisation purposes.[94]

The markets for digital platforms have characteristics that need to be taken into account when analysing their competitive conditions.[95] Platforms benefit from direct network effects when the utility of the service for one user increases directly with the number of other users of that service. Moreover, their versatile nature implies that cross-network (indirect) exter-

---

91 Rochet, Tirole, "Platform competition in two-sided markets," 2003, p. 990; Monopolkommission, above fn. 35, paras. 34 ff.; Bundeskartellamt, above fn. 35, pp. 3 ff. For definitions: Rochet, Tirole, "Two-Sided Markets: A Progress Report," 2006, p. 645, 645; Rysman, "The Economics of Two-Sided Markets," 2009, p. 125, 126.

92 Hoppner, "Defining Markets for Multi-Sided Platforms: The Case of Search Engines," 2015, p. 349.

93 Evans, Schmalensee, *Matchmakers: The New Economics of Multisided Platforms*, 2016, p. 8, 15.

94 WEF, "Platforms and Ecosystems," 2019, p. 11.

95 Farrel, Saloner, "Standardization, Compatibility and Innovation," 1985, p. 70.

nalities arise where a higher number of users leads to a higher provision of compatible goods, which in return makes the original product more valuable again. Direct and indirect network effects imply that the efficiency and utility for users of platforms increases with their size, which in turn influences the prices charged on the different sides of the platform.[96] Such network effects have been emphasised, for example, in the Commission's *Google/DoubleClick* merger decision[97] and by the *Bundeskartellamt* in its assessment of hotel booking platforms.[98] Another characteristic of platforms is economies of scale, as they have a relatively high share of fixed costs and low variable costs.[99]

Platforms differ in important ways, including how they generate income, their size, and their profitability.[100] Significant differences exist between platforms that generate revenue from advertising to fund 'free' user services (e.g., Google, Facebook) and those that charge transactional commissions or fees (e.g., Uber, Airbnb). In addition, a distinction can be made between transactional and non-transactional two-sided markets.[101] Such differences in revenue generation are important to understand the competitive dynamics in the relevant market. For example, multihoming (i.e., switching between or simultaneously using competitors' services) may be prevalent on one or both sides of the platform, depending on the platform's business model.[102] The relevance of user data to the operation of the platform also differs by revenue generation model. Moreover, the heterogeneous nature of platforms suggests that the subsidiarity principle is particularly relevant for the enforcement of EU competition law in this area.[103]

A comprehensive competition law assessment of platforms recognizes, on the one hand, their competition-enhancing effects and, on the other hand, their potential to disrupt free competition. Their assessment under competition law thus generally requires a balancing case-by-case consideration.

96 Pohlmeier, *Netzwerkeffekte und Kartellrecht*, 2004, p. 29.

97 Commission, 11.3.2008, M.4731 – *Google/DoubleClick*, para. 290.

98 Bundeskartellamt, 20.12.2013, Case B9–66/10 – *HRS*, para. 81; *Ellger*, in: Immenga and Mestmäcker, *EU-Wettbewerbsrecht*, 2019, Art. 101 Abs. 3 AEUV, paras. 602–605.

99 Duch-Brown, "The Competitive Landscape of Online Platforms," 2017, pp. 1, 4 f.

100 WEF, above fn. 43, p. 6.

101 Filistrucchi, Geradin, van Damme, Affeldt, "Market Definition in Two-Sided Markets: Theory and Practice," 2014, pp. 293, 298, 300–302.

102 WEF, above fn. 43, p. 6.

103 BMA, ACM, CDLCL, "Joint memorandum of the Belgian, Dutch and Luxembourg competition authorities on challenges faced by competition authorities in a digital world," 2019, p. 6.

To begin with, the digitalisation of the economy and the accompanying market success of large platforms has led to pro-competitive effects that are recognised by competition authorities.[104] First, even if they offer different products and services, platforms compete for the attention of the same users ('attention competition'), not least with the aim of attracting advertisers.[105] For the same reason, there is ongoing competition for the development of new technologies such as AI ('innovation competition'),[106] which should benefit consumers. Second, platforms can stimulate competition in external markets if they reduce logistics and payment processing costs for other undertakings, improve communication between suppliers and consumers, and provide personalised advertising opportunities.[107] By allowing all undertakings in a market to use the same digital distribution channel, platforms level the playing field to a certain extent.

In addition to their potential to increase competition, digital business models also raise competition concerns and questions about the suitability of the current legal framework. After a discussion of the cross-cutting issue of market definition, the remainder of this section addresses the implications for the three European antitrust 'pillars:' vertical restraints as defined in Art. 101 TFEU; abuse of market power as defined in Art. 102 TFEU; and catch-all problems of the existing merger control procedure.

A competitive analysis first correctly defines the relevant markets in order to be able to assess whether a dominant position exists in the market in question.[108] Digital markets can be defined as those in which undertakings develop new technologies and apply them to existing businesses or produce new services using digital capabilities.[109] They rely heavily on innovation, often have short product cycles, and are highly dynamic. In addition, market entry barriers are often low.[110] These characteristics go hand in hand with the need to frequently redefine cartel markets, as an already defined relevant market will soon no longer correspond to the economic realities.[111] Another special feature results from the fast and low-cost product differen-

104 ACCC, "Digital Platforms Inquiry: final report," 2019, p. 1.

105 Evans, "Attention Rivalry Among Online Platforms," 2013, p. 313.

106 Furman et al, above fn. 33, p. 20.

107 Walker, "Competition policy and digital platforms: six uncontroversial propositions," 2020, pp. 1–2.

108 Paal, above fn. 84, p. 45.

109 CMA, "The CMA's Digital Markets Strategy," 2019, p. 5.

110 Monopolkommission, above fn. 35, para. 19.

111 Pitofsky, "New Definitions of Relevant Market and the Assault on Antitrust," 1990, p. 1805, 1812.

tiation. As digitalisation further blurs the line between offline and online businesses, concepts such as digital markets may become highly relevant.

Additional problems arise in the market definition of platform markets. In multi-sided markets, it would be inappropriate to distinguish several isolated product markets, as they cannot be properly understood in isolation.[112] Scenarios in which a digital service is provided free of charge to a specific group of customers are also problematic. In defining the relevant market, the (allegedly) free side of the market can either be part of the platform market, which consists of the two sides of the market, or it could be conceived as one of the two separate relevant markets that together form the platform.[113] Similar issues arise in relation to the role of data in these markets: As *Evans* notes, the value of data is difficult to determine and can be seen as close to zero.[114] With a base price of zero, the SSNIP test for market definition is no longer functional.[115]

However, price is only one dimension of competition and in competition law analysis must be compared with other variables such as quality and innovation.[116] This makes it possible to take into account that customer attention/data is the real 'currency' in digital markets.[117] Thus, market boundaries can also be assessed by measuring the impact of a small but significant and non-transitory loss of quality (SSNDQ test).[118] If the customer's numbers can be quantified by data or attention, a test based on cost changes can be created (SSNIC test).[119] Thus, market definition remains an important step in antitrust analysis.

The case law to date illustrates numerous possibilities of vertical restraints of competition in the digital age.[120] Platforms can coordinate the behaviour of their various suppliers (e.g., sellers in a marketplace), whereby it is often difficult to decide whether these are hub-and-spoke cartels within the meaning of Art. 101(1) TFEU or merely vertical price moderation.[121]

---

112 Monopolkommission, above fn. 35, pp. 136–143.

113 Robertson, above fn. 25, p. 141.

114 Evans, "The Antitrust Economics of Free," 2011, p. 1.

115 Sharma, "SSNIP Test: A Useful Tool, Not a Panacea," 2011, p. 188.

116 Bruc, above fn. 39, pp. 188 f.

117 Newman, "Antitrust in Zero-price Markets: Foundation," 2015, p. 149, 202.

118 Gal, Rubinfeld, "The Hidden Costs of Free Goods: Implications for Antitrust Enforcement," 2016, p. 521, 551.

119 Newman, above fn. 117, p. 164.

120 For an overview: WEF, above fn. 43, p. 9.

121 Künstner, „Preissetzung durch Algorithmen als Herausforderung des Kartellrechts, " 2019, p. 36, 39.

Also relevant is 'resale price maintenance,' as the effects of this vertical price maintenance, which is prohibited under competition law, are intensified by the use of price algorithms and the associated reaction linkage of online traders.[122] Also worth mentioning are 'most favoured nation' clauses, where platforms (e.g. online travel agencies) seek parity between the price and other terms of sale on their platform and their own website and the sales channels and/or other platforms of the supplier (e.g. a hotel).[123] 'Selective distribution agreements' can further restrict merchants' ability to sell online. Most, if not all, of these vertical restraints lead to both efficiencies and reductions in free competition.

The traditional starting point for measuring market power is the market share of the company under investigation in the relevant market.[124] This approach needs to be adapted for multisided markets. In multi-sided markets, where prices do not reflect the value of a product/service to customers due to network effects, market shares are very volatile and less meaningful in terms of sustainable market power.[125] In such markets, innovation is often the more important competitive parameter.[126] Moreover, concentration on one side of the market may over- or underestimate the degree of market power if the influence of competitive conditions on the other side is not assessed.[127] Multihoming by customers should be taken into account as it may overcome the concentration tendency caused by network effects. The market position of competitors, barriers to entry, and countervailing buyer power are also decisive criteria for measuring market power.[128] In practice, it has been found that in digital markets there is competition for the market rather than competition in the market.[129] .

122 Künstner, ibid., p. 40. Similar: WEF, above fn. 43, p. 9.

123 Bundeskartellamt, 20.12.2013, Case B9–66/10 – *HRS*, para. 20. See also: Akman, "A Competition Law Assessment of Platform Most-Favoured-Customer Clauses", 2016, p. 781.

124 Collyer, Mullan, Timan, "Measuring Market Power in Multi-Sided Markets," 2017, p. 1.

125 Robertson, above fn. 25, p. 133; Ahlborn, Evans, Padilla, "Competition Policy in the New Economy: Is European Competition Law Up to the Challenge?," 2001, p. 156, 162.

126 Monopolkommission, above fn. 35, para. 8.

127 OECD, "Background Note: Latin American and Caribbean Competition Forum – Session III: Practical Approaches to Assessing Digital Platform Markets for Competition Law Enforcement," 2019, pp. 21ff.

128 WEF, above fn. 43, p. 10.

129 Geroski, "Competition in Markets and Competition for Markets," 2003, p. 151, 152.

Due to the network effects described above, there is a widespread perception that digital markets tend towards concentration or even natural monopolies.[130] Thus, there is a fear that data-driven markets can lead to an outcome where the winner takes all market share when further concentration is a likely outcome of market success.[131] This is particularly evident in AI-based feedback loops: the more data a dominant company has, the more its AI improves (which in turn improves the products or services it offers). As a crucial information hub, platforms also have considerable bargaining power between suppliers and consumers.[132] Empirical results confirm that rapid self-correction is not to be expected in markets dominated by digital platforms.[133] However, it should be noted that strong network effects make these markets not only concentrated but also effective. So far, there is no clear benchmark for efficient market structure in platform markets.[134]

In any case, market power does not yet constitute an offence punishable under Art. 102 TFEU. An indication of resulting competition law infringements is provided by recent decisions in the context of digital platforms, which concerned the transfer of market power to another market, exclusivity agreements, tying and bundling of products, and the combination of user data. It is to be expected that the 'exploitative abuse' approach, the role of platforms' terms and conditions, and the possible discrimination of third parties in platforms with a 'dual role,' as well as access to databases, will play a greater role in the future.[135] There are calls in the literature to facilitate competition law intervention against platforms by narrowing the market definition, stricter rules for unilateral conduct, avoiding the framework for market dominance altogether, or sanctioning strategies to prevent multi-homing.[136]

Due to the aforementioned network effects, the barriers to entry into digital markets are comparatively high, which is why the social costs of

130 WEF, above fn. 94, p. 16.

131 Bruc, above fn. 39, p. 206.

132 Lianos, Motchenkova, above fn. 14, p. 419.

133 Stigler Center for the Study of the Economy and the State, *Report of the Committee for the Study of Digital Platforms: Markets Structure and Antitrust Subcommittee*, 2019, p. 81.

134 Duch-Brown, above fn. 99, p. 7.

135 Mandrescu, "Applying EU Competition Law to Online Platforms: The Road Ahead – Part 2," 2017, p. 410.

136 For a summary, see: Bundesministerium für Wirtschaft und Energie, above fn. 36, pp. 62 ff., 157 f.

improper merger clearance are presumably higher than in traditional markets.[137] Nevertheless, not one of the more than 400 acquisitions made by GAFAM between 2008–18 was blocked by competition authorities.[138] These are not, contrary to some statements in the literature, 'killer acquisitions.'[139] The real danger for competition comes from the fact that market-dominant platforms buy up start-ups with a rapidly growing user base before the effects could be examined under the EU Merger Regulation.[140]

This raises two problems in particular for merger control review. First, acquisitions of start-ups by established technology undertakings do not always meet the turnover-based thresholds that trigger a merger review and/or notification obligation.[141] Second, the competitive assessment of the merger depends on the counterfactual situation that would have arisen without the acquisition, which can only be predicted with great uncertainty in dynamic markets.[142]

Therefore, in addition to stronger enforcement of merger control within the current framework,[143] it has been suggested that merger control should be reformed by covering more transactions (e.g., by changing the thresholds), stricter merger control standards, or the introduction of ex-post control.[144] In particular, voices in the Anglo-Saxon literature call for stricter control of vertical mergers,[145] which have so far been assessed as economically beneficial.[146] In contrast, individual authors point to the need for a credible 'exit' strategy to generate risk capital[147] and the possible technical synergies and spillovers that can be invoked in the context of an 'efficiency defence.'[148]

137 Lear, "Ex-post assessment of merger control decisions in digital markets," 2019, p. xiv.

138 Furman et al, above fn. 33, p. 12.

139 Bitton, Dolmans, Mostyn, Pearl, "Competition In Display Ad Technology: A Retrospective Look At Google/Doubleclick and Google/Admob," 2019.

140 BMA, ACM, CDLCL, above fn. 103, p. 2.

141 Furman et al, above fn. 33, p. 94.

142 Walker, above fn. 107, p. 7.

143 Salop, "Invigorating Vertical Merger Enforcement," 2018, pp. 1962, 1963–1966.

144 Lear, above fn. 137, pp. xii–xiv.

145 Khan, "Amazon's Antitrust Paradox," 2017, p. 710, 797.

146 For an empirical overview, see: Lafontaine, Slade, "Vertical Integration and Firm Boundaries: The Evidence," 2007, p. 629.

147 Sokol, "Vertical Mergers and Entrepreneurial Exit," 2018, p. 1357; WEF, above fn. 43, p. 12

148 Kokkoris, Valletti, "Innovation Considerations in Horizontal Merger Control," 2020, pp. 1, 32–34.

IV. Interim result

Most business models of digital platforms based on big data and self-learning algorithms lead to both positive and negative effects on competition and consumer welfare, with the former tending to be static and the latter more dynamic. As a result, a balancing decision usually has to be made by the competition authority. After this extensive overview of the basic problem areas and conflicts of opinion, the following section is devoted to the arguments submitted by various stakeholders in the context of the conference organised by the Commission on 'Designing Competition Policy in the Age of Digitalisation.'

C. Stakeholder Contributions

The Commission organised a conference on 'Designing Competition Policy in the Age of Digitalisation' on 17 January 2019 as part of a broader work stream, including preparation for the expert report mentioned in the introduction. Against this background, the Commission asked for contributions of up to ten pages from stakeholders 'involved in or affected by the digitisation of the economy' to improve legislative brainstorming through stakeholder engagement.[149] As the basis for the conference and expert report, the contributions, according to the Commission, 'made a valuable contribution' to its work.[150] The conference was positively received and is considered a 'milestone' in Vestager's tenure.

I. Overview

A total of 108 contributions with a total length of 901 pages were submitted, with the length of individual contributions varying from one page to 25 pages (mean: 8 pages). Almost all contributions were written in English. As can be seen in Figure 1, most contributions come from industry represen-

149 All contributions: https://ec.europa.eu/competition/scp19/media_en.html (15.05.2020). In the following, all references to individual stakeholder contributions will be made by referring to the name of the submitting party in italics. They are not listed separately in the bibliography.

150 Call for Contributions: https://ec.europa.eu/competition/scp19/ (accessed 5 May 2020).

tatives (26), undertakings (25), and academics (23). In contrast, representatives of civil society appear underrepresented (workers' associations: 3, NGOs: 4, think tanks: 14).

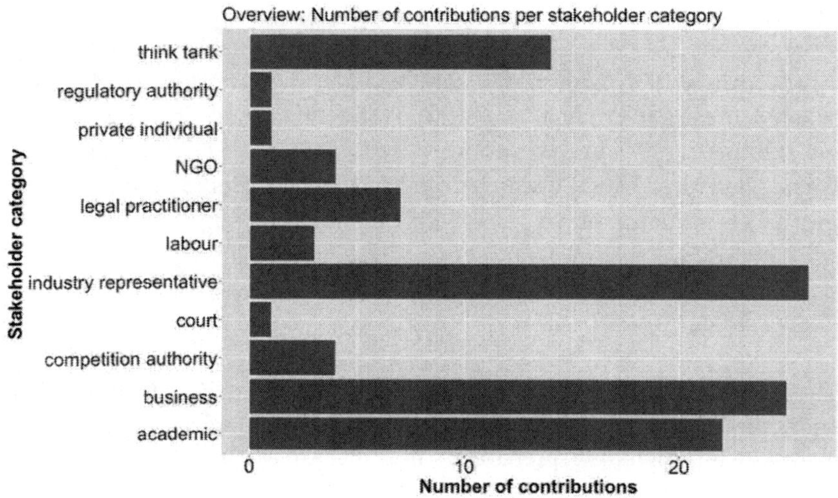

Figure 1

However, the influence of a particular interest group is not only determined by the absolute number of contributions submitted, but also by their length. Figure 2 illustrates the range as well as the average length of the contributions, again sorted by institutional background of the stakeholders. According to this, almost all stakeholders kept to the specified 10 pages.

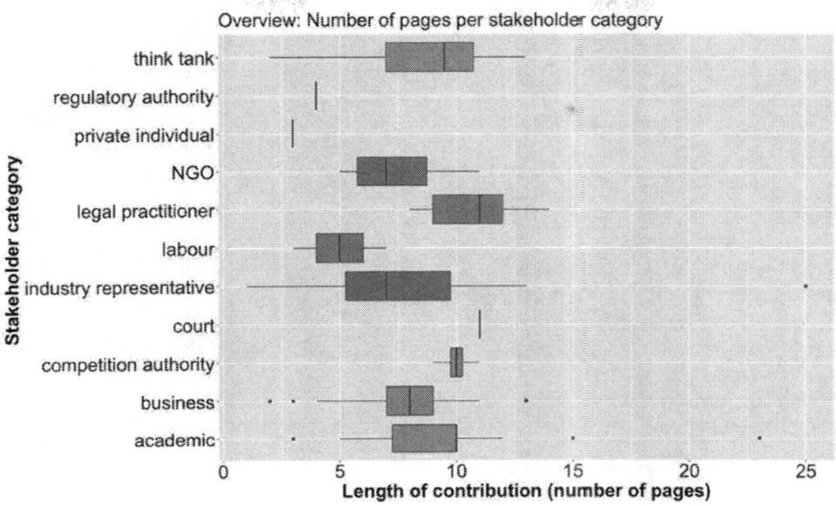

Figure 2

In addition to a breakdown by institutional background, the contributions submitted can be classified by the geographical origin and economic sector concerned (Figure 3). As can be seen from the resulting visual overview, most contributions came from stakeholders operating across Europe (26) or from stakeholders based in one of the three major European countries (UK: 15, Germany: 14, France: 11). However, there were also numerous contributions from international stakeholders (17), with a focus on the USA (8).

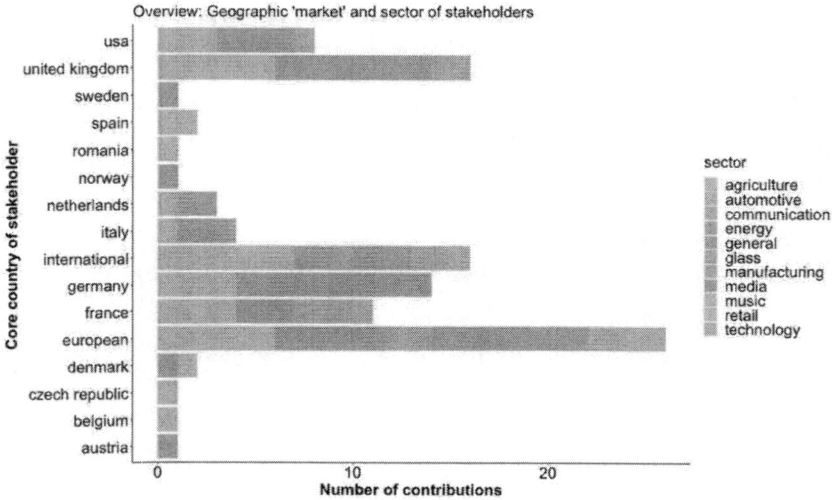

Figure 3

Due to the prominence of large platforms such as Google, the relationship between national and multinational undertakings (Figure 4) can also be brought into question. An exclusive consideration of the contributions submitted by undertakings shows a total of at least eight undertakings that are active multinationally (International: 4, USA: 4).

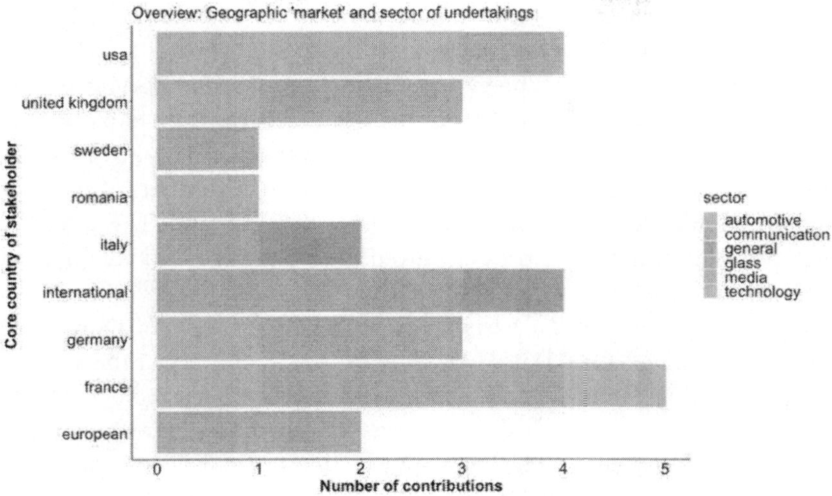

Figure 4

The lobbying literature assumes that regulatory protection decreases as the share of multinationals increases, and that the latter tend to have less—but still significant—political influence.[151] It is therefore necessary to examine to what extent the influence of contributions classified as American or international differs from the influence of contributions from European stakeholders. This will be done in the following, first in a quantitative way (by means of Topic Modelling) and then qualitatively (through close reading).

II. Quantitative analysis

Topic modelling is a probability-based method for exploring larger text collections, based on the algorithm developed by *Blei, Ng and Jordan*.[152] The method generates statistical models (topics) for mapping frequent

151 Hillman, Ursprung, "Multinational firms, political competition, and international trade policy," 1993, p. 347. See also: Grossman, Helpman, "Foreign investment with endogenous protection," 1996, pp. 199–223.

152 Blei, Ng, Jordan, "Latent Dirichlet Allocation," 2003, p. 993; Blei, "Probabilistic Topic Models," 2012, p. 77.

common occurrences of words.[153] The topic modelling method makes it possible to structure large amounts of text thematically in an objective way. It is assumed that a collection of texts consists of different discourses, the so-called 'topics,' which occur to varying degrees in the individual texts. A 'topic' is defined as a group of words that occur together in a text in a way that is statistically significant. For example, if the algorithm identifies a topic that contains the words 'competition,' 'law,' '101,' '102,' and 'TFEU' with a high probability, it can be manually given the label 'European competition law.'

In the following, a special variant of topic modelling, so-called Structural Topic Modelling (STM), is used and applied to the entirety of the submitted contributions with the help of the programming language 'R.'[154] STM has been successfully applied in a variety of different contexts in social science and the humanities.[155] The aim of this method is to analyse the relationship of the estimated topics to other information about the underlying texts, so-called metadata. This is done by taking metadata into account when the algorithm models the topics. Here, the institutional categories of stakeholders are used as metadata.

STM assumes a fixed, user-defined number of topics. There is no 'right' number of topics appropriate for a given corpus,[156] but researchers predominantly use a smaller number between 5 and 15.[157] In line with the literature, the following topic model estimates 10 topics, which also corresponds to the number of identified stakeholder categories.[158] The quantitative significance of the different discourses can be visually reflected by the distribution of the estimated topics within the corpus of contributions (Figure 5). Efficiency and innovation benefits of digitalisation (Topics 5 and 6), exploitation

153 Horstmann, "Topic Modeling," 2018; Jannidis, "Quantitative Analyse literarischer Texte am Beispiel des Topic Modeling," 2016, p. 24.

154 For the technical background, see: Silge, Robinson, above fn. 5; Roberts, Stewart, Tingley, "stm: R Package for Structural Topic Models," 2019, p. 1.

155 Küsters, Volkind, Wagner, "Digital Humanities and the State of Legal History. A Text Mining Perspective," 2019, p. 244. See also: Roberts, Stewart, Airoldi, "A model of text for experimentation in the social sciences," 2016, p. 988; Roberts et al, "Structural Topic Models for Open-Ended Survey Responses," 2014, p. 1064.

156 Grimmer, Stewart, above fn. 5, p. 267.

157 Wehrheim, "Economic history goes digital: topic modeling the Journal of Economic History," 2019, p. 83, 113; Ferri, Lusiani, Pareschi, "Accounting for Accounting History: A Topic modeling Approach (1996–2015)," 2018, p. 173.

158 For reasons of space, it was not possible to print the entire topic table with word profiles. On request, these results can be obtained from the author.

abuse (Topic 1) and data protection (Topic 4) issues are particularly prominent, followed by discussions about platforms (Topic 9) and algorithms (Topic 10) in general.

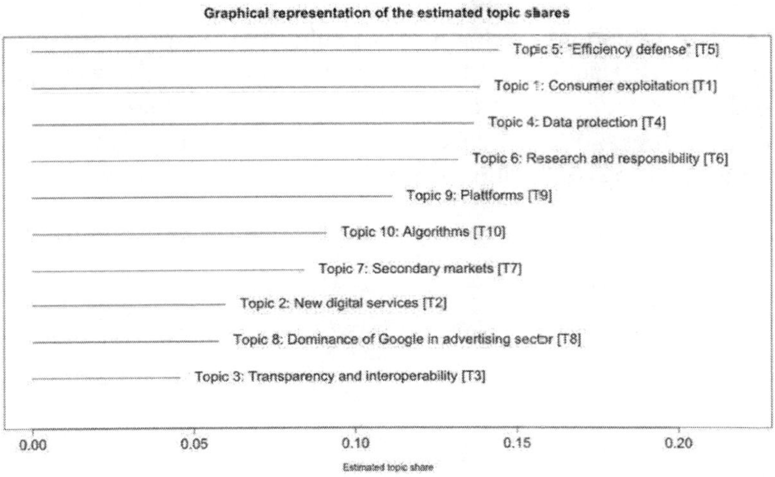

Figure 5

Not all of the estimated topics deal with competition law issues in the narrower sense, which statistically is to be expected. Nevertheless, four relevant discourses in particular can be identified which need to be substantiated in the subsequent qualitative analysis. First of all, it is striking that the word 'data' is distributed across various topics, while algorithms and platforms are each given their own clearly defined topic. This reflects, on the one hand, that data, as a central input, is a cross-cutting topic, but on the other hand also that some stakeholders, such as NGOs, focus on data protection aspects, for which a separate topic is thus appreciated (Topic 4). The hypothesis of an impending algorithmic collusion is reflected in detail by Topic 10, while Topic 9 theoretically receives platforms (including words like 'two-sided', 'eco-systems') and addresses the resulting limitations of 'multi-homing.' Finally, Topic 5 is worth mentioning, highlighting the pro-competitive effects of platforms such as 'efficiency,' 'scaling,' and 'innovation,' which could be invoked by undertakings in the context of an 'efficiency defence.'[159]

Compared to traditional topic models, STM is characterised by the fact that metadata is taken into account when modelling the topics. In the present case, the institutional context of the submitted contributions was taken into account in such a way that it influences the respective frequency with which a certain topic is discussed.[160] In line with the lobbying question posed at the beginning of this paper, the following figures compare the semantic contrast between the contributions submitted by undertakings on the one hand and competition authorities or academics, respectively, on the other.

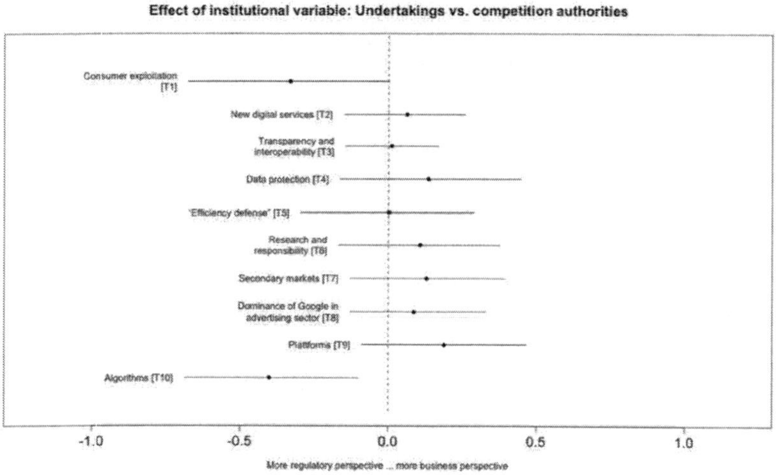

Figure 6

Figure 6 compares the different probabilities with which the ten topics that were estimated by the STM are mentioned by undertakings and competition authorities. Not surprisingly, consumer exploitation issues (Topic 1) and theoretical aspects of algorithms (Topic 10) are pre-dominantly addressed by competition authorities, while comments on the new digital

159 Riziotis, "Efficiency Defence in Article 82 EC," 2008, pp. 98–115. See also: Kuoppamäki, Torstila, "Is There a Future for an Efficiency Defence in European Merger Control?," 2015.

160 Roberts, Stewart, Tingley, above fn. 154, p. 1.

services (Topic 2) or the dominance of Google in the advertising sector (Topic 8) are more frequently found in corporate contributions. The central point of discussion among undertakings is clearly in the area of platforms (Topic 9).

Figure 7 shows the frequency with which the same ten topics are discussed by undertakings and academics. As expected, undertakings avoid the topic of data protection (Topic 4) and prefer to focus on the description of their new digital services (Topic 2) and their research efforts (Topic 6). Efficiency arguments are mentioned not only by undertakings but also by academics. Again, issues of consumer exploitation (the word profile of Topic 1 presumably includes concepts such as 'attention market'[161] and 'exploitation') are ignored by undertakings and only addressed by academics. And as in the case of the previous comparison, companies tend to focus on platforms and their underlying business models (Topic 9), while academics tend to focus on algorithms (Topic 10). On the one hand, this shows how strongly *Ezrachi and Stucke*'s well-known theoretical argument about algorithmic collusion has shaped the academic discourse of researchers at universities or in competition authorities recently. On the other hand, as the qualitative analysis in the next section shows, the platform focus on part of undertakings can be explained by the high proportion of European undertakings that want to subject their American competitors to stricter competition law treatment.

161 Evans, above fn. 105, p. 313.

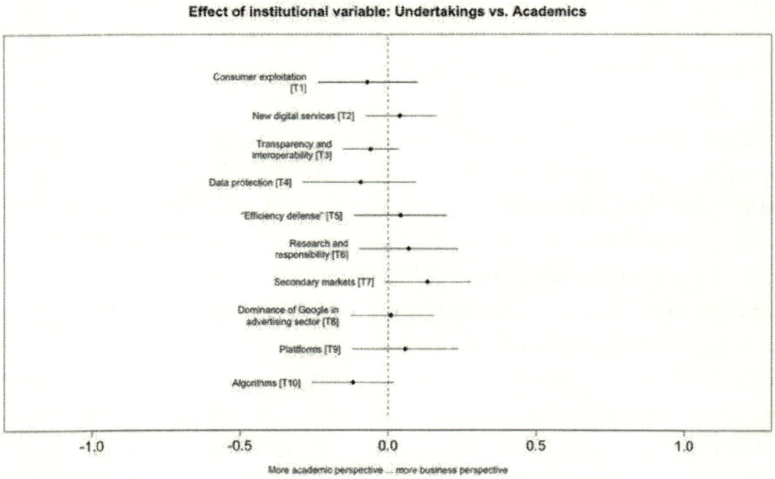

Figure 7

III. Qualitative Analysis

This section discusses the contributions submitted by undertakings (1) and academics (2) on a qualitative level and compares the differences in content between European and 'external' stakeholders against the background of the lobbying problem described in the introduction.

1. Undertakings

In fact, among the 25 undertakings represented, there are only two GAFAM representatives, namely Facebook and Microsoft. In their contributions, both undertakings describe that they are part of a dynamic industry characterised by disruptive innovation, low barriers to entry, and strong competition for the attention of consumers and advertisers.[162] In addition, Big Data is denied the characteristic of being a competitive 'bottleneck.'[163] All in all,

162 *Facebook*, pp. 1–6; *Microsoft*, p. 7.

163 *Facebook*, pp. 6–8; *Microsoft*, pp. 3–6. In this regard, Microsoft refers to the scheme developed with the law firms Herrington & Sutcliffe and Latham & Watkins in: Sivinski, Okuliar, Kjolbye, "Is big data a big deal? A competition law approach to big data," 2017, p. 199.

both undertakings see no need for a reform of the existing competition law, but rather plead for a cautious intervention in individual cases that takes into account their impact on innovation incentives.[164]

Against the background of the lobbying discourse discussed, the analysis of the footnotes is revealing.[165] Apart from a few standard references to the theoretical platform literature,[166] the Facebook contribution refers to *Evans*' work almost throughout;[167] not only to discuss the problems of SSNIP tests and market definition in relation to platforms,[168] but also to substantiate the claim that there is sufficient competition despite network effects.[169] Since Evans is financially supported by Google,[170] stands in the tradition of the Chicago School, and has represented Microsoft and Tencent in competition law cases, a bias in favour of large digital undertakings is quite conceivable here. Similarly, Microsoft cites a single paper written by *Sokol*[171] to prove that the buyout of start-ups by dominant undertakings is conducive to innovation.[172] Sokol is with a Palo Alto-based law firm that represented LinkedIn in its acquisition by Microsoft.

The rather one-sided presentation by Facebook and Google, which strongly resembles the chains of argumentation in the contributions by industry representatives, is complemented by the critical contributions of European entrepreneurs, especially from the communications and media sector. These describe how the mechanisms of the platform economy, especially network effects and free prices, would have produced American platform undertakings of unprecedented market and opinion power.[173] With reference to *Khan*'s foundational work,[174] among others, it is argued that

164 *Facebook*, p. 9; *Microsoft*, p. 9.

165 Conceptually: Hamann, above fn. 19, p. 501.

166 Armstrong, "Competition in two-sided markets," 2006, p. 668.

167 Evans, above fn. 105, pp. 318–321; Evans, "Why the Dynamics of Competition for Online Platforms Leads to Sleepless Nights, but Not Sleepy Monopolies," 2017; Evans, Noel, "Defining Antitrust Markets When Firms Operate Two-Sided Platforms," 2005, p. 667, 699–700.

168 *Facebook*, pp. 3 f., fn. 4–7.

169 *Facebook*, p. 6, fn. 18, 19.

170 See his own disclaimer in: Evans, "Multisided Platforms, Dynamic Competition, and the Assessment of Market Power for Internet-Based Firms," 2016, p. 1.

171 Sokol, above fn. 147, p. 1357.

172 *Microsoft*, p. 8.

173 *AT Internet*, p. 5; *Mediaset*, pp. 2–3; *Bertelsmann*, pp. 3–4; *Le Groupe La Poste*, pp. 1–3; *Telefonica*, pp. 1–2; *Vodafone*, p. 3.

174 Khan, above fn. 145, p. 710; Khan, "The Separation of Platforms and Commerce," 2018, p. 973.

platforms use their gatekeeper power to extort better terms from dependent users and to prevent innovation competition through low-price strategies, product bundling, and vertical integration.[175] Opposing competitive pressures do not exist, since both P2B and B2B consumers cannot leave the dominant platform ecosystem due to 'lock-in' effects.[176]

In contrast to the larger platforms, the contributions of European undertakings emphasise the key role of data in the development of competitive services.[177] The French company AT Internet writes that the competition for the best AI is mainly about the amount of data that feeds machine learning, and that it is obvious 'that Google, with its strategy of dumping and foreclosing the Google Analytics market, secure[d] one of the most powerful data sources in the digital market.'[178] In particular, media undertakings such as Bertelsmann, Mediaset, and ProSiebenSat.1 demand access to the data generated from the consumption of media content in order to enable competition on an equal footing.[179] Against this background, an adjustment of the EU merger control is also demanded in order to better cover start-up takeovers.[180]

In sum, European undertakings plead for a stricter competition law investigation of exploitative abuses and market foreclosure by platforms within the framework of Art. 102 TFEU,[181] urge data access,[182] and call for changes to the SSNIP test and market definition.[183] Telefonica's contribution stands out for its call for a new theory of harm that recognises privacy as a parameter of competition and thus enables new forms of market power abuse to be captured.[184] Complaints by European undertakings often go beyond purely competition law aspects and also address stricter regulation in the area of data protection or tax harmonisation.[185] Some European

175 *Le Groupe La Poste*, pp. 2, 3; *ProSiebenSat.1*, pp. 1–3, 7; *Telefonica*, p. 3; *Vodafone*, p. 4.

176 *ProSiebenSat.1*, pp. 3–6, 9–10; *Telefonica*, p. 9; *Vodafone*, p. 3.

177 E.g., *Telefonica*, pp. 1, 9 f.; *Vodafone*, p. 4. And quotes below.

178 *AT Internet*, p. 7.

179 *Bertelsmann*, p. 2; *Mediaset*, p. 5, *ProSiebenSat.1*, pp. 3, 8.

180 E.g., *Telefonica*, pp. 6, 11 f.

181 *Le Groupe La Poste*, p. 7.

182 Via the essential facility doctrine: *AT Internet*, p. 5.

183 *Telefonica*, pp. 8 f.

184 *Telefonica*, p. 11.

185 *AT Internet*, p. 6; *Bertelsmann*, p. 6; *Mediaset*, p. 9. Tax issues could be handled by EU state aid law: Calliess, Ruffert, Cremer, *EUV/AEUV*, 2016, AEUV Art. 107 Rn. 1–86.

undertakings also establish academic collaborations to support their arguments.[186] References to 'attention competition' by Facebook and Microsoft and complaints by European competitors about exploitation of network effects and consumers[187] reflect the vocabulary of Topic 1, in line with the thematic distribution estimated by the STM (see Figure 5).

2. Academics

A total of 22 papers were submitted by academics, of whom only two were of non-European origin. Of particular interest here is the paper written by Google Chief Economist *Varian* with *Dolmans* and *Baird*, who commented on all three panel themes of the conference. Since data of a non-rivalrous nature is easy to collect with an innovative product and is characterised by diminishing marginal utility, the paper argues, data is a negligible parameter from a competition law perspective.[188] Moreover, mandated data access should be rejected because it reduces incentives for innovation and raises data protection issues[189]—i.e., the same argument that has already been seen in the contributions of American undertakings. Interestingly, the assessment of data's increasingly diminished significance is supported by a footnote[190] that refers to an article written by researchers from the Chinese search engine provider Baidu.[191] As mentioned by *Varian et al.*, this article describes a 'power-law distribution' of model accuracy as a function of dataset size, which theoretically supports the thesis of a decreasing marginal utility of Big Data. However, the Baidu researchers also emphasise that real-world applications in areas such as voice or image recognition

186 For example, the French Post's contribution is largely based on three studies by *Borsenberger*, which in turn are based on close cooperation between *Groupe La Poste* and the *Toulouse School of Economics*: Borsenberger, "The Concentration Phenomenon in E-commerce," 2015, pp. 31–41; For the relevant references in the contribution: *Le Groupe La Poste*, pp. 4–6. Telefonica's proposals are based on an expert opinion commissioned by Finanzplatz München Initiative from Podszun, "Innovation, Variety & Fair Choice – New Rules for the Digital Economy: Expert Opinion for Finanzplatz München Initiative (FPMI)," 2017. Reference in *Telefonica*, p. 7, fn. 13.

187 *Telefonica*, p. 1.

188 *Varian/Dolmans/Baird*, pp. 1 f.

189 Ibid., pp. 3 f.

190 See: "according to a study by Hestness et al." ibid., p. 2.

191 Hestness, Narang, Ardalani et al., "Deep Learning Scaling is Predictable, Empirically," 2017, p. 1.

are still far from an area where adding data no longer brings about any practical improvement[192]—this point is concealed by *Varian et al.*

The market power of large digital platforms, the article continues, is also usually overestimated, as a dynamic perspective is necessary, numerous competitors exist in the advertising and commercial search engine market, and cloud computing allows cheap and fast market entry.[193] In addition, the standardisation of operating systems and smartphone applications has significantly reduced switching costs. However, given possible direct and indirect network effects, it is recognised that measures that would enable data portability and reduce barriers to multi-homing would be helpful in maintaining the ability to switch and thus competitive pressure. The *Varian et al.* paper concludes with two observations directed against competitive intervention in digital markets, particularly in the context of merger control.[194] First, they point out that technology undertakings invest more money in research and development than other sectors. They also argue that buying up innovative start-ups is a necessary means of 'rewarding' innovation, especially given the declining popularity of IPOs. Overall, the authors' proximity to Google is clearly noticeable in their argumentation.

In contrast, the contributions submitted by European academics are fundamentally more sceptical, despite a high degree of variance. Overall, a focus on various forms of exploitative abuse by platforms[195] and the integration of non-price competition parameters such as data protection and innovation into the competitive assessment is noticeable.[196] However, there are clear differences in the assessment of DG COMP's possibilities to intervene in a corrective way: While *Kupkic* optimistically states that it could be 'relatively easy to construct a big data sharing obligation in a way that does not compromise the protection of personal data,'[197] *Bott* and *Milkau*, following *von Hayek*, warn against a 'pretence of knowledge.'[198] Solutions that increase interoperability between platforms and thus reduce

192 They call this area 'irreducible error region.' Hestness, Narang, Ardalani et al, ibid., p. 11.

193 *Varian/Dolmans/Baird*, pp. 4–7.

194 Ibid., pp. 9 f.

195 *Geradin*; *Krämer/Schnurr*; *Thépot*, esp. p. 5. See also: *Bounie/Dubusz/Waelbroeck* and *Rabassa*.

196 *Esayas*; *Schrepel*. See also: *Chirita* and *Colangelo/Maggiolino*. Differing opinion: *Körber*.

197 *Kupcik*, p. 3.

198 *Bott/Milkau*, p. 8.

consumer lock-in are favoured on various occasions[199]—these solutions were also highlighted later in the expert report.

The argumentation of European academics does not, at least superficially, indicate any intended promotion of European undertakings. It is emphasised that European law jurisprudence sets clear limits to the competition law interventions sought by undertakings,[200] and has not yet been clarified with regard to mandated data access.[201] Indeed, in light of the claims, it should be noted that the existence of a direct disadvantage of economic operators cannot necessarily be equated with a restrictive effect on competition (*Meo*);[202] that EU competition law only deals with the exclusion of 'equally efficient' competitors (*Intel*);[203] that the anticompetitive effect of a particular practice cannot be purely hypothetical but must be probable (*Post Danmark II*);[204] and that the 'special responsibility' of dominant undertakings refers only to a responsibility to ensure effective and undistorted competition in the common market, but does not provide a basis for sanctioning non-competitive infringements (*Michelin*).[205]

IV. Interim result

All three dimensions of the digital age discussed in the previous part—data, algorithms, and platforms—play a role in the stakeholders' contributions, whereby the discussion of data focuses primarily on questions of data access and data protection. Thus, the qualitative analysis confirms the prominence and distribution of certain 'topics' estimated by the STM (Figure 5). As a result, the contributions also reveal a dividing line within the entrepreneurial camp, which—in line with the lobbying literature on the influence of multinational undertakings—leads to diverging statements by dominant American platforms and their European competitors. The same dividing line is also found in contributions by academics, making it difficult to differentiate between interest-driven and objective statements.

199 *Weston*; *Laborda*, pp. 8 f.; *Louven*, pp. 4, 6; *Thépot*, pp. 4f.
200 Colomo, above fn. 21, esp. pp. 5–7. Similar: *Körber*. See also: *Gerbrandy*, p. 3; *Geradin*, pp. 9 f.
201 *Louven*.
202 ECJ, Case C-525/16, ECLI:EU:C:2018:270 – *Meo*, para. 25.
203 ECJ, Case C-413/14, ECLI:EU:C:2017:632 – *Intel*, paras. 111, 136.
204 ECJ, Case C-23/14, ECLI:EU:C:2015:651 – *Post Danmark II*, paras. 65, 75.
205 ECJ, Case 322/81, ECLI:EU:C:1983:313 – *Michelin*, para. 57. See also: *Körber*, p. 8.

The Commission's task is to assess whether the complaints voiced by European undertakings are opportunistic behaviour or legitimate competition concerns. With this in mind, this paper now turns to the processing of these contributions by the expert report commissioned by the Commission (Part D).

D. Expert Report

What influence did the contributions submitted have for the competition law argumentation and elaboration of reform proposals in the expert report? In their introduction, the Special Advisors express their gratitude for 'the valuable contributions received during the consultation process as well as the conference "Shaping competition policy in the era of digitalization" organised by the European Commission on 17 January 2019,' emphasise that they 'greatly appreciated' them, and conclude by saying that all submissions were 'gratefully received and considered.'[206] The report was also praised in the literature for being particularly 'open' to an exchange of ideas.[207] In this final part of the paper, thematic foci and reform proposals of the expert report are first identified and compared with the stakeholder contributions (I). The two subsequent sections develop (II) and apply (III) criteria to examine whether the stakeholder consultation was effective, representative, and transparent.

I. Comparison

The comparison of the content of the expert report with the stakeholder contributions is made through a qualitative assessment of the extent to which the 'topics' estimated by the STM are addressed in the expert report (1); through a quantitative search for certain 'keywords' (2); and through an evaluation of the footnote apparatus (3).

206 *Expert Report*, pp. 17 f.
207 Cf. 'open-minded' in: De Pablo, above fn. 7, p. 1, 2.

1. Topics

The expert report defines competition in the digital age in terms of three characteristics: extreme economies of scale due to the low production costs for digital products and services, strong network effects, and the increasingly important role of data as a central competitive parameter.[208] From these characteristics follows the existence of strong economies of scope that favour the development of ecosystems and give incumbents a strong competitive advantage.[209] At this point, the special advisors mention that 'experience' shows that large digital incumbents are very difficult to displace, although there is 'little empirical evidence' of the associated efficiency losses.[210] While there is no direct reference to the consultation process at this point, it can be assumed that the contributions of European undertakings have substantiated or at least reinforced this 'experience' of the consultants – not least because of their focus on exploitative abuses by dominant American providers (cf. Topics 1, 7, 8 in the STM).

Taken together, these features of the digital economy greatly influence the forms of competition and therefore justify adjustments in the application of European competition law. The subsequent main statements of the expert report on substantive law can be separated into three areas. The special advisors discuss the application of competition rules to platforms as well as the significance of data under competition law and then ask whether European merger control needs updating.

Given features such as network effects, economies of scale, and dominant ecosystems, the expert report argues, digital markets often only offer space for a limited number of platforms. In order to create incentives for the provision of goods and services on reasonable terms and for innovation, competition law would have to protect competition 'for' the market in particular.[211] Although the Special Advisors emphasise that a case-by-case analysis is always required, they argue that actions by a dominant platform that hinder competitors or increase their costs without constituting genuine 'competition on the merits' should be treated with suspicion.[212]

208 *Expert Report*, pp. 19–29.

209 *Expert Report*, pp. 33–35.

210 *Expert Report*, p. 36.

211 *Expert Report*, p. 55. In contrast to competition 'in' the market. For this differentiation, see: Geroski, above fn. 129, p. 151.

212 *Expert Report*, pp. 55 f.

At this point, the expert report focuses on the example of most-favoured-nation clauses (MFNs)[213] and offers a differentiated assessment depending on the competitive situation on the relevant market. If the competition between platforms prevailing there is sufficiently strong, it may be sufficient to prohibit clauses that prevent sellers on a platform from differentiating prices between platforms (i.e., a prohibition of 'wide' MFNs). Clauses preventing the seller from offering lower prices on its own website ('narrow' MFNs) would still be allowed in this scenario. If competition between platforms was weak, the pressure on the dominant platforms could only come from other sales channels, so that in this case 'narrow' MFNs would also have to be sanctioned under competition law. Since MFNs are only given cursory attention in the consultation contributions,[214] this substantive focus seems to be motivated by the recent case law in the area of hotel booking platforms.[215]

According to the expert report, in order to promote diversity of supply, innovation, and consumer welfare in the area of platforms, it is necessary to ensure that 'multihoming' and 'switching' are possible and that market-dominant platforms do not hinder these pro-competitive factors.[216] Since platforms act as regulators by setting the interaction framework for their users,[217] dominant platforms have a 'responsibility' to ensure that their rules do not impede free and undistorted competition without objective justification, according to the special advisers.[218] For the attribution of such responsibility under competition law, the expert report refers to the *Meca-Medina* case law on sports federations in the context of Art. 101 TFEU.[219] A more obvious argument would have relied on the 'special responsibility' established by the ECJ in *Michelin I* in the context of Art. 102 TFEU,[220] as the Special Advisers explicitly emphasise that this enhanced responsibility should only concern dominant platforms. Although the expert report legitimises its characterisation of platforms as regulators with a reference to the

213 For an overview: Akman, above fn. 123, p. 781; Akman / Sokol, "Online RPM and MFN Under Antitrust Law and Economics," 2017, p. 488.

214 The only exception: *Epicenter*, p. 5.

215 Bundeskartellamt, 20.12.2013, Case B9–66/10 – *HRS*; *Ellger*, in Immenga and Mestmäcker, above fn. 98.

216 *Expert Report*, pp. 57 f.

217 See also: Tolón, "The Dynamics of Platform Business Value Creation," 2017.

218 *Expert Report*, p. 61.

219 ECJ, Case C-519/04 P, ECLI:EU:C:2006:492 – *Meca-Medina*.

220 ECJ, Case 322/81, ECLI:EU:C:1983:313 – *Michelin I*, para. 57.

"most recent economic literature,"[221] an influence of the contributions of European undertakings is plausible, as they repeatedly refer to the market-creating, regulating function of platforms.[222]

According to the expert report, the fact that platforms act as regulators should influence the treatment of 'leveraging' and 'self-referencing' facts.[223] In the context of the digital economy, there is a concern from a leveraging perspective that some firms will transfer their market power to a secondary market, not only to make greater profits, but also to prevent new competitors from entering their core market.[224] This is a concern also expressed by undertakings in the consultation process (Topic 7). The Special Advisors expect that dominant platforms will seek to bundle services and products where their control over consumer data and network effects is strong with other services and products where this is less so. In such cases, according to the expert report, the efficiency benefit of bundling is low, so that competition law sanctions should be particularly strict.[225]

As can be seen from the decision in *Google Shopping*, 'self-referencing' is not classified by the Commission as abusive per se but is subject to an effects test within the framework of Art. 102 TFEU. While it has been disputed in the literature so far whether the case constellation of 'self-preferencing' can constitute an abuse,[226] the special advisors position themselves clearly. In cases of vertically integrated dominant platforms in markets with high entry barriers, according to the expert report, platforms would have to prove, to the extent that they exercise a regulatory function, that the self-favouring in question does not lead to long-term exclusionary effects on product markets.[227] In the event that self-favouring has already led to 'significant' advantages for a subsidiary of the platform, 'restorative' remedies are proposed.

The section on data in the expert report begins by stating that the heterogeneity of data and its different uses should be taken into account.[228] Data are categorised into voluntarily given, observed, and inferred—here

---

221 *Expert Report*, p. 6, also p. 60.
222 *ProSiebenSat.1*, pp. 2 f., 5.
223 *Expert Report*, p. 65.
224 See also: De Corniere, Taylor, "Upstream Bundling and Leverage of Market Power," 2018.
225 *Expert Report*, p. 66.
226 Overview: Hoeren, Sieber, Holznagel, *Multimedia-Recht*, 2019, paras. 200–202.
227 *Expert Report*, pp. 66–68.
228 Ibid., p. 75.

the Special Advisors follow the non-legal distinction established in the literature (see part B above). Furthermore, data could be collected at different levels (individual/aggregated), be generated at different frequencies, and concern historical or real-time values. Finally, they could be of a personal or non-personal nature. Due to the GDPR, with its specific framework for personal data, access to personal or non-personal data must be treated differently.[229] Overall, according to the expert report, the assessment of data as a competition parameter under competition law must be determined for each individual case by the market specifics as well as the nature of the data and its use.

In the following, the expert report addresses the data access issues discussed earlier (see part B above) and for this purpose distinguishes between agreed data sharing and mandated access via Art. 102 TFEU. The report recognises that data sharing or pooling agreements will often be pro-competitive by addressing data bottlenecks, providing innovation opportunities, or enabling the development of new or better products or services (especially through improved training of algorithms).[230] At the same time, case constellations are described under which such agreements become anti-competitive. The report therefore calls for a separate investigation of the different types of data pooling and their respective pro- and anti-competitive aspects.[231] The proposal to implement the findings thus obtained by means of guidance letters, findings of inapplicability (Art. 10 Regulation No. 1/2003), a revision of the guidelines on horizontal cooperation, or, at a later stage, a block exemption regulation for data is a sensible approach, which could also be extended to other areas.[232]

When competitors request access to a dominant firm's data under Art. 102 TFEU, it must be examined whether such access is 'indispensable' (see part B above). The Special Advisors are of the opinion that Art. 102 TFEU is not suitable for dealing with data requests from applicants pursuing business purposes that are essentially unrelated to the market served by the dominant firm.[233] In particular, they emphasise data access for the purpose of training AI algorithms,[234] perhaps because such access was also

229 Ibid., pp. 77–82.

230 Ibid., pp. 94–98.

231 Ibid., p. 109.

232 As demanded by: De Pablo, above fn. 7, p. 10.

233 *Expert Report*, p. 98.

234 Ibid., pp. 76, 100.

requested by undertakings in consultation submissions.[235] As a result, the expert report considers the application of the essential facility doctrine to be misguided in such cases and prefers market-oriented solutions or new regulatory regimes.

The expert report comes to a different conclusion with regard to data requests for the purpose of serving complementary markets or secondary markets, i.e., markets that are part of the broader ecosystem served by the data controller.[236] The Special Advisors give the example of a machine manufacturer that does not give users access to the data of its machines sold, which could lead to a foreclosure of secondary markets.[237] In light of this, they propose an update of the traditional competition law analysis of secondary markets to take into account the specificities of data, as well as an increased application of Art. 102 TFEU to this area.[238] This focus on secondary markets has not been discussed much in the literature so far,[239] but was emphasised by numerous contributions in the consultation procedure (Topic 7 in the STM), so that a significant stakeholder influence can be assumed here.

The last section of the expert report critically examines the takeover of small start-ups with a fast-growing user base and significant competitive potential by dominant platforms. The expert report first summarises the criticism of the previous decision-making practice in this area, which is essentially known from the literature (see part B above), and then reviews the jurisdictional thresholds currently set out in the EU Merger Regulation as well as the substantive competitive assessment of a merger that has been customary to date.[240] With regard to the first issue, in stark contrast to the consultation contributions (see part C above), it is argued that a change in the jurisdiction thresholds of the merger regulation would be premature—it would be better to first evaluate the performance of the transaction

235 *EBU*, pp. 8–10.

236 For an overview: OECD, "Competition Issues In Aftermarkets: Background note by the Secretariat," 2017.

237 *Expert Report*, p. 90.

238 *Expert Report*, pp. 90 f., 101 f., 105 f., 125.

239 But: Kerber, Frank, "Data Governance Regimes in the Digital Economy: The Example of Connected Cars," 2017; Schweitzer, Haucap, Kerber, Welker, "Modernisierung der Missbrauchsaufsicht für marktmächtige Unternehmen," 2018.

240 *Expert Report*, pp. 110–121.

value-based thresholds recently introduced by some Member States and the functioning of the referral system.[241]

In contrast, the Special Advisers consider it necessary to review the substantive damages theories under the SIEC test ('significant impediment of effective competition').[242] In explicit reference to *Facebook/WhatsApp*,[243] they focus here on cases in which a dominant platform which benefits from strong network effects, privileged data access, and a dominant ecosystem acquires a start-up with low revenues but a large and/or fast-growing user base and a high future market potential. In such an acquisition, the threat to competition is not limited to foreclosing competitors' access to essential inputs, but also extends to strengthening market dominance, as the dominance of the entire ecosystem is reinforced. Since this simultaneously leads to a strengthening of network effects, which is to be regarded as efficiency in the sense of an objective justification, the Commission must determine in each individual case whether these effects can be realised by other means and, if this is not possible, whether the gain in efficiency outweighs the loss of competition. Against this background, it is remarkable that the treatment of a possible 'efficiency defence' only takes up about half of a page in the 127-page report,[244] while efficiency considerations were so frequently represented in the stakeholder contributions that the STM estimated a separate 'topic' for this (Topic 5).

2. Words

A quantitative method to approximate the influence of the stakeholder contributions on the content of the expert report is to determine the word frequency of central terms. First, we look for the three dimensions of the digital economy discussed in part B—data, algorithms, platforms—that correlate with Topics 4, 9 and 10. Accordingly, data is the main focus of the expert report (Figure 8). Algorithms were discussed relatively more frequently in the contributions (cf. Figure 5).

241 Ibid., pp. 115 f.

242 Zimmer, "Significant Impediment to Effective Competition," 2004, p. 250.

243 Commission, 3.10.2014, M.7217 – *Facebook/WhatsApp*; *Expert Report*, p. 122, fn. 218.

244 *Expert Report*, p. 123. Similar: Riziotis, abovefn. 159, pp. 98–115.

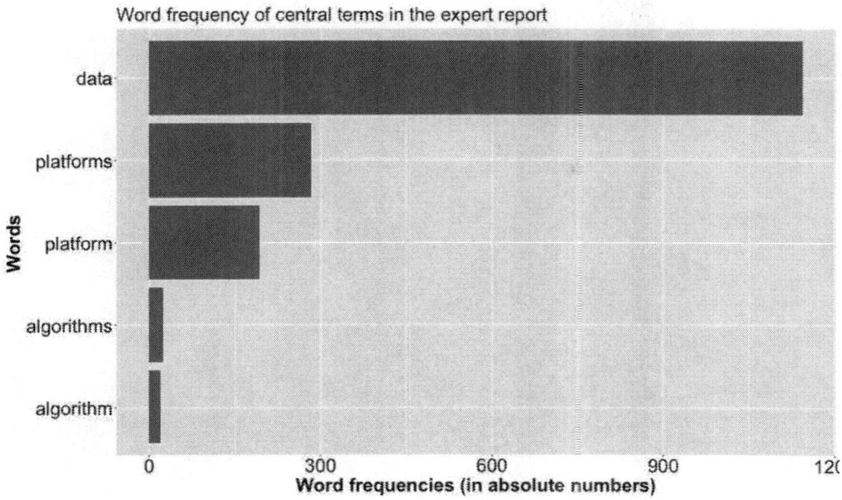

Figure 8

An alternative method is to identify central words in the stakeholder contributions and then determine their frequency in the expert report (Figure 9). Central terms in the contributions can be taken from the word profiles of the ten topics as estimated by the STM.[245] The result shows that in particular data access—for example in relation to secondary markets (Topic 7) and data protection issues (Topic 4)—new digital services (Topic 2), and interoperability measures to support open markets (Topic 3) were included by the expert report. In contrast, specific undertakings such as Google (Topic 8), descriptions of consumer abuse (Topic 1), or calls for more research (Topic 6) are comparatively less prominent.

245 By searching for two characteristic terms from their respective word profiles. T1: 'consumer,' 'exploitative;' T2: 'services,' 'markets;' T3: 'interoperability,' 'blockchain;' T4: 'privacy,' 'protection;' T5: 'innovation,' 'scale;' T6: 'research,' 'scientific;' T7: 'aftermarket,' 'access;' T8: 'google,' 'advertising.' T9 (algorithms) and T10 (platforms) are already covered by Figure 8.

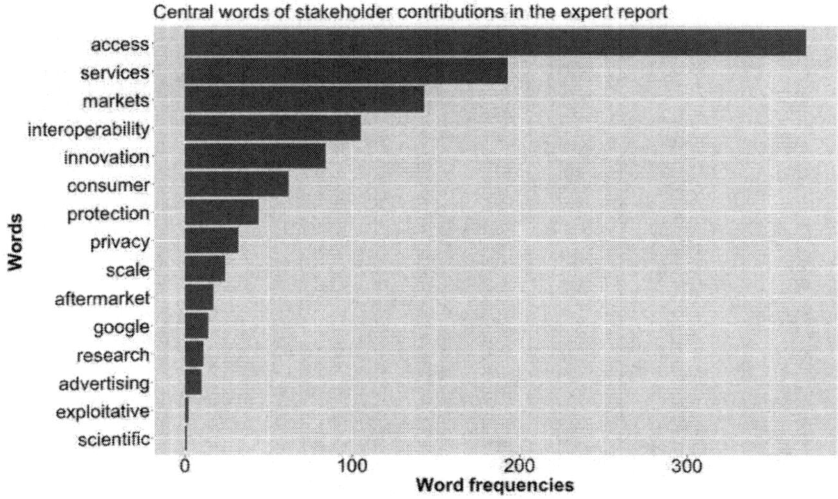

Figure 9

3. References

Direct references to stakeholder contributions are not to be found anywhere in the expert report. An indirect indicator is provided by the footnote apparatus, which gives a good overview of the literature received, the problem areas considered, and the "dialogue of authors."[246] All footnotes were categorised and arranged chronologically in Figure 10.

246 Schmidt, above fn. 19, p. 1123. See also: Hamann, above fn 19, 2014, p. 501.

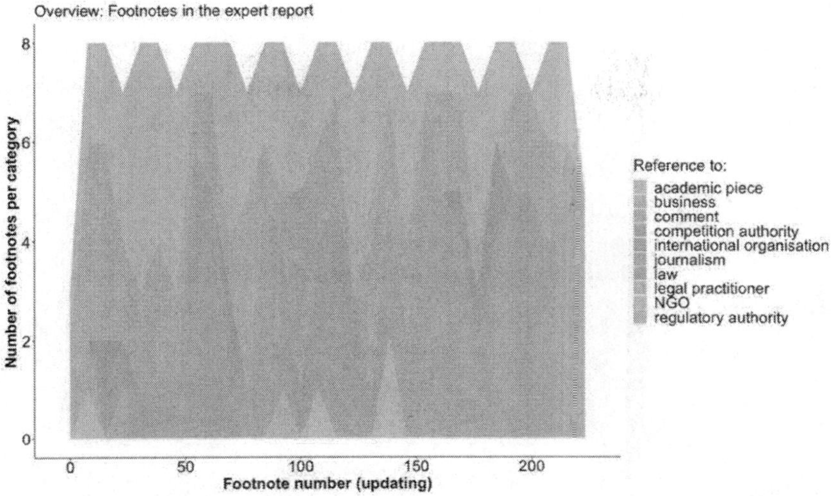

Figure 10

It can be seen that at the beginning of the expert report references to academic literature and general remarks make up the majority of the footnote apparatus, while in the course of the report, especially in the last third on EU merger control (from footnote 150 onwards), legal references increase strongly. Among these are references to Commission directives,[247] case law on the objectives of European competition law,[248] Bronner case law,[249] and merger control proceedings of apparent 'killer acquisitions.'[250] The few NGOs cited consistently hold views critical of GAFAM and advocate for the data protection and consumer welfare of European consumers.[251]

In the case of academic references, the national origin was also noted. French, German, and English references are not surprising as they are mostly self-references of the special advisors. As can be seen in Figure 11,

247 *Expert Report*, pp. 95 f., 123.

248 Ibid., p. 40.

249 Ibid., p. 99, p. 106.

250 Ibid., pp. 110, 118 f., 122.

251 The reference to the European consumer protection organisation BEUC can be found in *Expert Report*, p. 88, fn. 136. The only reference to a company, a crypto-messenger operator praised for its focus on data protection, points in the same direction.

American literature was exceptionally well received.[252] Among these references is, for example, the article 'Let the Right "One" Win,' written by *Weyl* and *White* in collaboration with Microsoft, according to which competition does not allow sufficient market concentration to optimally exploit network effects.[253]

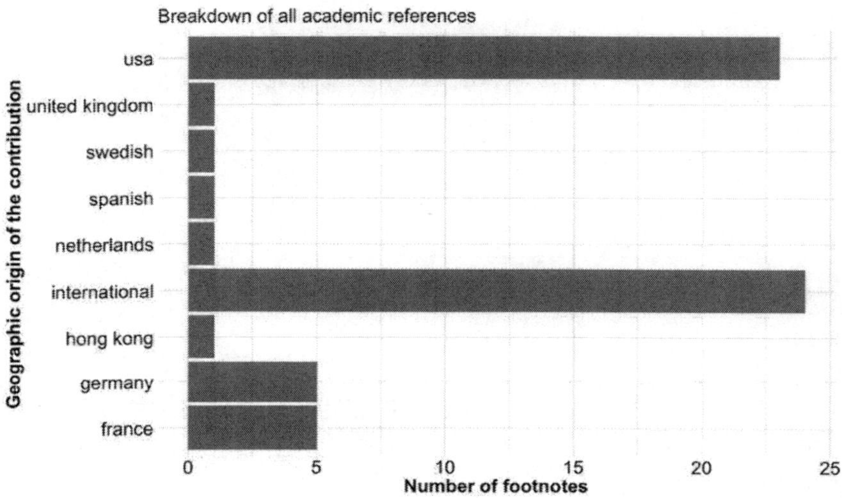

Figure 11

However, the high cumulative number of American references does not necessarily imply an adoption of pro-GAFAM arguments: some of the American authors cited, such as Wu, are highly critical of platforms and urge the break-up of large technology undertakings,[254] while other references to arguments in the American literature are criticised by the subsequent discussion in the expert report.[255] Moreover, the high number of articles resulting from international collaboration includes many intra-European academic collaborations. While the number of American references

252 The article "Digital Conglomerates and EU Competition Policy" by *Bourreau/de Streel* is cited most frequently, namely five times. *Expert Report*, fn. 182, 195, 210, 215, 217.

253 Weyl, White, "Let the Right 'One' Win: Policy Lessons from the New Economics of Platforms," 2014, p. 29; *Expert Report*, p. 23, fn. 21.

254 Wu, *The Curse of Bigness: Antitrust in the New Gilded Age*, 2018, p. 40, fn. 50.

255 As the reference to Lambrecht, Tucker, "Can big data protect a firm from competition?," 2015, p. 29, fn. 35.

is therefore not directly equivalent to an adoption of the arguments made there, the nationally disaggregated footnote apparatus is nevertheless surprising for a *European* expert report, especially in light of the geographical distribution of the stakeholders consulted (see Figure 3).

II. Assessment standard

Good legislative processes are evaluated in the literature according to various criteria ranging from gender neutrality[256] to influence through social media.[257] In the following, the focus will be on analytical criteria for an assessment of the processing of interest group contributions in the expert report. The participation of interest groups in the opinion-forming process is not only an essential element of a functioning democracy,[258] but also arises from the pragmatic realisation that complex or technical regulations require the expertise of stakeholders.[259] The problem, then, is not interest group influence per se, 'but how it is exercised, what we learn about it, and how policymakers deal with it for the common good.'[260] On this basis, there is a broad body of literature on criteria for good regulation[261] and the legal framework for appropriate interest group representation,[262] which emphasises three features: representativeness (1), effectiveness (2), and transparency (3).

1. Representativeness

The consultation process should allow for the meaningful and responsible participation of all relevant stakeholders, including affected citizens.[263] Discrimination against individual stakeholders must be avoided. Even before

256 Wersig, "Gesetzgebung ist nicht geschlechtsneutral," 2019, p. 244.
257 Voss, "Digitale Dynamik in Gesetzgebungsprozessen," 2019, p. 211.
258 Maunz, Dürig, *Grundgesetz-Kommentar*, 2019, Art. 9 GG, para. 158.
259 Pischel, Kopp, above fn. 8, § 1 para. 25.
260 Polk, "Die Drehtür der Demokratie," 2017.
261 Overview: Savary, *Regulierung dominanter Internetplattformen. Eigenheiten, Herausforderungen und Lösungsansätze im Licht von Ökonomie, Innovation und Recht*, 2017, p. 80.
262 Brouwer, above fn. 8, 2019, p. 2.
263 Savary, above fn. 261, p. 84.

the introduction of the so-called 'Better Regulation' (BR) principles,[264] there was criticism that the Commission's consultation practice showed a preference for certain actors[265] and that better procedures were needed to balance the unequal lobbying of interest groups in Brussels.[266] The evaluation of previous consultations identified similar shortcomings.[267]

2. Effectiveness

Once the contributions received in the consultation process have been representatively recorded and presented, it is necessary to clarify how this information is to be used. It is not clear from the BR guidelines what type and amount of empirical evidence is to be considered, who contributes this evidence, and how it will be taken into account in the final drafting and implementation of the regulation.[268] Therefore, it was criticised that additional guidance on the methods for evaluating the submissions received would have been useful.[269] There are several hurdles for the effective processing of the contributions submitted, such as the amount of data collected[270] or the question of weighting the different responses.[271]

264 Listorti, Basyte Ferrari, Acs et al., "The debate on the EU Better Regulation Agenda: a literature review," 2019. See also: Radaelli, "Whither Better Regulation for the Lisbon Agenda," 2007, p. 190; Kaeding, "In Search of Better Quality of EU Regulations for Prompt Transposition: The Brussels Perspective," 2008, p. 583; Radaelli, Meuwese, "Better Regulation in Europe: Between Public Management and Regulatory Reform," 2009, p. 639; Alemanno, "How Much Better Is Better Regulation? Assessing the Impact of the Better Regulation Package on the European Union: A Research Agenda," 2015, p. 344; Tombs, "Making Better Regulation, Making Regulation Better?," 2016, p. 332; Mödinger, *Bessere Rechtsetzung. Leistungsfähigkeit eines europäischen Konzepts*, 2020.

265 Franzius, "Demokratisierung der Europäischen Union," 2013, p. 655, 664.

266 Franzius, Preuß, *Die Zukunft der europäischen Demokratie*, 2012, p. 166.

267 Listorti, Basyte Ferrari, Acs et al., above fn. 264, p. 41.

268 Ranchordás, "Consultations, Citizen Narratives and Evidence-based Regulation: The Strange Case of the Consultation on the Collaborative Economy," 2017, p. 52.

269 Chase, Schlosser, "Better Regulation: An Ongoing Journey," 2015, p. 378.

270 Eliantonio, Spendzharova, "The European Union's New "Better Regulation" Agenda: Between Procedures and Politics," 2017, p. 3, 9.

271 Garben, "An 'Impact Assessment' of EU Better Regulation," 2018, p. 217, 235.

3. Transparency

Finally, transparency—an essential element of the BR agenda[272]—contributes to the 'through-put' legitimacy of the process.[273] Both of the preceding requirements for the consultation process should thus be transparent, i.e. transparency about which contributions have been received on the one hand, and transparency about the arguments considered relevant on the other, so that a third party can objectively assess whether an effective evaluation has taken place. Such transparent participation of stakeholders contributes to improving the quality of legislation and to the balance and acceptance of parliamentary decisions.[274] As a result, it is necessary that the outcome of the consultation, in this case the expert report, makes transparent which arguments were heard and which of them were considered important.

III. Comparison

Based on these three criteria (representativeness, effectiveness, and transparency), it is possible to assess the functioning of the consultation process in the case of the Commission's expert study on competition law in the digital age.

1. Representativeness of the report

The literature indicates that previous Commission consultation formats have predominantly involved industry associations, EU-funded transnational NGOs, and other established actors with privileged access.[275] It also offers rough guidelines for the evaluation of the characteristic of representativeness: *Denardis* and *Raymond* argue that the requirements for a form of 'multi-stakeholder governance' is only fulfilled if at least two different class-

272 Héritier, "Composite democracy in Europe. The role of transparency and access to information," 2013.

273 Schmidt, "Democracy and Legitimacy in the European Union Revisited: Input, Output and 'Throughput'," 2013, p. 2.

274 Brouwer, above fn. 8, p. 2.

275 Dawson, "Better regulation and the future of EU regulatory law and politics," 2016, p. 1209, 1219; Van den Abeele, above fn. 1, p. 5.

es of stakeholders are included.[276] *Almeida et al.* require the involvement of at least three stakeholders.[277]

The breakdown of the submitted contributions according to institutional background found a broad, representative selection of stakeholders (see part B above). Against this background, the expert report has equally reflected the core concerns of different stakeholders. Behavioural economics and data protection aspects that were important to NGOs were mentioned. The same applies to the efforts of European undertakings: for example, it was recognised that incumbent digital providers are very difficult to displace, that platforms exercise a market-creating, regulatory function, with important consequences for the competition law assessment of 'leveraging' and self-preferencing, and that there is a risk of market power being transferred to a secondary market or this being foreclosed through exclusive data use. American literature was received to the same extent as European literature. The arguments of some dominant American platforms were even implicitly taken up by focusing on ex-ante consultation and data mobility instead of interim measures.

Overall, these are definitely 'privileged' actors in the sense referred to in the literature—no influence of individuals or smaller institutional actors such as workers' organisation could be demonstrated. As a result, the criterion of representativeness can nevertheless be regarded as fulfilled in view of the above-mentioned benchmarks. It should also be noted that the expert report goes far beyond a mere analysis of the contributions: the discussion of MFNs, the rejection of the essential facility doctrine to legitimise data access for AI training purposes, as well as the retention of the ECMR thresholds are important elements that were either judged contrary to the stakeholders or were not prioritised by the latter.

2. Effectiveness of the report

In comparing the two 'inputs' of the digital economy (discussed in part B), the expert report places a clear emphasis on data, not least by devoting a separate chapter to it. In doing so, it implicitly positions itself in the larger competition law debate on whether a dominant position in digital markets

276 *DeNardis/Raymond*, Governance, p. 9. Quoted after: Savary, above fn. 261, p. 81, fn. 552.

277 *Almeida et al.*, Multistakeholder, p. 74. Quoted after: Savary, above fn. 261, p. 81, fn. 552.

tends to be induced by more data or by a better algorithm.[278] A significant portion of the literature argues that highly effective algorithms can be developed without overly large datasets, making technical innovation, rather than the scale of the underlying data, the key competition parameter.[279] Here, reference is often made to the 'non-rival' nature of Big Data,[280] based on two assumptions: First, the same data can be used by different undertakings at the same time.[281] Secondly, the value of the data is not in the information collected itself, but in the knowledge that can be gained from it.[282] Consequently, different undertakings could achieve the same knowledge by evaluating different datasets.[283] The non-rivalrous nature of data is also referred to in the consultation contributions of dominant platforms.[284]

This view is contrasted with statements by computer scientists,[285] industry insiders,[286] and empirical studies[287] that describe the amount of data as the essential competitive factor in the digital age—not only because of its cumulative importance in optimising algorithms and the products and services based on them, but also because of its role in preserving monopoly

278 Lambrecht, Tucker, above fn. 255.

279 Nazzini, "Google and the (Ever-stretching) Boundaries of Article 102," 2015, p. 301, 306. Similarly sceptical regarding the cumulative benefits of big data: Chiou, Tucker, "Search Engines and Data Retention: Implications for Privacy and Antitrust," 2014; Manne, Wright, above fn. 14, p. 212; Bork, Sidak, above fn. 15, pp, 688–691; differing opinion: Grunes, Stucke, "No Mistake about It: The Important Role of Antitrust in the Era of Big Data," 2015, pp. 7 f.; Stucke, Grunes, above fn 34, pp. 42–47, 288–301.

280 Lambrecht, Tucker, above fn. 255, p. 5.

281 Tucker, Wellford, "Big Mistakes Regarding Big Data," 2014, p. 1, 3; LeVine, "How Old Tech could roar back," 2018.

282 Manne, Sperry, "The Problems and Perils of Bootstrapping Privacy and Data into an Antitrust Framework," 2015, p. 1, 9.

283 Graef, "Market Definition and Market Power in Data: the Case of Online Platforms," 2015, p. 473, 479.

284 *Facebook*, p. 7; *Microsoft*, p. 3.

285 Russell, Norvig, *Artificial Intelligence. A Modern Approach*, 2016, p. 28; Banko, Brill, "Scaling to very very large corpora for natural language disambiguation," 2001, p. 26, 27; Fischbach, above fn 31, pp. 141 f.

286 Halevy, Norvig, Pereira, "The Unreasonable Effectiveness of Data," 2009, p. 8; Asay, "'Whole Web' is the OS of the future," 2010.

287 De Cnudde, Martens, Evgeniou, Provost, "A Benchmarking Study of Classification Techniques for Behavioral Data," 2017.

rents.[288] Moreover, it can be argued that data, even if non-rivalrous in nature, cannot necessarily be collected and used equally by all competitors.[289]

It is therefore to be welcomed that the expert report clearly positions itself in this debate,[290] taking the position of computer scientists and industry insiders who have the necessary expertise to make an appropriate assessment. In this respect, there is an effective weighting in the sense of the criterion to be examined here. This weighting implicitly leads to the expert report assigning less importance to the algorithm-induced case constructions emphasised in numerous contributions made by undertakings. In view of the theoretical and empirical problems of algorithmic damage theories identified, such as algorithmic collusion (see part B above), this is also a welcome weighting.

A second significant weighting in terms of content compared to the consultation contributions is taken by the expert report with regard to the pro-competitive, innovative, and efficient effects of digital business models that can be used in the context of an 'efficiency defence.' While these claim a significant share of the contributions (cf. Figure 5), the report does not include a discussion on how platforms can promote competition in and between markets.[291] The Special Advisers conclude, with reference to the concept of error costs, that platforms should bear the burden of proof for their pro-competitive behaviour.[292] This contradicts the common notion that vertical integration is pro-competitive, as *Colomo* also points out in his conference paper.[293] Moreover, consumer benefits arise when platforms reduce search costs, facilitate price and product comparisons, enable remote shopping, and create new areas of work, such as ride-hailing, through 'creative destruction' in *Schumpeter*'s sense.[294] The considerable economic value of 'free' platform services for consumers is difficult to quantify,[295] but recent studies suggest very high consumer benefits.[296]

288 Zuboff, above fn. 9, pp. 95, 161, 170, 187.

289 Autorité de la concurrence/Bundeskartellamt, above fn. 35, p. 42.

290 *Expert Report*, p. 103.

291 This is also criticised by: De Pablo, above fn. 7, p. 1, 8.

292 *Expert Report*, p. 7, 68.

293 Colomo, above fn. 21, p. 9.

294 WEF, above fn 43, p. 6; Bethell, Baird, Waksman, above fn. 42, p. 37.

295 OECD, "An Introduction to Online Platforms and their Role in the Digital Transformation," 2019, p. 31; Brynjolfsson, Collis, Eggers, "Using Massive Online Choice Experiments to Measure Changes in Well-Being," 2019, p. 7250.

296 Brynjolfsson, Collis, Eggers, "Using Massive Online Choice Experiments to Measure Changes in Well-being," 2018. See also: Brynjolfsson and Oh, "The Attention

Digitisation of the economy is a highly effective tool for promoting cross-border trade. Market integration considerations are essential to understanding EU competition law.[297] Once a plausible pro-competitive justification for an agreement has been found, according to settled case law, it is no longer possible to make a blanket judgement on a competition infringement by object—rather, an effects analysis is necessary, which requires a precise knowledge of the various pro-competitive and welfare-enhancing consequences of the competitive act.[298] *Walker* also emphasises that the enormous consumer benefits of digital services should be taken more into account when applying competition law to platforms.[299] In terms of the criterion of effectiveness to be examined here, the weighting of the arguments in this regard in the expert report therefore appears to be insufficient—a more effective consultation would have more appropriately appreciated the undertakings' efficiency and welfare arguments.

3. Transparency of the report

All contributions received were published on DG COMP's website. There is no similar transparency in the expert report. As shown above, many topics raised by the contributions were also mentioned in the report and the focus was mostly similar. But these influences were not made clear either by direct mention of the contributions in question in the main text or by the footnote apparatus, so that the criterion of transparency must be judged as insufficiently fulfilled.

IV. Interim result

The expert report is a representative and in parts effective, albeit insufficiently transparent, evaluation of the consultation contributions. In particular, the prominent presentation of data as a central competition parameter for achieving market power in the digital age should be emphasised, be-

Economy: Measuring the Value of Free Digital Services on the Internet, Proceedings of the 33rd International Conference on Information Systems 2012," 2012.

297 E.g., ECJ, Cases 56 and 58–64, ECLI:EU:C:1966:41 – *Consten-Grundig*, p. 388.

298 For a summary of the case law, see the recent judgment in: ECJ, C-228/18 – *Budapest Bank*, para. 83.

299 Walker, above fn. 107, p. 2.

cause it implicitly positions itself to a significant dispute of opinion. At the same time, a greater reception of efficiency and innovation aspects of platforms would have been desirable. In view of this result, it should be emphasised that knowledge about new technologies can be gained in particular through the interaction of the competition authority with the numerous stakeholders.[300] In addition, the preceding analysis has highlighted how digital methods themselves can be used to enrich this consultation process.

E. Result

This paper has quantitatively and qualitatively analysed the consultation process initiated by the Commission on the reform of EU competition law in the digital age. The consultation was representative as the special advisors addressed core concerns of various stakeholders, in particular behavioural economics and data protection, the persistence of market power in digital markets, the regulatory function of platforms, and the leveraging of market power and data access to secondary markets. The weighting of these concerns was largely effective, with a focus on data that made sense in light of the relevant literature. However, greater consideration of reasons for an 'efficiency defence' and more transparent handling of individual stakeholder contributions would have been desirable. By employing digital methods to analyse both stakeholder contributions and the expert report, this contribution also showed that besides challenging competition law from a substantive point of view, digital innovations can also enrich the methodological toolkit of competition law researchers and enforcers and thereby help to prepare EU competition law for the digital age.

The thematic and argumentative differences identified in this paper between European undertakings on the one hand and dominant US platforms and academics funded by them on the other support the thesis cited in the introduction of an increasing "polarization"[301] of the debate on European competition law in the digital age. The phenomenon itself is not new: the genesis of the German competition law was already marked by media

300 This is also mentioned by: Mehra, above fn 24, pp. 1369, 1371; Autorité de la concurrence, Bundeskartellamt, above fn 53, p. 77.

301 Shapiro, "Antitrust in a Time of Populism," 2018, p. 714; Colomo, above fn. 21.

debates between SMEs and heavy industry.[302] What is new about the debate under investigation, however, is the extent to which the lobbying efforts of large technology undertakings increasingly blur the line between academic and interest-driven debate contributions, as evidenced by numerous references to financial support or studies produced in cooperation with industry documented in this paper. Against this backdrop, the addition of text mining methods is ambivalent: While quantitative representations and word metrics are well suited to structuring large amounts of text thematically or according to specific categories, the jurisprudential evaluation of arguments and footnote apparatus requires knowledge of the literature and the biographical background of the authors. Quantitative evaluations are thus only suitable as a complementary methodology, not as an end in themselves.

Advocating for reform of European competition law in such a polarised situation is demanding, yet necessary. The expert report examined here presents numerous innovative and sensible proposals, of which the detailed conditions for data access under Art. 102 TFEU, the competition law analysis of behavioural economic aspects of digital ecosystems, the shifting of the burden of proof to the detriment of undertakings with market power, and the use of remedies to restore the ex-ante state of competition are particularly noteworthy. Of the proposals of the expert report, so far, the criticism of the usual market definition has been taken up in particular, as the Commission announced that it would revise the notice on the definition of the relevant market issued in 1997. At the time of writing, the Commission has also presented two proposals, the Digital Services Act and the Digital Markets Act, that include new rules for digital platforms, promise to ensure that small businesses can freely and fairly compete online, and echo the 'restorative' remedies mentioned in the expert report.

The expert report analysed here is important, but at the same time it is framed on an abstract level, so that the exact form of regulation remains open. Many of the issues addressed in the report are currently the focus of cases pending before EU courts, which provide an opportunity to explore the changes addressed under European law. In addition, continued discussions with stakeholders on 'best practices' and the current state of the art can help further refine analytical frameworks and regulatory

302 Kutzner, *Marktwirtschaft schreiben. Das Wirtschaftsressort der Frankfurter Allgemeinen Zeitung 1949 bis 1992*, 2019, pp. 117–39.

interventions and address novel competition infringements before they actually occur[303]—the consultation process examined in this paper, with its representative range of participants and broad thematic coverage, illustrates the potential of 'participatory antitrust' to promote 'better regulation' in the digital age. Admittedly, the subjective and self-interested consultation contributions should be treated with caution. But as *Gal* rightly points out, the anti-competitive concerns and welfare effects arising from technological developments in the digital economy are too important to ignore until detailed and more objective evidence is available.[304] For the same reason, DG COMP needs to develop a workforce with technical expertise.

It is essential for a competition authority to identify the areas in which it needs to expand its capabilities through structured case selection and ex-post reflection.[305] As shown throughout this paper, the digitalisation of the economy raises new types of competition law issues, which make extensive technical background knowledge in DG COMP irreplaceable—an observation that is also shared by numerous stakeholders in their contributions[306] as well as the relevant literature.[307] In this respect, it is surprising that the expert report does not contain a proposal for the creation of a special unit for digital markets or a separate digital authority, in strong contrast to other expert reports on the digital age that have been published in the past years.[308]

The integration of technological knowledge could proceed analogously to the integration of economic knowledge into the Commission's practice, i.e., via personnel expansion. The post of Chief Economist was created in 2003, mainly in response to a series of judgments annulling Commission merger decisions and convincing the Commission that its decisions should be subject to more rigorous internal economic scrutiny.[309] Similarly, a future

303 ACCC, above fn. 104, pp. 25, 464.

304 Gal, "Algorithms as Illegal Agreements," 2019, esp. pp. 117 f.

305 Kovacic, "Deciding What to Do and How to Do It: Prioritization, Project Selection, and Competition Agency Effectiveness," 2018, pp. 9, 22 f.

306 *Masmi-Dazi*, p. 8; *Mediaset*, pp. 1f.; *ProSiebenSat.1*, p. 11; *Telefonica*, p. 12; *DPA*; Submission to Panel 2, p. 4; *Stiftung Neue Verantwortung*, p. 10; *Oxera*, Algorithmic Competition, p. 8.

307 Autorité de la concurrence, Bundeskartellamt, above fn. 53, p. 74; Bernhardt, Dewenter, above fn 54, pp. 20 f.; Schwalbe, above fn. 70, p. 568; Mehra, above fn. 24, p. 1370.

308 Furman et al, above fn 33, pp. 5–6; ACCC, above fn. 104, pp. 13–14; Stigler Center for the Study of the Economy and the State, above fn 133, p. 9.

309 Jones, Sufrin, above fn. 37, pp. 59, 98 f.

Chief Technologist could answer technical questions in the application of competition rules to undertakings in digital markets, provide guidance in the analysis of datasets, 'white-box' algorithms (see part B above) and algorithmically set prices, and contribute to the development of new regulatory tools, most notably in relation to a privacy-sensitive regime for mandated data access. It may also be given a role in the future in more rigorously scrutinising the acquisition of start-ups.[310] Finally, there would be the possibility of developing algorithms for the competition authority's own use,[311] maybe similar to the STM algorithm used in this paper to structure the stakeholder contributions.

During the Eisenhower administration in the 1950s, the US Antitrust Division pushed to better disseminate the new technological knowledge by opening up the data processing, consumer electronics and telecommunications sectors to both American and foreign competitors through lawsuits against IBM, AT&T, and RCA, thus shaping the development of the 'electronic century.'[312] For the coming years, to mark the beginning of an equally welfare-enhancing 'digital century,' it is necessary for the Commission to open up and keep open digital markets in the same way—for this, a sufficient understanding of the complex underlying technologies is essential, which can be built not least through a representative, effective, and transparent evaluation of the different perspectives of relevant stakeholders. On this basis, it might even be possible to turn digital technologies from an object of competition law into a methodological toolkit that helps to guarantee the law's continued successful application in the 'digital century.'

Bibliography

Abadi, Martin, David Andersen, "Learning to Protect Communications with Adversarial Neural Cryptog-raphy," *arXiv*, 2016, https://arxiv.org/pdf/1610.06918.pdf (last accessed: 08.05.2020).

Australian Competition & Consumer Commission (ACCC), "Digital Platforms Inquiry: final report," 2019.

Ahlborn, Christian, David Evans, and Jorge Padilla, "Competition Policy in the New Economy: Is European Competition Law Up to the Challenge?," *ECLR* 22 (2001): 156–167.

310 BMA, ACM, CDLCL, above fn. 103, p. 4.

311 Schwalbe, above fn. 70, p. 568.

312 Stoller, *Goliath: The 100-Year War Between Monopoly Power and Democracy*, 2019, pp. 194 f.

Akman, Pinar, "A Competition Law Assessment of Platform Most-Favoured-Customer Clauses," *Journal of Competition Law and Economics* 12, 4 (2016): 781–833.

Akman, Pinar, and D. Daniel Sokol, "Online RPM and MFN Under Antitrust Law and Economics," *Rev. Indust. Org.* 50, 2 (2017): 133–155.

Alemanno, Alberto, "How Much Better Is Better Regulation? Assessing the Impact of the Better Regulation Package on the European Union: A Research Agenda," *European Journal of Risk Regulation* 6, 3 (2015): 344–356.

Argenton, Cédric, and Jens Prüfer, "Search Engine Competition with Network Externalities," *J Competition L & Econ* 8, 1 (2011): 73–105.

Armstrong, Mark, "Competition in two-sided markets," *Rand J. Econ.* 37, 3 (2006): 668–691.

Asay, Matt, "'Whole Web' is the OS of the future," *CNET*, 2010, https://www.cnet.com/news/tim-oreilly-whole-web-is-the-os-of-the-future (last accessed: 27 April 2019).

Autorité de la concurrence/Bundeskartellamt, "Algorithms and Competition," 2019.

Autorité de la concurrence/Bundeskartellamt, "Competition Law and Data," 2016.

Ballard, Dylan, and Amar Naik, "Algorithms, Artificial Intelligence, and Joint Conduct," *CPI Antitrust Chronicle* 1, 2 (2017): 29–35.

Banko, Michele, and Eric Brill, "Scaling to very very large corpora for natural language disambiguation," Proceedings of the 39th Annual Meeting on Association for Computational Linguistics 1, 2001, pp. 26–33.

Bernhardt, Lea, and Ralf Dewenter, "Collusion by code or algorithmic collusion," *European Competition Journal* 16, 2–3 (2020): 312–342.

Bethell, Oliver, Gavin Baird, and Alexander Waksman, "Ensuring innovation through participative antitrust," *Journal of Antitrust Enforcement* 8, 1 (2020): 30–55.

Bitton, Dan, Mauritius Dolmans, Henry Mostyn, and David Pearl, "Competition In Display Ad Technology: A Retrospective Look At Google/Doubleclick and Google/Admob," *CPI*, 2019, https://www.competitionpolicyinternational.com/competition-in-display-ad-technology-a-retrospective-look-at-google-doubleclick-and-google-admob (last accessed: 8 May 2020).

Blei, David, "Probabilistic Topic Models," *Communications of the ACM* 55, 4 (2012): 77–84.

Blei, David, Andrew Ng, and Michael Jordan, "Latent Dirichlet Allocation," *Journal of Machine Learning Research* 3, (2003): 993–1022.

BMA, ACM, and CDLCL, "Joint memorandum of the Belgian, Dutch and Luxembourg competition authorities on challenges faced by competition authorities in a digital world," (2019), https://www.belgiancompetition.be/sites/default/files/content/download/files/bma_acm_cdlcl.joint_memorandum_191002.pdf (last accessed: 08.05.2020).

Borgesius, Frederik Zuiderveen, and Joost Poort, "Online price discrimination and EU data privacy law," *Journal Consumer Policy* 40 (2017): 347–366.

Bork, Robert, and Gregory Sidak, "What Does the Chicago School Teach about Internet Search and the Antitrust Treatment of Google?," *J Competition L & Econ* 8, (2012): 663–700.

Borocas, Solon, and Andrew Selbst, "Big Data's disparate Impact," California Law Review 104, 3 (2016): 671–732.

Borsenberger, Claire, "The Concentration Phenomenon in E-commerce," in *Postal and Delivery Innovation in the Digital Economy*, ed. Michael A. Crew, Timothy J. Brennan, Springer International Publishing, 2015, pp. 31–41.

Broemel, Roland, and Hans-Heinrich Trute, "Alles nur Datenschutz?," *Berliner Debatte Initial* 27, 4 (2016): 50–65.

Brouwer, Tobias, "Lobby-Compliance: Wege zu einer besseren und transparenteren Gesetzgebung," *CCZ* 1, (2019): 2–11.

Bruc, Edouard, "Data as an essential facility in European law: how to define the 'target' market and divert the data pipeline?," *European Competition Journal* 15, 2–3 (2019): 177–224.

Brynjolfsson, Erik, Avinash Collis, and Felix Eggers, "Using Massive Online Choice Experiments to Measure Changes in Well-Being," *PNAS* 116, 15 (2019): 7250–7255.

Brynjolfsson, Erik, Avinash Collis, and Felix Eggers, "Using Massive Online Choice Experiments to Measure Changes in Well-being," NBER Working Paper, 2018, https://www.nber.org/papers/w24514.pdf (last accessed: 9 May 2020).

Brynjolfsson, Erik, Joo Hee Oh, "The Attention Economy: Measuring the Value of Free Digital Services on the Internet," Proceedings of the 33rd International Conference on Information Systems, 2012, https://aisel.aisnet.org/cgi/viewcontent.cgi?article=1045&context=icis2012 (last accessed: 9 May 2020).

Bundeskartellamt, "Arbeitspapier Marktmacht von Plattformen und Netzwerken," No. B6–113/15, 2016.

Bundesministerium für Wirtschaft und Energie, "Ein neuer Wettbewerbsrahmen für die Digitalwirtschaft: Bericht der Kommission Wettbewerbsrecht," 4.0, 2019.

Calliess, Christian, Matthias Ruffert, and Hans-Joachim Cremer, *EUV/AEUV*, 5th ed., München: C. H. Beck, 2016.

Camesasca, Peter et al, "Google: Why the EU and US Positions Are an Ocean Apart," *Global Competition Rev 16, 3* (2013): 35.

Chase, Peter, and Adam Schlosser, "Better Regulation: An Ongoing Journey," *EJRR* 6, 3 (2015): 378–379.

Chiou, Lesley, and Catherine Tucker, "Search Engines and Data Retention: Implications for Privacy and Anti-trust," MIT Sloan School Working Paper No. 5094–14, 2014, https://papers.ssrn.com/sol3/papers.cfm?abstract_id=2441333 (last accessed: 9 May 2020).

CMA, "Pricing Algorithms: Economic Working Paper on the Use of Algorithms to Facilitate Collusion and Per-sonalised Pricing," 2018.

CMA, "The CMA's Digital Markets Strategy," 2019, https://assets.publishing.service.gov.uk/government/uploads/system/uploads/attachment_data/file/814709/cma_digital_strategy_2019.pdf (last accessed: 8 May 2020).

Collyer, Kate/Mullan, Hugh/Timan, Natalie, "Measuring Market Power in Multi-Sided Markets," *CPI Antitrust Chronicle* 3, 44 (2017), https://www.competitionpolicyinternational.com/wp-content/uploads/2017/09/CPI-Collyer-Mullan-Timan.pdf (last accessed: 8 May 2020).

Colomo, Pablo Ibanez, "From a distance, literally and figuratively," Chillin' Competition Blog, 2020, https://chillingcompetition.com/2020/03/25/from-a-distance-literally-and-figuratively (last accessed: 8 May 2020).

Coupette, Corinna, *Juristische Netzwerkforschung. Modellierung, Quantifizierung und Visualisierung relationaler Daten im Recht*, Tübingen: Mohr Siebeck, 2019.

Coupette, Corinna, and Andreas Fleckner, "Quantitative Rechtswissenschaft. Sammlung, Analyse und Kommunikation juristischer Daten," *JZ* 73, 8 (2018): 379–389.

Crane, Daniel, "Search Neutrality and Referral Dominance," *J Competition L & Econ* 8, 3 (2012): 459–468.

D'Souza, Deborah, "Tech Lobby: Internet Giants Spend Record Amounts, Electronic Firms Trim Budget" *Investopedia*, 2019, https://www.investopedia.com/tech/what-are-tech-giants-lobbying-trump-era (last accessed: 15 April 2020).

Dawson, Marc, "Better regulation and the future of EU regulatory law and politics," *CMLRev* 53, 5 (2016), 1209–1235.

De Cnudde, Sofie, David Martens, Theodoros Evgeniou, and Foster Provost, "A Benchmarking Study of Classi-fication Techniques for Behavioral Data," Dept. of Engineering (University of Antwerp) Research Paper No. 5, 2017, https://econpapers.repec.org/paper/antwpaper/2017005.htm (last accessed: 9 May 2020).

De Corniere, Alexandre, and Gregg Taylor, "Upstream Bundling and Leverage of Market Power," CEPR Discussion Paper No. DP13083, 2018, https://papers.ssrn.com/sol3/papers.cfm?abstract_id=3222597 (last accessed: 9 May 2020).

De Pablo, Alfonso Lamadrid, "Shortcuts and Courts in the Era of Digitization," *CPI Antitrust Chronicle* 1, 2 (2019): 1–11.

Delibašić, Boris, "White-Box or Black-Box Decision Tree Algorithms: Which to Use in Education?," *IEEE Trans Educ* 56, 3 (2012): 287–291.

Dolmans, Mauritius, and Tobias Pesch, "Should we disrupt antitrust law?," *CLPD*, 2019, https://www.clearygottlieb.com/-/media/files/should-we-disrupt-antitrust-law-pdf.pdf (last accessed: 8 May 2020).

Duch-Brown, Néstor, "The Competitive Landscape of Online Platforms," European Commission JRC Digital Economic Working Paper No. 04, 2017: 1–35.

Eckert, Andreas, "Danksagungen gegen den Strich lesen," *FAZ*, 27 April 2020.

Eliantonio, Mariolina, and Aneta Spendzharova, "The European Union's New 'Better Regulation' Agenda: Between Procedures and Politics," *European Journal of Law Reform* 19, 1–2 (2017): 3–15.

Emmerich, Volker, *Kartellrecht: Ein Studienbuch*, 11th ed., München: C. H. Beck, 2008.

Evans, David, "Attention Rivalry Among Online Platforms," *J. Competition L. & Econ.* 9, 2 (2013): 313–357.

Evans, David, "Multisided Platforms, Dynamic Competition, and the Assessment of Market Power for Internet-Based Firms," Coase-Sandor Working Paper Series in Law and Economics No. 753, 2016, pp. 1–31.

Evans, David, "The Antitrust Economics of Free," Chicago John M. Olin Law & Economics Working Paper No. 555, 2011, pp. 1–26.

Evans, David, "Why the Dynamics of Competition for Online Platforms Leads to Sleepless Nights, but Not Sleepy Monopolies," *SSRN*, 2017 https://papers.ssrn.com/sol3/papers.cfm?abstract_id=3009438 (last accessed: 9 May 2020).

Evans, David, and Michael Noel, "Defining Antitrust Markets When Firms Operate Two-Sided Platforms," *Colum. Bus. L. Rev.* 3 (2005): 667–702.

Evans, David, and Richard Schmalensee, *Matchmakers: The New Economics of Multi-sided Platforms*, Boston: Harvard Business Review Press, 2016.

Ezrachi, Ariel, and Maurice Stucke, "Artificial Intelligence & Collusion: When Computers Inhibit Competition," *University of Illinois Law Review* 5 (2017): 1775–1810.

Ezrachi, Ariel, Maurice Stucke, "Two Artificial Neural Networks Meet in an Online Hub and Change the Future (of Competition, Market Dynamics and Society)," Oxford Legal Studies Research Paper No. 24, 2017, https://papers.ssrn.com/sol3/papers.cfm?abstract_id=2949434## (last accessed: 8 May 2020).

Ezrachi, Ariel, and Maurice Stucke, "Virtual Competition," *Journal of European Competition Law & Practice* 7, 9 (2016): 585–586.

Farrel, Joseph, and Garth Saloner, "Standardization, Compatibility and Innovation," *RAND Journal of Economics* 16, 1 (1985): 70–83.

Faust, Florian, and Hans-Bernd Schäfer, *Zivilrechtliche und rechtsökonomische Probleme des Internet und der künstlichen Intelligenz. 15. Travemünder Symposium zur ökonomischen Analyse des Rechts*, Tübingen: Mohr Siebeck, 2019.

Ferri, Paolo, Maria Lusiani, and Luca Pareschi, "Accounting for Accounting History: A Topic modeling Approach (1996–2015)," *Accounting History* 23, 1–2 (2018): 173–205.

Filistrucchi, Lapo, Damien Geradin, Eric van Damme, Eric, and Pauline Affeldt, "Market Definition in Two-Sided Markets: Theory and Practice," *JCL&E* 10, 2 (2014): 293–339.

Fischbach, Rainer, "Big Data – Big Confusion. Weshalb es noch immer keine künstliche Intelligenz gibt," *Berliner Debatte Initial* 31, 1 (2020): 136–147.

Foroohar, Rana, *Don't Be Evil: The Case Against Big Tech*, London: Allen Lane, 2019.

Franzius, Claudio, "Demokratisierung der Europäischen Union," *EuR* 48 (2013): 655–668.

Franzius, Claudio, and Ulrich Preuß, *Die Zukunft der europäischen Demokratie*, Baden-Baden: Nomos, 2012.

Furman, Jason et al., "Unlocking Digital Competition: Report of the Digital Competition Expert Panel," 2019.

Gal, Michael, "Algorithms as Illegal Agreements," *Berkeley Technology Law Journal* 34 (2019): 67–118.

Gal, Michal, and Niva Elkin-Koren, "Algorithmic Consumers," *Harv JL & Tech* 30 (2016): 309–353.

Gal, Michal, and Daniel Rubinfeld, "The Hidden Costs of Free Goods: Implications for Antitrust Enforcement," *Antitrust Law Journal* 80, 3 (2016): 521–580.

Garben, Sacha, "An 'Impact Assessment' of EU Better Regulation," in *The EU Better Regulation Agenda: A Critical Assessment*, ed. Sacha Garben and Inge Govaere, Oxford: Hart Publishing, 2018, pp. 217–242.

Gassler, Martin, "Why the introduction of a new transaction-value jurisdictional threshold for the EUMR has been postponed, at least for now," *Oxford Competition Law*, 2019, https://oxcat.ouplaw.com/page/775 (last accessed: 9 May 2020).

Geroski, Paul, "Competition in Markets and Competition for Markets," *Journal of Industry, Competition and Trade* 3, 3 (2003): 151–166.

Gitelman, Lisa, "'Raw Data' is an Oxymoron," Cambridge (MA): The MIT Press, 2013.

Goodfellow, Ian, Yoshua Bengio, and Aaron Courville, *Deep Learning*, Cambridge (MA): The MIT Press, 2016.

Graef, Inge, *EU Competition Law, Data Protection and Online Platforms: Data as Essential Facility*, Alphen aan den Rijn: Wolters Kluwer, 2016.

Graef, Inge, "Market Definition and Market Power in Data: the Case of Online Platforms," *World Competition* 38, 4 (2015): 473–506.

Graf, Thomas, and Henry Mostyn, "European Union – Access to Online Platforms and Competition Law," *GCR*, 2019, https://globalcompetitionreview.com/insight/e-commerce-competition-enforcement-guide-second-edition/1209647/european-union---access-to-online-platforms-and-competition-law (last ac-cessed: 8 May 2020).

Grimmer, Justin, and Brandon Stewart, "Text as Data: The Promise and Pitfalls of Automatic Content Analysis Methods for Political Texts," *Political Analysis* 21, 3 (2013): 267–297.

Grossman, Gene, and Elhanan Helpman, "Foreign investment with endogenous protection," in *The Political Econ-omy of Trade Policy*, eds Robert Feenstra, Gene Grossman, and Douglas Irwin, Cambridge (MA): The MIT Press, 1996, pp. 199–223.

Grossman, Gene, and Elhanan Helpman, *Interest Groups and Trade Policy*, Princeton: Princeton University Press, 2002.

Grunes, Allen, and Maurice Stucke, "No Mistake about It: The Important Role of Antitrust in the Era of Big Data," Antitrust Source, 2015, https://papers.ssrn.com/sol3/papers.cfm?abstract_id=2600051## (last accessed: 9 May 2020).

Halevy, Alon, Peter Norvig, and Fernando Pereira, "The Unreasonable Effectiveness of Data," *Intelligent Systems, IEEE* 24 (2009): 8–12.

Hamann, Hanjo, "Die Fußnote, das unbekannte Wesen – Potential und Grenzen juristischer Zitationsanalyse," *ReWiss* 4 (2014): 501–534.

Hamburger, Tom, and Matea Gold, "Google, Once Disdainful of Lobbying, Now a Master of Washington Influence," *Washington Post*, 2014, https://www.washingtonpost.com/politics/how-google-is-transforming-power-and-politicsgoogle-once-disdainful-of-lobbying-now-a-master-of-washington-influence/2014/04/12/51648b92-b4d3-11e3-8cb6-284052554d74_story.html (last accessed: 15 March 2020).

Harrington Jr, Joseph, "Developing Competition Law for Collusion by Autonomous Price-setting Agents," *SSRN*, 2017, https://papers.ssrn.com/sol3/papers.cfm?abstract_id=3037818 (last accessed: 8 May 2020).

Havenstein, Heather, "Spring comes to AI winter," *Computerworld* 39, 7 (2015): 28–29.

Héritier, Adrienne, "Composite democracy in Europe. The role of transparency and access to information," *Journal of European Public Policy* 10, 5 (2013): 814–833.

Hestness, Joel, Sharan Narang, Newsha Ardalani, et al., "Deep Learning Scaling is Predictable, Empirically," *arxiv*, 2017, https://arxiv.org/abs/1712.00409 (last accessed: 27 April 2020).

Hillman, Arye, *The Political Economy of Protection*, London: Harwood Academic Publishers, 1989.

Hillman, Arye, and Heinrich Ursprung, "Multinational firms, political competition, and international trade policy," *Int. Econ. Rev.* 34, 2 (1993): 347–363.

Hoeren, Thomas, Ulrich Sieber, and Bernd Holznagel, *Multimedia-Recht*, 50th ed., München: C. H. Beck, 2019.

Hoppner, Thomas, "Defining Markets for Multi-Sided Platforms: The Case of Search Engines," *World Competition* 38, 3 (2015): 349–366.

Hoppner, Thomas, "Google: Friend or Foe of Ad-Financed Content Providers?," *J Media L* 5, 1 (2013): 14–30.

Horstmann, Jan, "Topic Modeling," *forTEXT*, 2018, https://fortext.net/routinen/methoden/topic-modeling (last accessed: 09.05.2020).

Hu, Han, and Yonggang Wen, et al., "Toward Scalable Systems for Big Data Analytics: A Technology Tutorial," *IEEE Access* 2 (2014): 652–687.

Immenga, Ulrich, and Ernst-Joachim Mestmäcker, *EU-Wettbewerbsrecht*, 6th ed., München: C. H. Beck, 2019.

Jannidis, Fotis, "Quantitative Analyse literarischer Texte am Beispiel des Topic Modeling," *Der Deutschunterricht* 68, 5 (2016): 24–35.

Jones, Alison, and Brenda Sufrin, *EU Competition Law*, Oxford: Oxford University Press, 2014.

Kaeding, Michael, "In Search of Better Quality of EU Regulations for Prompt Transposition: The Brussels Perspective," *European Law Journal* 14, 5 (2008): 583–603.

Kalbheim, Jan, "Der Einfluss der Richter des Europäischen Gerichtshofs auf dessen Rechtsprechung – eine empirisch-statistische Analyse der Rolle des Berichterstatters," *ZVglRWiss* 115 (2016): 431–382.

Kerber, Wolfgang, and Jonas Frank, "Data Governance Regimes in the Digital Economy: The Example of Con-nected Cars," *SSRN*, 2017, https://papers.ssrn.com/sol3/papers.cfm?abstract_id=3064794 (last accessed: 30 April 2020).

Khan, Lina, "Amazon's Antitrust Paradox," *Yale L.J.* 126 (2017): 710–805.

Khan, Lina, "The Separation of Platforms and Commerce," *Columbia Law Review* 199 (2018): 973–1094.

Kokkoris, Ioannis, and Tommaso Valletti, "Innovation Considerations in Horizontal Merger Control," *Journal of Competition Law & Economics* 16, 2 (2020): 220–261, https://academic.oup.com/jcle/advance-article-abstract/doi/10.1093/joclec/nhaa008/5820042 (last accessed: 8 May 2020).

Kovacic, William, "Deciding What to Do and How to Do It: Prioritization, Project Selection, and Competition Agency Effectiveness," *Competition Law Review* 13, 1 (2018): 9–26.

Künstner, Manuel, "Preissetzung durch Algorithmen als Herausforderung des Kartellrechts," *GRUR* (2019): 36–42.

Kuoppamäki, Petri, and Torstila, Sami, "Is There a Future for an Efficiency Defence in European Merger Control?," *SSRN*, 2015, https://ssrn.com/abstract=2727171 (last accessed: 9 May 2020).

Küsters, Anselm, "Artificial Intelligence, Law and Legal History," *Die Funzel* 4, 1 (2020): 27–29.

Küsters, Anselm, Laura Volkind, and Andreas Wagner, "Digital Humanities and the State of Legal History. A Text Mining Perspective," *Rg 27* (2019): 244–259.

Kutzner, Maximilian, *Marktwirtschaft schreiben. Das Wirtschaftsressort der Frankfurter Allgemeinen Zeitung 1949 bis 1992*, Tübingen: Mohr Siebeck, 2019.

Lafontaine, Francine, and Margaret Slade, "Vertical Integration and Firm Boundaries: The Evidence," *J Econ Literature* 45, 3 (2007): 629–685.

Lambrecht, Anja, and Catherine Tucker, "Can big data protect a firm from competition?," *Competition Policy International*, 2015, https://www.competitionpolicyinternational.com/can-big-data-protect-a-firm-from-competition/ (last accessed: 9 May 2020).

Lear, "Ex-post assessment of merger control decisions in digital markets," *Lear*, 2019, https://www.learlab.com/wp-content/uploads/2019/06/CMA_past_digital_mergers_GOV.UK_version-1.pdf (last accessed: 8 May 2020).

LeVine, Steve, "How Old Tech could roar back," *Axios* (2018), https://www.axios.com/big-tech-newrivals-old-tech-ibm-uber-facebook-1519609801-80daea23-cee2-44bf-ad54-f65336a996c2.html (last accessed: 9 May 2020).

Lianos, Ioannis, and Evgenia Motchenkova, "Market Dominance and Search Quality in the Search Engine Mar-ket," *J Competition L & Econ* 9, 2 (2013): 419–455.

Listorti, Giulia, Egle Basyte Ferrari, Svetlana Acs, et al., "The debate on the EU Better Regulation Agenda: a literature review," 2019, https://ec.europa.eu/jrc/en/publication/debate-eu-better-regulation-agenda-literature-review (last accessed: 9 May 2020).

Louven, Sebastian, "Datenmacht und Zugang zu Daten," *NZKart* 5 (2018): 217–222.

Louven, Sebastian, "Datenzugangsverhältnis, FRAND und Wettbewerbsrecht," *K&R* 4 (2018): 230–236.

Luchetta, Giacomo, "Is the Google Platform a Two-sided Market?," *J Competition L & Econ* 10 (2013): 185–222.

Mandrescu, Daniel, "Applying EU Competition Law to Online Platforms: The Road Ahead – Part 2," *European Competition Law Review* 28, 9 (2017): 410–422.

Manne, Geoffrey, and Raymond Sperry, "The Problems and Perils of Bootstrapping Privacy and Data into an Antitrust Framework," *CPI Antitrust Chronicle* 5 (2015), https://papers.ssrn.com/sol3/papers.cfm?abstract_id=2617685 (last accessed: 9 May 2020).

Manne, Geoffrey, and Joshua Wright, "Google and the Limits of Antitrust: The Case Against the Antitrust Case Against Google," *Harvard J L Public Policy* 34 (2011): 171–244.

Matzner, Tobias, "Beyond data as representation: The performativity of Big Data in surveillance," *Surveillance & Society* 14, 2 (2016): 197–210.

Maunz, Theodor, and Günter Dürig, *Grundgesetz-Kommentar*, 88th ed., München: C. H. Beck, 2019.

Mehra, Salil, "Antitrust and the Robo-Seller: Competition in the Time of Algorithms," *Minnesota Law Review* 100 (2016): 1323–1375.

Mödinger, Maximilian, *Bessere Rechtsetzung. Leistungsfähigkeit eines europäischen Konzepts*, Tübingen: Mohr Siebeck, 2020.

Monopolkommission, "Wettbewerbspolitik: Herausforderung digitale Märkte," Sondergutachten No. 68 (2015).

Mullins, Brody, and Jack Nicas, "Paying Professors: Inside Google's Academic Influence Campaign," *The Wall Street Journal*, 2017, https://www.wsj.com/articles/paying-professors-inside-googles-academic-influence-campaign-1499785286?mod=e2tw (last accessed: 15 April 2020).

Murray, Grant, "European Commission conference on 'Shaping competition policy in an era of digitisation': 5 key points and practical implications," *Kluwer Competition Law Blog*, 2019, http://competitionlawblog.kluwercompetitionlaw.com/2019/01/24/european-commission-conference-on-shaping-competition-policy-in-an-era-of-digitisation-5-key-points-and-practical-implications/ (last accessed: 9 May2020).

Nazzini, Renato, "Google and the (Ever-stretching) Boundaries of Article 102," *Journal of European Competition Law & Practice* 6, 5 (2015): 301–313.

Newman, John, "Antitrust in Zero-price Markets: Foundation," *University of Pennsylvania Law Review* 164, 1 (2015): 149–206.

OECD, Working Party on Privacy and Security in the Digital Economy, "Summary of the OECD Privacy Expert Roundtable. Protecting Privacy in a Data-driven Economy: Taking Stock of Current Thinking," 2014, www.oecd.org/officialdocuments/publicdisplaydocumentpdf/?cote=dsti/iccp/reg(2014)3&doclanguage=en (last accessed: 12 October.2016).

OECD, "An Introduction to Online Platforms and their Role in the Digital Transformation," 2019.

OECD, "Background Note: Latin American and Caribbean Competition Forum – Session III: Practical Approaches to Assessing Digital Platform Markets for Competition Law Enforcement," 2019.

OECD, "Competition Issues In Aftermarkets: Background note by the Secretariat," *DAF/COMP* 2 (2017), https://one.oecd.org/document/DAF/COMP(2017)2/en/pdf (last accessed: 9 May 2020).

Paal, Boris, "Missbrauchstatbestand und Algorithmic Pricing," *GRUR* (2019): 43–53.

Pasquale, Frank, *The Black Box Society: The Secret Algorithms that Control Money and Information*, Cambridge (MA): Harvard University Press, 2016.

Patterson, Mark, "Conflicts of Interest in Scientific Expert Testimony," *William & Mary L. Rev.* 40, 4 (1999): 1313–1394.

Petit, Nicolas, "Antitrust and Artificial Intelligence: A Research Agenda," *Journal of European Competition Law & Practice* 8, 6 (2017): 361–362.

Pischel, Gerhard, and Reinhold Kopp, *Compliance für Wirtschaftsverbände*, München: C. H. Beck, 2017.

Pitofsky, Robert, "New Definitions of Relevant Market and the Assault on Antitrust," *Columbia L Rev 90* (1990): 1805–1864.

Podszun, Rupprecht, "Conference Debriefing (6): Shaping the Future of Competition Policy," *D-Kart Blog*, 2019, https://www.d-kart.de/blog/2019/01/22/conference-debriefing-6-shaping-the-future-of-competition-policy/ (last accessed: 9 May 2020).

Podszun, Rupprecht, "GWB10: Die Lage," *D-Kart Blog*, 2020, https://www.d-kart.de/blog/2020/01/30/gwb10-die-lage-1/ (last accessed: 8 May 2020).

Podszun, Rupprecht, "Innovation, Variety & Fair Choice – New Rules for the Digital Economy: Expert Opinion for Finanzplatz München Initiative (FPMI)," *SSRN*, 2017, https://ssrn.com/abstract=3243403 (last accessed: 9 May 2020).

Podszun, Rupprecht, and Marius Leber, "Internetkartellrecht," *Kölner Zeitschrift zum Wirtschaftsrecht* 6, 4 (2015): 316–328.

Pohlmeier, Julia, *Netzwerkeffekte und Kartellrecht*, Baden-Baden: Nomos, 2004.

Polk, Andreas, "Die Drehtür der Demokratie," *Spiegel Online*, 2017, https://www.spiegel.de/politik/deutschland/politik-und-lobbyismus-die-drehtuer-der-demokratie-gastbeitrag-andreas-polk-a-1167806.html (last accessed: 14 May 2020).

Potters, Jan, and Randolph Sloof, "Interest groups: a survey of empirical models that try to assess their influence," *Eur. J. Polit. Econ.* 12, 3 (1996): 403–442.

Radaelli, Claudio, "Whither Better Regulation for the Lisbon Agenda," *Journal of European Public Policy* 14, 2 (2007): 190–207.

Radaelli, Claudio, and Anne Meuwese, "Better Regulation in Europe: Between Public Management and Regulatory Reform," *Public Administration* 87, 3 (2009): 639–654.

Ranchordás, Sofia, "Consultations, Citizen Narratives and Evidence-based Regulation: The Strange Case of the Consultation on the Collaborative Economy," *European Journal of Law Reform* 19, 1–2 (2017): 52–73.

Ritschel, Gregor, and Thomas Müller, "Big Data als Theorieersatz?," *Berliner Debatte Initial* 27, 4 (2016): 4–12.

Riziotis, Dimitris, "Efficiency Defence in Article 82 EC," in *Abuse of Dominant Position: New Interpretation, New Enforcement Mechanisms?*, ed. Mark-Oliver Mackenrodt, Beatriz Conde Gallego, and Stefan Enchelmaier, Berlin: Springer, 2008, pp. 98–115.

Roberts, Margaret, et al., "Structural Topic Models for Open-Ended Survey Responses," *American Journal of Political Science* 58 (2014): 1064–1082.

Roberts, Margaret, Brandon Stewart, and Edoardo Airoldi, "A model of text for experimentation in the social sciences," *Journal of the American Statistical Association* 111, 515 (2016): 988–1003.

Roberts, Margaret, Brandon Stewart, and Dustin Tingley, "stm: R Package for Structural Topic Models," *Journal of Statistical Software* 91, 2 (2019): 1–40.

Robertson, Viktoria, "Delineating Digital Markets under EU Competition Law: Challenging or Futile?," *CompLRev* 12, 2 (2017): 131–151.

Rochet, Jean-Charles, and Jean Tirole, "Platform competition in two-sided markets," *Journal of the European Economic Association* 1, 4 (2003): 990–1029.

Rochet, Jean-Charles, and Jean Tirole, "Two-Sided Markets: A Progress Report," *RAND J of Economics* 37, 3 (2006): 645–667.

Russell, Stuart, and Peter Norvig, *Artificial Intelligence. A Modern Approach*, 3rd ed., Harlow: Pearson, 2016.

Rysman, Marc, "The Economics of Two-Sided Markets," *J of Economic Perspectives* 23, 3 (2009): 125–143.

Salop, Steven, "Invigorating Vertical Merger Enforcement," *Yale L.J.* 127 (2018): 1962–1994.

Savary, Fiona, *Regulierung dominanter Internetplattformen. Eigenheiten, Herausforderungen und Lösungsansätze im Licht von Ökonomie, Innovation und Recht*, Zürich: Dike, 2017.

Schmidhuber, Jürgen, "Deep Learning in Neural Networks: An Overview," *Neural Networks* 61 (2015): 85–117.

Schmidt, Karsten, "Zueignung aus Zuneigung – Vorstudien zu einer juristischen Dedikationslehre," *JuristenZeitung* 45, 23 (1990): 1121–1123.

Schmidt, Vivien, "Democracy and Legitimacy in the European Union Revisited: Input, Output and 'Through-put'," *Political Studies* 61, 1 (2013): 2–22.

Schwalbe, Ulrich, "Algorithms, Machine Learning, and Collusion," *Journal of Competition Law & Economics* 14, 4 (2018): 568–607.

Schweitzer, Heike, Jacques Crémer, and Yves Montjoye, "Report on Competition Law in the Digital Age," 2019, https://ec.europa.eu/competition/publications/reports/kd0419345enn.pdf (last accessed: 8 May 2020)

Schweitzer, Heike, Thomas Fetzer, and Martin Peitz, "Digitale Plattformen: Bausteine für einen künftigen Ordnungsrahmen," Zentrum für Europäische Wirtschaftsforschung GmbH Discussion Paper No. 16–042, 2016, http://ftp.zew.de/pub/zew-docs/dp/dp16042.pdf (last accessed: 8 May 2020).

Schweitzer, Heike, Justus Haucap, Wolfgang Kerber, and Robert Welker, "Modernisierung der Missbrauchsaufsicht für marktmächtige Unternehmen," 2018, https://www.bmwi.de/Redaktion/DE/Publikationen/Wirtschaft/modernisierung-der-missbrauchsaufsicht-fuer-marktmaechtige-unternehmen.pdf?__blob=publicationFile&v=15 (last accessed: 8 May 2020).

Shapiro, Carl, "Antitrust in a Time of Populism," *Int'l J Indus Org* (2018): 714–747.

Sharma, Kaushal, "SSNIP Test: A Useful Tool, Not a Panacea," *Competition LR* 1 (2011): 178–182.

Siems, Mathias, "Statistische Rechtsvergleichung," *RabelsZ* 72, 2 (2008): 354–390.

Silge, Julia, and David Robinson, *Text Mining with R: A Tidy Approach*, Newton (MA): O'Reilly, 2020, https://www.tidytextmining.com (last accessed: 9 May 2020).

Sivinski, Greg, Alex Okuliar, and Lars Kjolbye, "Is big data a big deal? A competition law approach to big data," *European Competition Journal* 13, 2–3 (2017): 199–227.

Sokol, Daniel, "Vertical Mergers and Entrepreneurial Exit," *Florida Law Review* 70 (2018): 1357–1378.

Speth, Rudolf, and Annette Zimmer, *Lobby Work. Interessenvertretung als Politikgestaltung*, Berlin: Springer, 2015.

Stigler Center for the Study of the Economy and the State, "Report of the Committee for the Study of Digital Platforms: Markets Structure and Antitrust Subcommittee," 2019.

Stoller, Matt, *Goliath: The 100-Year War Between Monopoly Power and Democracy*, New York: Simon & Schuster 2019.

Stucke, Maurice, and Allen Grunes, *Big Data and Competition Policy*, Oxford: Oxford University Press, 2016.

Sukhbaatar, Sainbayar, Arthur Szlam, and Rob Fergus, "Learning Multiagent Communication with Backpropa-gation," *NIPS* (2016), https://papers.nips.cc/paper/6398-learning-multiagent-communication-with-backpropagation.pdf (last accessed: 8 May 2020).

Telle, Sebastian, "Konditionenmissbrauch durch Ausplünderung von Plattform-Nutzerdaten," *WRP 7* (2016): 814–820.

Tolón, Eliana, "The Dynamics of Platform Business Value Creation," *CPI Antitrust Chronicle*, 2017, https://www.competitionpolicyinternational.com/the-dynamics-of-platform-business-value-creation/ (last accessed: 9 May 2020).

Tombs, Steve, "Making Better Regulation, Making Regulation Better?," *Policy Studies* 37, 4 (2016): 332–349.

Tucker, Darren, and Hill Wellford, "Big Mistakes Regarding Big Data," *Antitrust Source* 14, 2 (2014), https://papers.ssrn.com/sol3/papers.cfm?abstract_id=2549044 (last accessed: 9 May 2020).

Van de Geer, Ruben, et al., "Dynamic Pricing and Learning with Competition: Insights from the Dynamic Pricing Challenge at the 2017 INFORMS RM & Pricing Conference," *Journal of Revenue and Pricing Management* 18, 3 (2019): 185–203.

Van den Abeele, Eric, "'Better Regulation': A Bureaucratic Simplification with a Political Agenda," ETUI Working Paper No. 04, 2015, https://ssrn.com/abstract=2628067.

Van Gorp, Nicolai, Olga Batura, et al., "Challenges for Competition Policy in a Digitalised Economy," Study for the ECON Committee, 2015, https://www.europarl.europa.eu/thinktank/en/document.html?reference=IPOL_STU%282015%29542235 (last accessed: 8 May 2020).

Verhaert, Joyce, "The Challenges Involved with the Application of Article 102 TFEU to the New Economy: a Case Study of Google," *Eur Competition L Rev* 35, 6 (2014): 265–370.

Vogel, Friedemann, Hanjo Hamann, and Isabelle Gauer, "Computer-Assisted Legal Linguistics: Corpus Analysis as a New Tool for Legal Studies," *Law & Social Inquiry* 43, 4 (2018): 1340–1363.

Völcker, Sven, and Robert Benditz, "Die Entwicklung des europäischen Kartellrechts in den Jahren 2018 und 2019," *EuZW* 31, 7 (2020): 259–269.

Voss, Axel, "Digitale Dynamik in Gesetzgebungsprozessen," *ZRP* (2019): 211–213.

Walker, Mike, "Competition policy and digital platforms: six uncontroversial propositions," *European Competition Journal* 16, 1 (2020): 1–10.

Weck, Thomas, "Current Issues of Competition Policy in E Commerce, 2nd CoRe Conference Proceedings: Current Issues of Competition Policy in E-Commerce," 2019, https://core.lexxion.eu/data/article/13913/pdf/core_2019_01-016.pdf (last accessed: 8 May 2020).

WEF, "Competition Policy in a Globalized, Digitalized Economy," 2019.

WEF, "Platforms and Ecosystems," 2019.

Wehrheim, Lino, "Economic history goes digital: topic modeling the Journal of Economic History," *Cliometrica* 13, 1 (2019): 83–125.

Wersig, "Gesetzgebung ist nicht geschlechtsneutral," *ZRP* (2019): 244–247.

Weyl, Glen, and Alexnader White, "Let the Right 'One' Win: Policy Lessons from the New Economics of Platforms," *Competition Policy International* 10, 2 (2014): 29–51.

Wiedemann, *Kartellrecht*, 4th ed., München: C. H. Beck, 2020.

Woodcock, Ramsi, "The Bargaining Robot," *CPI Antitrust Chronicle* 40 (2017), https://ssrn.com/abstract=2972228 (last accessed: 8 May 2020).

Wu, Tim, *The Curse of Bigness: Antitrust in the New Gilded Age*, New York: Columbia Global Reports, 2018.

Zander-Hayat, Helga, Lucia Reisch, and Christine Steffen, "Personalisierte Preise – Eine verbraucherpolitische Einordnung," *VuR* (2016): 403–409.

Zimmer, Daniel, "Significant Impediment to Effective Competition," *ZWeR* 2 (2004): 250.

Zuboff, Shoshana, *The Age of Surveillance Capitalism*, New York: PublicAffairs, 2019.

Contributors (in alphabetical order)

Philip Maximilian Bender

Dr. Philip Maximilian Bender, LL.M. (Yale), Maître en droit (Paris II), is Legal and Policy Officer at the European Commission in Brussels.

Lei Cheng

Dr. Lei Cheng is an Associate Professor at Renmin University Law School, Beijing, China, and a post-doctoral fellow of the Chinese Academy of Social Sciences.

Henning Glaser

Henning Glaser is Founding Director of the German-Southeast Asian Center of Excellence for Public Policy and Good Governance (CPG) at the Faculty of Law of Thammasat University, Bangkok, Thailand, where he concurrently serves a lecturer for Comparative Public Law.

Makoto Hong

Makoto Hong is an Assistant Director at the Infocomm Media Development Authority, Singapore, and former State Counsel at the Attorney General's Chambers Academy, Singapore.

Matthias Krüger

Prof. Dr. jur. Matthias Krüger is Professor of Criminal Law and Criminal Procedure Law at the Faculty of Law of Ludwig Maximilian University of Munich, Germany.

Anselm Küsters

Dr. Anselm Küsters is the Head of Department for Digitalization / New Technologies at the Berlin office of the Centre for European Policy and an Associate Researcher at the Max Planck Institute for Legal History and Legal Theory in Frankfurt and at Humboldt University of Berlin.

Sorawit Limparangsri

Sorawit Limparangsri is Chief Judge of the Office of the President of the Supreme Court, Thailand.

Van Quang Nguyen

Dr. Van Quang Nguyen in an Associate Professor of Law at Hanoi Law University, Vietnam, where he also serves as Editor in Chief of the Journal of Legal Studies.

Rinat Kitai-Sangero

Professor Rinat Kitai-Sangero is a staff member at the Law School and the head of the Multidisciplinary Studies at Zefat Academic College, Israel.

Pokpong Srisanit

Dr. Pokpong Srisanit is Associate Professor of Law and Dean of the Faculty of Law, Thammasat University, Thailand.

Karam Chand Vohrah †

Dato Karam Chand Vohrah was Consultant at Lee Hishammuddin Allen & Gledhill, Kuala Lumpur, Malaysia, and Chair of the Institutional Reforms Committee, established under former Prime Minister Dr. Mahathir Mohamad to gather input from various civil society organizations and stakeholders to strengthen governance systems.

Denise Wong

Denise Wong is Assistant Chief Executive of the Data Protection and Innovation Group at the Infocomm Media Development Authority, Singapore, and Deputy Commissioner at the Personal Data Protection Commission, Singapore.